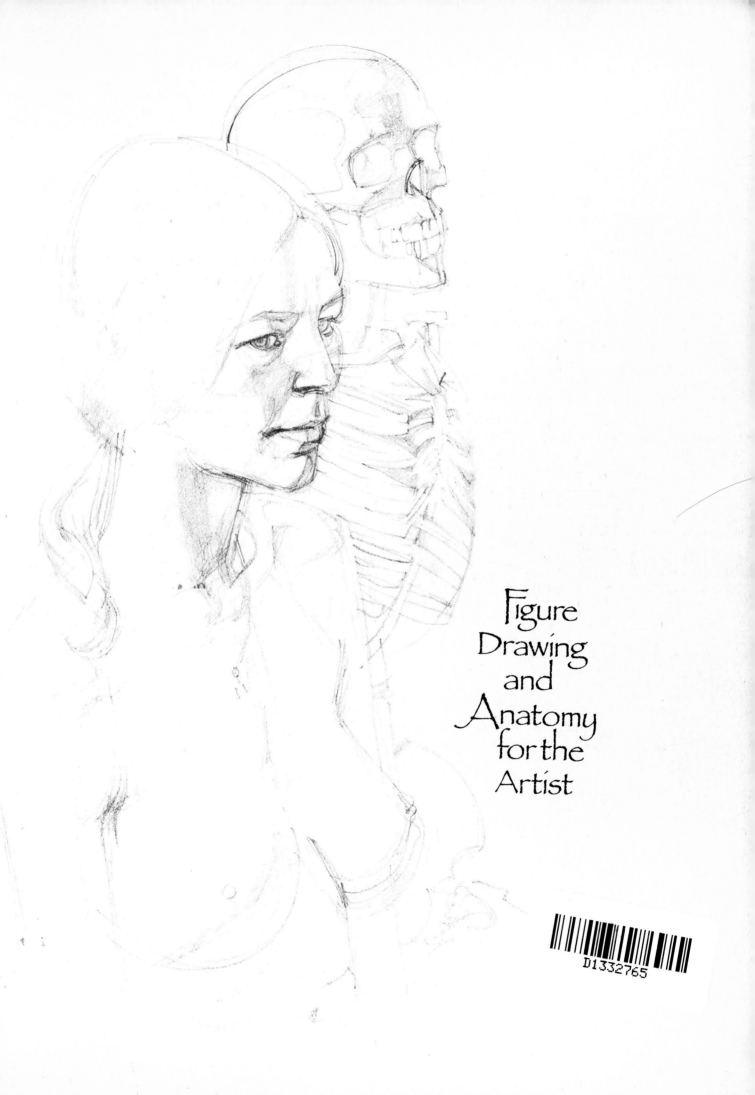

Figure
Drawing
and
Anatomy
for the
Artist

Hamlyn

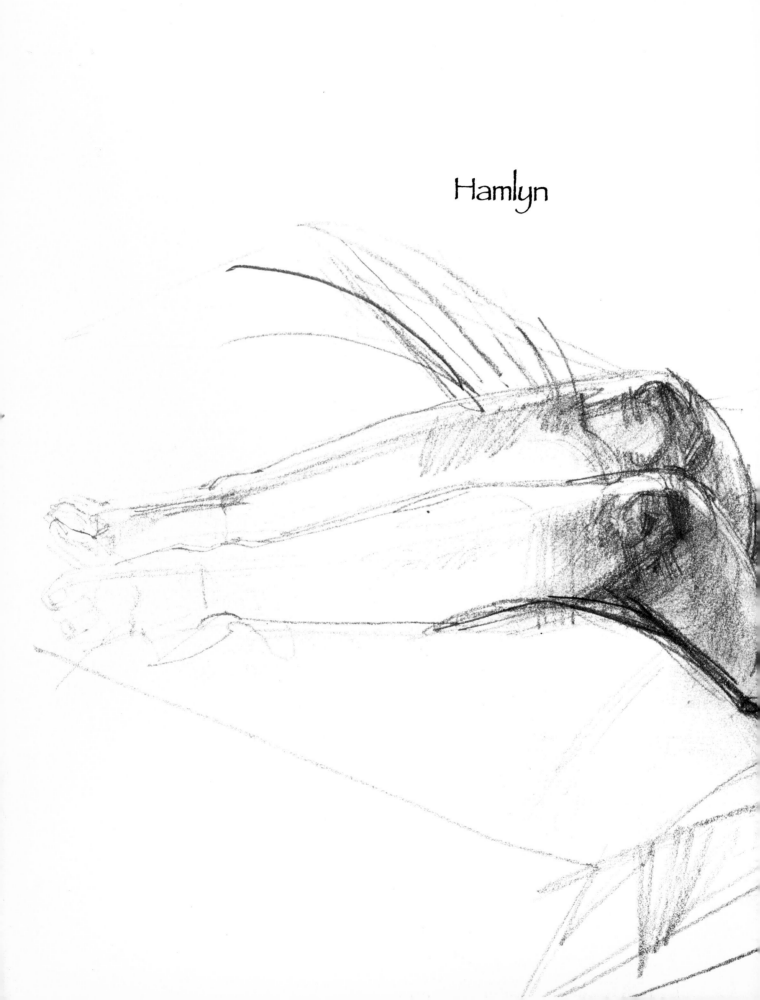

Figure Drawing and Anatomy for the Artist

John Raynes

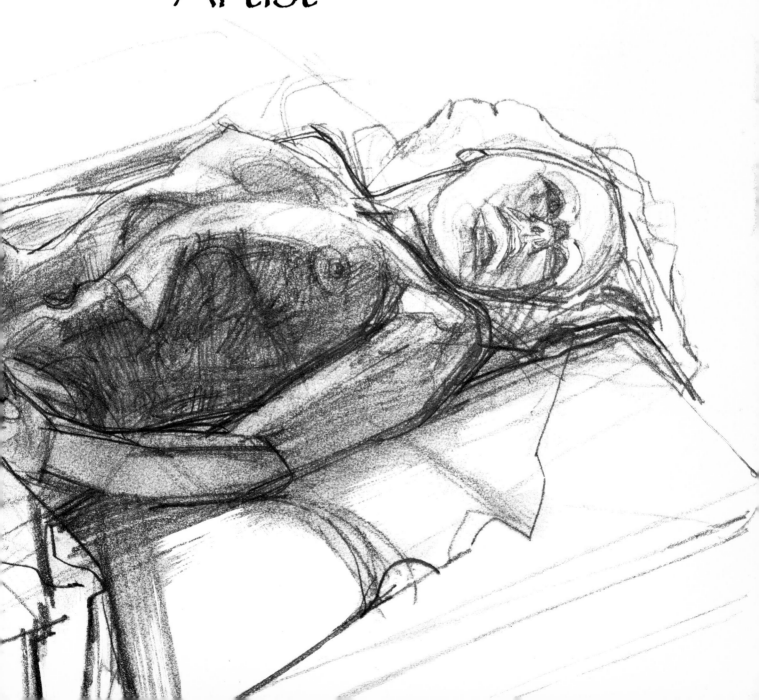

Published by
The Hamlyn Publishing Group Limited
a division of The Octopus Publishing Group
Michelin House, 81 Fulham Road, London SW3 6RB

ISBN 0 600 33394 9

Produced by Mandarin Offset
Printed and bound in Hong Kong

Acknowledgements

Photographs
The illustration on page 7 is reproduced by the gracious permission of
Her Majesty the Queen.
Graphische Sammlung Albertina, Vienna 9, 247, 248 top, 248 bottom;
British Museum, London 8; City Art Gallery, Manchester 241;
Courtauld Institute of Art, London 238; Durand-Ruel & Cie 246;
Newnes Picture Library 240 bottom; Kodak Museum, Harrow 204-5;
Kunstmuseum, Basel 234-5; Museum Boymans-von Beuningen,
Rotterdam 237; Philadelphia Museum of Art, Pennsylvania 205;
Roger-Viollet, Paris 6; Tate Gallery, London 239, 242 top, 242 bottom,
244, 245, 249, 250; Victoria and Albert Museum, London 233, 236 left,
236 right, 240 top, 251, 252.

© A.D.A.G.P. Paris, 1981, 205, 244.

The remaining photographs are by the author.

Drawings
The drawings in the book are the work of the author, except those on
pages 14, 21, 22, 29, 31, 35-7, 45, 50, 51, 53, 177, 180, 207, 208, which
are the work of Polly Raynes.

Contents

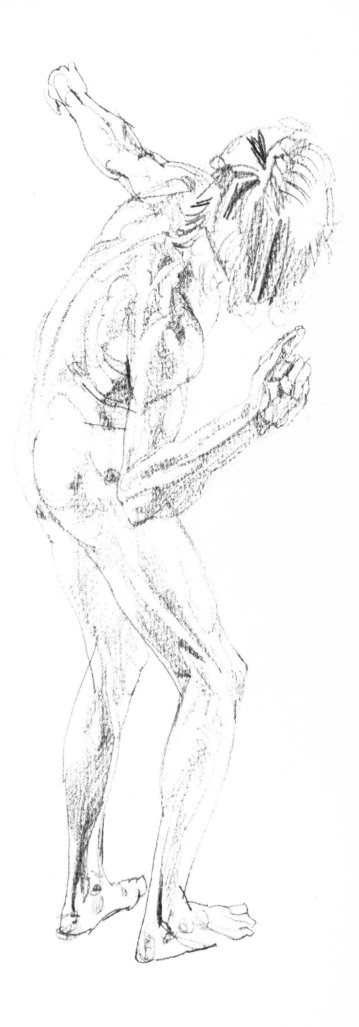

Introduction

Drawing can be one of several different things.

It can be a representation of visual imagery existing only in the imagination or in dreams.

It can be the intuitive making of abstract shapes with no attempt to produce anything recognizable as observable reality.

It can be plans and sections of known or visualized objects, as by an architect or a technical draughtsman, which explain unseen internal workings and structure.

It can also be the making of images drawn from direct observation, with the intention of representing what is seen. In this type of drawing an attempt is made to discover the essential appearance of an object by close study, which is not to say that the knowledge so gained may not feed the imagination with images which can later find their way into more creative work.

This last is known as *objective* drawing, and it is with this approach to drawing that I am primarily concerned in this book.

Even within this one area of specifically objective drawing, there is an immense variety of ways of seeing: the same object can be seen and drawn in many ways, each just as 'real' and true as the others.

The earliest drawings known are those on the walls of the cave dwellings of our prehistoric ancestors. They are often, perhaps surprisingly, beautiful to our modern eyes, and they are nearly always accurate depictions of the shape of the animals then living. Early man's survival depended on these animals and it was important that they should be recognized and identified quickly and accurately. The cave artist's concentration on linear outline drawings of the animals, filled-in silhouettes in some cases, show just the information that is needed to identify an animal at a distance; colour, markings and even some suggestion of form are there too, but above all they are accurate outline drawings.

To represent and recognize a solid three-dimensional object by linear outline was already a huge intellectual leap to have made. A line does not in reality exist to mark the boundaries of an object against its surroundings or against other objects. Tone, colour, three-dimensional vision and movement tell us where the edges of objects are in real life.

The linear outline is a translation, an invented language, or rather the first phrases of a language with which we have learned to represent the visual world. Only higher primates seem to have the

Detail from a wall painting in Tassili (Algeria)

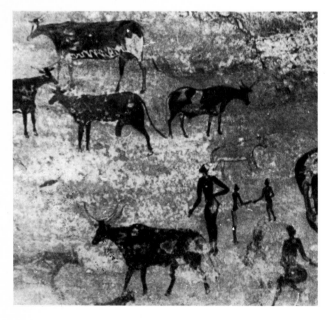

6

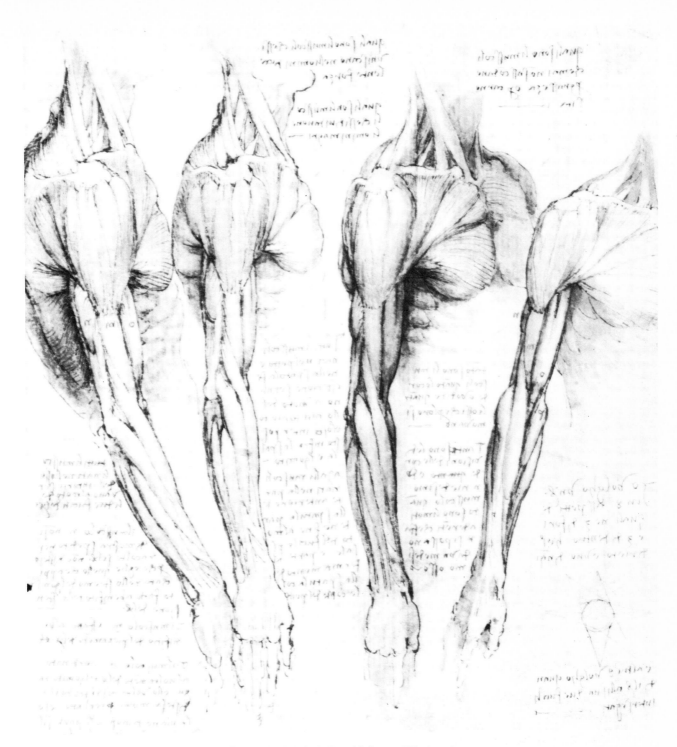

Study of the arm and shoulder muscles by Leonardo da Vinci. Royal Library, Windsor Castle

ability to read such statements, even domestic dogs and cats, living in homes where drawn images abound, seem to show no capability of recognizing other animals or themselves from outline drawings.

It is now so natural to accept an outline drawing as a depiction of reality, that it is sometimes thought of as the *only* way to draw, and that edges and perhaps sharp creases are the only features to be represented by these lines.

This is to forget that the outline *is* a series of invented marks which we humans have learned to interpret, and that therefore drawing in its most fundamental form is not a copying exercise as when a camera or a retina records, but an interpretation, and as such a great amount of different visual information can be depicted in many different ways as the language of visual expression evolves.

Early drawing was mainly linear and symbolic. Although the Greeks of the Golden Age had achieved extraordinarily naturalistic and lifelike, albeit idealized, human forms in their sculpture, little comparable drawing survives. Not until the 15th century, in the so-called Italian Renaissance, do we see the real flowering of figure drawing and detailed studies from life.

Michelangelo and Leonardo da Vinci set standards of observation, fluency and power that had never been seen before. These masters, drawing with pen and ink, charcoal, chalk and silverpoint on paper or prepared surfaces, were trying to extract from their models the information required for their paintings. While still depending on a linear outline, they used it in conjunction with vigorous linear hatching and cross-hatching to suggest form and movement. Human anatomy was studied in detail and well understood.

For Leonardo it was not enough to observe and draw the model. To answer the questions he had to know how the mechanism worked. At Windsor Castle there is a large collection of Leonardo's anatomical drawings, essentially notes made while dissecting cadavers.

All the best figure drawings try to make a visual statement about the observed object. They do not try to convey all the possible information, but try to tell the truth succinctly and clearly about a chosen aspect. Good drawings are selective and single minded.

The following sequence of exercises is intended to help the beginner to draw objectively from the human figure using this necessity to be selective as the guiding principle.

If used as a course, pursued with tenacity and enthusiasm, it should give a totally inexperienced and relatively inept beginner at least the ability to draw with understanding and honesty.

For those with some natural talent for whom the figure does not present so formidable a problem, I hope that following this ordered sequence will help to clarify aims and concentrate attention on enquiry and discovery.

Theoretically, in order to draw the human figure, knowledge of what lies beneath the surface of the skin is not absolutely necessary. If observation of the surface is acute enough and the planes and undulations and depressions are accurately recorded, the underlying structure will be evident.

The difficulty is that such faithful rendering of every such detail in its proper relationship to other details and surfaces is very non-selective and pretty difficult too. How are you to decide which bump or depression is superficial and could in some instances be ignored, and which ones give evidence of the fundamental structure and are therefore probably more vital?

Some knowledge of human anatomy is therefore

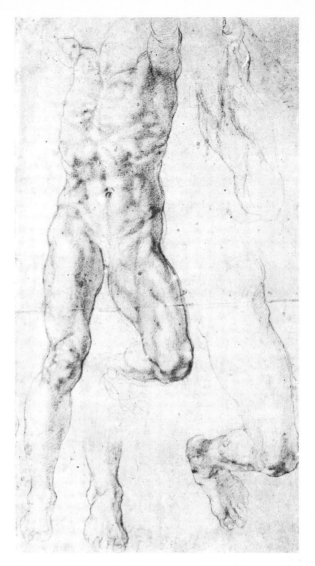

Drawing of Haman by Michelangelo. British Museum, London

useful; enough at least to enable you to recognise those surface features which indicate the disposition of underlying structure.

To understand anatomy fully you should first begin with the bony skeleton, and the way it articulates, and then discover how cartilage, tendon and successive layers of muscle wrap the structure together, tension it and power the struts and levers to produce movement.

The first half of this book is devoted to a fairly detailed exposition of the body skeleton and musculature of the human body.

Much of the information offered may be considered to be too detailed for the student to assimilate, and indeed it is not intended that all the anatomy should be fully understood before embarking on the projects in the second half of the book.

Perhaps the pages on surface form could be the first reading on the subject, further detail being sought as curiosity evolves.

For those who *do* read the anatomy section completely there can be hidden rewards in that the subject has its own fascination apart from its utility in drawing the figure.

It is absolutely vital to understand that drawing anything well requires more than technique. It is much more important to be honest and self critical, treating each drawing as a genuine search for greater knowledge. Curiously enough, setting out to draw a truthful rather than a beautiful drawing will often result in one that is truthful *and* beautiful. Some of the world's best drawings were made by artists who did not possess natural facility.

For me, and I am sure for most others who like me have been drawing all their lives, the excitement and challenge of drawing never diminishes. There is always something more to learn, some simpler more direct ways to express things seen or experienced.

Good draughtsmanship is not acquired quickly or easily; there are no real short cuts. Tackling all the projects in this book may seem a daunting prospect, but taken one at a time and not looking too far ahead, I hope that the progressive discoveries you can make will carry you enthusiastically from project to project.

On the other hand, I would not want you to consider the order of the projects to be sacrosanct. Perhaps a project may spark off further ideas, or the type or availability of models and locations may make it difficult to comply exactly with the instructions. The sequence of projects may eventually be treated as a general outline only, or as something to fall back on if other ideas falter. It is also to be expected that some projects will need to be repeated, either because the objective has not been reached or perhaps because it *did* go well and pointed the way to further exploration on the same lines. All this is fine: the book is to be *used*; it does not provide all the answers. The answers are only to be found through the actual activity of drawing.

Perhaps some diffidence may be felt by a beginner asked to draw complete figures in the first session. I feel strongly that this method is preferable to the teaching sequence in which block drawings, simple diagrams of masses, anatomy and similar disciplines have to be mastered before progressing to real human beings.

It is much less dreary to plunge in boldly, draw what is seen with as few preconceptions as possible, learning the niceties and difficulties to be dealt with later as they are encountered.

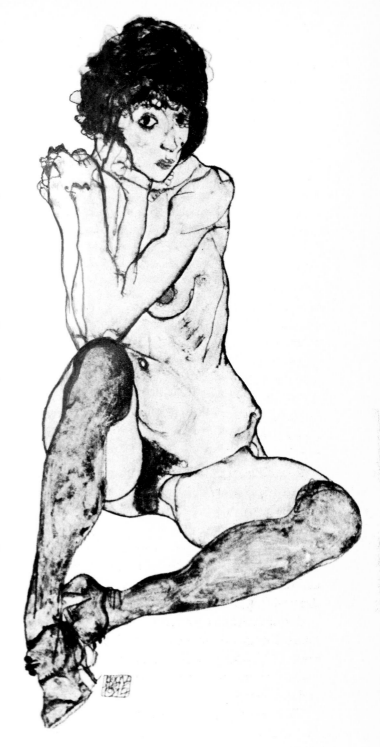

Sitting nude with her arm leaning on her right knee,
by Egon Schiele. Albertina, Vienna

The skeleton

An understanding of human anatomy must begin with the skeleton. The whole structure comprises 179 main bones, all splendidly specialized for their purpose and combining together to form a very strong but light framework.

All drawings of the skeleton are, in a sense, an invention. The vertebrate skeleton falls apart when robbed of muscle, tendon and cartilage. The skeletal drawings here are therefore from real skeletons or plastic replicas threaded together with copper wire, bolts and wing nuts and variously contrived hinges. Great ingenuity in this assembly has simulated most of the freedom and restriction of actual human movement, but, perforce, articulation cannot be fully or precisely represented.

The drawings on this page show frontal views of complete male and female adult skeletons.

The most important support structure in the body is the spine or *vertebral column*, the lower end of which is virtually one piece with the pelvis or hip bone. In fact three separate bones make up the pelvis, but they are bound together so securely that, although some movement is possible, for practical drawing purposes they can be considered as a single rigid structure. A complicated and strong system of musculature rather like the rigging of a ship, maintains the curved but basically upright stance of the vertebral column, and the strong links between this flexible mast and the stable deck of the pelvis support the rest of the structure so fundamentally that they nearly always provide the key to analyzing the essence of any pose.

The *femurs* or thigh bones, very strong bones with extensive surfaces to which the large buttock and thigh muscles are attached, are located by their domed upper ends into hemispherical sockets in the pelvis. Two long bones make up the lower leg, the *tibia* or shin bone and the *fibula*; their upper ends combine with the *patella* or kneecap to form a compound joint with essential movement in only one plane. Their lower ends are recognizable as the protuberances normally known as the ankle, and they form a joint with the true ankle bones of the foot, the *tarsal* bones, the longest of which is the heel bone or *calcaneus*. Together with the long foot bones, or *metatarsus*, they form a strong arch capable of supporting great weight. The toe bones are named collectively the *phalanges*.

Attached to the vertebral column and supported by its upper sections, there is a cage composed of thin curved bones – the ribs. This system actually does perform the function of a protective cage around vital organs such as the heart, but it is primarily a kind of bellows alternately compressing and expanding the lungs for inhalation and exhalation. A third function of the rib cage is to support the shoulder girdle and arms.

1 *Cranium*
2 *Mandible*
3 *Clavicle*
4 *Sternum*
5 *Humerus*
6 *Rib cage*
7 *Vertebral column (24 bones)*
8 *Pelvis*
9 *Radius*
10 *Ulna*
11 *Carpus (8 bones)*
12 *Metacarpus (5 bones)*
13 *Phalanges–hand (14 bones)*
14 *Femur*
15 *Patella*
16 *Tibia*
17 *Fibula*
18 *Tarsus (7 bones)*
19 *Metatarsus (5 bones)*
20 *Phalanges–foot (14 bones)*

Frontal view

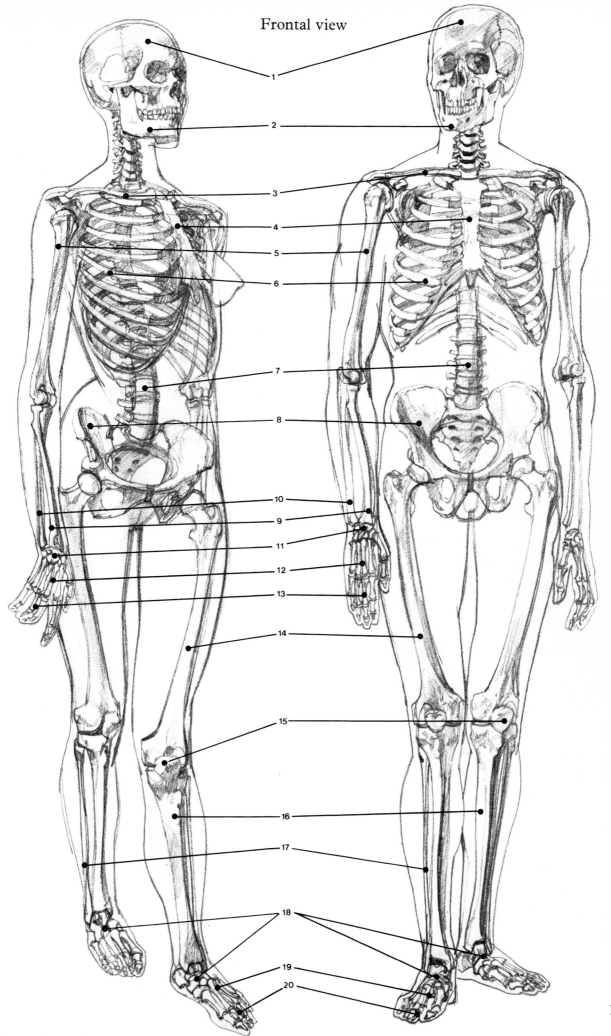

1
2
3
4
5
6
7
8
10
9
11
12
13
14
15
16
17
18
19
20

A complex system of mainly flat muscles interlace the rib cage or *thorax* and complete the frontal links with the pelvis to make a strong flexible whole, the trunk. The relative positions of the pelvis and thorax, the consequent variation in shape of the thorax and the linking curve of the vertebral column, together constitute a vital relationship which the artist must analyze with precision.

Resting on the upper back of the thorax and on either side of the vertebral column are two flattish triangular bones: the shoulder blades or *scapulae*. Approximately in line with the tops of the scapulae but on the front of the rib cage are the collar bones or *clavicles* which join the breast bone (*sternum*) to extensions of the outer corners of the scapulae; this system makes up the shoulder girdles. The domed end of the upper arm bone or humerus is inserted into the loosely formed cavity under this girdle to form a joint similar to the ball-and-socket of the hip but even more mobile. The elbow joint between the lower end of the humerus and the two bones of the lower arm (the *ulna* and the *radius*) resembles the knee joint. Eight small, irregularly shaped bones called the *carpals* form the wrist, the five hand bones are known as the *metacarpals* and the finger and thumb bones, the *phalanges*.

At the top end of the vertebral column are two very complicated and specialized vertebrae, the *axis* and the *atlas*. Their special function is to provide movement and support for the skull. A skull is for the most part an ovoid boney protection for the brain. At the front there are eye sockets, a nasal opening and the upper jaw containing teeth. The lower jaw or *mandible* is a separate bone, in which the lower teeth are set. It hinges on processes at the side of the skull, or *cranium*, to open and close the mouth.

This is a very simple description of the human skeleton and may seem to contain some self-evident statements. However, it is useful to establish an impression of the basic functions of the complete system. It is all too easy to see the skeleton as a slightly ghoulish collection of indeterminately shaped remains – only a slight change of approach is needed to reveal the beauty of the highly efficient supports, levers, bearings and enclosures, all perfectly shaped for their individual functions and combining together with marvellous precision.

In order to speak of the skeleton in more detail, it is necessary to define some terms normally used in anatomical description. *Anterior* means near to the front of the body, *posterior* near to the back. Bones which fit together at a joint are said to *articulate* with each other at that point and the parts of the bones which meet in the joint are called their *articular surfaces* or *facets*.

1 *Cranium*
2 *Mandible*
3 *Clavicle*
5 *Humerus*
6 *Rib cage*
7 *Vertebral column (24 bones)*
8 *Pelvis*
9 *Radius*
10 *Ulna*
11 *Carpus (8 bones)*
12 *Metacarpus (5 bones)*
13 *Phalanges–hand (14 bones)*
14 *Femur*
16 *Tibia*
17 *Fibula*
18 *Tarsus (7 bones)*
19 *Metatarsus (5 bones)*
20 *Phalanges–foot (14 bones)*
21 *Scapula*

Rear view

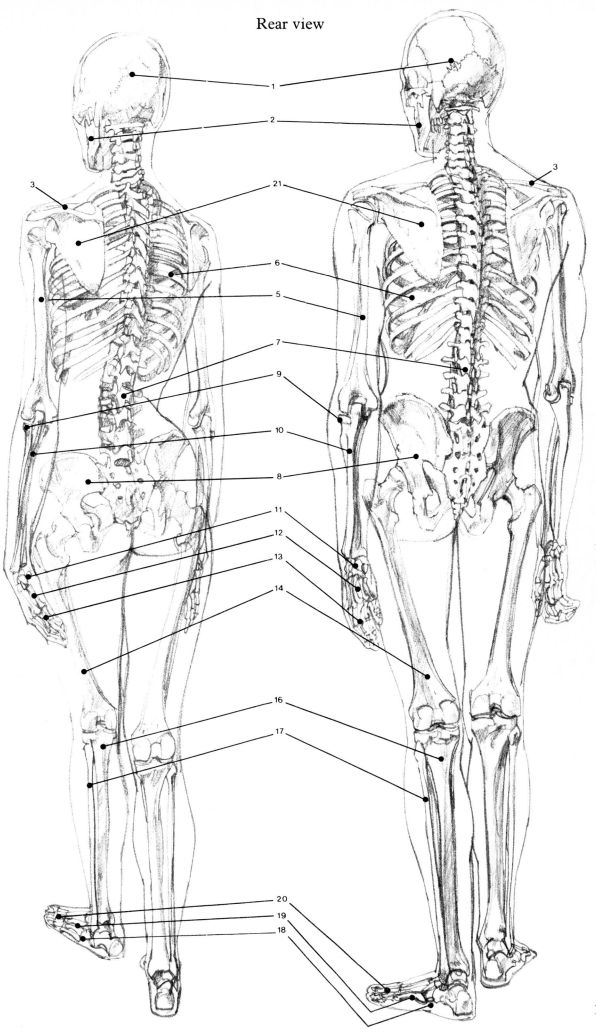

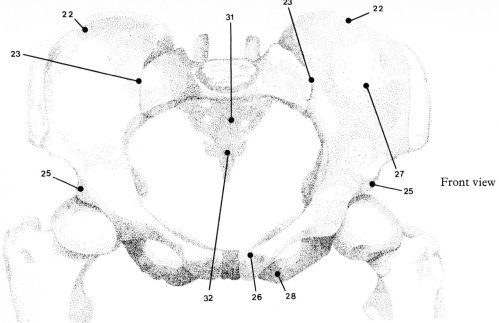

Front view

For the artist, the exact position of the pelvis relative to the rest of the skeleton and to the ground plane is almost always the key to the correct analysis of a pose.

In both sexes the pelvis is a strong, rigid support structure made up of the two hip bones, called the *innominate bones*, and the *sacrum*. Each innominate bone is a combination of three bones joined by cartilage in the young, but fused together in the adult. The upper part is called the *ilium*, the upper edge of which is the *iliac crest*, the most obvious and easily identified feature of the pelvis in the live figure.

The pubis forms the anterior part of each innominate bone. These are joined together by cartilage at the pubic symphysis, to form the pubic crest. The crest and its lateral extensions, to which the muscles and fascia of the abdominal wall are attached along the upper edge, form the lower boundary of the trunk, which is clearly visible in life. The *ischium* is the lower, posterior part of the innominate bone and forms most of the inverted arch created by the combined rami of the ischium and

22 *Iliac crest*
23 *Sacro-iliac joint*
24 *Anterior superior iliac spine*
25 *Anterior inferior iliac spine*
26 *Pubic arch*
27 *Ilium*
28 *Ramus of ischium*
29 *Ischium*
30 *Posterior superior iliac spine*
31 *Sacrum*
32 *Coccyx*
33 *5th lumbar vertebra*
56 *Acetabulum*

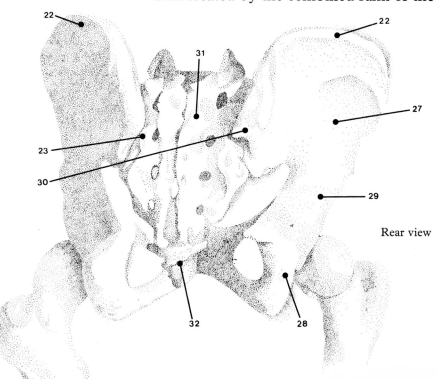

Rear view

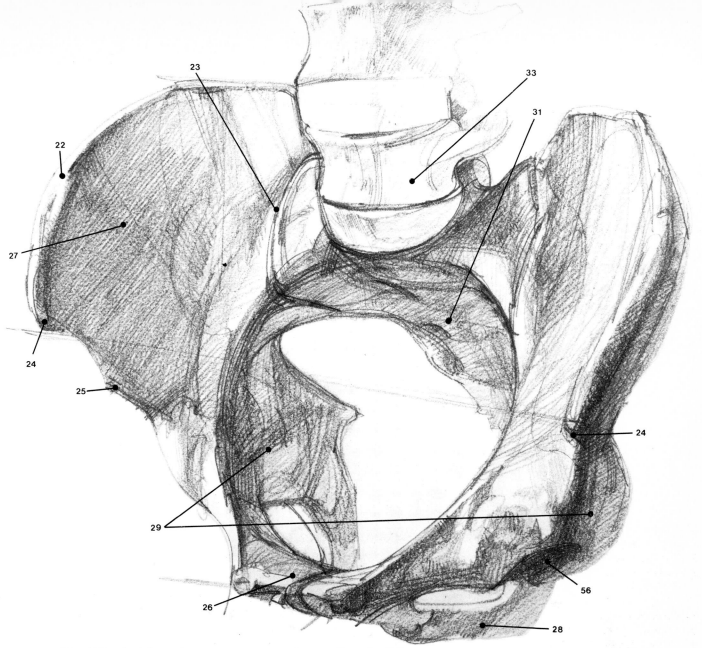

pubis. The ischium is never near to the surface in life,
but it provides attachment for a number of the powerful
muscles of the thigh, and the two ischial tuberosities
also provide a firm base for the sitting figure.

All three parts of the hip bone come together at a
triple junction which, on the lateral (external) side
forms the socket, the *acetabulum*, for the head of the
femur. The triangular wedge of the sacrum joins the
two innominate bones posteriorly. Its shape is visible in
life chiefly by reference to the prominences of the
posterior superior iliac spines. The sacrum is described
more fully on page 34.

Most of the obvious differences in male and female
skeletons are to be found in the pelvis. In view of the
heavier weight and musculature in the male, the male
pelvis is generally more massive and rugged than the
female. To facilitate childbirth the female pelvis is
wider, more open and less deep, and it normally adopts
a more forward-tilted attitude so that the upper surface
of the sacrum is more nearly horizontal.

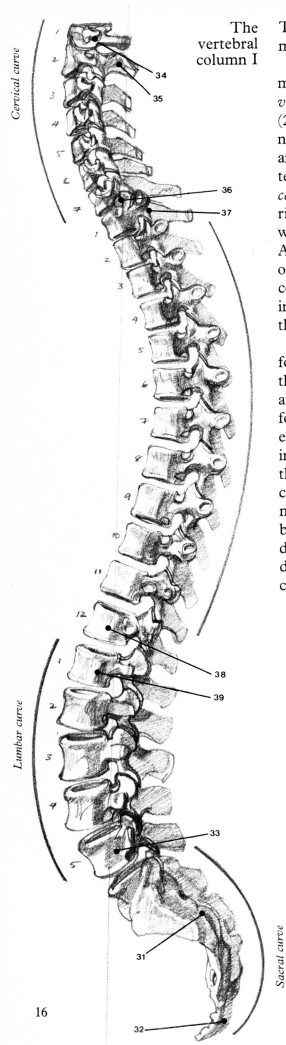

The pelvis is rigid in itself, but it acquires considerable mobility from the movement of the spine.

The spine or vertebral column is the key to human mobility. It is composed of 24 individual bones, the *vertebrae*, linked together into a column about 60–70 cm (24–28 in) long. Each vertebra is separated from the next by a fibro-cartilage disc, which cushions shocks and allows tilting and torsion between adjoining vertebral bodies. At the top, or neck end, there are seven *cervical vertebrae*; the next twelve vertebrae support the ribs and are called *thoracic vertebrae*, and the last five, which link to the pelvis, are the *lumbar vertebrae*. Although the sacrum has been considered here as part of the pelvis, it is really a continuation of the vertebral column, in that it is five vertebrae fused together and includes another four or five small fused vertebrae in the *coccyx*, the residual tail.

In normal upright posture, the vertebral column has four curves: the cervical curve is convex forwards, the thoracic concave, the lumbar convex forwards again and the sacro-coccygeal concave downwards and forwards. These curves help to cushion shocks and enable the column to bear vertical pressure better. The intervertebral discs are elastic and compressible, and therefore augment the cushioning action of the vertebral curves in taking up and neutralizing the shocks of muscle pull and weight thrust, which may be imparted by violent activity such as running and jumping. The degrees of curvature vary from race to race and individual to individual, and change with age; they must be carefully observed as the spine posture is fundamental to the analysis of a standing figure.

The cervical curvature begins at the atlas, continues until the second thoracic vertebra and then begins to change into the contrary curve of the thoracic. It is the least extreme of the four curves and when the head is bent forwards it may become a concave forwards curve. The forward concave curvature of the thoracic is most extreme at the sixth thoracic vertebra and merges into the lumbar curve at the twelfth. Its curvature is caused by the fact that each vertebral body is slightly wedge-shaped – the posterior parts of the vertebral bodies are deeper than the anterior. The lumbar curve, on the other hand, is mainly caused by the slight wedge-shape of the discs rather than of the vertebral bodies. Lumbar curvature is more pronounced in the female than the male, but lessens with age in both sexes.

The amount of movement between one vertebra and the next is in fact rather small, but when added together throughout the column the degree of flexibility is considerable, allowing *flexion* (forward bending), *extension* (backward bending), bending to one or other side and rotation or twisting. Most of the flexion and extension movement occurs in the cervical and lumbar regions, least in the thoracic; sideways bending can take place in any part of the column but also is most free in the cervical and lumbar areas. Rotation too is slight between individual vertebrae, but over the whole column the degree of twist is considerable, although it is least in the lumbar region. In any one action of the body the vertebral column may exhibit combinations of all these movements.

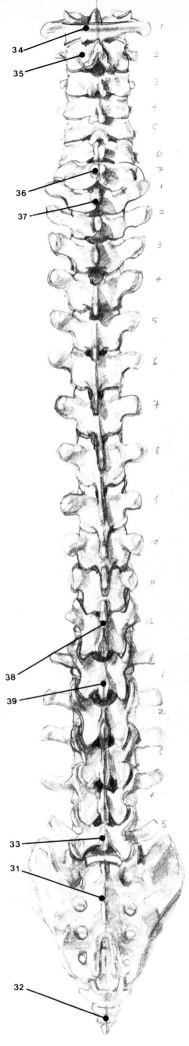

31 *Sacrum*
32 *Coccyx*
33 *5th lumbar vertebra*
34 *Atlas*
35 *Axis*
36 *7th cervical vertebra*
37 *1st thoracic vertebra*
38 *12th thoracic vertebra*
39 *1st lumbar vertebra*
Note: slight lateral curvature in the thoracic region; directed towards left in left-handed people, to the opposite side in the right-handed.

The
vertebral
column II

Each of the separate vertebrae is in itself quite a complex and precise structure. In most vertebrae there is a more or less cylindrical part called the *body* of the vertebra, the flat surfaces of which are joined to the next by the intervertebral discs. Most of the weight supported by the vertebral column in the normal upright posture is transmitted through the bodies of the vertebrae. However, the articular processes of the vertebrae are also in contact and contribute to the weight-taking and the general strength of the complete column, especially in flexion and extension. These surfaces are lever-like processes which extend from an arch on the posterior or dorsal side of the body. The arch encloses a space known as the *vertebral foramen*, and protects the spinal cord which occupies it.

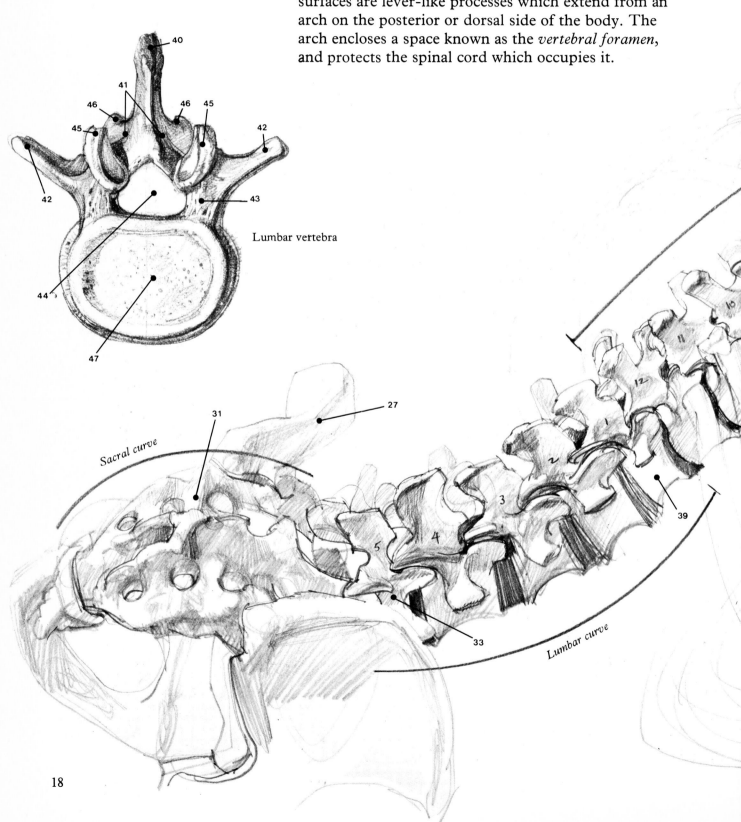

Lumbar vertebra

There are seven processes projecting from the vertebral arch, four of which articulate with the neighbouring vertebra, two with the one above and two below. The others are one spinous and two transverse processes, which function as levers, since muscles for extension and rotation of the vertebral column are attached to them.

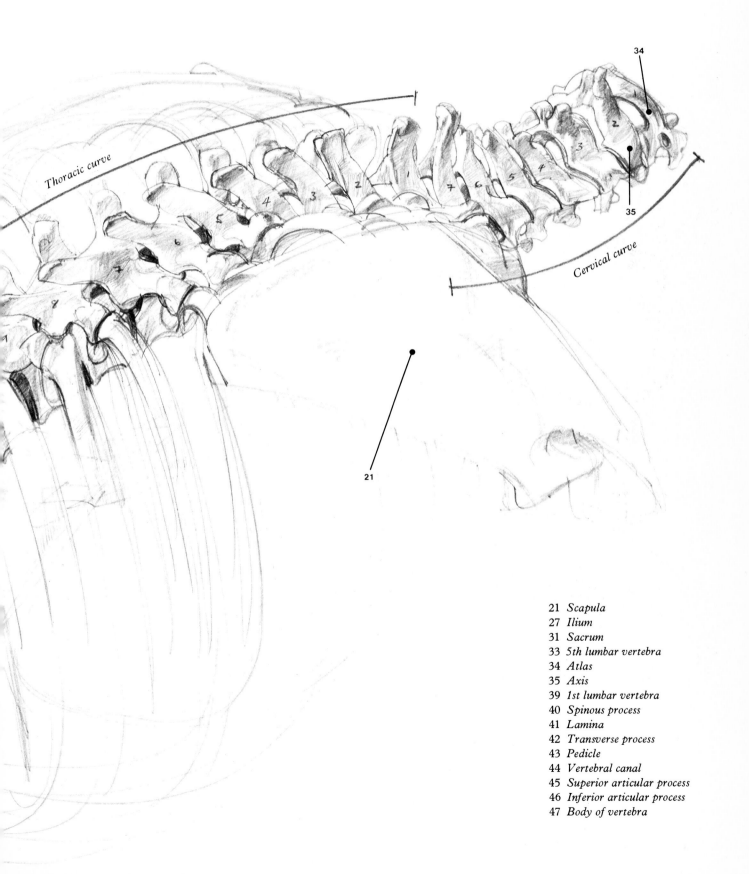

21 Scapula
27 Ilium
31 Sacrum
33 5th lumbar vertebra
34 Atlas
35 Axis
39 1st lumbar vertebra
40 Spinous process
41 Lamina
42 Transverse process
43 Pedicle
44 Vertebral canal
45 Superior articular process
46 Inferior articular process
47 Body of vertebra

Typically, the seven cervical vertebrae have comparatively small broad bodies and large foramens. The articular processes combine together on each side to form articular pillars; the spinal process is sometimes double-ended, and the transverse processes are perforated by foramina. As a group, these cervical vertebrae constitute the neck of the human skeleton; they interlock closely to form a relatively smooth and neat profile.

Only the top cervical vertebra, the *atlas*, noticeably stands out from its fellows, not least because it lacks a body. It supports the head (hence its name) and is able to pivot freely on a vertical projection from the front of the *axis*, or second cervical vertebra. The transverse processes are larger than those of the other cervicals and there is virtually no spinous process, just a posterior tubercle which gives the atlas a rather ring-like form. Movement, especially rotation of the skull, is facilitated by long and slightly convex articular facets, which slide on the corresponding facets of the axis beneath.

As mentioned above, the axis has, jutting vertically from its body, a strong peg-like process on which the atlas and the head rotate. Otherwise, for the purposes of this study it appears essentially as a typical neck vertebra.

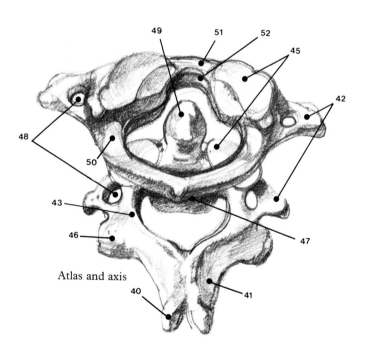

Atlas and axis

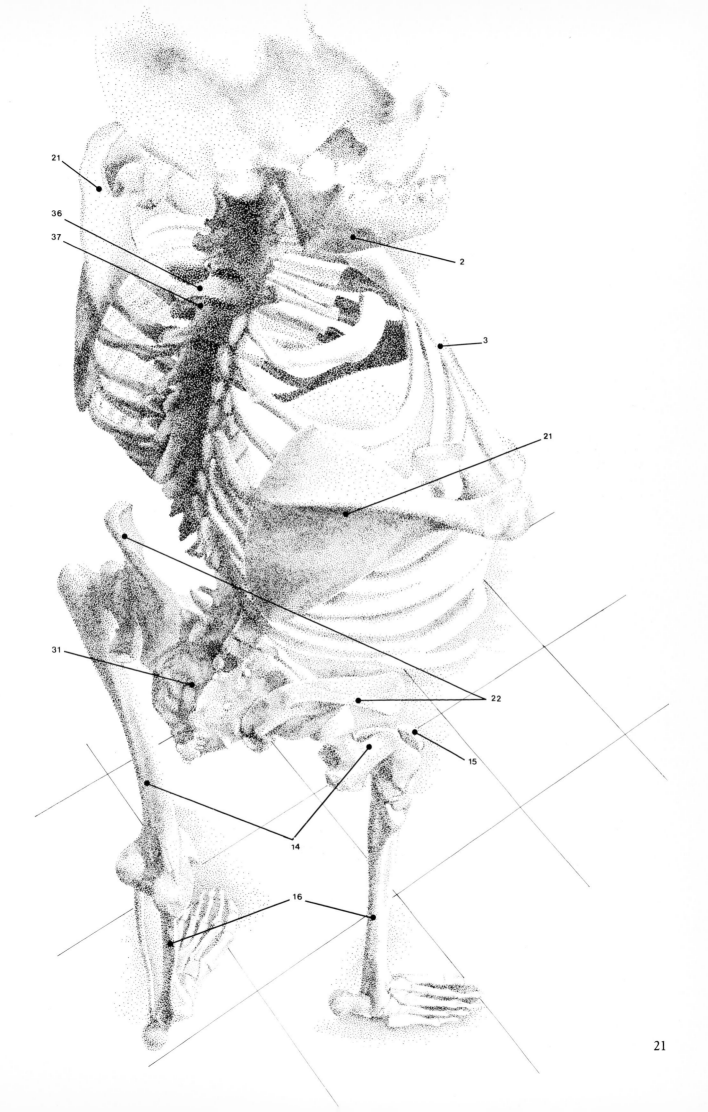

21

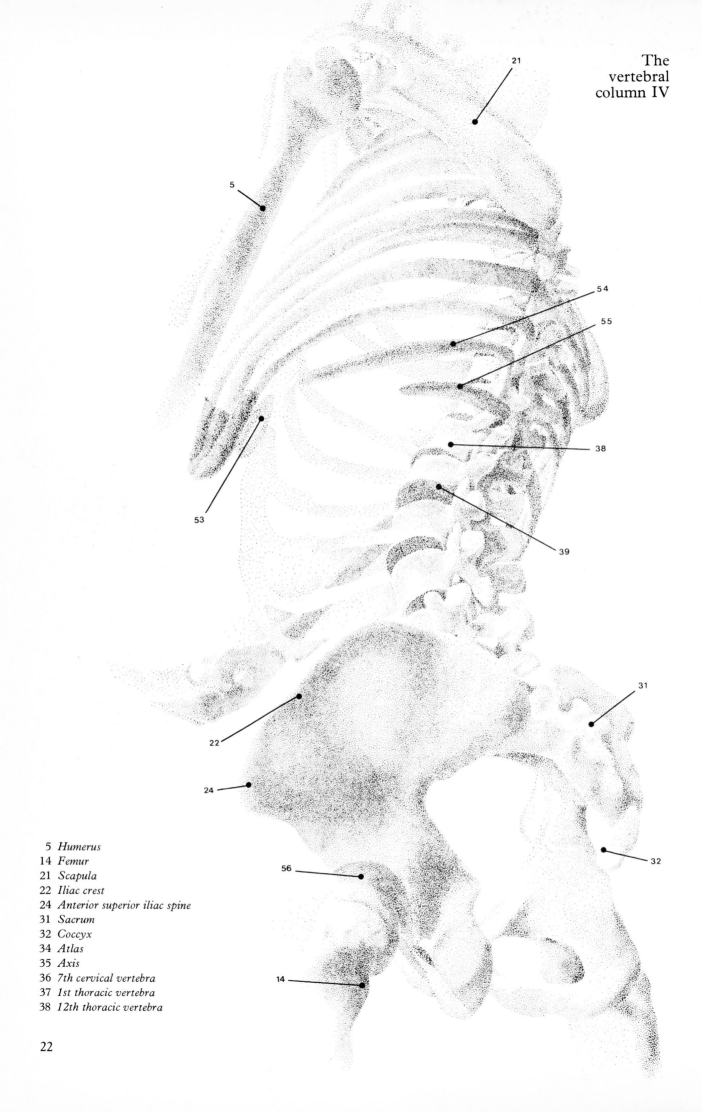

5 *Humerus*
14 *Femur*
21 *Scapula*
22 *Iliac crest*
24 *Anterior superior iliac spine*
31 *Sacrum*
32 *Coccyx*
34 *Atlas*
35 *Axis*
36 *7th cervical vertebra*
37 *1st thoracic vertebra*
38 *12th thoracic vertebra*

Only at the seventh cervical vertebra is there any further deviation from the relatively smooth column; this vertebra has a much longer spinous process. This is especially important as it is nearly always visible through the skin in the living subject; for this reason the seventh cervical is sometimes called the *vertebra prominens*. A number of important muscles are attached near the tip of this spine, including those responsible for extension of the neck and head, and the deep muscles of the upper back.

Thoracic vertebrae have costal facets on the sides of their bodies and, but for the last two or three vertebrae, on the transverse processes. These provide for articulation with the tubercles and heads of each pair of ribs, in a manner that will be described later. A general increase in size is apparent down the column, especially in the thoracic vertebrae, the last or twelfth of which is almost of the lumbar type in its solidity and bulk. All the thoracic vertebrae have closely interlocking articular spines, very prominent transverse processes and even more prominent and downward-slanting spinal processes.

Lumbar vertebrae, five in number and the last of the separate vertebrae, are very large and strong. They play a vital role as support structures for the whole upper skeleton. The body of a lumbar vertebra is wider from side to side than back to front, and a little deeper in the front than the back. The spinous process is almost horizontal, square-ended and thicker at its edges, which are roughened for muscle attachment. All but the fifth have relatively thin, long transverse processes, the fifth's being much more massive and emanating partially from the vertebral body itself rather than from the vertebral arch.

39 *1st lumbar vertebra*
40 *Spinous process*
42 *Transverse process*
45 *Superior articular process*
46 *Inferior articular process*
47 *Body of vertebra*
48 *Foramen transversarium*
49 *Dens*
53 *Xiphoid process*
54 *11th rib*
55 *12th rib*
56 *Acetabulum*
57 *1st rib*
58 *2nd rib*
59 *Vertebral foramen*

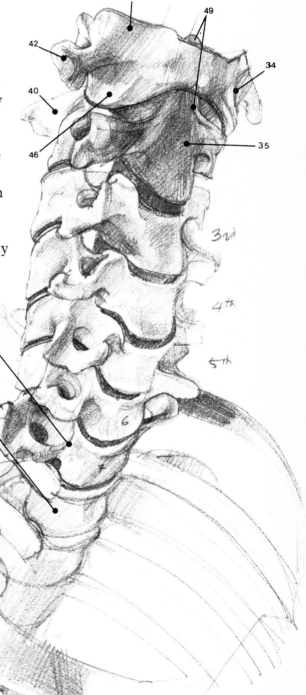

2nd cervical vertebra

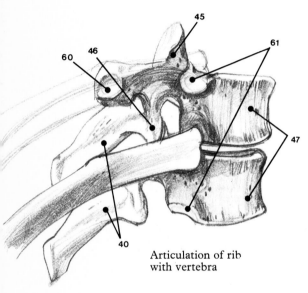

Articulation of rib
with vertebra

Suspended from the thoracic vertebrae are twelve pairs of elastic arches of bone forming the greater part of the *thorax* or rib cage. The first seven pairs are connected by lengths of cartilage (shown darker in the skeletal drawings) to the *sternum*. Of the remaining five pairs of ribs, three – the eighth, ninth and tenth – are joined to the cartilage of the rib immediately above, and the last two pairs are free at the anterior ends. These three types of ribs are described as true, false and floating ribs respectively.

From the vertebral column, each rib curves backwards before swinging round and downwards to the front (anterior) surface where it meets the sternum. Consequently a cross-section of the thorax is kidney-shaped, and the back (posterior) surface has two wide and deep grooves running alongside the spinous processes of the thoracic vertebrae. Occasionally an extra pair of ribs may develop on the seventh cervical or the first lumbar vertebra, or there may be only eleven ribs, owing to the absence of the lower pair of floating ribs.

Each rib has a shaft, a posterior and an anterior end. The shaft is flat, curved and slightly twisted in such a way as to follow the curves of the complete thorax and make up a smoothly contoured surface. The posterior end, which articulates with the thoracic vertebrae, has a head, a neck and a tubercle. The head has two facets, the lower, larger one for articulation with the appropriate thoracic vertebral body and the upper, smaller one for the body of the vertebra above. Between the two facets is a ridge, called the *crest*, which attaches to the disc between the two vertebrae. The tubercle has a facet which articulates with the transverse process of the numerically corresponding vertebra. In total, for a typical rib, there are thus four points of contact with the vertebral column. Only the last three ribs are exceptions, in that the tenth has only one articular head facet, and the floating ribs only one facet and no tubercle.

The small upper opening of the thorax, known as the *inlet*, slopes downwards and forwards; the lower opening or *outlet* is bounded at the sides by the twelfth ribs and in front by the cartilages of the tenth, ninth, eighth and seventh ribs. As these ribs ascend from each side to the lower end of the sternum they form an angle, called the *infrasternal angle*. There is great variety of size and shape of thorax depending on sex, race, age and individual build. Thin people usually have a long narrow thorax, whereas stocky figures have a broad, short one. In females the thorax is generally smaller, actually and proportionately to the rest of the body, and the slope of the inlet is greater.

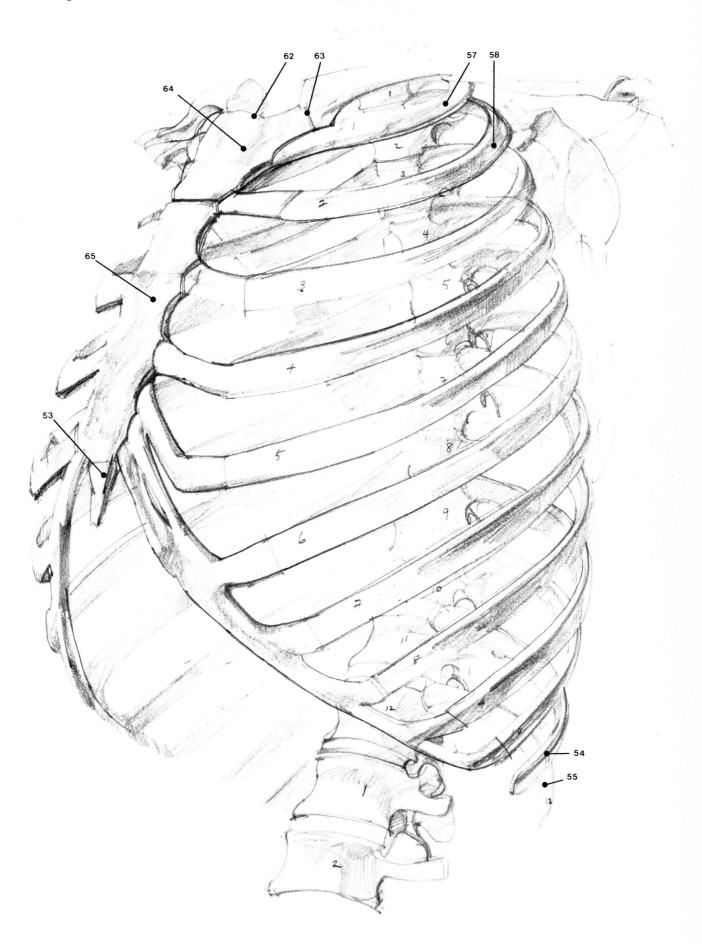

For the figure artist the capabilities and limitations of movement in the spinal column are of paramount importance. Skeletons for demonstration, whether real or manufactured, are always made up so that the shoulder, elbow, wrist, hip, knee and ankle joints approach as nearly as possible the articulation they enjoy in life, but the vertebral column is normally threaded on to a rigid rod, curved to simulate the upright, symmetrical posture.

In life such a position is rarely maintained; weight transferences from leg to leg are continual in walking and running. Even when standing, most people take their weight more on one leg than the other, shift from one foot to the other and transfer weight from the heel to the ball of the foot as the muscles involved begin to tire. Every action of the head, arms or legs affects the curvature of the spine to a lesser or greater degree.

For this reason the restraining rod was removed from the vertebral column of the skeleton used as reference for the illustrations on pages 27–35, and was replaced with a flexible cable, in order to simulate the movements possible in life. There is a risk of inaccuracy in such a procedure, for the absence of the restraining ligaments means that the only restriction to movement is the natural shape of the bodies of the vertebrae and their articular processes, and, in the thoracic region, the limitations of thorax flexibility.

The ligaments that hold the vertebrae securely together possess a varying but relatively small degree of elasticity, greater in the young than in the old. The intervertebral discs, too, can only be deformed to a limited extent, although the thickest ones, in the lumbar and cervical areas, can be squashed rather more than the thinner thoracic discs. When the vertebral column is bent back in extension, the anterior longitudinal ligament is stretched and the vertebrae tend to pivot over their articular processes. The possible movement, which is greatest in the lumbar and cervical regions, is limited by the tension of the anterior longitudinal ligament and the proximity of the spinous processes. In the lumbar region of the young the movement can be extreme and the spine very supple.

Flexion or forward bending is not as free as extension, since the posterior longitudinal ligament, the *ligamenta flava*, interspinous and supraspinous ligaments all limit the amount of movement. As in extension, the thoracic area has least flexibility, so that interference with breathing is kept to a minimum. Flexion is freest in the cervical vertebrae, although Gray's *Anatomy* insists that 'Flexion is arrested just beyond the point where the cervical convexity is straightened: the movement is checked by the apposition of the projecting lower lips of the bodies of the subjacent vertebrae.' Maybe the

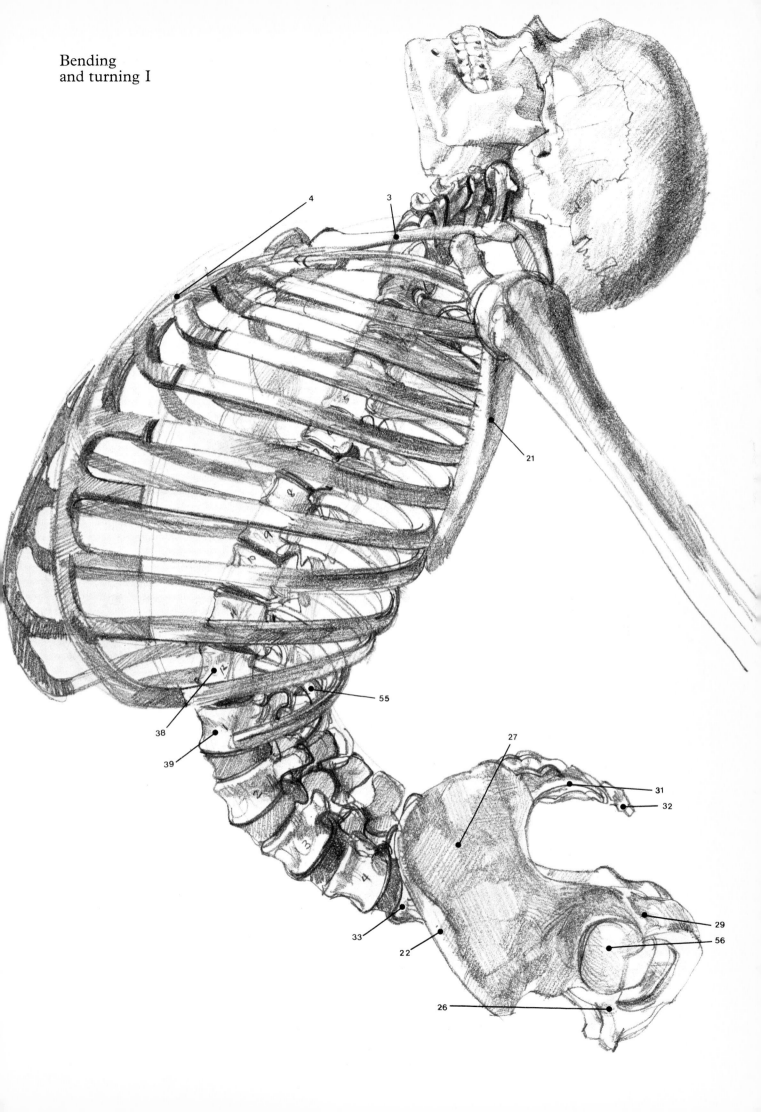

Bending
and turning I

degree of flexion shown in these drawings then is a little excessive, but great individual variation does exist; the lumbar region of a trained acrobat, for instance, can be extremely extended.

Lateral flexion, bending to one side or the other, is accompanied by some rotation of the vertebrae on each other, especially in the neck. This is caused by the relative angles of the articular processes. In life this may not be obvious, for the head can be counter-rotated on the axis to compensate exactly, but if the head is allowed to fall freely to the side from the upright, face-forward position, it will tend to turn towards that side too.

In the thoracic area lateral flexion crowds the ribs together on one side and spreads them on the other, thus limiting movement. Nevertheless, this plane of movement is the freest in the thoracic area, since the vertical disposition of the articular processes hinders forward and backward bending. Again, the lumbar region has a considerable range of lateral bend, widely variable according to age and flexibility. Rotation has been mentioned in the context of lateral flexion in the neck; but rotation unaccompanied by extension or forward or lateral flexion is possible between all vertebrae only to a very slight degree. It is only when these slight movements are added together along the whole column that any appreciable degree of twist is achieved. In the living human figure most actions, other than

14 *Femur*
21 *Scapula*
27 *Ilium*
28 *Ramus of ischium*
36 *7th cervical vertebra*
37 *1st thoracic vertebra*
39 *1st lumbar vertebra*
56 *Acetabulum*
66 *Interspinous ligament*
67 *Supraspinous ligament*
68 *Ligamentum flavum*
69 *Posterior longitudinal ligament*
70 *Anterior longitudinal ligament*
71 *4th lumbar vertebra*

Cross-section of
vertebral column showing
lateral flexion

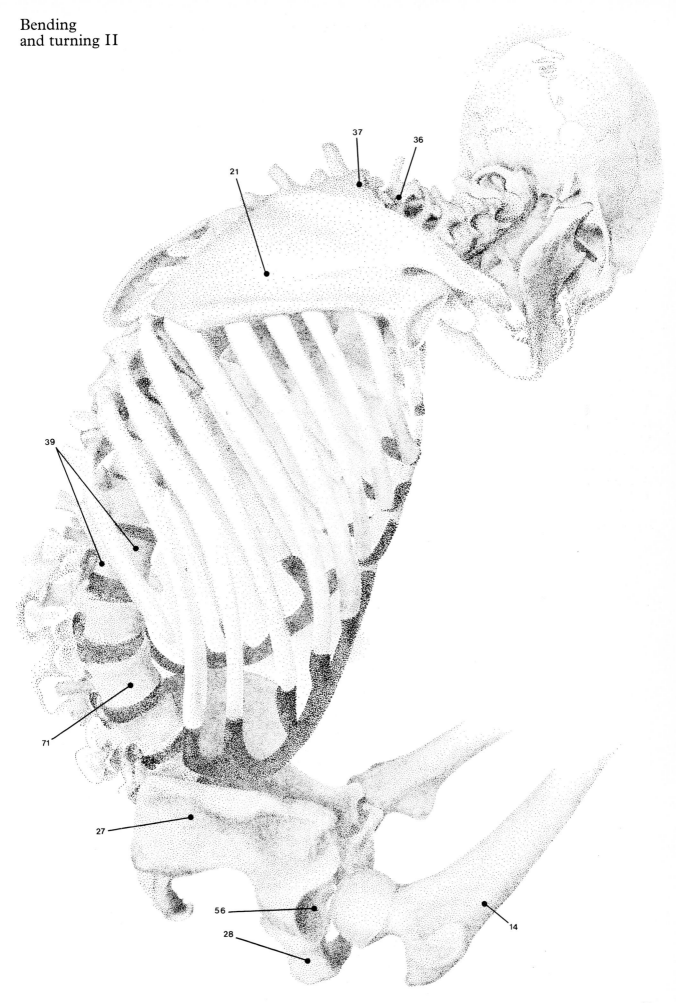

formal exercises, involve the vertebral column in a combination of two or more of the movements discussed.

In the pose on the opposite page, the whole column is showing rotation; from the lower lumbar to the top of the thoracic, rotation appears clockwise from this angle and is accompanied by some lateral flexion in the lumbar area. The cervical region rotates in the other direction and also involves passive lateral flexion. The degree of twist or rotary movement between pelvis and thorax shown here is about as much as most people could normally manage comfortably, although the relaxation of musculature and the relief of pressure on the inter-vertebral discs brought about by the lying position would increase the degree of flexibility in the vertebral column.

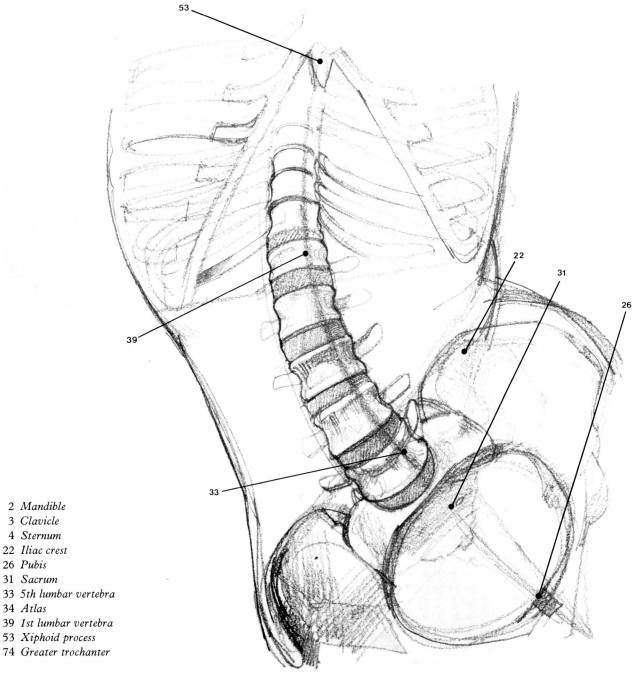

2 *Mandible*
3 *Clavicle*
4 *Sternum*
22 *Iliac crest*
26 *Pubis*
31 *Sacrum*
33 *5th lumbar vertebra*
34 *Atlas*
39 *1st lumbar vertebra*
53 *Xiphoid process*
74 *Greater trochanter*

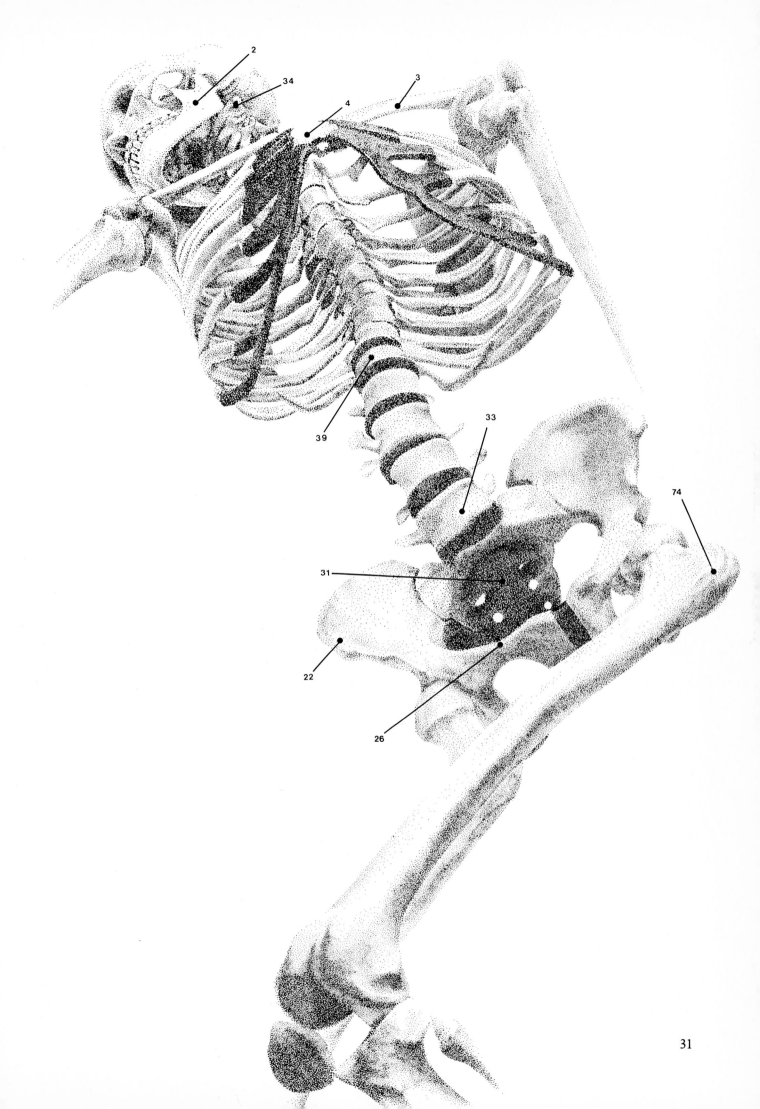

31

The drawings on this page show the disparity between theoretical range of movement and that possible or reasonable in real life. To achieve the amount of twist in the lumbar region of the skeleton, the model would have to align her left hip bone almost with the centre of the thorax outlet; an extraordinary degree of distortion would have to be accommodated by relaxing the abdominal and lower back musculature and ligaments.

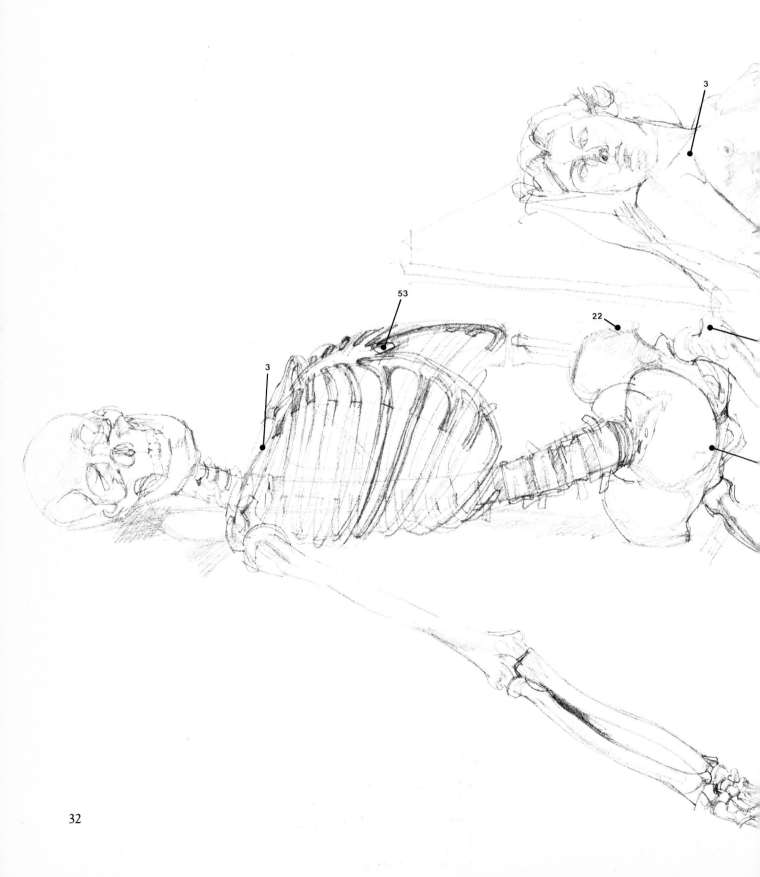

In short, it would be impossible. The limited rotation between each vertebra and the next has been increased and concentrated to an unrealistic degree.

It is worth mentioning that it is possible to bend laterally sufficiently to cause a confluence of the lower edge of the thorax and the iliac crest, and it is more likely that the lower ribs would tuck slightly into the pelvic cavity than the other way round.

3 *Clavicle*
15 *Patella*
22 *Iliac crest*
26 *Pubis*
53 *Xiphoid process*
72 *Greater trochanter*

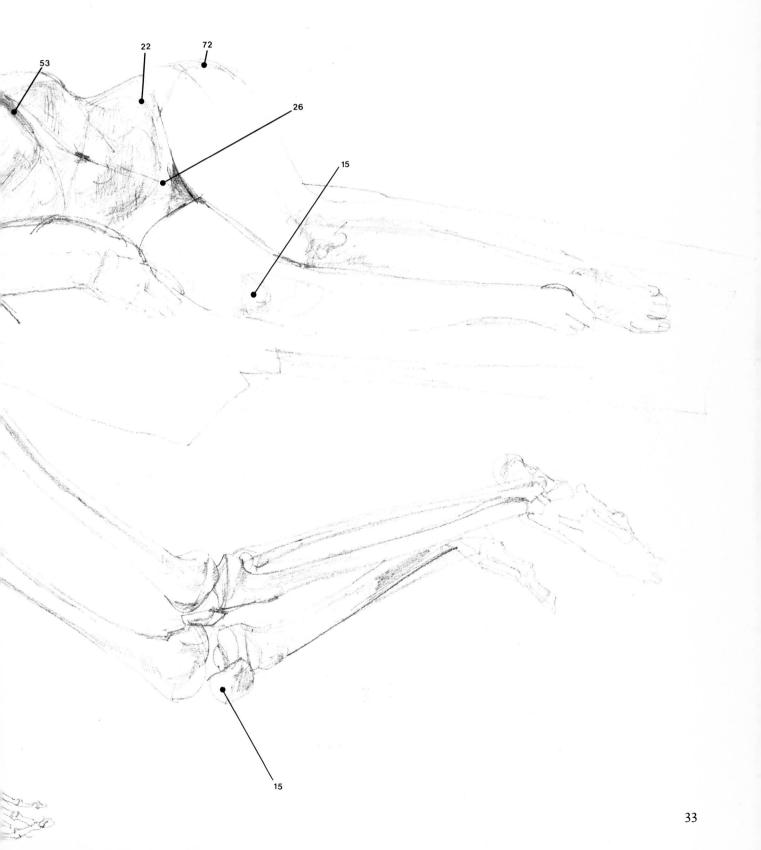

On the opposite page the vertebral column shows, in an exaggerated form, all the possible directions of movement combining together into a sinuous curve. The lumbar area is extended, laterally flexed and rotated, the thoracic is forward and laterally flexed with slight rotation and the cervical area is forward and laterally flexed and rotated.

In nearly every case of spinal bending and torsion some small movement occurs between the sacrum and the innominate bones at the sacro-iliac joint. Although for the purposes of an anatomy for artists, the sacrum is usually considered to be a firmly fixed part of the rigid structure of the pelvis, this small degree of movement does occur, and greatest change derives from the movement from lying to standing posture. Sacro-iliac movement is small, but the angle of the sacrum relative to the lumbar curve has a great effect on the appearance of the whole pelvic area and indeed on the whole stance of the body, by virtue of the counter-balancing adjustments of the rest of the vertebral column. A brief description of this part of the pelvis as a separate entity is thus appropriate at this stage. In life, however, the pelvic girdle should be observed in its entirety.

The sacrum is a large triangular bone formed by the fusion of five vertebrae, and a cross-section reveals the remains of intervertebral discs and tubercles and residual spinous processes on the upper surface.

The region known as the base of the sacrum is rather confusingly at the top when the pelvis is in the upright position; it makes more sense when one thinks of it as the base of the spine, articulating with and supporting the fifth lumbar vertebra. The articular surface consists of the body, which is larger and wider than those of other vertebrae, and two articular processes. In the erect position the sacrum projects backwards to form an angle with the fifth lumbar vertebra, called the *sacro-vertebral angle*. Its dorsal (back) surface is convex and

The sacrum— anterior view

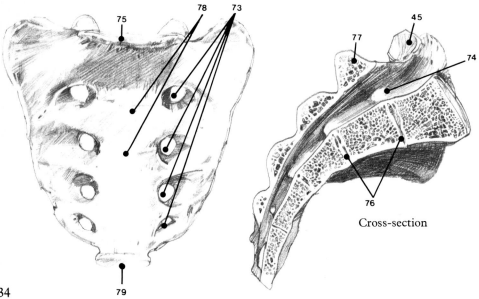

Cross-section

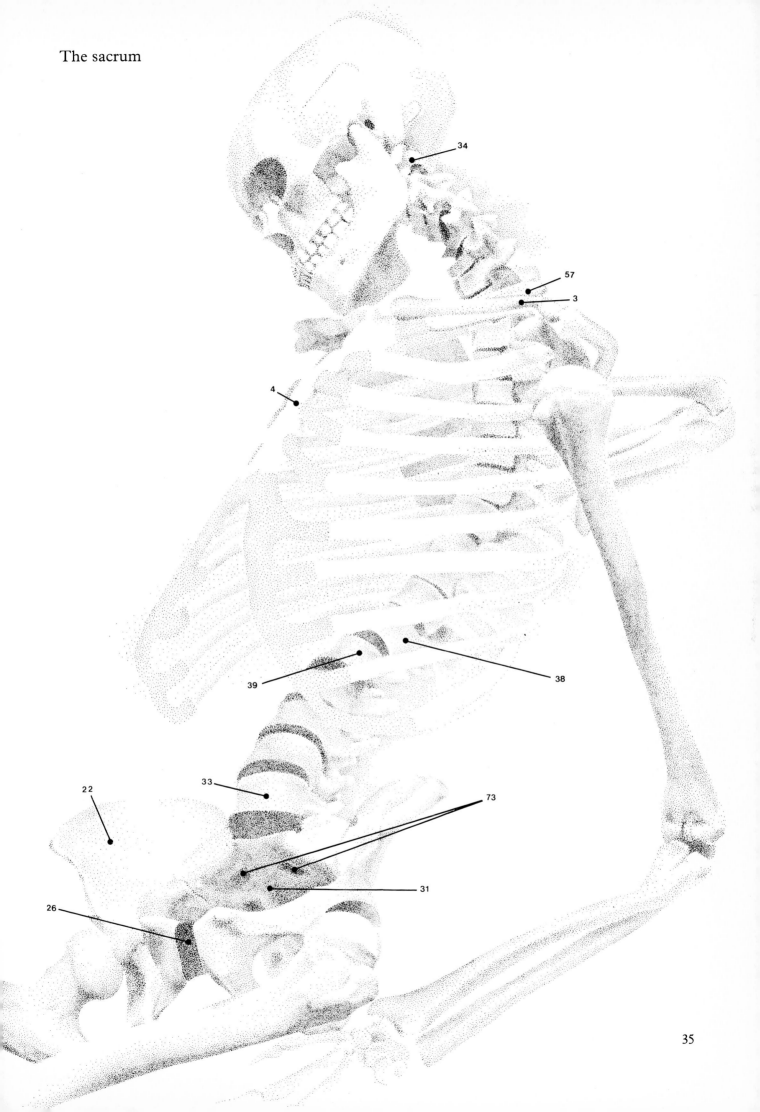

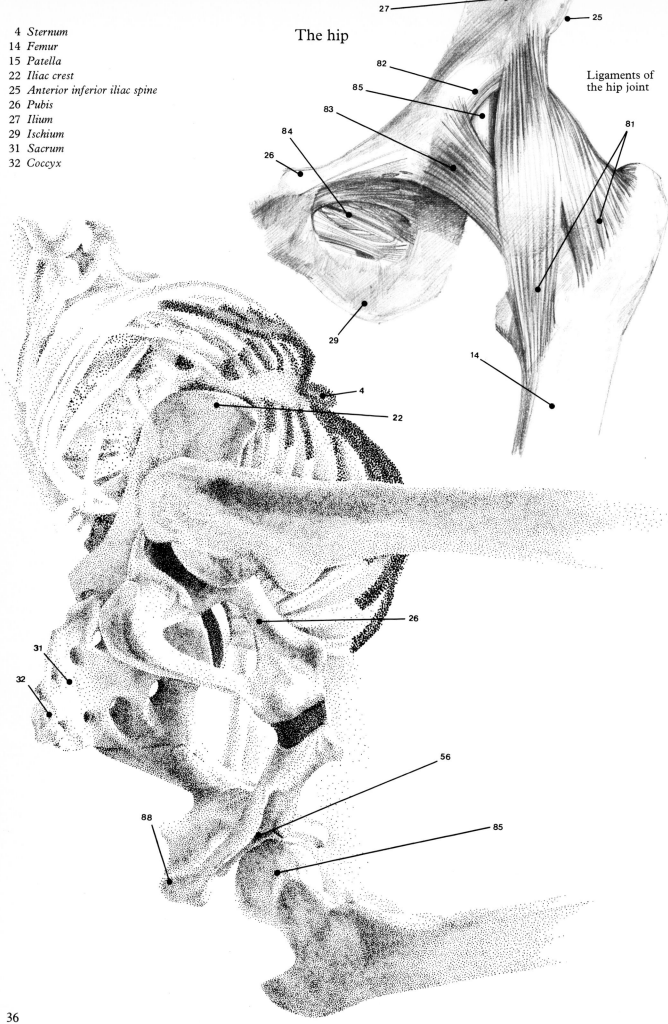

The hip

Ligaments of the hip joint

4 *Sternum*
14 *Femur*
15 *Patella*
22 *Iliac crest*
25 *Anterior inferior iliac spine*
26 *Pubis*
27 *Ilium*
29 *Ischium*
31 *Sacrum*
32 *Coccyx*

very uneven with spinous and transverse tubercles providing large attachment areas for the strong spinal muscles. The *apex* is at the lower, inferior edge, and articulates with the coccyx, and the whole is held in position like a wedge between the hip bones by a strong web of ligaments (see pages 14 and 84).

Although well covered by ligament and muscular attachments, the triangular area is outlined on the surface of the figure by the two posterior superior iliac spines and the coccyx, and is a useful landmark.

We now come to the connection of the skeleton of the torso with the legs – the hip joint.

This joint is of the ball-and-socket type; the slightly more than hemispherical head of the femur articulates in the cup shape of the *acetabulum*. From a small roughened pit a little below and behind the centre of the head, a ligament connects the head to the interior of the acetabulum, but the strongest connections are secured by a number of ligaments which completely cover the head and most of the neck of the femur. Within this binding of ligaments the femur has a vast range of movement, allowing the thigh to swing forward (flexion of the hip joint), backward (extension), outward (abduction), and inward (adduction). It can also rotate so that the leg faces outward (lateral rotation) and to point knees inward (medial rotation). The first three movements can be of a large degree in the young or very flexible, as is evident when a dancer or a gymnast rotates the trunk through 180° while the legs remain in the 'splits' position. It is also very securely constructed; when a footballer takes a swinging kick at the ball, his whole body rotates about the hip joint of the leg in contact with the ground.

56 *Acetabulum*
72 *Greater trochanter*
81 *Ilio-femoral ligament*
82 *Labrum acetabulare*
83 *Pubo-femoral ligament*
84 *Obturator membrane*
85 *Head of femur*
86 *Lesser trochanter*
87 *Pubic tubercle*
88 *Ischial tuberosity*

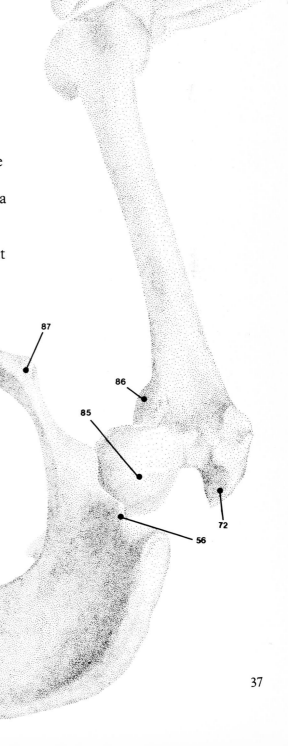

37

The leg I

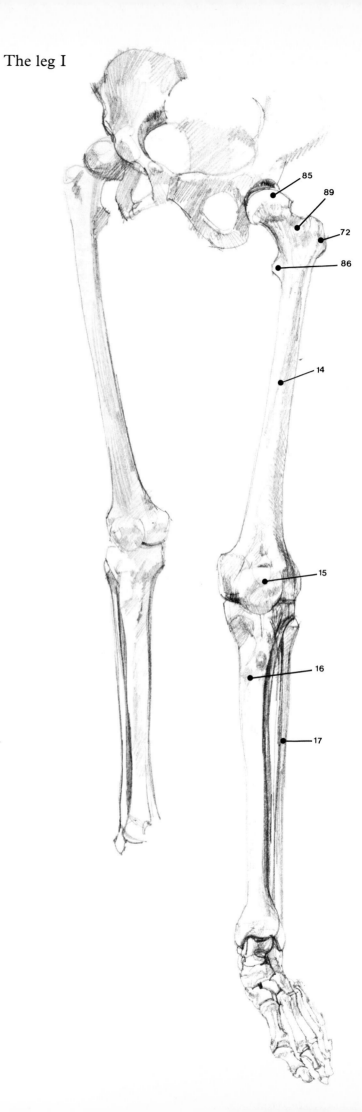

14 *Femur*
15 *Patella*
16 *Tibia*
17 *Fibula*
72 *Greater trochanter*
85 *Head of femur*
86 *Lesser trochanter*
89 *Neck of femur*
90 *Adductor tubercle*
91 *Medial condyle*
92 *Lateral condyle*
93 *Patellar surface*

The *femur* is the longest and heaviest bone in the body, and is a quarter or even a third the length of the total body. The head, which has been described, is separated from the main shaft by about 5 cm (2 in) of neck which is angled at around 125° to the main shaft. At the outside of the shaft, where it joins the neck, there is a large prominence, named the *greater trochanter*; this lies close to the surface and is identifiable in life either as a lump at the widest part of the hips or at least as the point where the plane of the flank changes to that of the thigh. Most of the shaft, covered with tuberosities, grooves and ridges, affords attachment to or is covered by muscles. Although it is deep in the leg, its direction is evident at the surface by the tubular form of the thigh, with its familiar, slightly diagonal appearance from hip to knee, as seen from the front.

The lower end is made up of two large condyles separated posteriorly by a deep division called the *intercondylar notch*. At the anterior (front) side the condyles are joined together and form an articular surface for the *patella* or kneecap. The lower surfaces articulate with the upper end of the tibia. Much of the lower end of the femur and most of the upper end of the tibia is close to the surface in life, and together with the patella gives shape to the outer form of the knee.

The knee is the largest joint in the body and is structurally complicated. Basically it is a hinge, with the convex condyles of the lower end of the femur sliding in the loosely matched hollows of the upper condyles of the tibia. In the fully straightened (extended) position the knee joint 'screws' itself into tight contact, ligaments and muscles reach the limit of their travel and the knee locks securely. This description of the locking mechanism of the knee is over-simplified and rather unenlightening, but the medical descriptions of the action are extremely complicated and the precise role of all factors is still a matter of dispute. From the point of view of the artist complete understanding of the dynamics is not really vital, but there is one modification of the simple hinge concept which is worth taking into account.

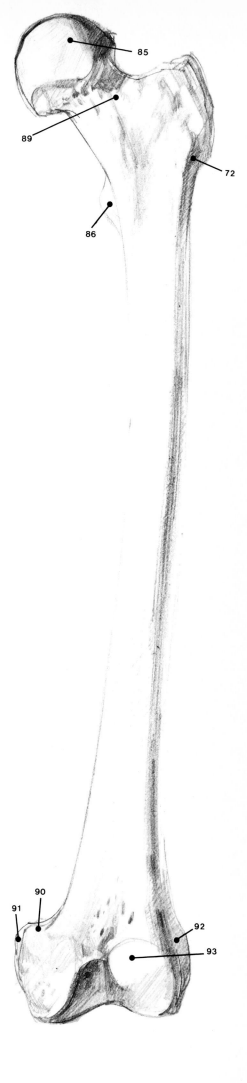

The leg II   As the knee joint nears locking point in full extension, the femur has to rotate a little inward (medially) in order to make close contact with the unequally sized 'receiving hollows' of the tibia. Consequently the inner condyle of the femur acquires more prominence from the front view when the knee is locked, and is rather more noticeable from the medial side when the knee is bent back.

An instantly recognizable part of the external form of the knee, especially in the male, is the thinly covered tuberosity of the tibia. The sharp front edge of the triangular section shaft of the tibia is also close to the

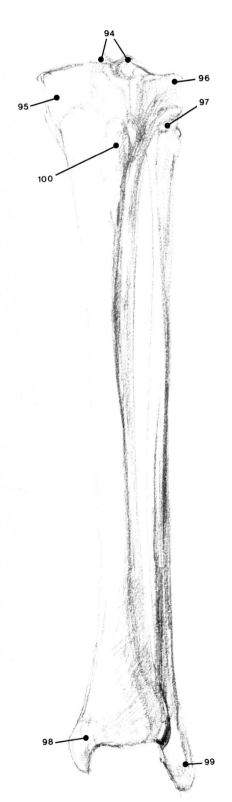

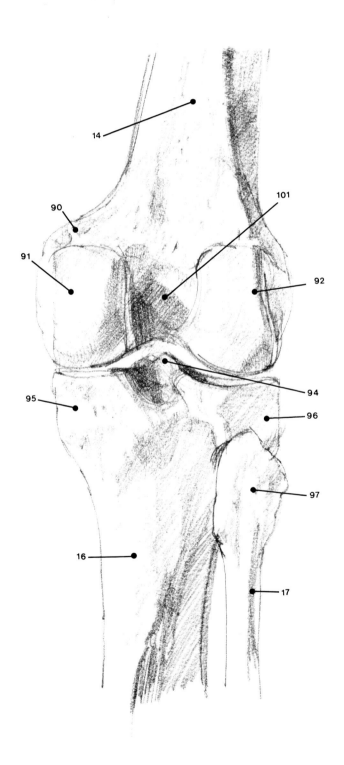

skin in life, and the whole of the medial face of its shaft is free of muscular attachments, and therefore presents another useful fixed line of reference for the artist.

Alongside the tibia on the outside (lateral side) of the leg is the slim bone named the *fibula*. It does not have to share support of the body weight, but functions as a bracing rod for the ankle articulation and also provides attachments for many muscles of extension and flexion. The head of the fibula is enlarged and articulates with the under-side of the lateral condyle of the tibia by means of a small circular facet. It is superficial in life and contributes to the outer form of the knee.

14 *Femur*
15 *Patella*
16 *Tibia*
17 *Fibula*
90 *Adductor tubercle*
91 *Medial condyle–femur*
92 *Lateral condyle–femur*
94 *Intercondylar eminences–tibia*
95 *Medial condyle–tibia*
96 *Lateral condyle–tibia*
97 *Head of fibula*
98 *Medial malleolus*
99 *Lateral malleolus*
100 *Tibial tuberosity*
101 *Intercondylar fossa*
102 *Calcaneus*
103 *Talus*
104 *Navicular*

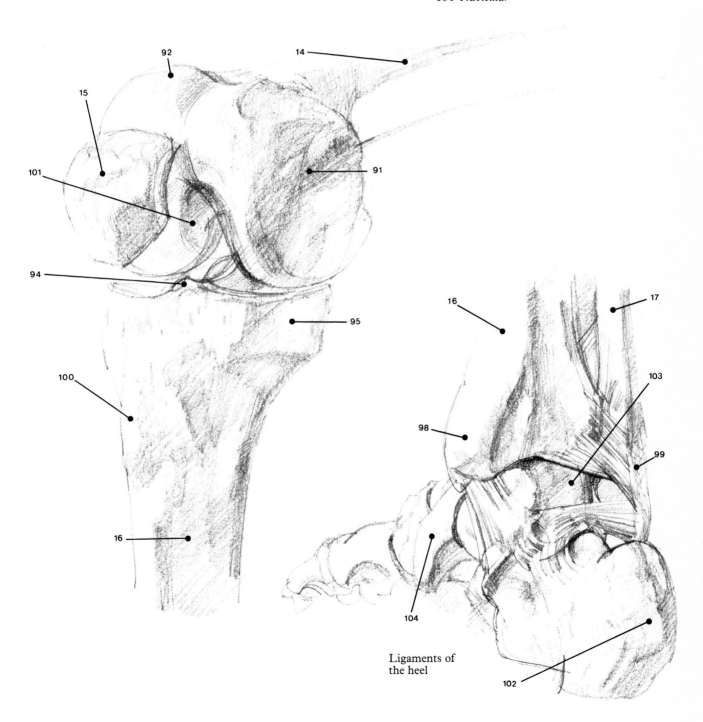

Ligaments of
the heel

The foot

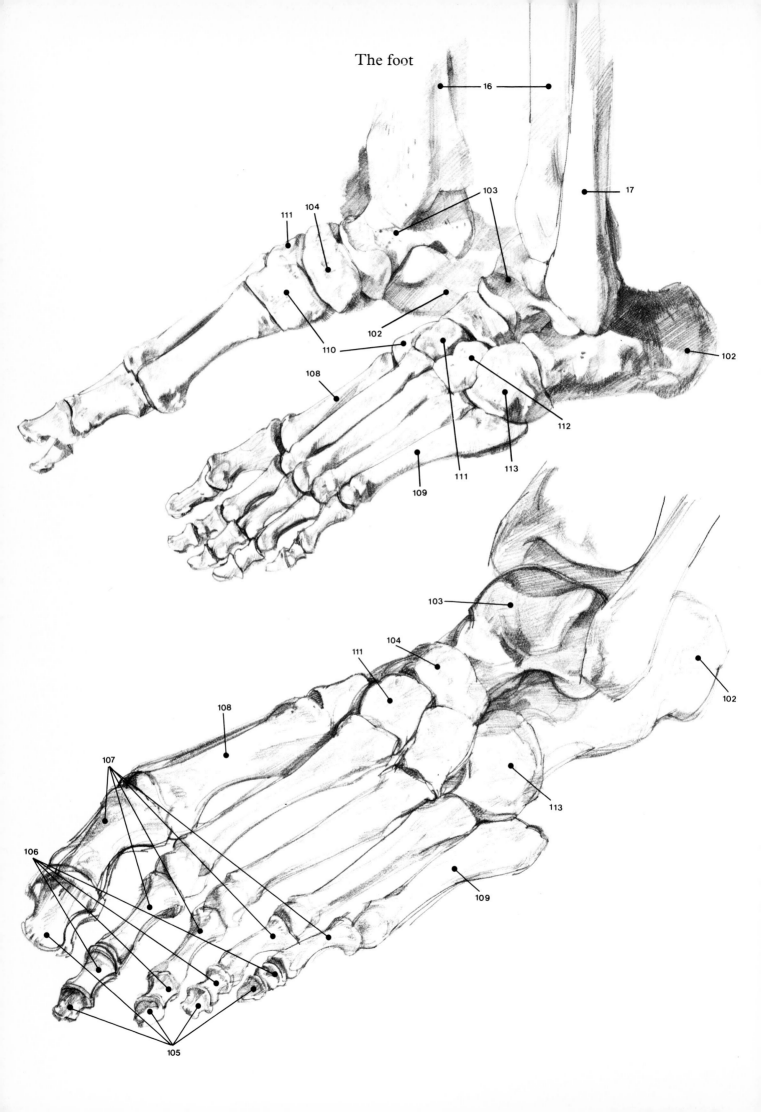

At the ankle end of the lower leg the medial edge of the tibia projects down and outwards to form the *medial malleolus*, while the fibula extends even further down on the lateral side, becoming the *lateral malleolus*. These are important prominences in life in all but the very fat, and are responsible for the familiar ankle form, in which the inner 'ankle' is always higher than, and forms a constant angle with, the outer one.

The *talus* has a complex shape, consisting mainly of articular surfaces, but consideration of its shape and detailed function relative to the adjacent bones of the foot would be beyond the needs of a study of anatomy for artists. Its articulation with the lower leg, however, is comparatively simple and important, allowing flexion and extension by a rocking motion in line with the foot.

To avoid confusion with the terms describing toe movements, flexion or drawing the foot upwards is called *dorsiflexion*, and extension or pointing the foot is called *plantarflexion*.

In dorsiflexion the broadest part of the articulating surface of the talus is wedged into the space between the malleoli, forcing them apart slightly and holding the foot very securely. Plantarflexion reduces the tension; although the malleoli spring back to retain their grasp on the sides of the talus, there is a small amount of side-to-side motion possible when the toe is fully pointed (in full plantarflexion).

By their muscular and cartilaginous connections the bones of the foot form a series of springy arches which act as a strong platform for the support of the body. It is astonishing that such a small structure is capable of absorbing the enormous loads to which it is subjected, but the complex of small bones and ligaments in the foot is beautifully contrived to do just this and it deserves careful observation. The form of the whole structure is easily seen through the skin in life. There are three arches – one transverse arch across the foot at about the line of the joints between metatarsus and tarsus, and one longitudinally on each side of the foot. Both longitudinal arches have the posterior part of the *calcaneus* or heel bone as the posterior pillar. From here the *lateral arch*, which is very low, continues through the body of the calcaneus (which joints with the *cuboid bone*), on into the lateral two metatarsal bones. Body weight or pressure is transmitted to this arch through the joint between the talus and the posterior facet on the upper surface of the calcaneus.

Much higher and more important is the *medial arch* comprising calcaneus, talus, navicular, the cuneiforms and the three metatarsal bones. The weight of the body is imposed directly on to the talus. This arch is the most pliable and resilient and probably the most active in absorbing imposed forces.

16 *Tibia*
17 *Fibula*
102 *Calcaneus*
103 *Talus*
104 *Navicular*
105 *Distal phalanges*
106 *Middle phalanges*
107 *Proximal phalanges*
108 *1st metatarsal*
109 *5th metatarsal*
110 *Medial cuneiform*
111 *Intermediate cuneiform*
112 *Lateral cuneiform*
113 *Cuboid*

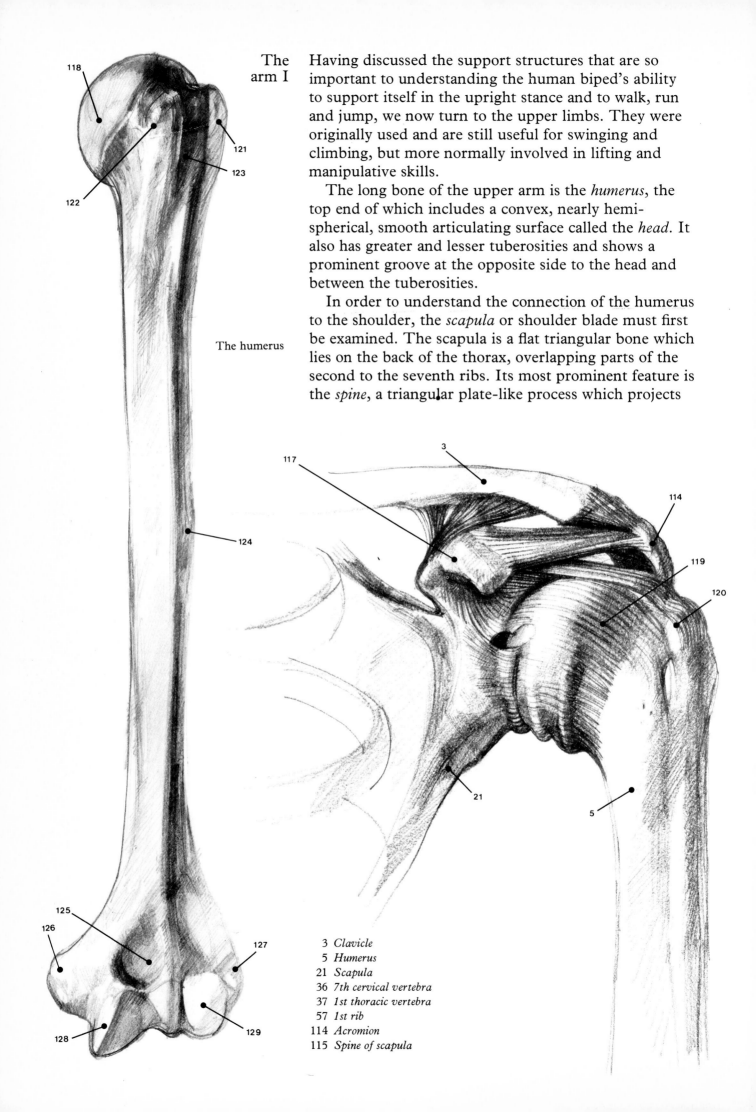

The arm I

Having discussed the support structures that are so important to understanding the human biped's ability to support itself in the upright stance and to walk, run and jump, we now turn to the upper limbs. They were originally used and are still useful for swinging and climbing, but more normally involved in lifting and manipulative skills.

The long bone of the upper arm is the *humerus*, the top end of which includes a convex, nearly hemispherical, smooth articulating surface called the *head*. It also has greater and lesser tuberosities and shows a prominent groove at the opposite side to the head and between the tuberosities.

In order to understand the connection of the humerus to the shoulder, the *scapula* or shoulder blade must first be examined. The scapula is a flat triangular bone which lies on the back of the thorax, overlapping parts of the second to the seventh ribs. Its most prominent feature is the *spine*, a triangular plate-like process which projects

The humerus

3 *Clavicle*
5 *Humerus*
21 *Scapula*
36 *7th cervical vertebra*
37 *1st thoracic vertebra*
57 *1st rib*
114 *Acromion*
115 *Spine of scapula*

from the dorsal surface of the scapula, extending outward and curving forward to form the bony upper edge of the shoulder known as the *acromion*. Nearly the whole of the crest of this spine, as well as the acromion, is just under the skin in life, and is clearly visible either as a prominence or a depression, depending on individual musculature.

On the upper border of the scapula the *coracoid process* projects forward and slightly laterally. Between the coracoid and the acromion, on the top outer corner (its *lateral angle*), lies the *glenoid cavity* which, although small and shallow, functions as the socket for articulation with the head of the humerus. When the *clavicle* is in position the shoulder girdle is formed, with the bony ridge of the scapula spine continuing over the shoulder at the acromion and across the front via the clavicle. A space is defined by the underside of the shoulder girdle, the glenoid cavity, and by the coracoid process, which dictates the freedom of movement of the humerus.

116 *Glenoid cavity*
117 *Coracoid process*
118 *Head of humerus*
119 *Capsular ligament*
120 *Groove for long tendon of biceps*
121 *Greater tubercle*
122 *Lesser tubercle*
123 *Intertubercular sulcus*
124 *Deltoid tuberosity*
125 *Coronoid fossa*
126 *Medial epicondyle*
127 *Lateral epicondyle*
128 *Trochlea*
129 *Capitulum*

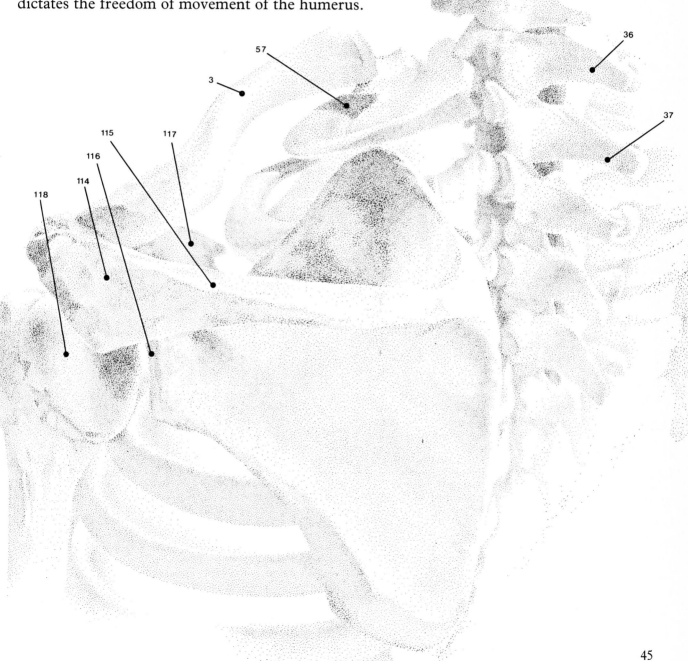

The arm II

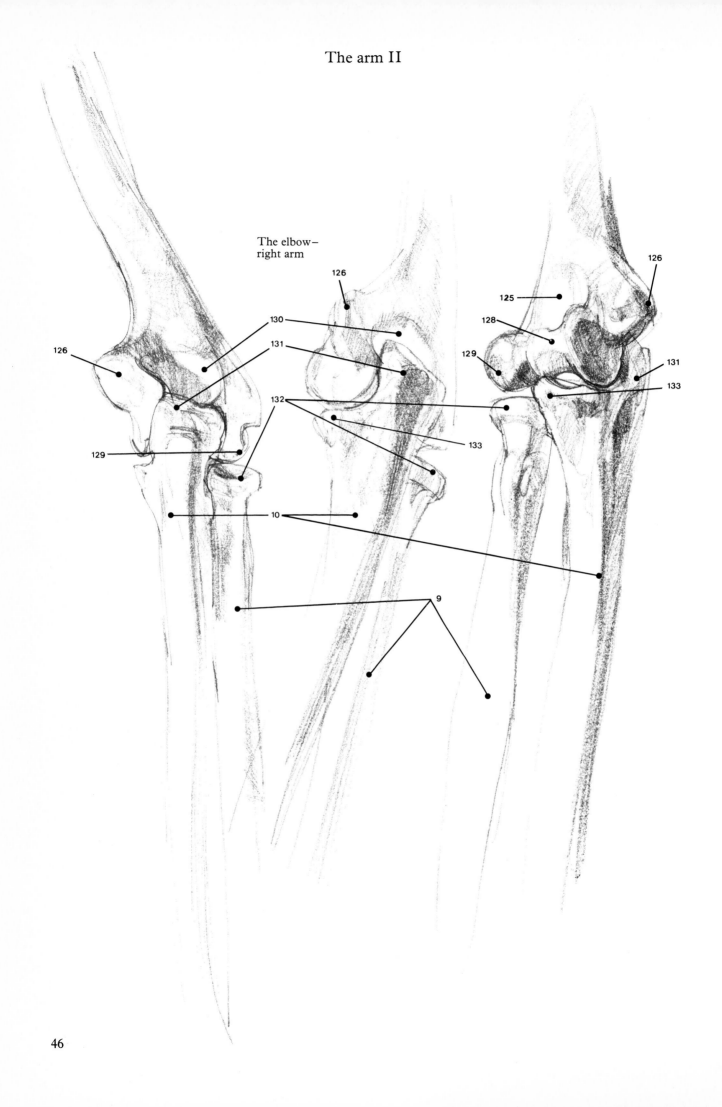

The elbow –
right arm

The shaft of the humerus is fairly long, about one-fifth the length of the total body. It is almost cylindrical in its upper half but flattens and widens in the lower half to culminate in a condyle or knuckle-shaped articular surface. From the front view the articular surface can clearly be seen to consist of a smooth, concave, pulley-like surface, the *trochlea*, and a hemispherical convex one, the *capitulum*. The medial epicondyle is also prominent and is seen in life as the inner point of the elbow joint.

Articulating on the capitulum is the cupped upper surface of the upper end of the *radius*, the shorter of the two forearm bones. The upper end of the other forearm bone, the *ulna*, has a notch, called the *trochlear notch*, which fits neatly round the trochlea at the bottom end of the humerus and articulates with it, enabling the joint to execute flexion and extension movements. There is a large projection forming the upper end of the ulna, called the *olecranon*; this inserts into a fossa (depression) on the humerus at full extension, preventing further movement and locking the arm. When the arm is *supinated* (with the palm of the hand uppermost or forward), the forearm bones are side by side, but when it is *pronated*, the hand and wrist turn inward and carry the radius across the ulna obliquely to the medial side, so that the two forearm bones cross and the lower ends rotate into reverse positions.

The lower ends of the radius and ulna form the beginning of the wrist, the end of the ulna being smaller than that of the radius. Both have styloid processes which can be seen on the surface, with that of the ulna normally more prominent. Their combined articular surfaces embrace the articular surfaces of the *triquetral*, *lunate* and *scaphoid* carpal bones of the wrist.

5 Humerus
9 Radius
10 Ulna
125 Coronoid fossa
126 Medial epicondyle
127 Lateral epicondyle
128 Trochlea
129 Capitulum
130 Olecranon fossa
131 Olecranon
132 Head of radius
133 Coronoid process

47

9 *Radius*
10 *Ulna*
134 *Styloid process–radius*
135 *Styloid process–ulna*
136 *Trapezium*
137 *Trapezoid*
138 *Scaphoid*
139 *Capitate*
140 *Lunate*
141 *Hamate*
142 *Triquetral*
143 *Pisiform*
144 *5th metacarpal*
145 *1st metacarpal*
146 *Proximal phalanges*
147 *Middle phalanges*
148 *Distal phalanges*

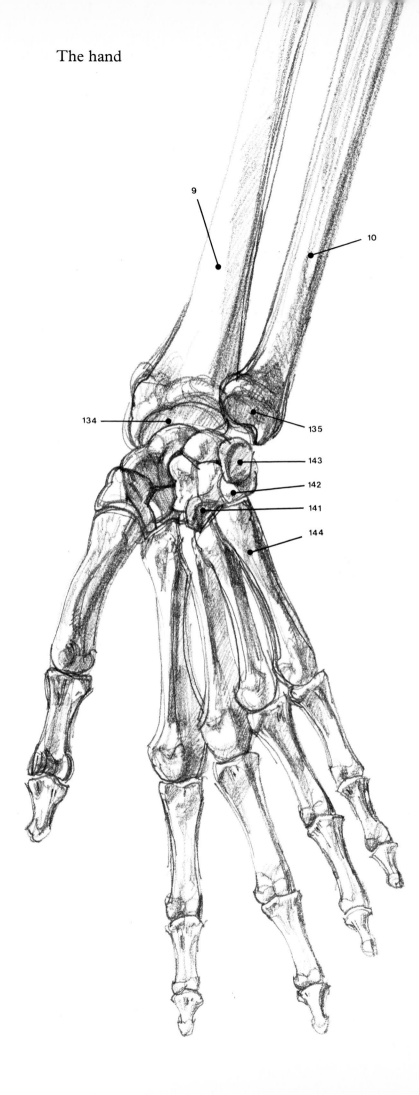

The wrist is a mobile joint that allows free movement in virtually all planes. Rotational movement within the wrist itself is limited, but since the whole wrist can be rotated this is scarcely too restricting.

Other than the triquetral, lunate and scaphoid bones, the remaining five carpals articulate on each other but in fact move very little. Their motions are mostly small sliding or rocking ones to accommodate to or extend the larger wrist movements.

Four of the *metacarpal* bones of the hand proper articulate with the distal (nearest to the free end of the limb) row of carpal bones and with each other, while the fifth metacarpal or thumb bone articulates with the *trapezium* and the first metacarpal in the familiar disposition of opposition to the hand. At their distal ends or heads, the metacarpal bones are rounded.

The fingers of the hand are made up of three *phalanges*, the thumb only two. Each phalanx, like the metacarpal bones, is a 'miniature' long bone, with a proximal end (nearest the wrist), called the base, a shaft and distal end called the *head*. The proximal phalanx of a digit is the largest, and has a concave base to articulate with the appropriate metacarpal and a pulley-shaped head. The middle phalanx is smaller and has the reverse-shaped base to articulate with the pulley shape of the first, and a similar but smaller pulley-shaped head, on which articulates the third or distal phalanx. This phalanx is distinguished by a rough horseshoe-shaped tuberosity to which the soft tissues of the finger tip attach. The two phalanges of the thumb resemble the proximal and distal phalanges of the fingers without the middle one.

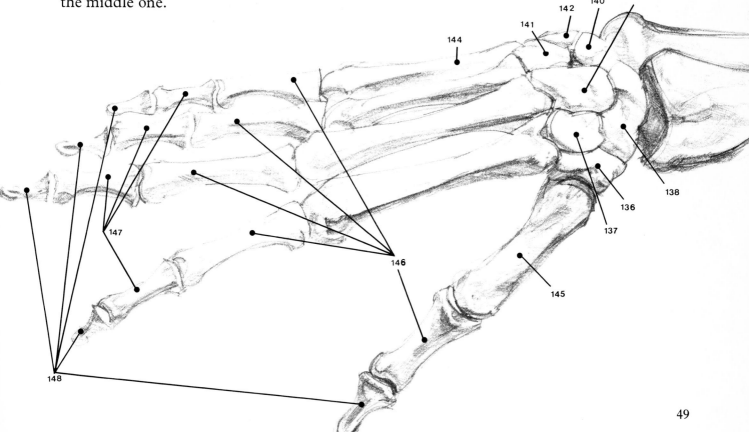

49

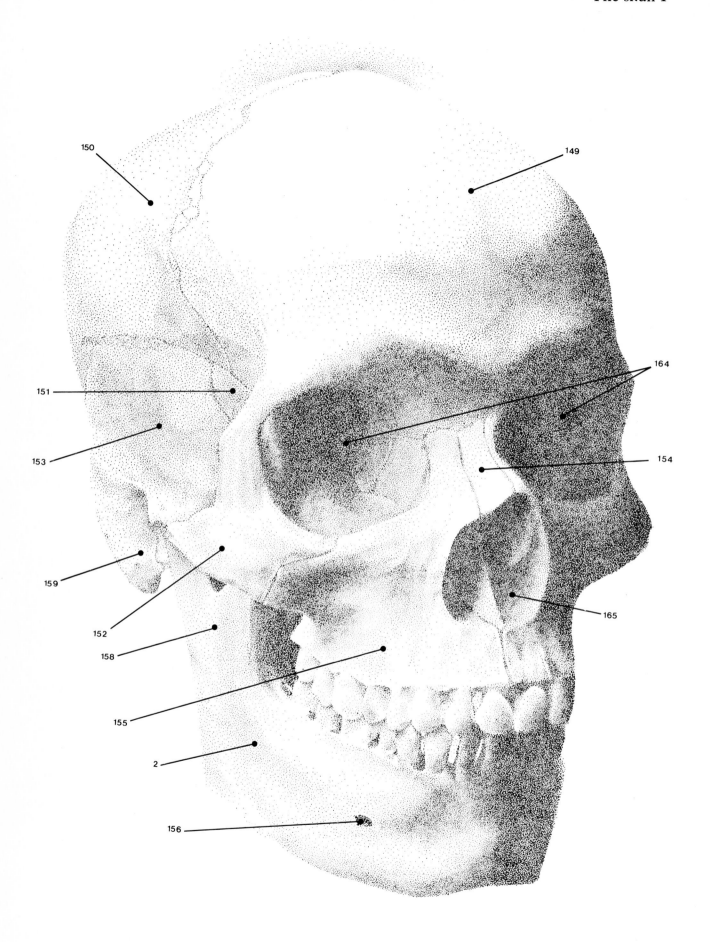

150

149

151

164

153

154

159

152

158

165

155

2

156

In terms of separate moving parts, the skull consists of only two bones: the *mandible* or jaw bone and the rest, which constitutes the *cranium*. In fact the cranium is made up of a total of 21 bones which operate as a single joined unit, but can be separated from each other. In an infant's skull the bones are only loosely joined with some gaps, but during the second year of life they knit together firmly and throughout life the joints gradually disappear and neighbouring bones fuse together. For the most part the cranium forms a box to enclose the brain. The rest of the skull is called the facial skeleton.

The forehead area is composed of a large bone called the *frontal*, which also forms the eyebrow ridges and the upper parts of the eye sockets. While it clearly forms part of what is normally considered to be the face, it is also the front part of the brain box. Next to the frontal are the two large *parietal bones*, joined together at the top centre of the cranium and forming the greater part of the sides and back. Between the parietals at the back is the *occipital bone*, leaf-shaped and bent to form the back and base of the cranium. It has a very rough surface for attachment of the powerful extensor muscles of the neck and spine.

The *temporal bones* are found at the sides of the skull beneath the parietals and extend a little into the base of the skull. The temporal bone includes the external *acoustic meatus*, or ear hole, the area immediately behind which is known as the *mastoid temporal*.

2	*Mandible*
149	*Frontal bone*
150	*Parietal bone*
151	*Greater wing of sphenoid bone*
152	*Zygomatic bone*
153	*Temporal bone*
154	*Nasal bone*
155	*Maxilla*
156	*Mental foramen*
157	*Occipital bone*
158	*Ramus of mandible*
159	*Mastoid process*
164	*Orbit*
165	*Nasal cavity*

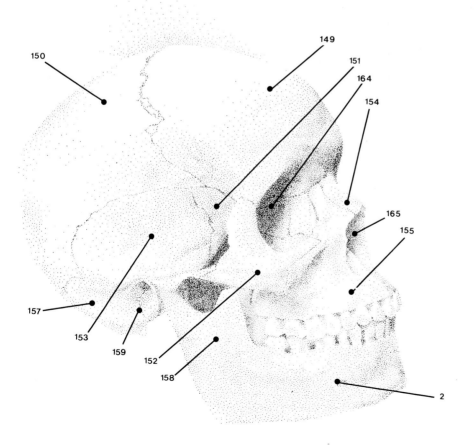

The skull II
There are two other subdivisions of the temporal. The *zygomatic process* of the temporal is a projection from the *squamous part*, or large area above the ear passage. A small plate of bone, called the *tympanic plate*, forms the front and rear wall of the ear passage and the *styloid process* projects downward from it. The remainder of the temporal is called the *petrous part*. It is situated deep in the base of the skull and as such is of little importance to the artist.

The *sphenoid bones* complete the enclosure of the cranium and form more of the eye sockets. Contributing to the generally conical space and squarish outlets of the eye sockets (*orbits*) are the *ethmoid* and the *lacrymal* bones. These largely determine how far apart the eyes are set. The bridge of the nose is formed by the two *nasal bones*. There are a number of thin plates of bone within the nasal cavity which again have no effect on surface form and are of little interest to the artist-anatomist.

The *maxillae* and the *zygomatics* are very prominent in the surface form of the face. The two maxillae form the upper jaw and extend at their upper edges into the orbits, and also join with the nasal bones to form the bony shape of the sides of the nose. Parts of the maxillae extend into the interior of the nasal cavity (the rear-facing area under the zygomatic) and also form the bony palate. The lower part of the anterior wall, known as the *alveolar process*, includes the teeth sockets and provides the basic form of the upper lip area.

The zygomatic bones are the cheek bones and form part of the outer lower rims of the eye sockets. Together with the zygomatic processes of the maxillae and the *zygomae* of the temporal bones, they form the zygomatic arches.

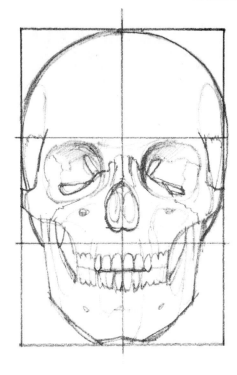
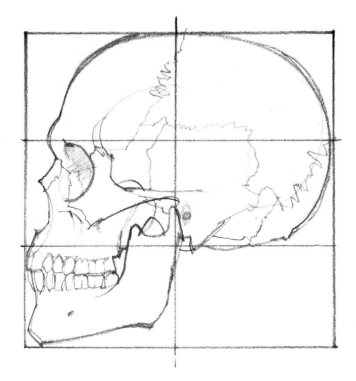

The lower teeth are situated in the lower jaw, or mandible, which has a rounded V-shaped body and two flat broad rami that project upward from the posterior ends. Each ramus has two upward-projecting processes; the anterior non-articulating one is the *coronoid process* and the posterior one, called the *condyloid process*, articulates with the temporal bone to form the *mandibular joint*.

Relative sizes, shapes and distances between the mandible, maxillae, nasal bones, zygomatics, eye orbits and frontal bones are infinitely varied and subtle and make possible the uniqueness of each and every face. Musculature and surface tissue of course fill out the basic forms, but although the superficial features change throughout life, the underlying bone structure is so fundamental to appearance that recognition of the individual throughout maturation and aging is almost always easy. Even the lengthening of the maxillae, which principally takes place between the ages of six and twelve years and alters the childish roundness into a more adult length, does not completely change the individuality of the face beyond recognition.

Viewed from above, the skull can be seen to have

  2 *Mandible*
149 *Frontal bone*
150 *Parietal bone*
152 *Zygomatic bone*
153 *Temporal bone*
154 *Nasal bone*
155 *Maxilla*
160 *Bregma*
161 *Superciliary arch*
162 *Sagittal suture*
163 *Coronal suture*
164 *Orbit*
165 *Nasal cavity*

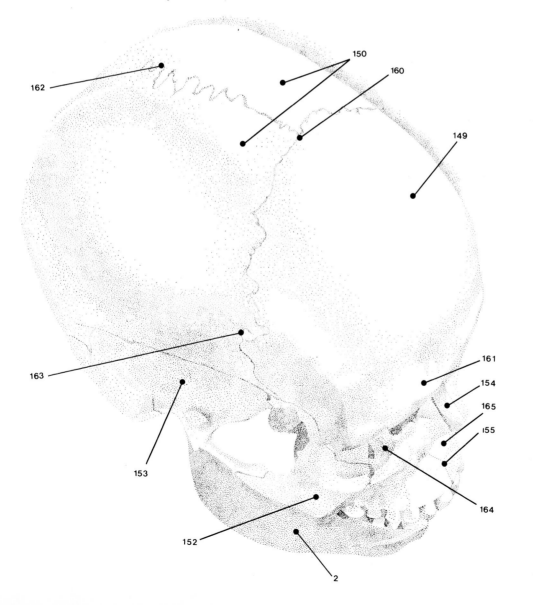

The skull III   convex contours; although there is great ethnic variation, European skulls are normally ovoid from this view,
with a flattened narrow end forming the facial surface.
The skull is widest across the cranium, nearer the
occipital than the frontal region. From the front the
outline is again somewhat ovoid, sometimes widest at
the zygomatic and sometimes across the cranium a little
higher up. The great variation in shape and size of the
mandible has an important influence on the general
shape from this view. The side view of the skull and
mandible can be seen as fitting into a square, so that the
cranium occupies the upper two-thirds and the mandible occupies half the remaining third.

   At the base of the skull, on the occipital bone, there
are two condyles, one each side of the foramen magnum,

for articulation with the atlas vertebra. This makes up the *atlanto-occipital* joint. The movements possible at this joint are flexion and extension (nodding the head) and a little tilting from side to side.

Most of the mobility of the head depends on the movement between the atlas and the axis, and the combinations of movement in the other cervical vertebrae. The articulation between atlas and axis takes place in two ways: as well as the normal sliding, rocking contact between their opposed articular processes, there is also a special one involving rotation of the anterior arch of the atlas around the upward-projecting odontoid process of the axis. Rotation, flexion, extension and lateral tilting can be combined to produce great mobility for the head and neck.

3 *Clavicle*
4 *Sternum*
34 *Atlas*
35 *Axis*
37 *1st thoracic vertebra*
57 *1st rib*
152 *Zygomatic bone*
155 *Maxilla*
157 *Occipital bone*
158 *Ramus of mandible*
159 *Mastoid process*
161 *Superciliary arch*
165 *Nasal cavity*
166 *External acoustic meatus*
167 *Coronoid process—mandible*
168 *Condylar process—mandible*

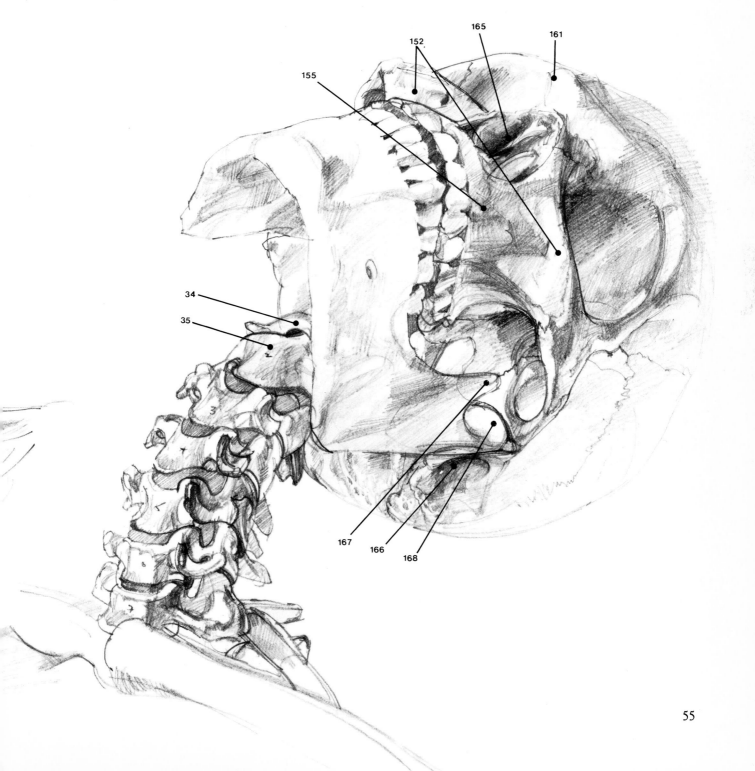

The muscles

Just as a decision has to be made as to how detailed a knowledge of human skeletal structure is useful to the figure artist, so priorities must be allocated in the study of musculature. Surface form is finally our only interest, but it is not always the feature immediately below the surface that is principally responsible for this form. Over large areas of the body the musculature is multi-layered; in some cases all the layers are of flat sheets of muscle, while sometimes the form is defined by rounded muscles at or near the top layer, and at other times by those forming the deep layer. There is such diversity of movement, so many combinations of muscular activity, that to choose at which layer the artist should stop is very difficult.

As a result, this part of the book starts from the deep layers and works to the surface, with comment and detailed description relevant to the likely ultimate effect of each muscular group on surface form.

Probably the most significant deep muscle group in the body from the point of view of the artist is that complex of muscles known as the *erector spinae*. As the name suggests, they function as rigging for the spinal column. It is made up of many separate muscles, with complicated attachments to ribs and transverse and spinous vertebral processes, but the overall appearance of the group is of two thick ropes of muscle stretching from the coccyx to the base of the skull. It is especially prominent in the sacro-lumbar area, where it is covered by a *fascia* (a band or sheet of connective tissue), and is rather more flattened in the thoracic area and prominent again in the neck.

As can be seen in the cross-section, the erector spinae group generally lies in and overfills the grooves formed by the transverse and spinous processes of the vertebral column. It is responsible for the characteristic appearance in life of the central line of the spine lying in the hollow formed by these two powerful columns of muscle.

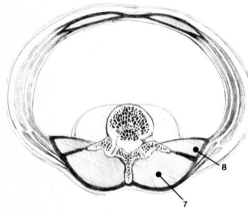

Cross-section
of thorax

The back I

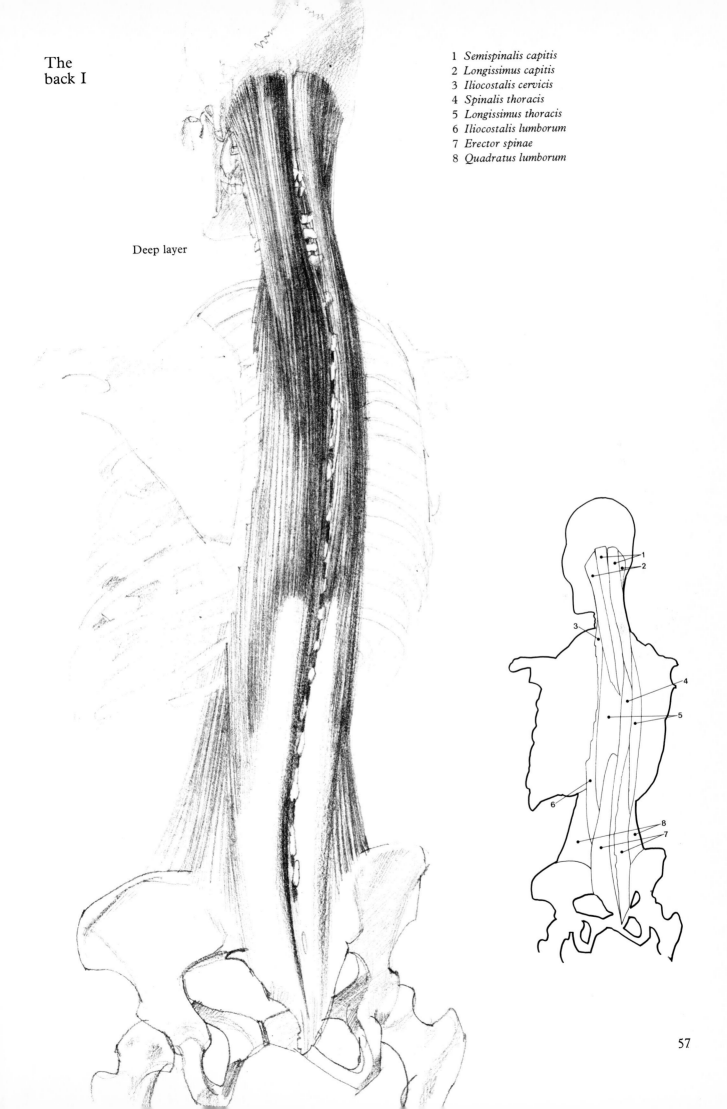

1 *Semispinalis capitis*
2 *Longissimus capitis*
3 *Iliocostalis cervicis*
4 *Spinalis thoracis*
5 *Longissimus thoracis*
6 *Iliocostalis lumborum*
7 *Erector spinae*
8 *Quadratus lumborum*

Deep layer

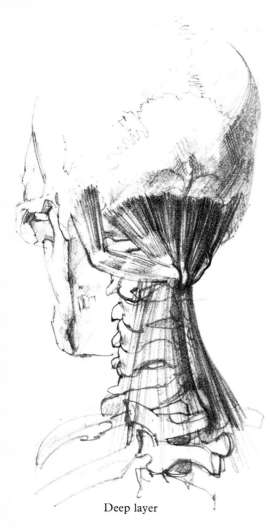

Deep layer

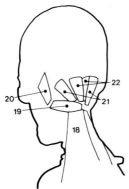

For the artist, the viscera can be considered as being contained in a more or less elastic sack which sits in the cup form of the pelvis and extends into the lower part of the thorax. Above is the diaphragm containing the lungs which are activated by the muscular expansion and contraction of the rib cage. The heart sits in its own sack, the *pericardium*, within the rib cage muscles. The shape of the trunk therefore depends firstly on the size of the gut that it contains and secondly on the elasticity and strength of the muscle layers that hold it in place.

There are three layers of flat muscle which perform this function, as well as more actively operating the trunk in its extension, flexion and twisting movements. The lowest layer is the *transverse abdominis*, shown in the drawing on page 62. It consists largely of an *aponeurosis* (a flat sheet of tendon-like substance, white in colour and smoother than contractile muscle fibre). Immediately above this muscle lies the layer called the *obliquus internus*. Its fibres run at an angle of about 45° to the transverse abdominis; they are shown from the back on the opposite page. The upper part of the erector spinae is overlaid by *rhomboideus major* and *minor*, together arising from the seventh cervical and the first to fifth thoracic vertebral spines, and attaching to the medial edge of the scapula.

Attaching to the same medial edge but on the inner, costal surface is another sheet-like muscle, the *serratus anterior*, which wraps around the chest to widespread insertions in (attachments to) the upper eight, nine, or even ten ribs. The *serratus posterior inferior* is a small muscle acting upon the lower ribs; it has little or no effect on surface form.

Rounding out the form of the back of the neck are several layers of muscle. Those shown as numbers 19 to 22 on this page are concerned with the fine control of head movements and cannot be discerned superficially, but the extensions of the erector spinae, the *semispinalis cervicis* and the *semispinalis capitis* partially overlayed by the *splenius capitis* all contribute to the rounded form of the back of the neck.

On the surface of the scapula are a group of muscles which are in the main superficial. They are the *infraspinatus*, the *teres minor* and *teres major*. The first two arise from the surface of the scapula and insert into the top of the humerus. The teres major threads under the long head of the *triceps* to insert into the underside of the upper humerus.

The back II

Intermediate layer

1 *Semispinalis capitis*
7 *Erector spinae*
8 *Quadratus lumborum*
9 *Splenius capitis*
10 *Supraspinatus*
11 *Infraspinatus*
12 *Teres minor*
13 *Teres major*
14 *Rhomboideus major*
15 *Serratus anterior*
16 *Serratus posterior inferior*
17 *Obliquus internus*
18 *Semispinalis cervicis*
19 *Obliquus capitis inferior*
20 *Obliquus capitis superior*
21 *Rectus capitis posterior major*
22 *Rectus capitis posterior minor*

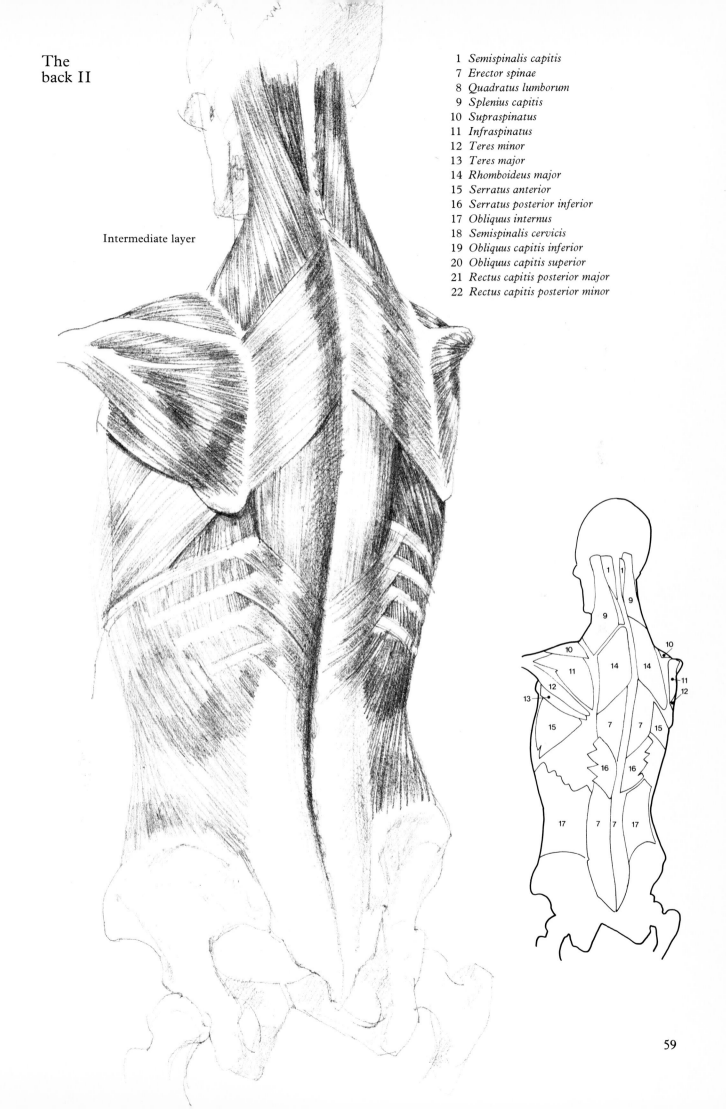

The dominating muscles of the upper back are the *trapezius* muscles, large flat triangles which together form the trapezium shape from which the name derives. They are attached to the base of the skull at the occipital, to the *ligamentum nuchae* (which covers the first six cervical spines), the seventh cervical and all the thoracic vertebral spinous processes. The upper fibres run downwards to insert in the lateral third of the clavicle and the medial border of the acromion. The middle fibres are nearly horizontal and insert into the upper edge of the spine of the scapula and the lower fibres proceed upwards to a flat triangular tendon which attaches to the tubercle of the scapula spine. All of the spinal attachments from about the sixth cervical to the third thoracic vertebral spines are by means of short tendinous fibres and the tendon extends to form a diamond-shaped depressed area between the two trapezius muscles.

The *latissimus dorsi* wraps a large area of the lower back. Although it is extensive, it is quite thin, so that underlying forms are still discernible. It arises from the spines of the lower six thoracic vertebrae, the posterior lumbar fascia, the spines of the lumbar vertebrae, the sacrum and the iliac crest. The lateral border also arises directly from the outer lip of the iliac crest and several muscular slips (extra fibres) arise from the lower three or four ribs. The muscle converges into a narrow tendon inserting into the upper humerus with a twist by which, with the arm in the resting position, the muscle is turned over on itself. Raising the arm above the head to an extent unwraps this twist. The lower angle of the scapula lies under, and can be observed through, the upper edge of the latissimus dorsi.

The third side of the 'frame' around the scapula is completed by the *deltoid* muscle, which extends right around the shoulder. From the back, the fibres attached to the lower edge of the crest of the scapula spine can be seen to pass downward and outward to converge into a short tendon attached to the deltoid tuberosity about halfway down the shaft of the humerus.

All but a small part of the medial border of the scapula is covered by superficial muscle, but the outline of its form is normally fairly easily seen. That medial border is seen as a groove between the swellings of the infraspinatus on one side and a triangle of rhomboideus major, which appears from under the trapezius. The raised level of the scapula and the thickness of the fibres of the lower trapezius mean that the visible triangle of the rhomboideus sometimes appears as a depression. This is known as a *triangle of auscultation*.

Finally the third, top layer of the frontal and lateral trunk covering, the *obliquus externus*, is also visible.

The back III

Superficial layer

11 *Infraspinatus*
12 *Teres minor*
13 *Teres major*
14 *Rhomboideus major*
23 *Sternocleidomastoid*
24 *Trapezius*
25 *Deltoid*
26 *Latissimus dorsi*
27 *Obliquus externus*

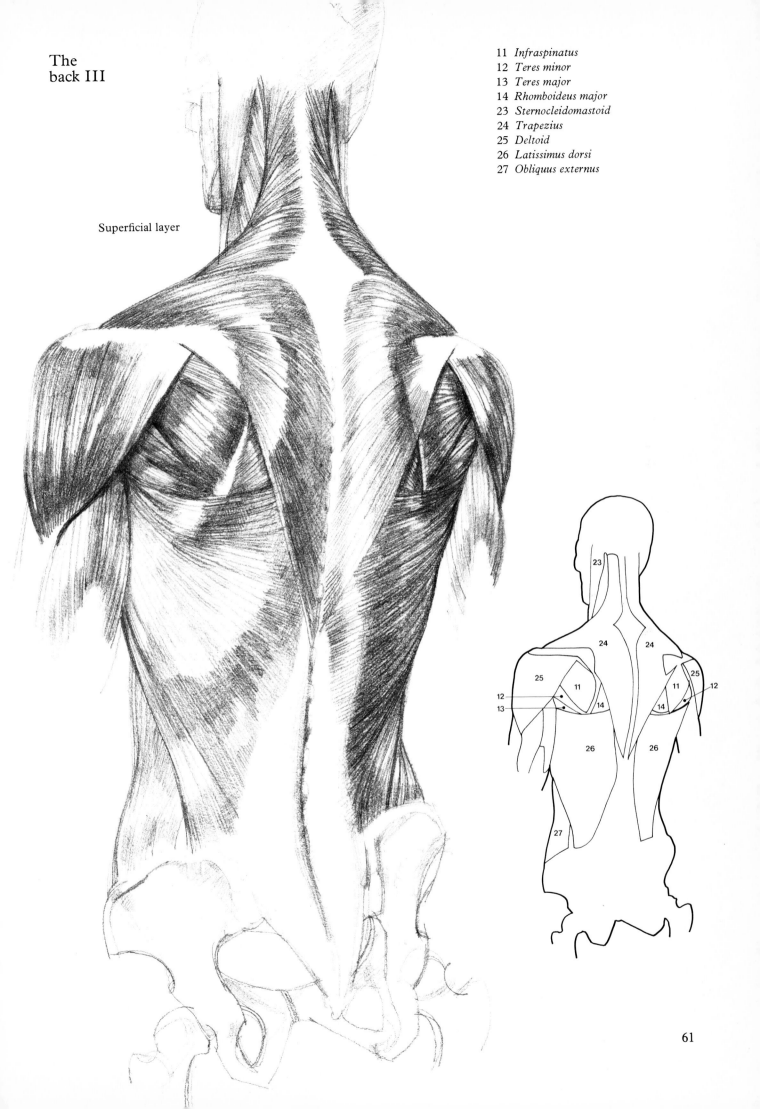

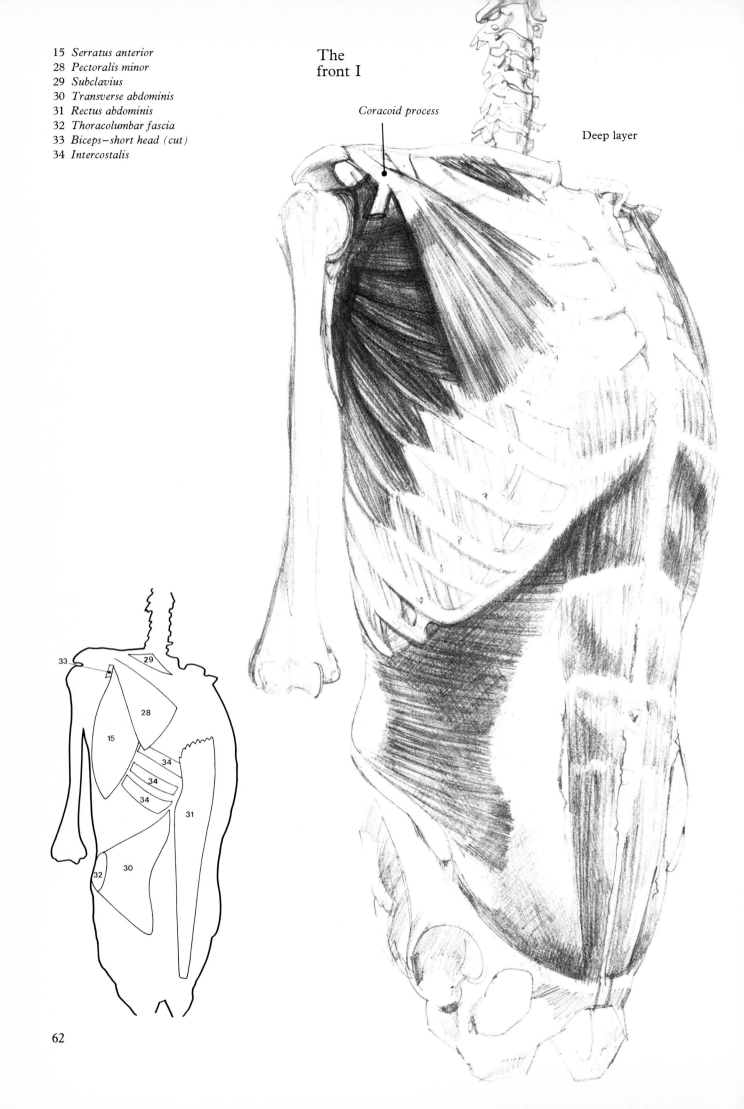

15 *Serratus anterior*
28 *Pectoralis minor*
29 *Subclavius*
30 *Transverse abdominis*
31 *Rectus abdominis*
32 *Thoracolumbar fascia*
33 *Biceps—short head (cut)*
34 *Intercostalis*

The
front I

Coracoid process

Deep layer

On the opposite page the illustration shows the deep muscles of the trunk viewed from three-quarter front.

The *serratus anterior* has been considered and illustrated on page 58 as a muscle of the back; here its attachments to the upper eight or nine ribs at the side of the chest can be seen. The small drawing on this page shows the full extent of the muscle. The lower four or five digitations converge on to the bottom medial border of the scapula, those from the middle attach in a sheet a little higher up the same border, and the major length of the upper medial border is occupied by fibres from the first two ribs only. Although only the medial ends of the lower four or five digitations of the serratus anterior with the ribs (costal digitations) are visible in life, and they are often mistakenly thought to be ribs rather than muscle fibres, it is in fact a strong muscle and is the prime mover in all reaching and pushing movements. It also positively anchors the scapula in rotated positions to provide a firm shoulder joint.

The *pectoralis minor*, in life, is almost entirely hidden under the large surface muscle of the chest, the *pectoralis major*. In the larger drawing it can be seen to attach by a flat tendon to the coracoid process of the scapula, and it can be continuous with the coraco-acromial ligament or can even pass through it to blend with ligaments attaching to the humerus. Occasionally a slip, called *pectoralis minimus*, joins the first rib to the coracoid process.

In this context it is worth mentioning that there is great variation between people in muscular origins and insertions throughout the body. Muscles often have non-standard additional slips and some muscles may be totally absent. The rectus abdominis, for example, which is a prominent and important muscle extending along the front of the abdomen from the pubis to attachments into the fifth, sixth and seventh costal cartilages, sometimes attaches by a slip to the fifth rib proper, and sometimes not, and it may even reach the fourth or third rib.

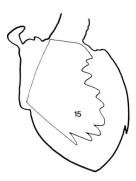

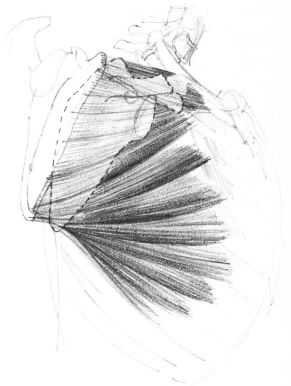

Serratus anterior

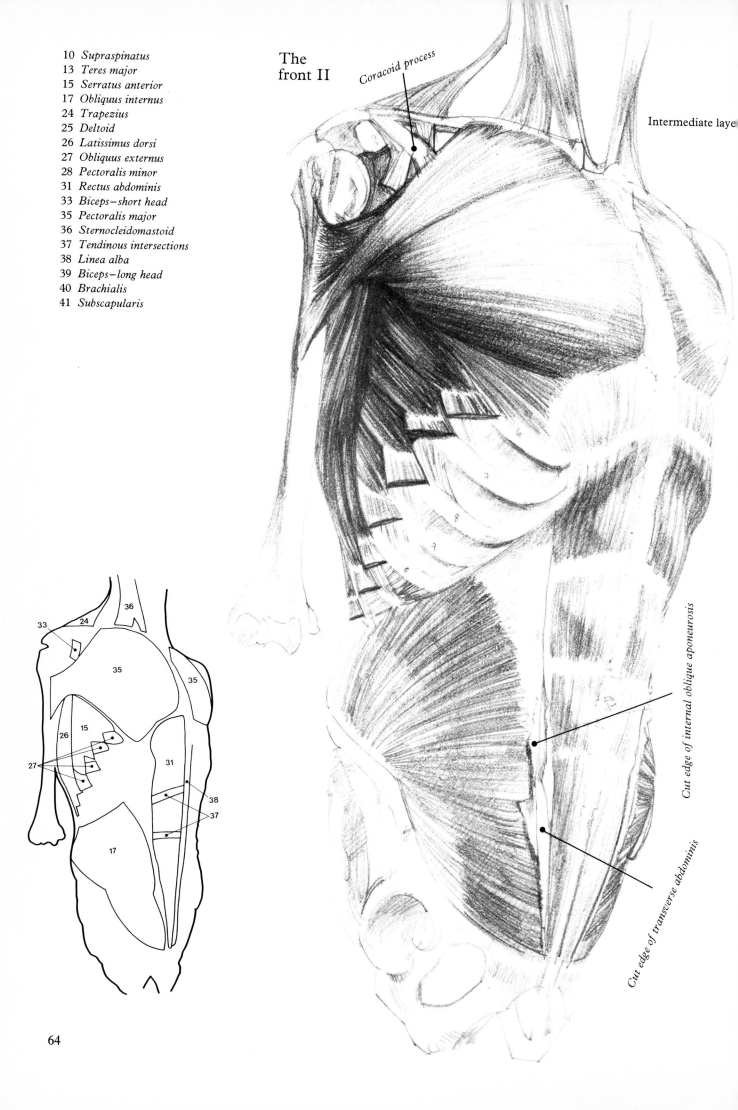

The
front II

Coracoid process

Intermediate laye

Cut edge of internal oblique aponeurosis

Cut edge of transverse abdominis

64

The most obvious addition shown on the opposite page is the large muscle of the chest, the *pectoralis major*. It is of thick triangular form, arising from the medial half of the clavicle, half the breadth of the sternum and the cartilages of the first or second to the sixth or seventh ribs and the aponeurosis of the obliquus externus abdominis. At the other end the muscle converges into a flat tendon which twists over to insert high into the humerus. The precise manner of this twisting is complicated to describe, since not all the fibres are involved; but the sternal part of the pectoralis is mainly involved in the twist and the clavicular part inserts more directly into the tendon. The small drawing clarifies the relationship of the pectoralis major to the pectoralis minor which it almost completely covers, and to the long head of the biceps around which it wraps. Slightly higher and medial to the insertion of the pectoralis major tendon on the humerus can be seen the tendon of the latissimus dorsi, described on page 60.

Returning to the larger illustration, the *rectus abdominis* is again shown, but the edges of the transverse abdominis and the internal oblique aponeurosis have been cut to show that the lower fibres of the rectus abdominis are covered by these two layers of aponeurosis, and emerge gradually as the muscle progresses upward. In fact there is a third layer, the obliquus externus, covering the complete rectus abdominis so that even the top third is not quite superficial. Nevertheless the coverings are thin and smooth, so the rectus abdominis is strongly visible at the surface, especially in fit and lean people, on whom the tendinous intersections can be clearly seen.

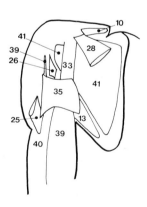

Pectoralis major
and minor

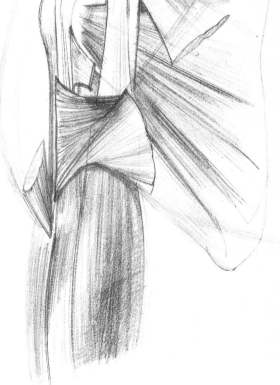

65

15 *Serratus anterior*
24 *Trapezius*
25 *Deltoid*
26 *Latissimus dorsi*
27 *Obliquus externus*
36 *Sternocleidomastoid*
42 *Clavicular part of pectoralis major*
43 *Sternocostal part of pectoralis major*
44 *Biceps*

The front III

Superficial layer

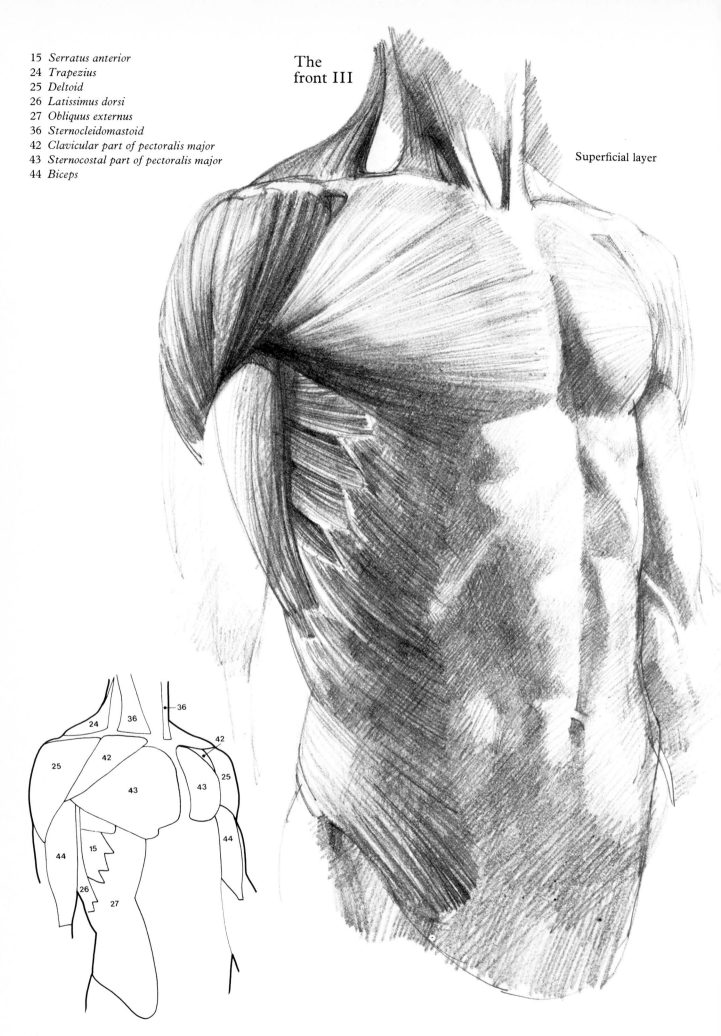

We come now to the surface musculature of the front of the trunk.

The insertion of the deltoid into the humerus, and attachments to the spine of the scapula have already been described. Here its frontal attachments to the lateral third of the clavicle are visible, and the small drawing shows the complete extent of the muscle. In life the deltoid provides the rounded form of the shoulder and in action it can appear corrugated and complex in form. This is caused by the fact that the intermediate part of the muscle is 'multi-pennate', or composed of a bundle of groups of fibres, separated by intramuscular strips of tendon converging into the main tendon. Its insertion securely wraps around the deltoid tuberosity on the humerus and also has connections with the deep *brachial fascia* (muscles underlying the biceps, described on page 72) and can thereby sometimes even reach the forearm. It is a powerful muscle and is active in almost all shoulder movements; the acromial fibres especially are capable of strong contraction when the arm is raised (see page 71).

The most superficial flat abdominal covering is the *obliquus externus abdominis*, arising by eight slips from the lower eight ribs and interdigitating as shown here (and pages 62 and 64) with the digitations of the serratus anterior and latissimus dorsi. Its fibres pass downward and forward as shown, to join a large flat aponeurosis covering the front of the trunk from around the sixth rib down to the pubic crest.

This drawing tries to suggest the appearance in life of the rectus abdominis as seen through the layers of aponeurosis. Of the linear tendinous intersections discussed on page 65, the one near the navel is normally the lowest, this and the next one up normally being the most clearly visible. The top tendinous intersection is usually nearly coincident with the lower edge of the thorax, and there are sometimes one or two extra ones below the navel (although the subject must be particularly lean for these to be visible under three layers of aponeurosis).

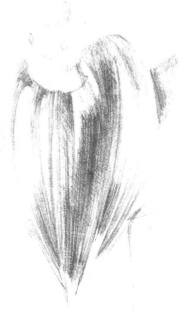

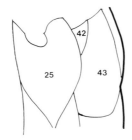

Deltoid muscle

On this spread and the next the musculature described on the previous pages is shown in action and from less familiar angles.

The figure on this page with the raised left arm demonstrates the rotation of the scapula associated with this action. The dotted lines indicate the resting and rotated positions of the scapulae spines. The upper medial angle of the scapulae is visible through the lower trapezius fibres, and the medial border appears superficially between the infraspinatus and the slightly more exposed rhomboideus major and is then covered at its lower angle by the latissimus dorsi.

The lateral edge of the scapula in this action projects laterally and thus changes the outline of the back from this view. Active and therefore contracted fibres of the upper trapezius bunch the form of the upper shoulder and similarly the intermediate fibres of the deltoid effectively bury the acromion at their conjunction.

The drawing on the opposite page views the

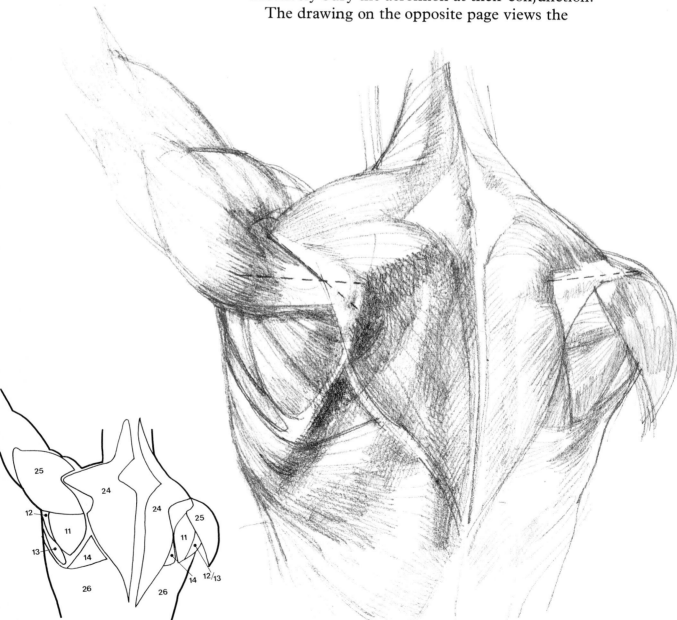

musculature of the back from above, to reveal the extension of the trapezius attachments along the scapula spine and the acromion to the outer third of the clavicle. The extent of this clavicular attachment is variable, sometimes reaching as far as halfway along; it may even blend with the edge of the sternomastoid, which is shown here connecting the inner third to half of the clavicle with the mastoid process. In the interval between these two can be seen a series of thin muscles which are variously active in swallowing, speech, and head rotation, flexion and so on. These are described in more detail on page 98.

From this view the spinous process of the seventh cervical vertebra may be prominent near the centre of the tendinous diamond of the two trapezius muscles. More noticeable is the difference in direction of the combined infraspinatus and teres minor, and the teres major, which results from their different insertions and their separation by the long head of the triceps.

11 *Infraspinatus*
12 *Teres minor*
13 *Teres major*
14 *Rhomboideus major*
23 *Sternocleidomastoid*
24 *Trapezius*
25 *Deltoid*
26 *Latissimus dorsi*
35 *Pectoralis major*

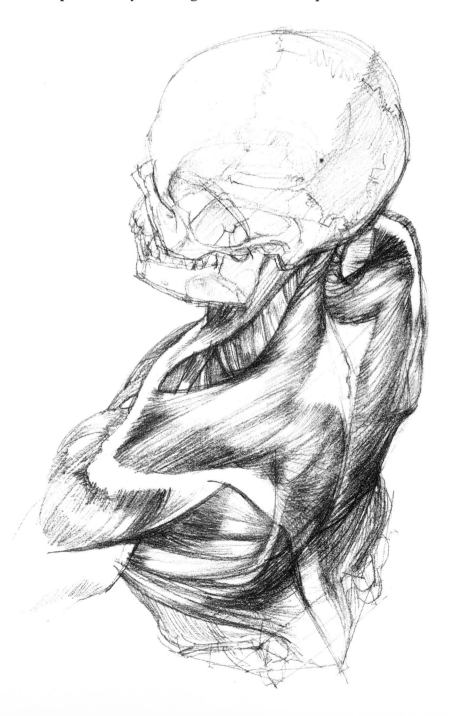

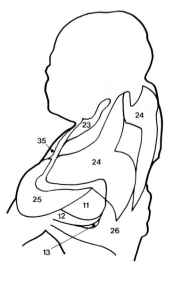

69

The shoulder II

From the front the raised arm always seems to present difficulties to the anatomy student but its form is really quite straightforward if the insertions of the muscles involved are understood and taken into account.

The dominant underarm feature in this position is probably the combined form of the teres major and the latissimus dorsi. Both insert into the upper humerus by means of closely adjacent tendons and have to relax and elongate considerably to allow the arm to be raised above the head. They both pass medially to the triceps, while the teres minor and infraspinatus pass the other side of the triceps to their insertions in the head of the humerus.

The pectoralis major, with its upper humerus insertion, is also stretched by the arm raising. One result of the upward stretching of the latissimus dorsi and pectoralis major is to reveal more of the serratus anterior, which becomes prominent through the rotation of the scapula. A small section of the pectoralis minor

11 *Infraspinatus*
12 *Teres minor*
13 *Teres major*
14 *Rhomboideus major*
15 *Serratus anterior*
24 *Trapezius*
25 *Deltoid*
26 *Latissimus dorsi*
28 *Pectoralis minor*
35 *Pectoralis major*

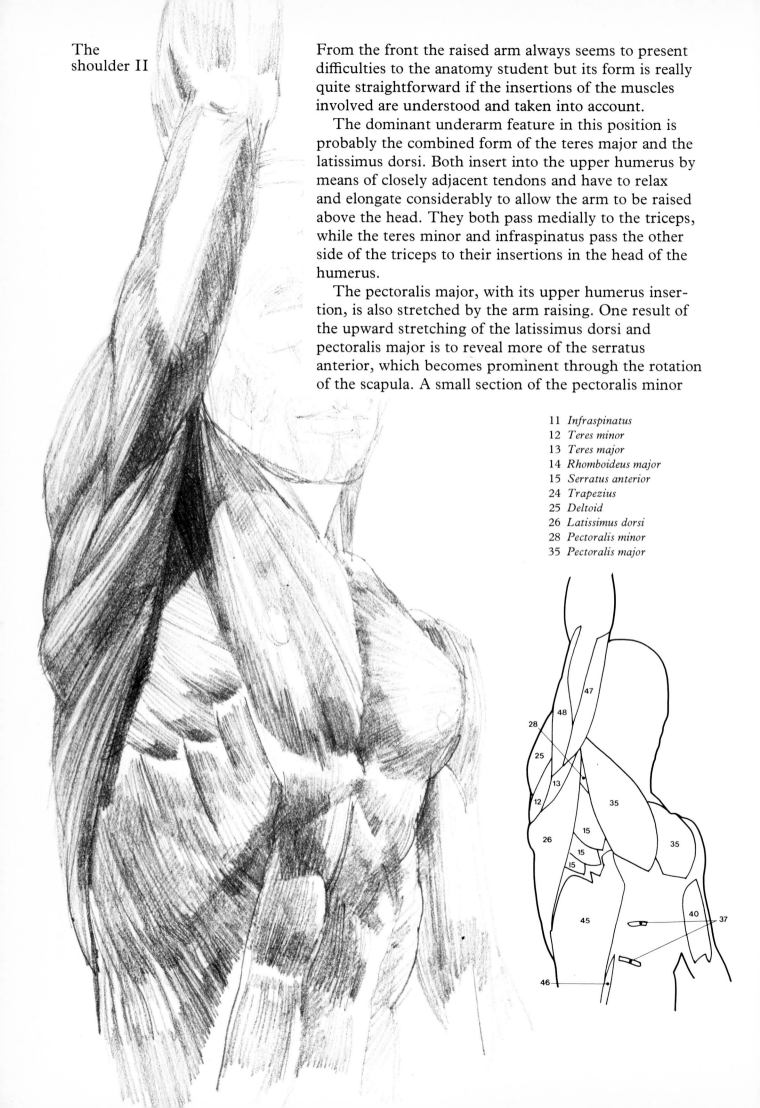

may also be revealed in the armpit but it is rarely visible as a separate form.

The lengthened and relaxed fibres of the deltoid arising from the rotated spine of the scapula can be seen pulled upwards by the tendon shared with the active acromial fibres. The triceps itself is only active and tensed if the arm is held rigidly straight (in extension); indeed the whole arm can be quite relaxed, and all the work done by the combined action of the deltoid, trapezius and scapula muscles.

The drawing shown on this page is a rear view of exactly the same action. This drawing is based on a photograph, like several others in this book; they are intended to show clearly how the activity of the musculature fits with the actual form observed. The model in this case was well developed; most of the features are recognizable in a less pronounced form in slighter individuals, although the outline of the scapula assumes greater importance as the muscle size diminishes.

36 *Sternocleidomastoid*
37 *Tendinous intersections*
40 *Brachialis*
44 *Biceps*
45 *Obliquus externus abdominis*
46 *Linea semilunaris*
47 *Triceps—long head*
48 *Triceps—lateral head*

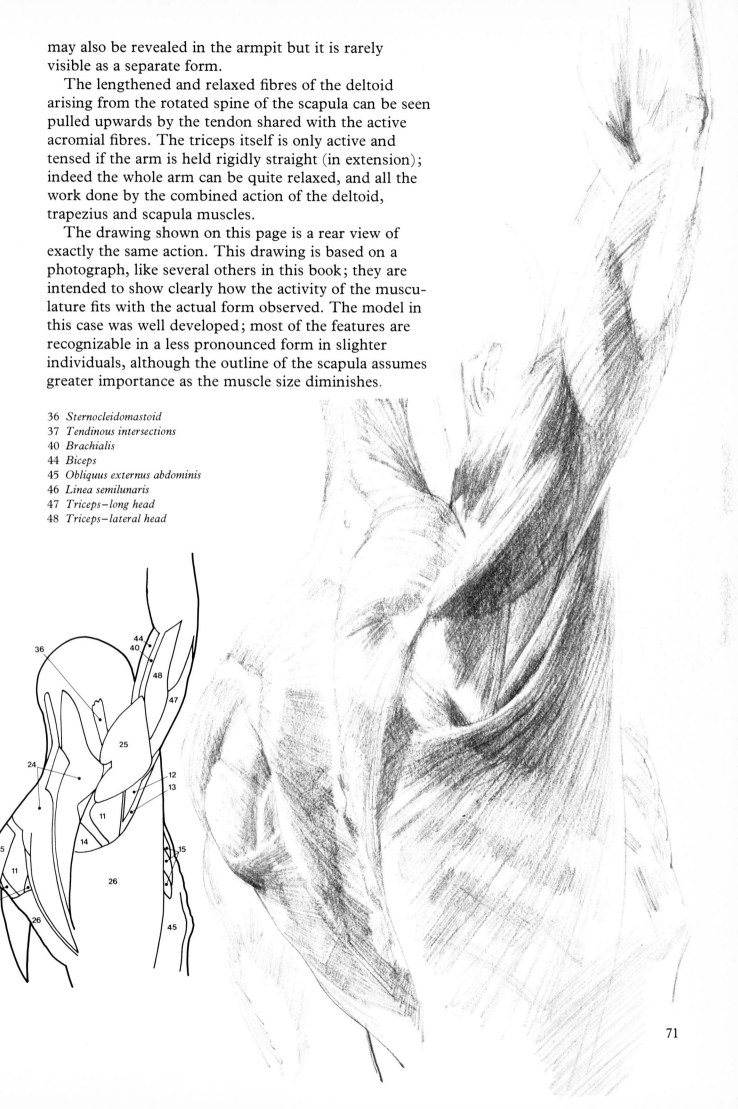

The arm I   In considering the muscles of the limbs it is useful to distinguish between *flexor* groups and *extensor* groups. Basically, the muscles of the front of the arm in the supinated position (with the palm of the hand facing forwards) are flexors, in that they are used in flexion or bending of the arm. The muscles of the back of the arm power the extension or straightening of the arm and are therefore extensors.

The flexor muscles of the arm can be considered as two-layered on the upper arm and three-layered on the forearm. The deepest forearm layer is shown on this page. The largest muscle making up this deep layer is the *flexor digitorum profundus*, arising from the upper three-quarters of the ulna. Its attachments extend on to the *interosseus membrane* (a strong fibrous sheet between radius and ulna). Four long tendons attach the muscle to the fingers, the one for the index finger directly connected, the others interconnected by tissue and tendinous slips. Next to it is the *flexor pollicis longus*, which arises from an adjacent and similar area, including three-quarters of the radius and some of the interosseus membrane.

Just visible under the ligaments of these two muscles lies the *pronator quadratus* which extends across the front of the lower radius and ulna and is chiefly responsible for the pronation, or turning inwards, of the forearm.

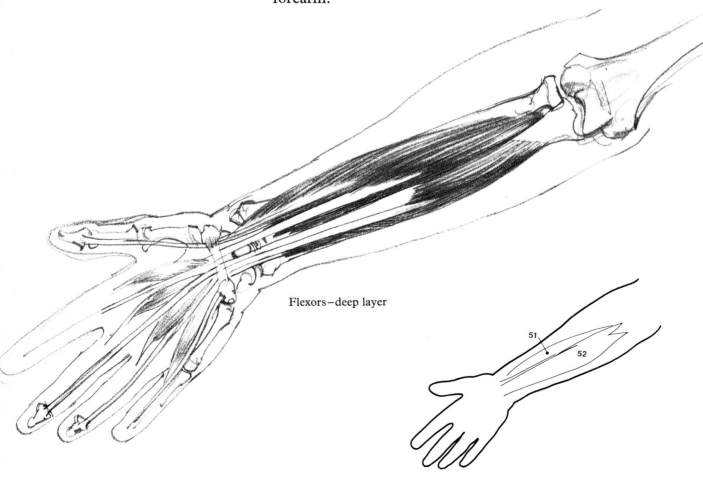

Flexors—deep layer

51
52

The second layer of the right forearm and the deep layer of the upper arm are shown in the drawing below. At the front of the humerus is the *brachialis* arising from its lower half and inserting by a short but strong tendon into the coronoid process and the tuberosity of the ulna. The *coracobrachialis* arises from the tip of the coracoid process of the scapula and attaches to the medial border of the humerus about midway along its length.

Almost entirely covering the deep muscles of the forearm, the *flexor digitorum superficialis* arises by two heads, the humero-ulnar and the radial. The humero-ulnar is the main origin, springing from the medial epicondyle of the humerus and adjacent area; the radial head is a thin sheet of muscle arising from the upper two-thirds of the anterior border of the radius.

40 *Brachialis*
50 *Coracobrachialis*
51 *Flexor pollicis longus*
52 *Flexor digitorum profundus*
53 *Flexor digitorum superficialis*

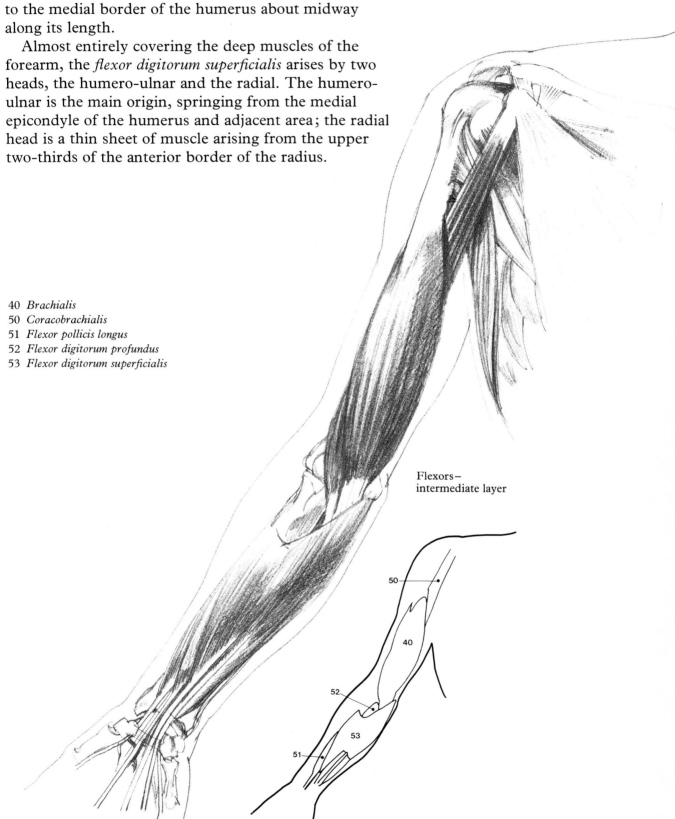

Flexors – intermediate layer

73

Flexors–
superficial layer

Coracoid proce.

Head of humerus

Superficial muscles of the front of the arm are shown in the drawing opposite although they are not all flexors: two extensors have curved over from the other side. These two, numbered 58 and 59, are described with the extensors on page 78.

The top layer of the forearm flexors comprises the *flexor carpi ulnaris*, the *palmaris longus*, the *flexor carpi radialis*, and the *pronator teres*. All four arise wholly or partially from the medial epicondyle of the humerus, and the first three have long tendons which progress to the radial, palmar and ulna areas of the hand as their names suggest. Their insertions are shown in more detail on page 80.

Both the flexor carpi ulnaris and the pronator teres have ulnar as well as humeral attachments; the pronator teres progresses not to the hand but obliquely across the forearm to halfway down the outside of the radius, thus helping to rotate the arm.

Lastly, the big flexor of the upper arm is the *biceps*. It has two heads, the short head arising from the coracoid process, and the long head from within the shoulder joint just above the glenoid cavity of the scapula. The tendon of the long head passes over the head of the humerus and descends in the groove of the *intertubercular sulcus* to the belly of the muscle, which is separate from and lies alongside the muscle of the short head, until they combine in a flattened tendon that inserts into the radial tuberosity. The bicipital aponeurosis is an additional attachment of this tendon to the deep fascia of the flexors of the forearm.

Medial view

Medial epicondyle

Olecranon

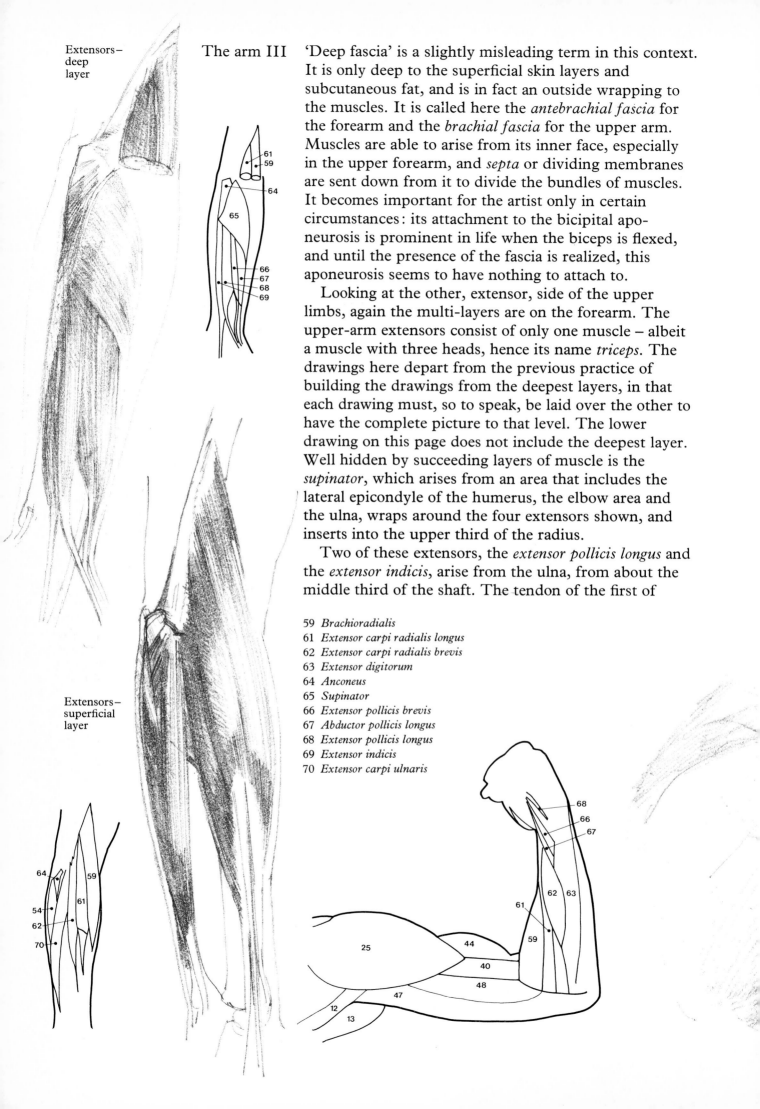

Extensors –
deep
layer

The arm III

'Deep fascia' is a slightly misleading term in this context. It is only deep to the superficial skin layers and subcutaneous fat, and is in fact an outside wrapping to the muscles. It is called here the *antebrachial fascia* for the forearm and the *brachial fascia* for the upper arm. Muscles are able to arise from its inner face, especially in the upper forearm, and *septa* or dividing membranes are sent down from it to divide the bundles of muscles. It becomes important for the artist only in certain circumstances: its attachment to the bicipital aponeurosis is prominent in life when the biceps is flexed, and until the presence of the fascia is realized, this aponeurosis seems to have nothing to attach to.

Looking at the other, extensor, side of the upper limbs, again the multi-layers are on the forearm. The upper-arm extensors consist of only one muscle – albeit a muscle with three heads, hence its name *triceps*. The drawings here depart from the previous practice of building the drawings from the deepest layers, in that each drawing must, so to speak, be laid over the other to have the complete picture to that level. The lower drawing on this page does not include the deepest layer. Well hidden by succeeding layers of muscle is the *supinator*, which arises from an area that includes the lateral epicondyle of the humerus, the elbow area and the ulna, wraps around the four extensors shown, and inserts into the upper third of the radius.

Two of these extensors, the *extensor pollicis longus* and the *extensor indicis*, arise from the ulna, from about the middle third of the shaft. The tendon of the first of

59 *Brachioradialis*
61 *Extensor carpi radialis longus*
62 *Extensor carpi radialis brevis*
63 *Extensor digitorum*
64 *Anconeus*
65 *Supinator*
66 *Extensor pollicis brevis*
67 *Abductor pollicis longus*
68 *Extensor pollicis longus*
69 *Extensor indicis*
70 *Extensor carpi ulnaris*

Extensors –
superficial
layer

these extends along the thumb to the distal phalanx, whereas that from the second goes to the index finger. The *abductor pollicis longus* and the *extensor pollicis brevis* are closely associated and arise from the middles of radius, ulna and interosseus membrane, the abductor inserts into the wrist and base of thumb and the extensor into the first joint of the thumb.

Three muscles which combine to make a single prominent form at the surface, separated from the other extensors, are drawn at the bottom of the opposite page. They are the *brachioradialis*, the *extensors carpi radialis longus* and *brevis*. All three arise from the lower lateral part of the humerus, the last from as low down as the lateral epicondyle. The brachioradialis attaches by a flat tendon to the lower end of the radius, and the other two muscles go to the second and third metacarpal bones respectively.

As can be seen more clearly in the drawing on page 79, the two deep muscles, the *abductor pollicis longus* and the *extensor pollicis brevis* become superficial near the wrist and curve over the tendons of brachioradialis and the carpi radialis extensors to their own insertions.

Also shown here is the *anconeus* muscle, which is partially overlapped by the extensor carpi ulnaris, as shown overleaf, and covered by a fascia extension from the triceps, but is still visible at the surface in some circumstances. It is a small triangular muscle, arising from the surface of the lateral epicondyle of the humerus and attaching to the upper quarter of the back of the ulna up to the olecranon.

12 *Teres minor*
13 *Teres major*
25 *Deltoid*
40 *Brachialis*
44 *Biceps*
47 *Triceps–long head*
48 *Triceps–lateral head*
54 *Flexor carpi ulnaris*

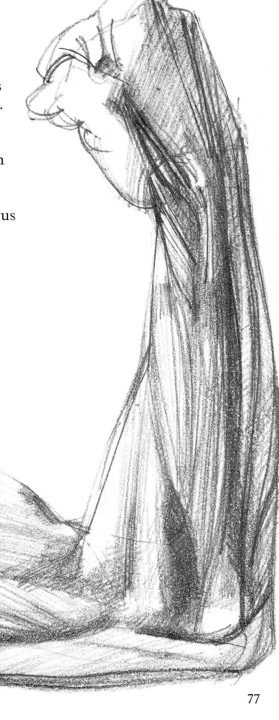

Lateral view

The arm IV

The viewpoint for the drawings opposite has been moved more to the rear. In the forearm in the left-hand drawing the muscles shown are a combination of those in the two drawings on page 76, viewed from this slightly modified position.

In contrast to the multi-layered forearm, the upper arm tensor musculature consists of only one muscle, the *triceps*. Its three heads are the long, the medial and the lateral. The long head arises by a flat tendon from just below the shoulder joint on the scapula, the lateral head from a narrow ridge high on the back of the humerus, and the medial head from a large area comprising three-quarters of the posterior surface of the humerus. Although large, the medial head is almost entirely covered by the long head from this view.

The triceps tendon begins about the middle of the muscle and is in two layers, the outer one presenting a large tendinous area in the centre of the back of the upper arm as shown. Its insertions are into the olecranon of the ulna, and, by a band of fibres, over the anconeus into the deep fascia of the forearm. The triceps muscle is very powerful – the medial head is principally active in normal lightly loaded movements, but all three act together when straightening the arm against resistance, as in weight-lifting or push-up exercises. In these circumstances the lateral head contracts into a very prominently outlined form.

In the right hand drawing the *deltoid* has been added, covering the upper tendinous attachments of the triceps, and rounding out the shoulder form.

Prominent in extension of the wrist and fingers is the *extensor digitorum*. It arises by the common extensor tendon from the lateral epicondyle of the humerus, from intermuscular septa and the antibrachial fascia, and divides below into four tendons, one for each finger.

Sharing the common extensor tendon from the lateral epicondyle and also arising from the posterior border of the ulna, the *extensor carpi ulnaris* passes downward close to the edge of the ulna to insert in the base of the little finger. It is attached to the ulna by means of an aponeurosis shared with the two flexor muscles from the other side of the arm, the *flexor carpi ulnaris* and the *flexor digitorum profundus*, but the ulna can be felt and usually seen as a depression between the flexors and the extensors.

Finally, the *extensor digiti minimi* also arises from the common extensor tendon by a thin tendinous slip and various intermuscular septa. It is small and lies mostly under the extensor digitorum; it only emerges as a tendon to the little finger, and has little effect on surface form.

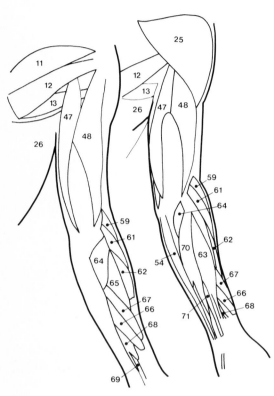

11 *Infraspinatus*
12 *Teres minor*
13 *Teres major*
25 *Deltoid*
26 *Latissimus dorsi*
47 *Triceps—long head*
48 *Triceps—lateral head*
54 *Flexor carpi ulnaris*
59 *Brachioradialis*
61 *Extensor carpi radialis longus*
62 *Extensor carpi radialis brevis*
63 *Extensor digitorum*
64 *Anconeus*
65 *Supinator*
66 *Extensor pollicis brevis*
67 *Abductor pollicis longus*
68 *Extensor pollicis longus*
69 *Extensor indicis*
70 *Extensor carpi ulnaris*
71 *Extensor digiti minimi*

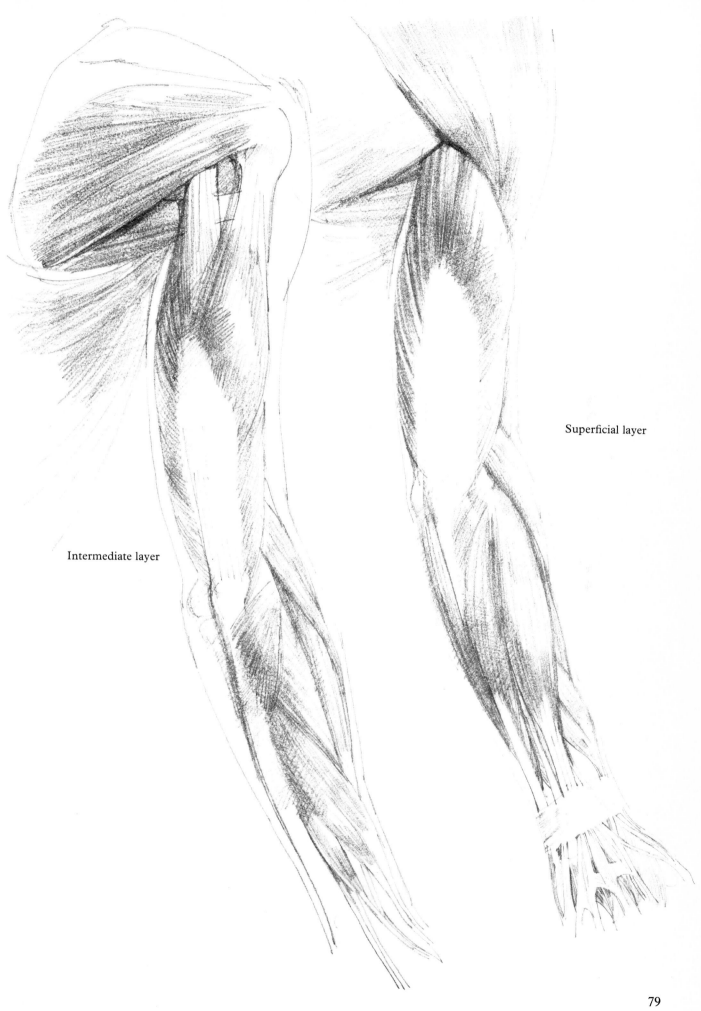

Intermediate layer

Superficial layer

79

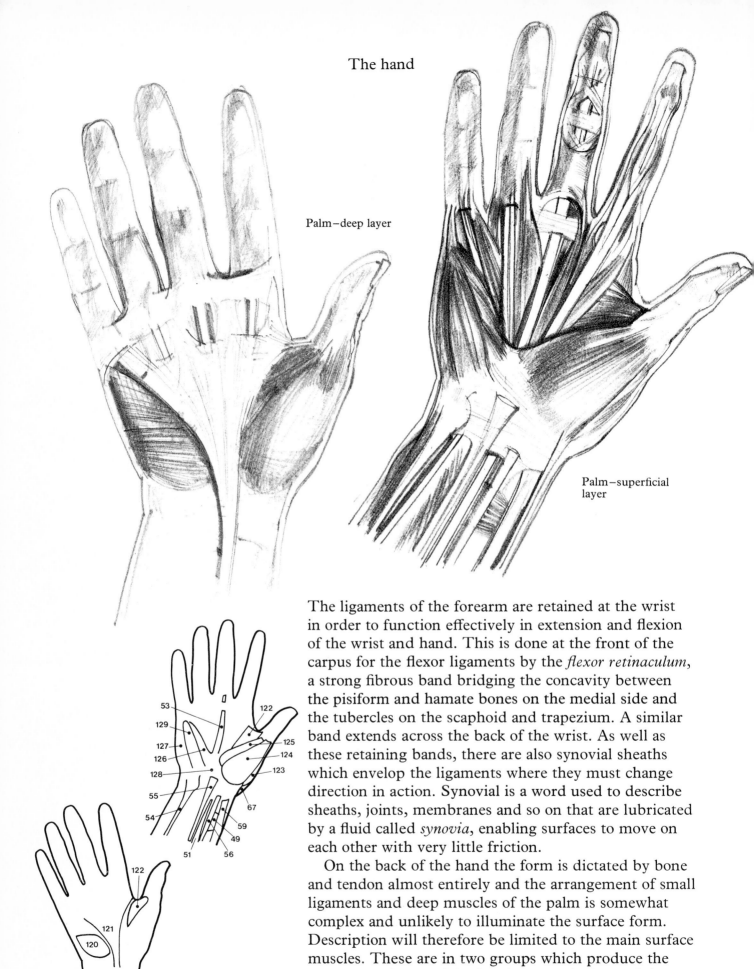

The hand

Palm–deep layer

Palm–superficial
layer

The ligaments of the forearm are retained at the wrist
in order to function effectively in extension and flexion
of the wrist and hand. This is done at the front of the
carpus for the flexor ligaments by the *flexor retinaculum*,
a strong fibrous band bridging the concavity between
the pisiform and hamate bones on the medial side and
the tubercles on the scaphoid and trapezium. A similar
band extends across the back of the wrist. As well as
these retaining bands, there are also synovial sheaths
which envelop the ligaments where they must change
direction in action. Synovial is a word used to describe
sheaths, joints, membranes and so on that are lubricated
by a fluid called *synovia*, enabling surfaces to move on
each other with very little friction.

On the back of the hand the form is dictated by bone
and tendon almost entirely and the arrangement of small
ligaments and deep muscles of the palm is somewhat
complex and unlikely to illuminate the surface form.
Description will therefore be limited to the main surface
muscles. These are in two groups which produce the
two convex forms of the hand, one at the base of the
thumb and the other on the little finger side of the palm.

On the surface of the *thenar eminence*, as the thumb

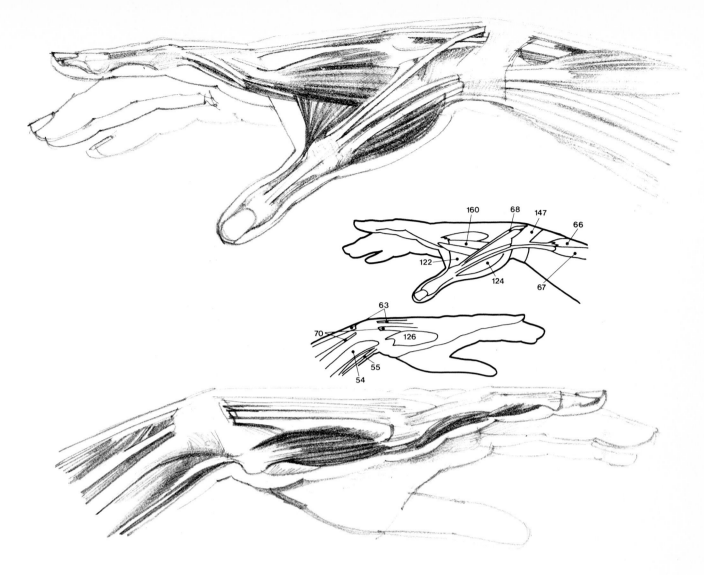

base is called, are two closely associated muscles, the *abductor pollicis brevis* and the *flexor pollicis brevis*. The abductor is thin, reflecting the shape of the fatter muscle underneath, whereas the flexor has both surface and deep parts, the surface head sharing attachments to the flexor retinaculum with the abductor. Both muscles insert at the base of the proximal phalanx of the thumb. Underneath the abductor and giving it form, is a fatter muscle called the *opponens pollicis*. This arises from the flexor retinaculum and the trapezium bone of the wrist, and inserts into the length of the outer edge of the first metacarpal or thumb bone.

On the other, little finger side, three muscles make up the *hypothenar eminence*. They are the *opponens digiti minimi*, the *abductor digiti minimi* and the *flexor digiti minimi*. The opponens is deep to the other two, arising from the hamate bone of the wrist and the flexor retinaculum, and inserting along the length of the fifth metacarpal. Side by side over the opponens, the flexor and the abductor both insert into the base of the little finger. The first arises from the hamate bone and the flexor retinaculum, the second from the pisiform bone and the ligament of the flexor carpi ulnaris.

49 *Pronator quadratus*
51 *Flexor pollicis longus*
53 *Flexor digitorum superficialis*
54 *Flexor carpi ulnaris*
55 *Palmaris longus*
56 *Flexor carpi radialis*
59 *Brachioradialis*
63 *Extensor digitorum*
66 *Extensor pollicis brevis*
67 *Abductor pollicis longus*
68 *Extensor pollicis longus*
70 *Extensor carpi ulnaris*
120 *Palmaris brevis*
121 *Palmar aponeurosis*
122 *Adductor pollicis*
123 *Opponens pollicis*
124 *Abductor pollicis brevis*
125 *Flexor pollicis brevis*
126 *Opponens digiti minimi*
127 *Abductor digiti minimi*
128 *Flexor retinaculum*
129 *Flexor digiti minimi brevis*
147 *Extensor retinaculum*
160 *1st dorsal interosseus*

89 *Glutèus minimus*
90 *Gemellus superior*
91 *Obturator internus*
92 *Gemellus inferior*
93 *Quadratus femoris*
94 *Adductor magnus*
95 *Vastus lateralis*
100 *Biceps femoris—long head*
101 *Biceps femoris—short head*
102 *Gracilis*
103 *Semimembranosus*
104 *Sartorius*
105 *Vastus medialis*
106 *Semitendinosus*
110 *Adductor longus*
116 *Rectus femoris*

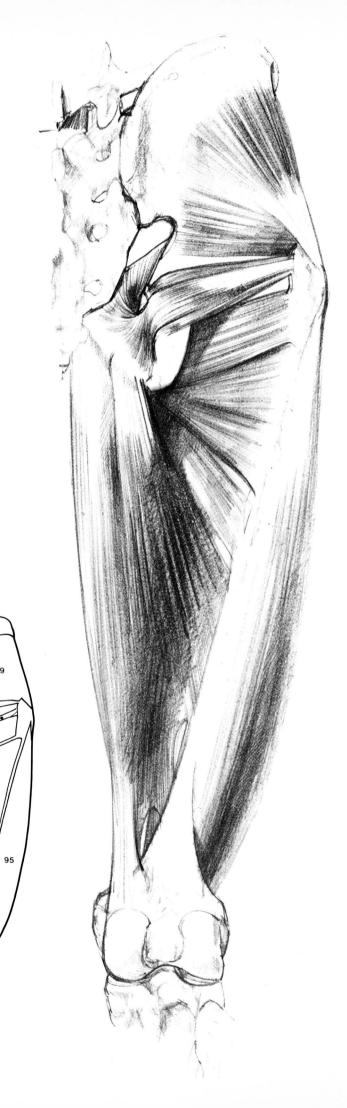

It is important for the anatomist to have a complete understanding of the musculature of the lower limb and its connections with the pelvis. Accordingly, the thigh and pelvic musculature will be examined first, followed by the lower leg. The drawing opposite shows the deep muscles of the *gluteal* (buttock) region and of the flexor aspect of the thigh.

The *adductor magnus* is a very large triangular muscle arising from the ramus of the ischium, fanning out and attaching to the femur from just below the lesser trochanter, down the whole length of the shaft to the medial condyle. Most of the muscle is flat in form, deep in the centre of the thigh and affecting surface form not at all, but the near-vertical medial fibres make a thicker mass which does remain superficial and is responsible for the typical shape of the inside of the thigh.

The *vastus lateralis* is prominent in this drawing, but it is really one of the extensor group of thigh muscles and will be described later.

The *gluteus minimus* is the deepest of three layers of gluteal muscles. Fan-shaped, it arises from the outer surface of the ilium and converges to a deep aponeurosis which ends in a tendon that inserts into the surface of the greater trochanter.

In the section below, which is taken through approximately the middle of the right thigh, the great thickness of the adductor magnus is evident. Its relationship to the superficial flexor muscles of the thigh is illuminating; it is not always easy to read the form in the round from anatomy drawings or even from life – the occasional cross-section is sometimes surprising.

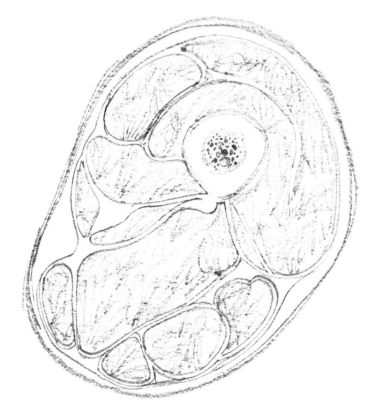

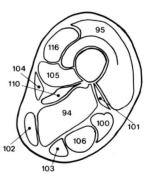

Thigh–cross-section

89 *Gluteus minimus*
90 *Gemellus superior*
91 *Obturator internus*
92 *Gemellus inferior*
93 *Quadratus femoris*
94 *Adductor magnus*
95 *Vastus lateralis*
96 *Gluteus medius*
97 *Piriformis*
98 *Obturator externus*
99 *Gluteus maximus*
   (*attachment of deeper fibres*)
100 *Biceps femoris—long head*
101 *Biceps femoris—short head*
102 *Gracilis*
103 *Semimembranosus*
104 *Sartorius*
105 *Vastus medialis*
106 *Semitendinosus*
107 *Obliquus abdominis externus*
108 *Obliquus abdominis internus*
109 *Gluteal fascia*

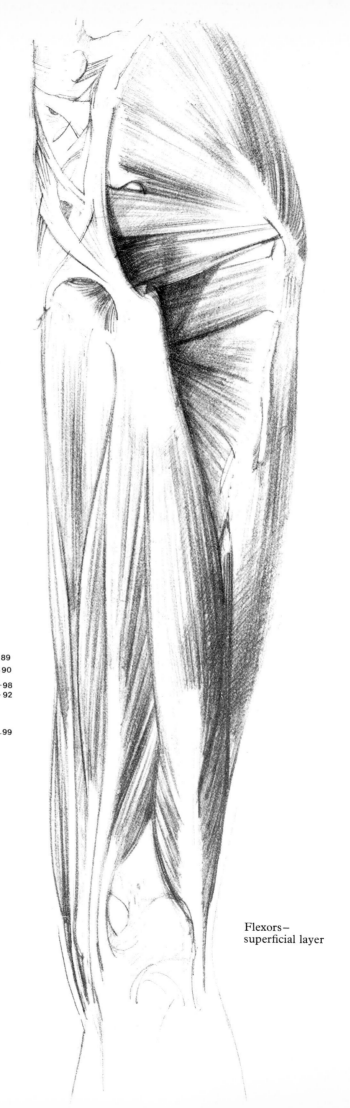

Flexors—
superficial layer

All the superficial muscles of the flexor side of the thigh are shown in the drawing opposite, with the exception of the *gluteus maximus*, which is shown wrapping over to form the familiar buttock shape in the drawing below. Partially underlying the gluteus maximus is the *gluteus medius*. The superficial part is covered by the *gluteal fascia*; this is continuous with the *iliotibial tract*, described later.

All three superficial flexor muscles of the thigh arise from the ischial tuberosity. They are the *semimembranosus*, the *semitendinosus* and the *biceps femoris*: the last of these has two heads, the short head giving the biceps an additional thin origin along a posterior ridge of the femur. Both heads combine together in a tendon that mainly attaches to the head of the fibula, although there are lesser insertions in the surrounding ligaments.

Because of its short muscle fibres and very long tendon, the semitendinosus overlies but does not obscure the semimembranosus. The upper part, close to the origin, is actually connected to the long head of the biceps femoris. About halfway down the thigh its long tendon swings medially, curves round the medial condyle of the tibia and inserts into the upper part of the bone close to the tendons of two muscles from the inside of the thigh, the *gracilis* and the *sartorius*.

The semimembranosus arises from the ischial tuberosity underneath the ligament of the semitendinosus and the biceps femoris and its fibres are partially interwoven with theirs. Its attachments in the middle of the thigh involve deep aponeuroses and are rather complex, but the main tendon emerges to insert on the back of the medial condyle of the tibia. These three muscles are important in flexing the leg and extending the hip joint in order to hold the trunk upright and maintain or regain balance.

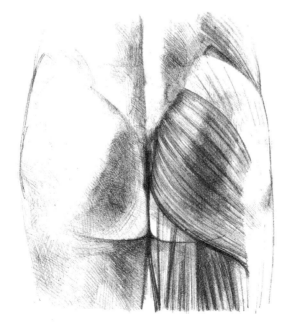

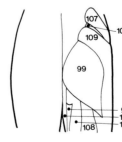

The buttocks

To the left of the dotted line in the drawing on this page lie the *quadriceps femoris*, comprising the four separately named muscles which together form the great extensor of the thigh. In this drawing the superficial central element, called the *rectus femoris*, has been removed to reveal the full extent of the combined *vastus lateralis*, *intermedius* and *medialis*.

The vastus medialis arises from the lower three-quarters of the length of the medial shaft of the femur, and the vastus intermedius from the upper two-thirds of the front and lateral surfaces. The vastus lateralis arises by a broad aponeurosis attached to the upper third of the back of the femur and including the anterior borders of the greater trochanter. It is largely covered by the *iliotibial tract*, which is a thickened and strengthened band of the fascia that covers all of the area, and runs down the lateral surface of the thigh.

All three vastus muscles also arise from the principal intermuscular septum which divides the extensors from the adductors and flexors, and all three converge to share the quadriceps femoris tendon inserting into the base of patella (some fibres blend with the *ligamentum patellae* in its top surface), and continuing from there to the tubercle of the tibia.

On the right side of the dotted line in the same drawing lie the medial femoral muscles. They are the *pectineus*, the *adductors brevis* and *longus*, and the already described *adductor magnus*. The adductor longus, lying next to the adductor magnus, arises by a thin tendon from the pubis and spreads to insertion by a very thin,

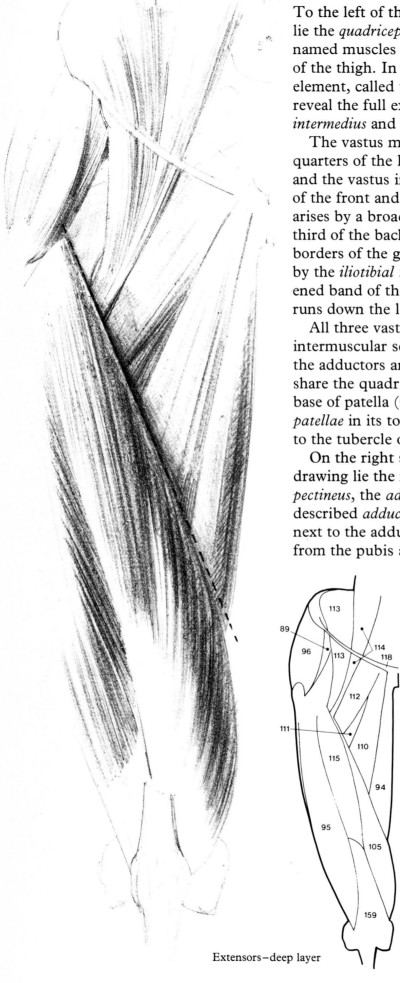

Extensors—deep layer

wide tendon into the middle third of the back of the femur. There is only a little space remaining on the middle of the femur shaft for insertions, as the vastu muscles are wrapped around about five-sixths of its circumference. Into this space the adductor longus, th adductors brevis and magnus all manage to insert by thin tendons. Next there is the pectineus, arising from farther out on the pubic ridge of the pelvis and inserting in the femur higher up, near to the lesser trochanter.

The thigh muscles added to complete the superficial musculature in the drawing on this page are the *sartorius* and the *rectus femoris*.

The rectus femoris covers the vastus intermedius, lying to some extent in a trough between the vastus lateralis and medialis. Its fibres are arranged in a bi-pennate form, as shown. It originates from the anterior inferior iliac spine and a rough groove above the hip joint, and gives rise to a single tendon which emerges between the *tensor fasciae latae* and the sartorius and extends over the front of the muscle, sometimes as far as the middle of the thigh. A narrow tendon inserts into the base of the patella with the common quadriceps tendon.

An unusual muscle, very long and strap-like, the sartorius arises from the anterior inferior iliac spine, sweeps across to the inside of the thigh, neatly separating the extensor group from the medial group, and accentuating the angled form of the frontal thigh. It inserts into the medial surface of the tibia shaft and the surrounding fascia and ligament.

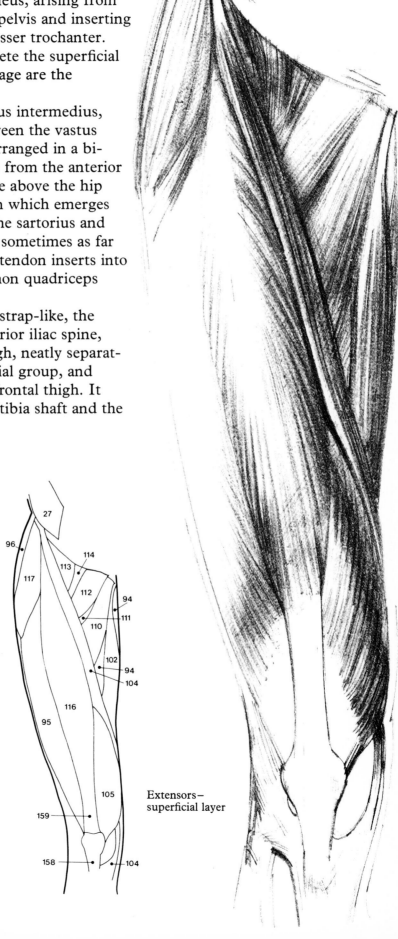

Extensors–
superficial layer

27 *Obliquus externus*
89 *Gluteus minimus*
94 *Adductor magnus*
95 *Vastus lateralis*
96 *Gluteus medius*
102 *Gracilis*
104 *Sartorius*
105 *Vastus medialis*
110 *Adductor longus*
111 *Adductor brevis*
112 *Pectineus*
113 *Iliacus*
114 *Psoas major*
115 *Vastus intermedius*
116 *Rectus femoris*
117 *Tensor fasciae latae*
118 *Inguinal ligament*
158 *Ligamentum patellae*
159 *Quadriceps tendon*

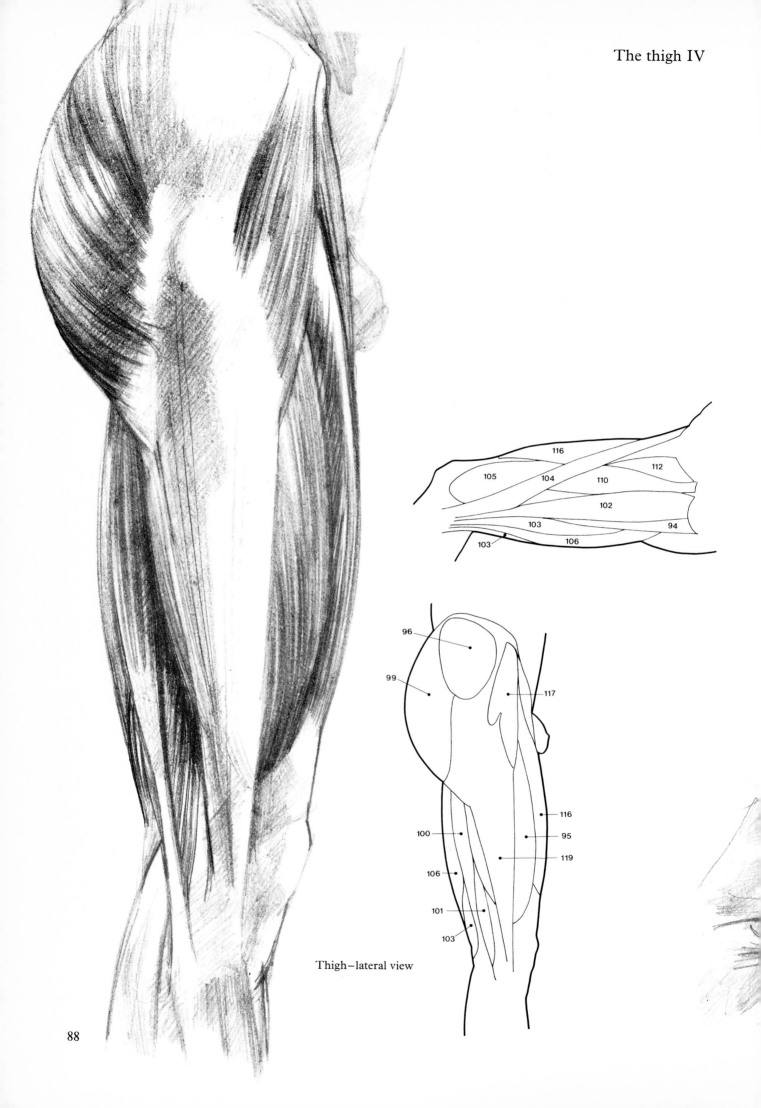

116
105   104   110   112
102
103   94
103   106

96
99
117

100   116
95
106   119

101
103

Thigh–lateral view

There is such a radical difference in the aspects of the outer and inner sides of the thigh that it is necessary to draw them separately although no new undescribed muscles are brought to light by so doing, but the relationship between the extensor, medial and flexor groups is, I hope, further clarified. The drawing below is based on a leg which is being flexed, rotated and slightly adducted at the same time. As a result the sartorius is prominent and takes a straighter than usual line from origin to insertion, rising from the surface at its pelvis origin to leave a pronounced hollow on its medial side.

The mass of the adductors, which includes the adductor longus, gracilis and adductor magnus, can be seen as one large form emerging from the groin. By contrast the rectus femoris and vastus extensors are lying flat and inactive.

On the opposite page the lateral view of the thigh is represented, and the reader's attention is directed especially to the extent and direction of the iliotibial tract. This and other strengthened fascia around the knee, are in fact localized thickenings of the general fascia that covers the whole leg, called in this area the *fascia lata*. In order to clarify the musculature, it is not normally represented in the areas where it is thin and functions mainly as an envelope, but shown only where it becomes akin to a ligament and provides attachments for muscles.

The iliotibial tract is a particularly strong and well-defined example of this local thickening, and it has a flattening effect on the form of the outside of the thigh. Its edges, especially from halfway down the thigh to the knee, are frequently visible under the skin in life. The front edge can appear as a thin groove in the convexity of the thigh, and the lower end of the back edge may appear sufficiently sharply to resemble a muscle's tendon of insertion.

94 *Adductor magnus*
95 *Vastus lateralis*
96 *Gluteus medius*
99 *Gluteus maximus*
100 *Biceps femoris—long head*
101 *Biceps femoris—short head*
102 *Gracilis*
103 *Semimembranosus*
104 *Sartorius*
105 *Vastus medialis*
106 *Semitendinosus*
110 *Adductor longus*
112 *Pectineus*
116 *Rectus femoris*
117 *Tensor fasciae latae*
119 *Iliotibial tract*

Thigh—medial view

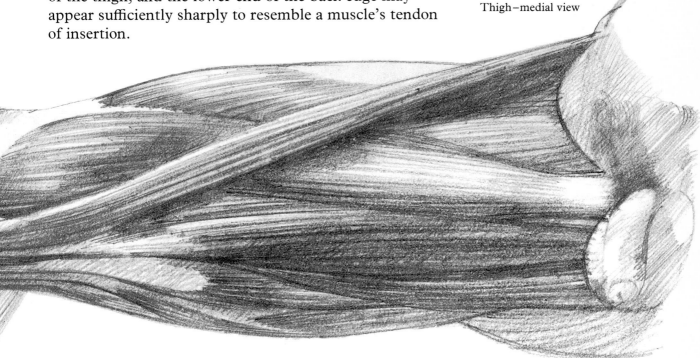

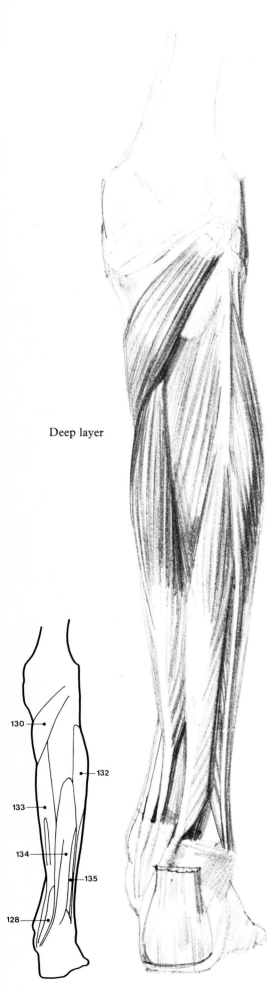

Deep layer

130 —
132 —
133 —
134 —
135 —
128 —

At the back of the lower leg there are effectively three layers of muscles, the deepest of which is drawn on the left, the two intermediate and superficial layers being shown in the drawings opposite.

The deepest of the deep group is the *tibialis posterior*, which has extensive origins, including the shafts of tibia and fibula, the interosseus membrane and surrounding fascia and septa. Its tendon has a synovial sheath which facilitates it to change direction around the medial malleolus to multiple insertions in the navicular, cuneiform and calcaneus bones and the bases of the second, third and fourth metatarsals.

The *popliteus* arises by a tendon from the lateral condyle of the femur, and sweeps across the back of the knee joint to insert into the back of the upper shaft of the tibia. Its tendon of origin emerges from beneath the fibrous capsule of the knee joint.

Two deep flexors, the *flexor digitorum longus* and the *flexor hallucis longus*, also have tendons in synovial sheaths which are led around the underside of the medial malleolus to insertions under the foot; the tendon of the hallucis inserts only into the base of the distal phalanx of the big toe, but the digitorum inserts into the lateral four toes. Their origins are from the shafts of fibula and tibia respectively.

Entirely covering the bodies of these two flexors, the *soleus* muscle is the biggest muscle of the lower leg and is largely responsible for its characteristic outline. Its triple origin is from the upper fibula, a fibrous arch high up between tibia and fibula and a large part of the middle of the tibia shaft. The deeper fibres of this muscle are longer than the superficial ones, and reach down almost to the ankles on each side before joining the main tendon of the heel, the *tendo calcaneus*, known popularly as the Achilles tendon. Shorter superficial fibres join the under-surface of a broad membranous tendon which eventually becomes fused with the tendo calcaneus. A small fleshy muscular slip, called the *plantaris*, arises from above the lateral condyle of the femur and becomes a long, thin tendon which descends over the soleus to insert close to the medial side of the tendo calcaneus.

Overlying the soleus, and often thought to comprise the bulk of the calf muscle, is the *gastrocnemius*. It is in fact relatively thin and mainly tendinous, but the ability of its two heads, especially the medial one, to contract and shorten severely makes it a conspicuous feature of the back of the leg. The medial head arises from above the medial epicondyle of the femur, and the lateral head from slightly lower on the lateral condyle. Both arise by strong tendons and the bellies of the two remain separate from each other. They insert together into the tendo calcaneus.

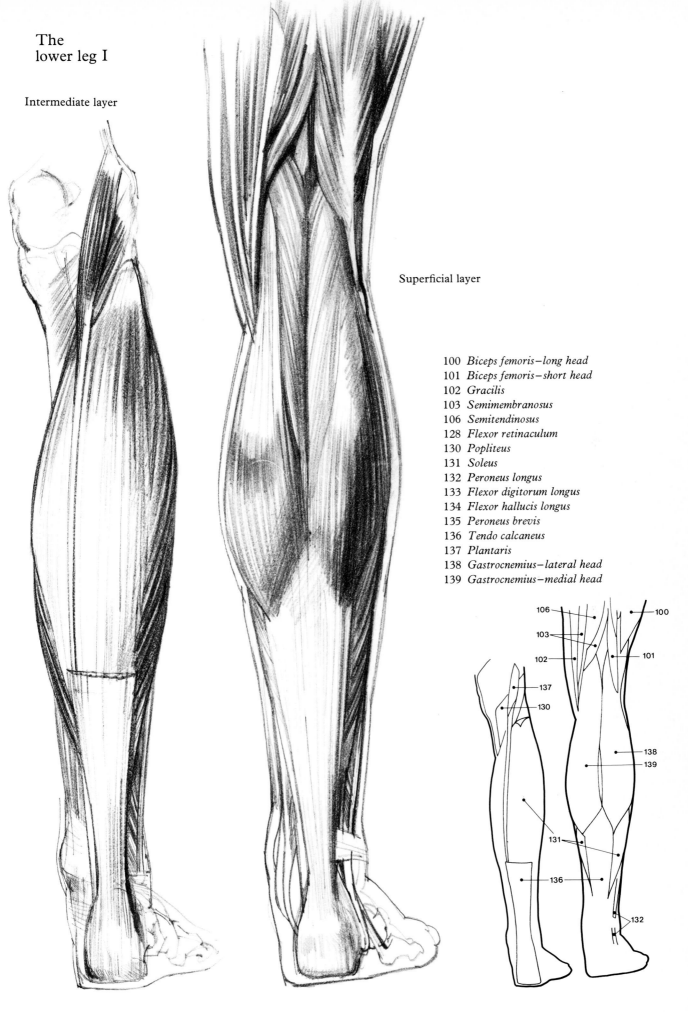

The lower leg I

Intermediate layer

Superficial layer

100 *Biceps femoris—long head*
101 *Biceps femoris—short head*
102 *Gracilis*
103 *Semimembranosus*
106 *Semitendinosus*
128 *Flexor retinaculum*
130 *Popliteus*
131 *Soleus*
132 *Peroneus longus*
133 *Flexor digitorum longus*
134 *Flexor hallucis longus*
135 *Peroneus brevis*
136 *Tendo calcaneus*
137 *Plantaris*
138 *Gastrocnemius—lateral head*
139 *Gastrocnemius—medial head*

Front view

Lateral view

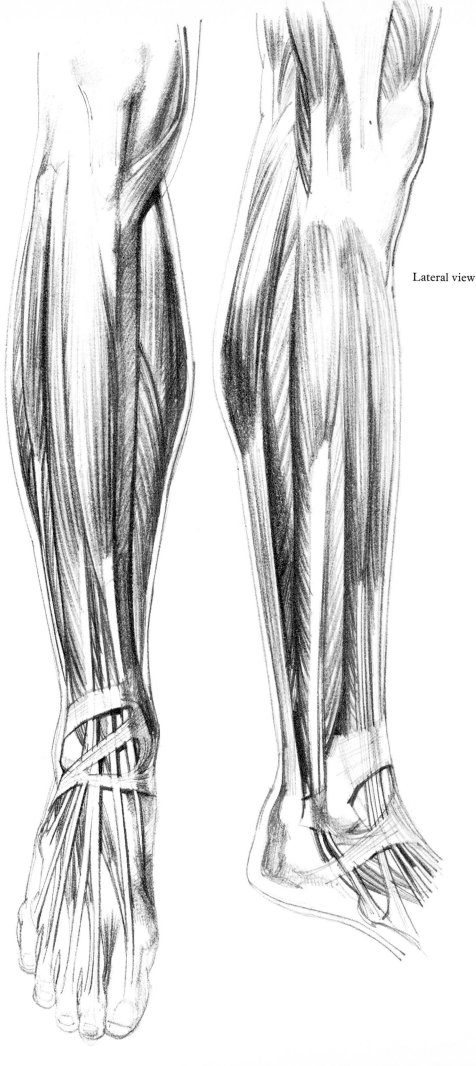

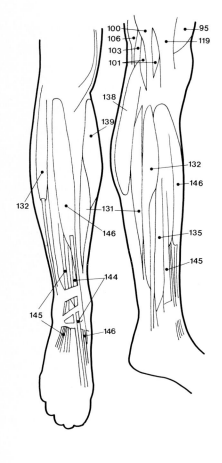

92

The main extensor muscle at the front of the lower leg is the *tibialis anterior*. It lies alongside the tibia, lateral to it and for its whole length, although its tendon crosses medially to insert into the medial cuneiform bone and the adjoining part of the base of the first metatarsal bone. It arises from the lateral condyle and from almost half the length of the lateral surface of the tibia, the interosseus membrane and adjoining fascia and septa. The tendon can be clearly seen when the muscle is flexed, as in dorsiflexion, and when the foot is turned inward at the ankle joint (inversion). Both movements are combined in walking when the heel is presented to the ground at the beginning of each step.

The *extensor digitorum longus* is the main extensor of the toes, arising from the lateral condyle of the tibia and the upper three-quarters of the fibula, the interosseus membrane and other associated fascia and septa. Its tendon divides into four on the top or dorsal surface of the foot, fanning out to insertions in the distal phalanges of the second to fifth toes. From between this muscle and the tibialis anterior, emerges the lower part of the *extensor hallucis longus* and its tendon, which extends to the distal phalanx of the big toe. It arises from the middle three-fifths of the fibula next to the origin of the extensor digitorum longus.

Last in this group of extensors come the *peroneus longus* and *brevis*. They are properly described as the lateral group operating as evertors, or turning muscles of the foot, but they are certainly also active in dorsiflexion, and if keeping to the simple division into flexors and extensors, they must stay with the latter.

The peroneus longus arises from the head and upper two-thirds of the fibula, alongside the other extensors, and other fascia and septa. It ends in a long tendon which is led by a groove around the lateral malleolus in a synovial sheath shared by the peroneus brevis. Its tendon then dives under the foot, crossing the sole obliquely to insert into the lateral side of the medial cuneiform bone and the base of the first metatarsal.

The peroneus brevis arises lower on the shaft of the fibula, and descends behind the peroneus longus. Its tendon shares the path round the lateral malleolus with the peroneus longus but attaches to the lateral side of the foot at the base of the fifth metatarsal bone.

As at the wrist, all the tendons, except the big tendo calcaneus, are retained at the ankle by retinacula. At the front of the ankle there are two, the upper and lower *extensor retinacula* and on the medial side, the single *flexor retinaculum*. Some tendons are led under one and through a loop in the other; some tendons even go through one retinaculum, or beneath two or more. All are positioned and lubricated by synovial sheaths as they pass the retinacula.

The leg

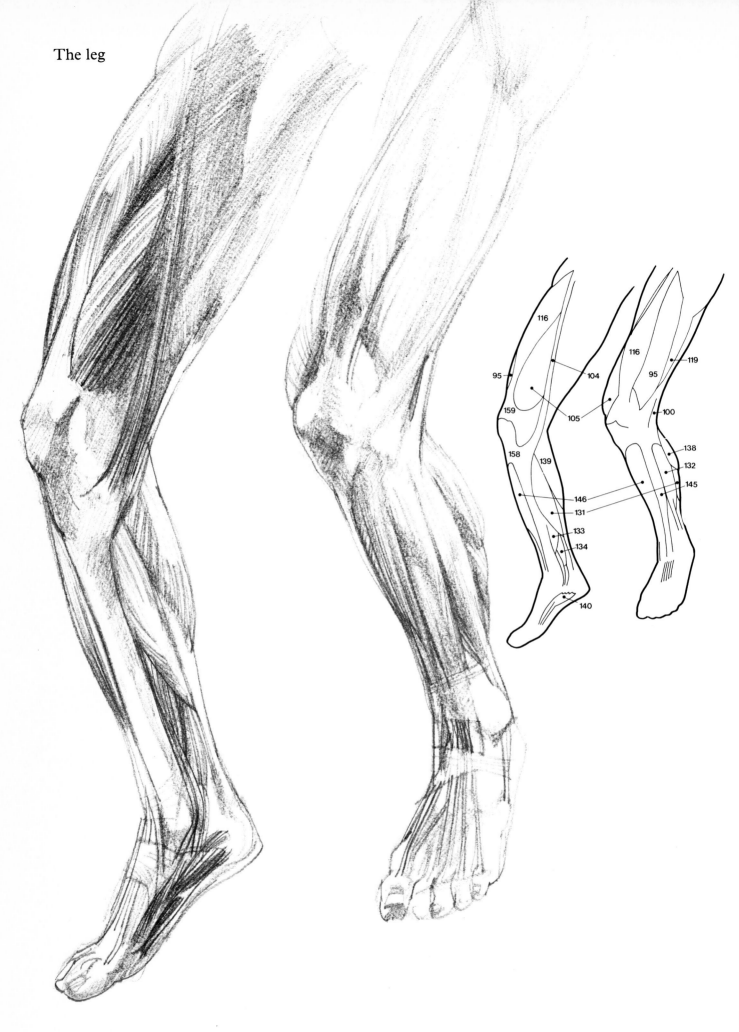

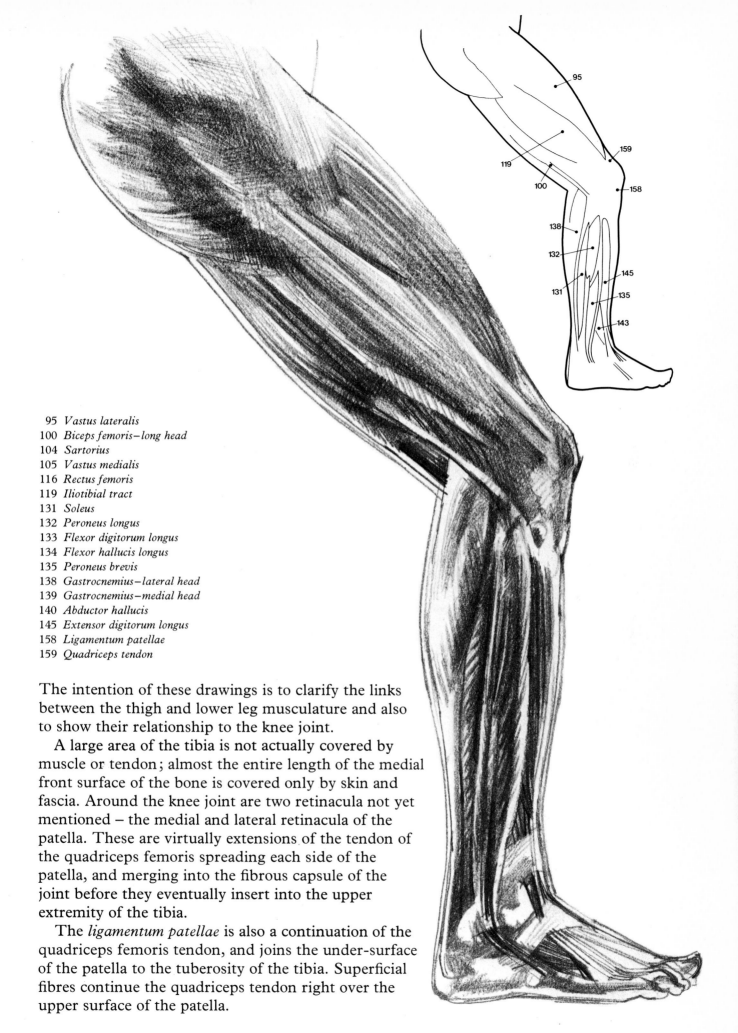

95 *Vastus lateralis*
100 *Biceps femoris—long head*
104 *Sartorius*
105 *Vastus medialis*
116 *Rectus femoris*
119 *Iliotibial tract*
131 *Soleus*
132 *Peroneus longus*
133 *Flexor digitorum longus*
134 *Flexor hallucis longus*
135 *Peroneus brevis*
138 *Gastrocnemius—lateral head*
139 *Gastrocnemius—medial head*
140 *Abductor hallucis*
145 *Extensor digitorum longus*
158 *Ligamentum patellae*
159 *Quadriceps tendon*

The intention of these drawings is to clarify the links
between the thigh and lower leg musculature and also
to show their relationship to the knee joint.

A large area of the tibia is not actually covered by
muscle or tendon; almost the entire length of the medial
front surface of the bone is covered only by skin and
fascia. Around the knee joint are two retinacula not yet
mentioned – the medial and lateral retinacula of the
patella. These are virtually extensions of the tendon of
the quadriceps femoris spreading each side of the
patella, and merging into the fibrous capsule of the
joint before they eventually insert into the upper
extremity of the tibia.

The *ligamentum patellae* is also a continuation of the
quadriceps femoris tendon, and joins the under-surface
of the patella to the tuberosity of the tibia. Superficial
fibres continue the quadriceps tendon right over the
upper surface of the patella.

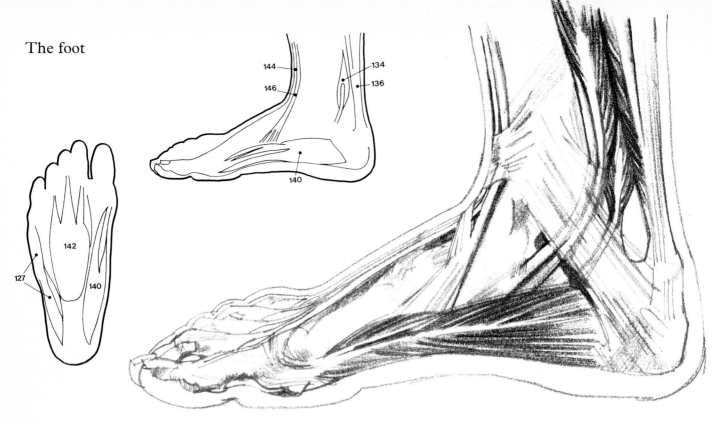

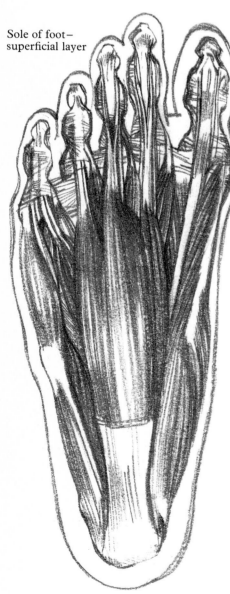

Sole of foot–
superficial layer

Most of the musculature of the foot is extrinsic; in other words it consists of tendon extensions of muscles of the leg. The intrinsic muscles are almost all on the sole or plantar surface; on the top or dorsal surface there is only one: the *extensor digitorum brevis* which arises from the upper lateral surface of the calcaneus bone and ligaments and fascia in that area. It divides into four fleshy parts from which narrow tendons extend to join the tendons of the extensor digitorum longus to insert into the upper surface of the second, third and fourth toes. Another tendon slants across the foot to join the tendon of the extensor hallucis longus to the big toe. Although the muscle is small and is deep to the long extensor, its main belly can often be seen at the surface, just above the tendon of peroneus brevis.

In the sole of the foot there are four layers of muscles. Overlaying them all is the *plantar aponeurosis*, the central part of which is quite thick. Superficial to that there are the layers of fat and the skin; on the parts of

127 *Abductor digiti minimi*
132 *Peroneus longus*
134 *Flexor hallucis longus*
135 *Peroneus brevis*
136 *Tendo calcaneus*
140 *Abductor hallucis*
141 *Plantar aponeurosis*
142 *Flexor digitorum brevis*
143 *Peroneus tertius*
144 *Extensor hallucis longus*
145 *Extensor digitorum longus*
146 *Tibialis anterior*
147 *Extensor retinaculum*
160 *Extensor digitorum brevis*

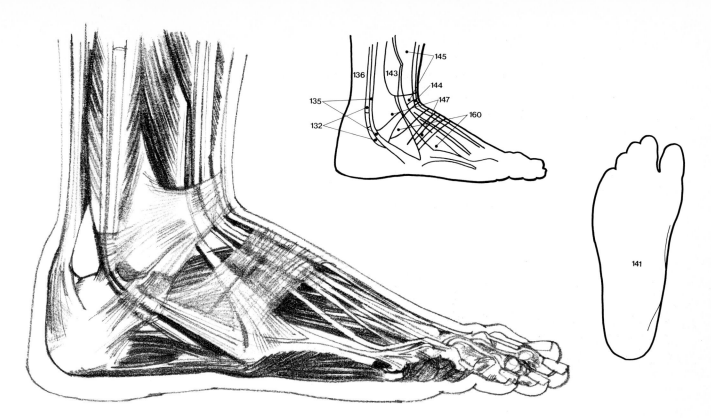

the sole that make contact with the ground these are
especially thick. In view of the relative unimportance of
the deep muscle layers of the palmar foot in affecting
outer form, only the superficial layer is described here.

The *abductor hallucis* arises by a short tendon from
the medial side of the calcaneus and from the plantar
retinaculum, and runs along the medial side of the foot
to insert, together with a deeper muscle, the *flexor
hallucis brevis*, into the base of the big toe.
The *flexor digitorum brevis* lies centrally in the foot,
immediately deep to the central plantar aponeurosis. It
arises by a narrow tendon from the calcaneus, from the
centre plantar aponeurosis and adjacent fascia and septa,
and inserts by four tendons into the lateral four toes.
The superficial muscle of the outer edge of the foot is
the *abductor digiti minimi*. It arises from tuberosities of
the calcaneus and surrounding tissue, and passes over
the base of the fifth metatarsal by a smooth groove
and inserts into the base of the little toe.

Sole of foot –
aponeurosis

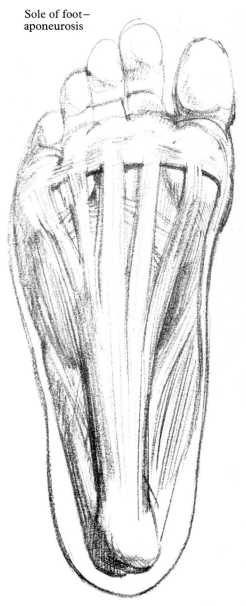

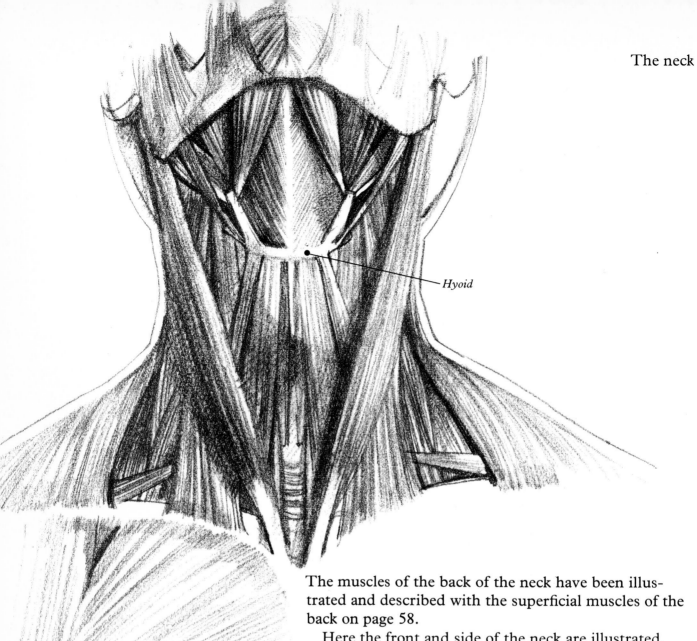

Hyoid

The muscles of the back of the neck have been illustrated and described with the superficial muscles of the
back on page 58.

Here the front and side of the neck are illustrated.
Involved in nearly all the muscular arrangements at the
front of the neck is a bone not previously mentioned. It
is the *hyoid*, a small U-shaped bone which is suspended
by the styloid processes of the temporal bones of the
skull by the *stylohyoid ligaments*. Virtually its whole
surface is occupied by muscular insertions. In life it
takes up a position at the junction of the underside of
the jaw with the neck, just above the thyroid cartilage
or Adam's apple.

The *digastric, mylohyoid* and *stylohyoid* muscles are
all above the hyoid bone and occupy the space under
the mandible in a manner that can be understood better
by reference to the illustration than by description. The
digastric perforates the stylohyoid, its posterior belly
attaching to the temporal bone.

Attaching to the lower surface of the hyoid bone and
pulling downwards are two more paired muscles, the
omohyoid and the *sternohyoid*. The latter arises from the
medial end of the clavicle, behind the *sternocleidomastoid* and proceeds directly upwards to the body of

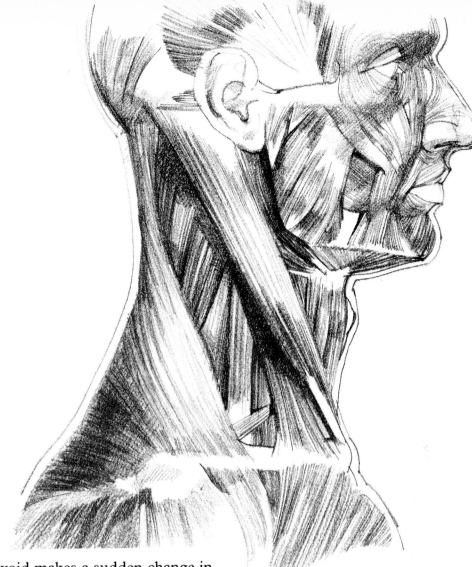

the hyoid. The omohyoid makes a sudden change in direction about two-thirds of the way down its length, the lower part inclining outwards to its origin on the upper border of the scapula. To maintain this turning angle, a band of fascia attached to the first rib and the clavicle ensheaths the intermediate tendon at the point of the turn, holding it down.

The *scalenus muscles*, anterior, medius and posterior, join the first and second ribs to the transverse processes of the axis and third, fourth and fifth cervical vertebrae.

The most prominent surface form in the front and side of the neck is the *sternocleidomastoid*. At its lower end it has two heads, the medial head attaching to the *manubrium* of the sternum, the lateral to the medial third of the clavicle. They unite almost immediately and assume together a more rounded form, ascending obliquely to insert by a strong flat tendon into the lateral surface of the mastoid process. The form of the sternocleidomastoid is especially noticeable in life when the head is turned strongly to one side.

Overlaying the whole of the front and side of the neck is a broad sheet of fascia called the *platysma*, which is only evident in extreme facial expressions of horror or anguish, or when great effort is being exerted.

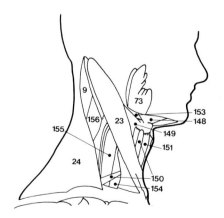

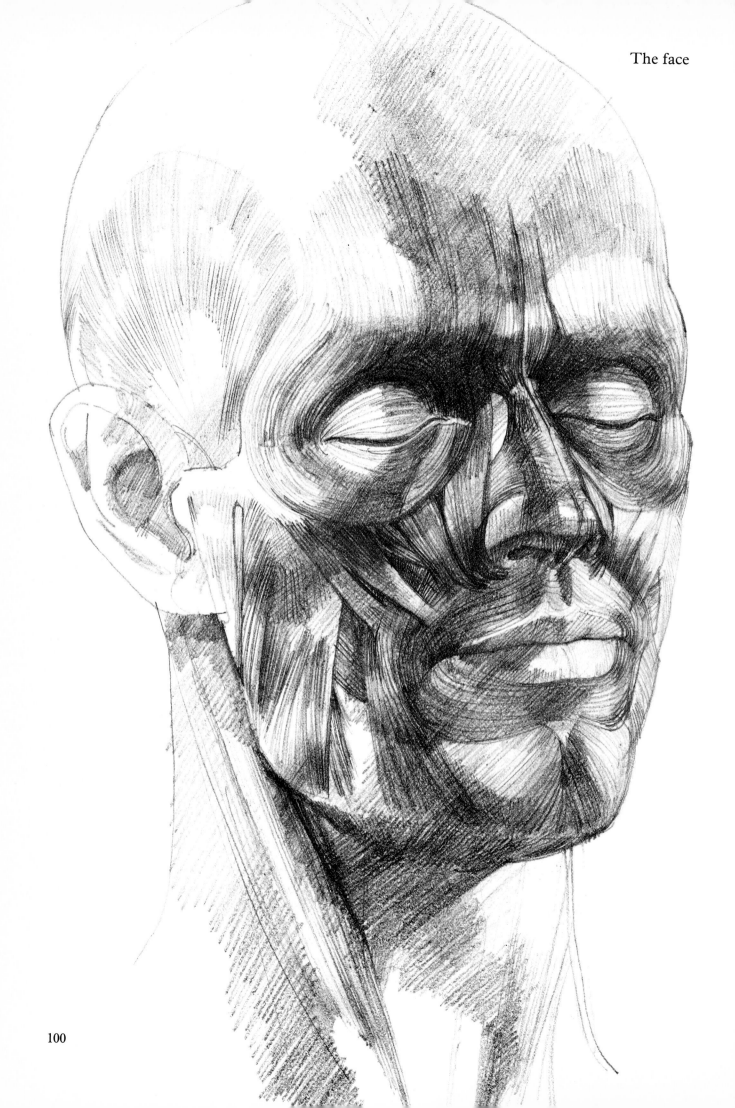

The muscles of the head and face modify the form established by the bony structure comparatively little. When the face is relaxed, the musculature fills the hollows and smooths the angular transitions, but otherwise allows the basic form of the skull to show through. Most of the muscles are concerned with movement of the features where little force is required.

The muscles acting on the mandible are exceptions to this. Known as the muscles of mastication, they are capable of exerting considerable force – the circus performer, for instance, can suspend the whole body from the clenched teeth. The *masseter* is the most prominent of this group, and can be seen at the angle of the jaw when it is clenched. Its three layers all arise from the zygomatic arch and insert into the mandible.

The *temporalis* is a large fan-shaped muscle, and its origin fills the whole depression of the temporal area. It converges to a tendon passing behind the zygomatic arch to its insertion; this virtually covers the coronoid process and extends down the front border of the ramus of the mandible.

Returning to what might be called the muscles of expression, one that produces its own form to some degree, rather than following what underlies it, is the *depressor anguli oris*. It arises from the mandible just lateral to the chin and blends into the corner of the mouth and the *orbicularis oris*.

The *depressor labii inferioris* covers the chin and when inactive its form is responsible for the rounded shape of the chin in life. Intermingled fat in the superficial fibres also contributes to this, and possibly also to the frequently dimpled surface when the muscle is active.

The orbicularis oris, usually depicted as a band simply surrounding the mouth, is rather more complicated than this, comprising fibres from most of the surrounding muscles enmeshed together.

Muscles numbered 81–84 on the drawing opposite are all considered to be muscles of the mouth. The first, the *levator labii superioris alaeque nasi* arises from the upper part of the frontal maxilla, between eye and nose, running downwards to insertions by two slips into the cartilage of the nose and into the upper lip. The *levator labii superioris*, the *zygomaticus major* and *minor* arise from just below the zygomatic arch.

The *orbicularis oculi*, on the other hand, is a fairly simple sphincter-like muscle, although the *palpebral* or eyelid parts can act independently of the orbital parts.

Covering the whole of the dome of the skull from the eyebrows to the base of the skull is a broad fibro-muscular layer called the *occipito-frontalis*. The frontal muscular layers are thus joined to the occipital parts by an aponeurosis called the *galea aponeurotica*.

23 Sternocleidomastoid
72 Temporalis
73 Masseter
74 Buccinator
75 Occipito-frontalis
76 Corrugator supercilii
77 Oculi–orbital part
78 Oculi–palebral part
79 Procerus
80 Compressor naris, dilatator naris
81 Levator labii superioris alaeque nasi
82 Levator labii superioris
83 Levator anguli oris
84 Zygomaticus major
85 Zygomaticus minor
86 Depressor anguli oris
87 Depressor labii inferioris
88 Orbicularis oris

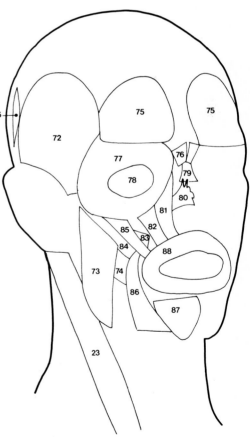

Shape

In this section the emphasis will be upon learning how to see and draw the overall shape of the figure, simply and directly, with no attention to detail. The objective is to introduce an abstract view of the human figure to help clear away the many preconceptions which will have been built up in the mind, and which obscure accurate observation.

A fundamental requirement in drawing is the ability to see the real shape of an object without subjective distortion. I will try to explain what I mean by the term 'subjective distortion'.

In normal everyday life we have to react quickly and intuitively to our surroundings in order to move about and perform actions with safety and certainty. To achieve this our brain selects from the mass of visual information supplied by the eye, only those aspects which are useful in recognizing objects, judging distances, speeds of movement etc. A very important part of this interpretation is the ability of the brain to deduce from one view of an object, not only what it is, but what it would look like from another view, and it nearly always converts an unusual view into a normal one, so that it can be recognized by matching with its stored memory image. For example the remembered image of say a wine bottle will always be an upright, longish form. But a bottle in life may be observed from above (fig.1), so that perhaps only a very small amount of its length can be seen. In this circumstance the bottle may actually present a shape to the eye which is very near to being circular, but in most cases the brain has no difficulty in interpreting the object and making a fair estimate of what its length and its shape would be if it was returned to the more familiar eye-level position. It does this by reference to the perspective distortion of the surroundings of the bottle, by reference to the usual length and appearance of other bottles, by comparing the slightly different views which the left eye and right eyes give (depth vision) and other subtle clues. It is very complicated and yet we do it instantly and are doing it all the time. Our judgment of whether to cross a road in front of a car depends on being able to judge the real distance of the vehicle and the real width of the road and from this and other facts the likelihood of reaching the other side safely. You do this time and time again, usually accurately, despite the fact that your eye records the *width* of the road as rather smaller than it does the same length applied across your vision.

Consider fig.2. Although dimension (a) representing the height of the building is much larger than dimension (b) representing the width of the road, the various perspective clues would lead your brain to deduce the *actual* width of the road that has to be crossed as perhaps as much as or more than the height of the building.

Now the important fact for you as an objective draughtsman is that it is the unprocessed, observed dimensions (a) and (b) that most concern you, not as in life, the calculated 'real' distance.

It may seem that I am dwelling unduly on this aspect but it really is at the root of *the* most common difficulty encountered in drawing by beginners. When attempting to draw the road and building, the brain tries to process what the eye sees so that the dimension (b) is stretched and drawn to occupy more depth in the picture despite its observed depth, because

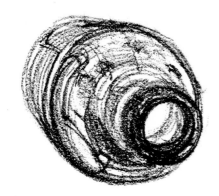

Fig.1

the brain knows that it is in reality a longer distance than it appears. But you must learn to ignore the interpretations of your subconscious brain and draw what your eye sees. It is hard to do this; the brain does not give up easily and is constantly processing your vision and catching you out. Luckily there are many ways of combatting this and helping your eye to see in the special direct way that it must in order to draw objectively.

One way is to train yourself to look for the overall flat shape occupied by an object, rather than assessing its height and width separately. If an object or part of an object can be loosely contained by a square or a circle, even if it does not fit precisely, it is very useful to imagine or even draw the square or circle around it. Triangles, rectangles, ovals, and irregular shapes close to these, are all easier to

judge relatively one to the other by eye than are linear dimensions.

The human form of course is *not* square, or any geometrical shape; it is its own shape or rather its own multitude of shapes depending on pose and viewpoint, but in many circumstances it is very useful to see it *contained* by one or other of these abstractions.

For projects 1 to 4 I suggest that soft pencil, chalk or, best of all, charcoal should be used for speed and simplicity.

Fig.2

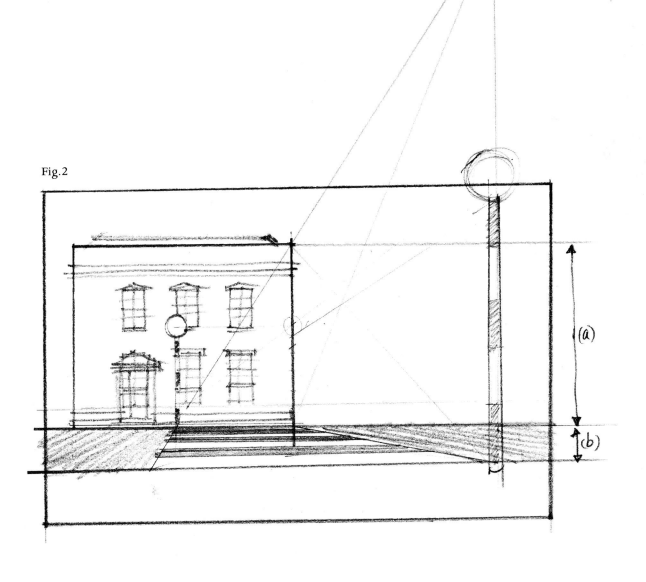

Shape

Project 1

For the first project, very quick, very simplified but complete drawings are to be attempted.

The purpose is to develop your ability to see the whole shape of the figure in almost one glance and also, right from the start, to rid you of the preconceptions of the figure as a torso with long appendages. We all know it *is* that, but in order to draw well, relating the parts properly to the whole, you must try to empty your mind of preconceptions and see what it is in front of you as though it is entirely new. Arms and legs, when entwined with and enclosed by the torso, are as one form.

Ask your model to adopt a series of curled up poses, wrapping arms, legs, head and neck as far as possible into one combined form, as though sculpted from a square block. Start with poses held for ten minutes at first, then five.

Look at the complete pose and try to decide if most of it would fit into a square, a rectangle, a circle or some other regular geometrical shape.

If it does more or less fit one of these shapes, either draw the geometric shape and then the figure contained within it, or draw the figure contained by the shape in your mind's eye. Ignore details – forget the fact that entwined or hidden arms and legs can in other circumstances unravel and separate; draw what you see as one lumpy form. It can be a simple outline or a silhouette, but it must include the whole figure. It is better to draw an almost abstract shape which suggests the general shape of the pose than to complete only an arm, hand or head, no matter how beautifully it is drawn. To do this is to miss the point of the exercise.

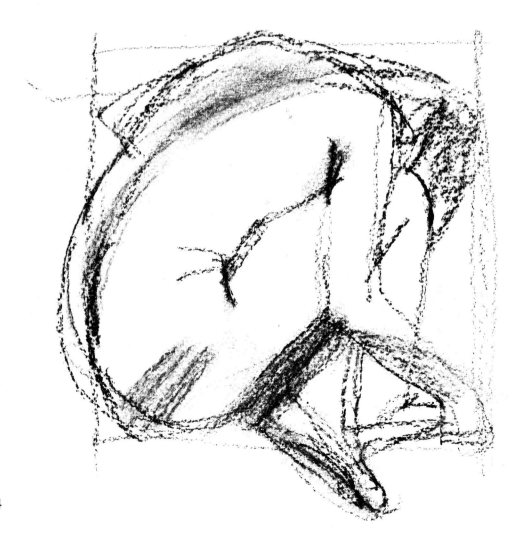

Fig.1

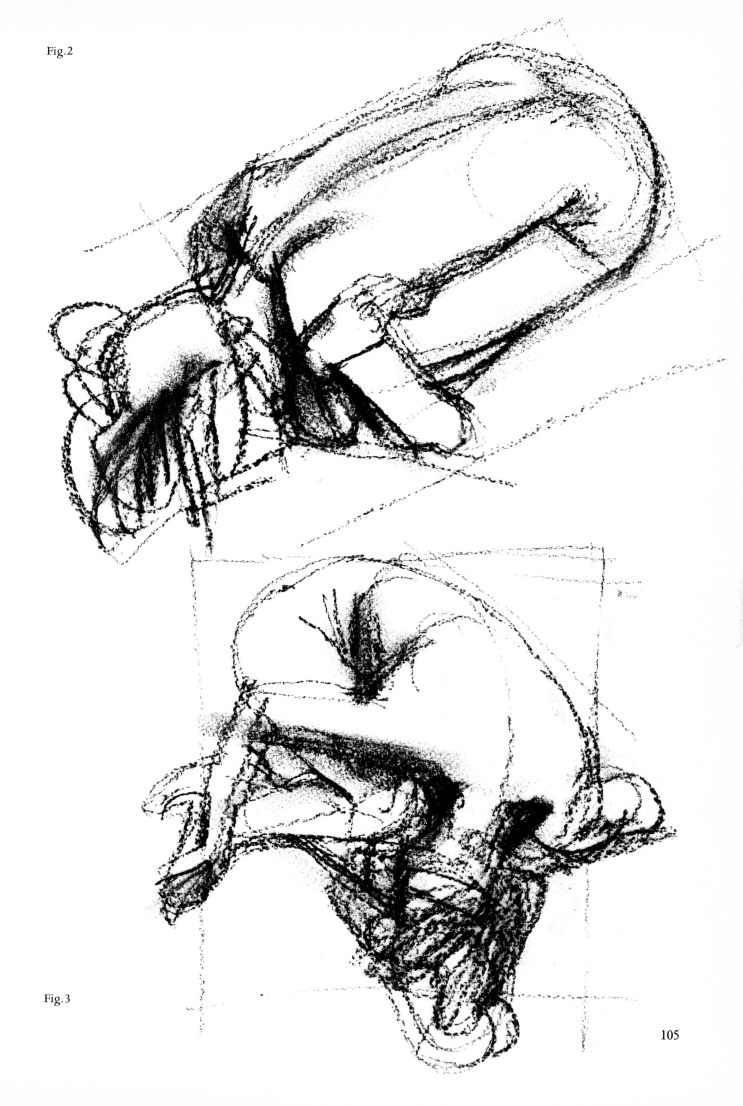

Fig.2

Fig.3

105

Shape

Project 2

Ask the model to take up a simple, sitting or semi-reclining pose on the floor. Aim for something fairly compact, not so curled up as before perhaps, but keeping arms and legs quite closely into the main form. The purpose is to appreciate the figure as a form arising from and defining the ground plane.

Having seen how the complete figure can be thought of as occupying a flat geometric shape and then a three dimensional block, I would like you to think of the block sitting on the floor or ground plane.

The live model, in every situation where studied drawing is possible (i.e. not flying, falling or floating), will be in contact with the floor, either directly or indirectly. It is vitally necessary to consider all the planes of the figure relative to this 'ground plane'. Only by

cultivating an acute awareness of the positions of a figure with reference to the plane of the floor can the structure and balance of the figure supporting itself against the downward pull of gravity be properly understood and analysed.

Described in words, this concept sounds more complex than it is in reality. It is really only necessary to divert attention to the way in which the figure is, so to speak, erected on the ground plane, for it to be clearly seen and appreciated. However, it is not always so easy to *define* the ground plane by drawing. A regular grid pattern on the floor, as tiles or carpet squares, is very helpful in this respect.

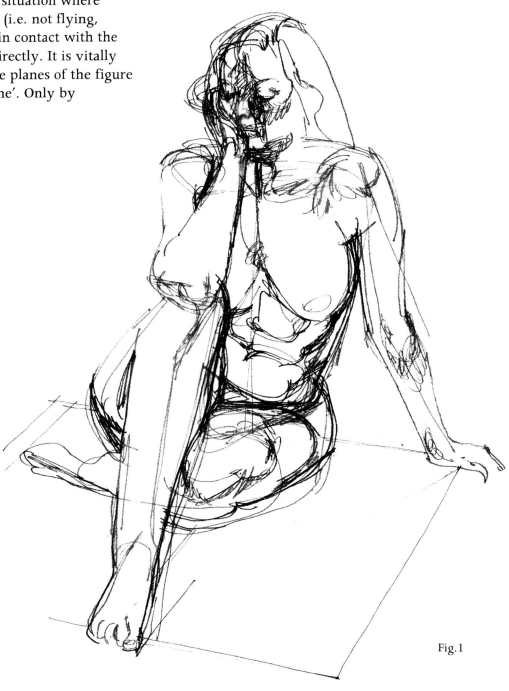

Fig.1

106

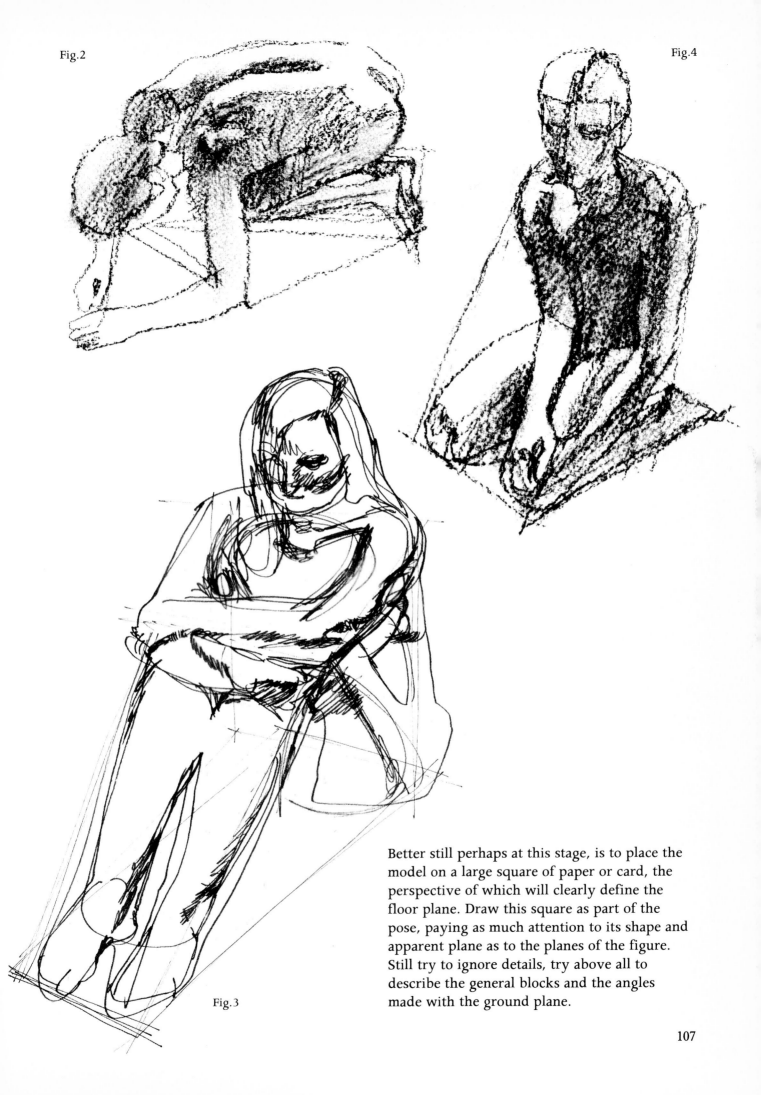

Fig.2

Fig.4

Fig.3

Better still perhaps at this stage, is to place the model on a large square of paper or card, the perspective of which will clearly define the floor plane. Draw this square as part of the pose, paying as much attention to its shape and apparent plane as to the planes of the figure. Still try to ignore details, try above all to describe the general blocks and the angles made with the ground plane.

Shape

Project 3

Probably the most commonly adopted pose in life drawing is that of the seated model. For this reason it is sometimes felt to be rather boring but if some thought is given to the nature of the event when the human figure achieves equilibrium by close association with a series of struts and supports called a chair, there is really no necessity for boredom!

The model should initially be asked to sit on a chair in a simple posture, well and firmly located, feet flat on the floor and not too far from the legs of the chair, bottom well back into the angle between seat and chair back.

A space visitor, unfamiliar with either chairs or humans, would have no reason to suppose that this composite object could be separated into two parts, the animate part moving away from the inanimate support.

You should try to see the object in the same way. Draw the six-legged object as a complete structure arising from the ground plane even higher than the structures in the previous project.

Although there may be quite a lot of space between the chair seat and the floor, the legs of the chair are just as securely supporting the

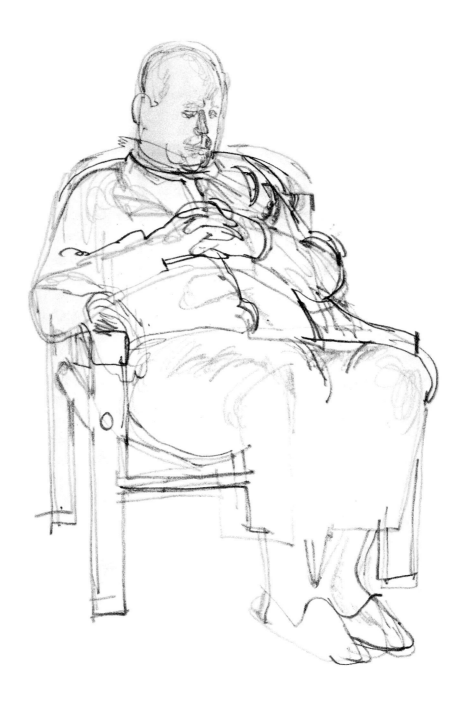

Fig.1

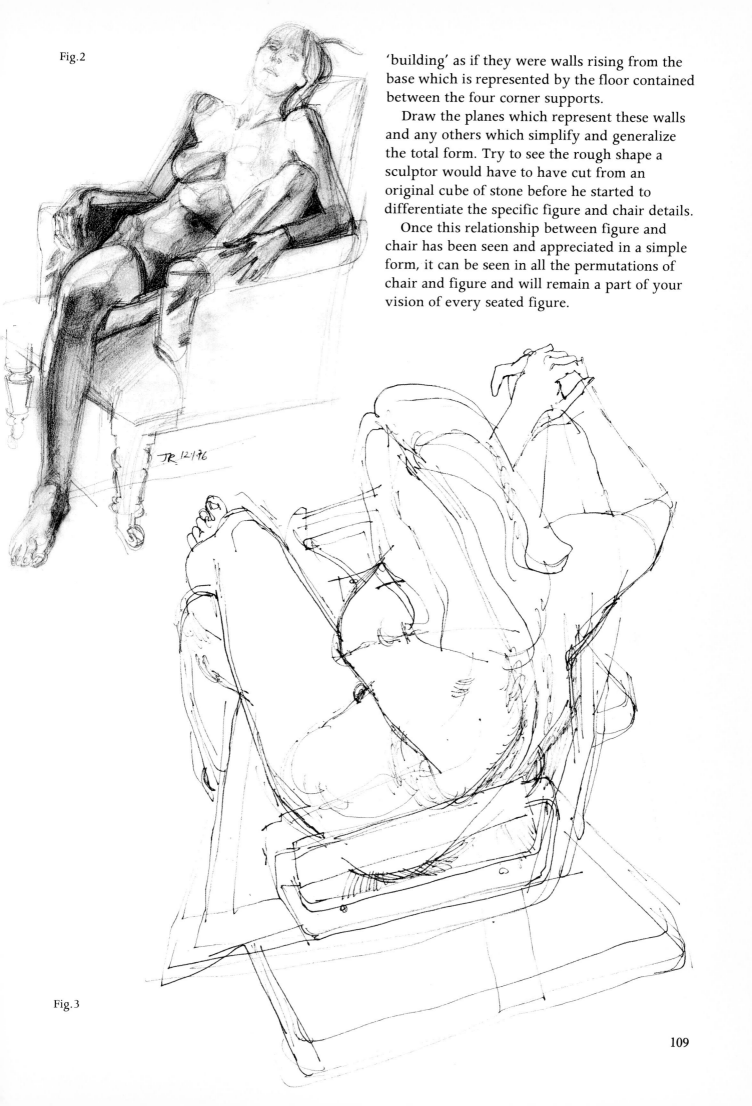

Fig.2

'building' as if they were walls rising from the base which is represented by the floor contained between the four corner supports.

Draw the planes which represent these walls and any others which simplify and generalize the total form. Try to see the rough shape a sculptor would have to have cut from an original cube of stone before he started to differentiate the specific figure and chair details.

Once this relationship between figure and chair has been seen and appreciated in a simple form, it can be seen in all the permutations of chair and figure and will remain a part of your vision of every seated figure.

Fig.3

109

Shape

Project 4

For this exercise the erection of the figure from the ground plane is completed: we have the standing figure.

Now before preconceptions about the human figure intervene, I want you to hold in your mind that idea of the standing figure as the thinnest shape you have yet considered in these exercises, but still a peg, a monolith, staying balanced upright because its base is at right angles to its centre line.

Of course, the actual ground contact area of a standing human figure is limited to the soles of the feet, but the weight of overhanging larger forms higher up is distributed so that gravity pulls equally all round and balance is maintained.

If you imagine strings falling vertically from the widest points all around a standing figure, you will have a sort of three-dimensional diagram of the forces which must be balanced (see fig.1).

The shape delineated on the floor represents its cast shadow if it were lit directly from above, and each pose will have a characteristic 'shadow', its shape and the position of the foot-contact areas within it representing its own particular diagram of forces.

Draw this diagram from observation of your

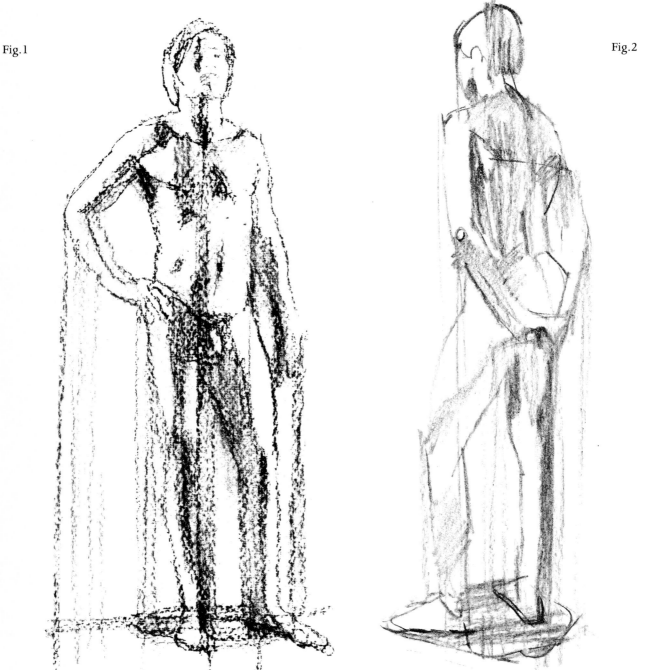

Fig.1   Fig.2

Fig.3

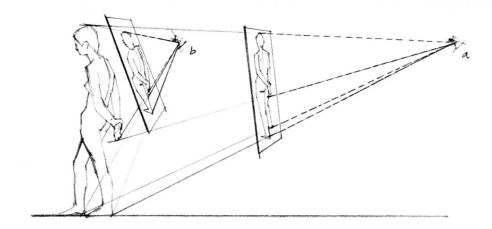

Fig.4

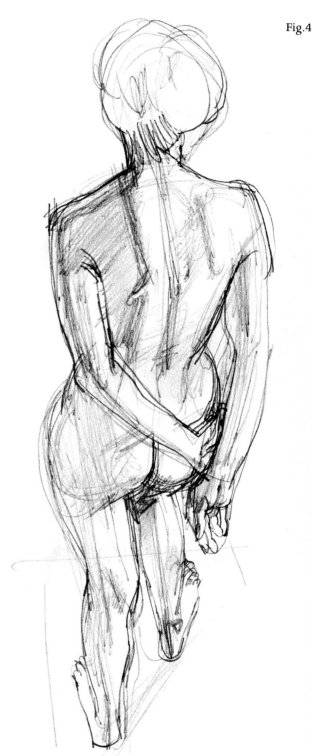

model's standing pose from several angles and distances.

You will find that it is easier to see both the 90–degree angle that the figure makes with the ground and the 'shadow' more clearly when the viewpoint is either rather raised or close to the model.

Another advantage of this is that the outline shape seen from close proximity or from any but an eye-to-eye level is unfamiliar and unexpected, which makes it less likely that you will draw what you think you know rather than what you see.

Look at fig.4. Objective observation of this standing figure tells us, for example, that the hands appear to be very close to the toes of the right foot. There is, of course, considerable *spatial* distance between them: we know this to be true because no human beings have arms which hang down to their feet – but this is a stumbling block – it is *because* we know this elementary fact that we tend to modify what we see to fall in with what we know.

Fig.3, shows diagrammatically how parts of an object which are situated on a line of sight will appear together two dimensionally although there may be considerable actual three-dimensional space between them. From the longer viewpoint A, the hands will be seen to rest in the 'normal' expected place i.e. fingertips about half way down the thigh. Approach to position B though, and the lines of sight bring hands and forward foot into close confluence, and widen the distance between the feet, which are now viewed from almost directly above.

The whole secret of foreshortening is contained in this concept.

Heads, hands and feet

Having used ten pages of drawings and text to urge you to observe and draw the figure as one simple entity, it may seem rather retrogressive of me to suggest that the head, hands and feet should now be singled out for special attention.

I *do* feel that it is generally rather dangerous to make lots of unrelated studies of small sections of the body, especially separate facial features. I consider that too much of this fragmented drawing makes it more difficult when you come to draw the complete figure to see its essential unity.

The complete head however, and to a lesser extent, the hands and feet, are rather exceptional and often present special difficulties for the beginner.

Part of the trouble lies in the comparative complexity of these forms, but much more fundamental is the difficulty of seeing them clearly and objectively. In everyday life we are continually reacting to visual messages from the facial features of other people, with or without the support of speech. We are capable of

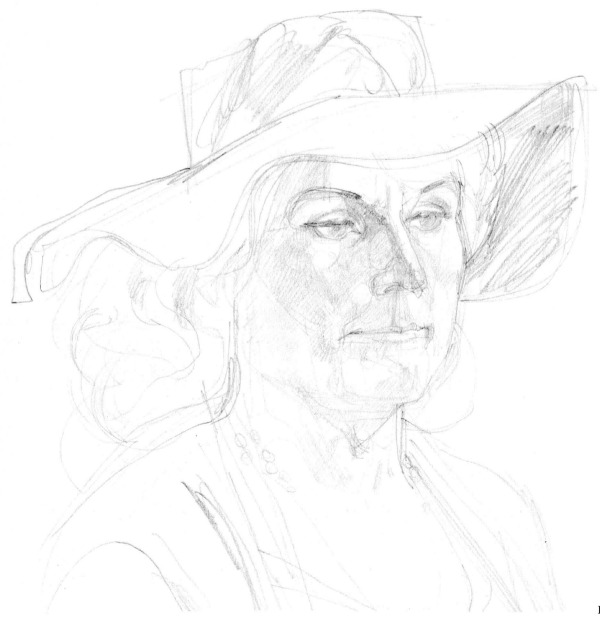

Fig.1

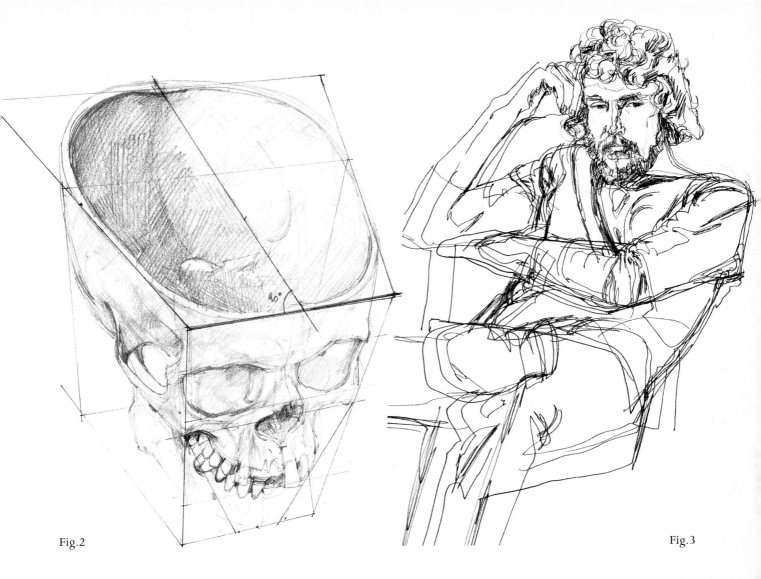

Fig.2

Fig.3

detecting very subtle changes in the shape of eyes and mouth and surrounding areas which interact with these features, and we can and do deduce a great variety of information by reading the signs.

We should know what such a familiar thing as the human head looks like. Unfortunately it is precisely the fact that we think we *do* know what it looks like that prevents us from looking at it objectively. We are so used to reading signals from especially expressive areas of the face and unconsciously rejecting comparatively blank areas that it carries over into our observation of the head when we want to make a drawing, with the result that the *same* interesting bits monopolise our attention.

The result is a sort of symbol of a head in which the facial area looms large and the eyes, nose and mouth occupy an inordinately large area within that.

To draw the head as it is, we have to combat this 'processing' of the picture received by our eyes, and learn to consider the less expressive

areas *between* the features and to give the facial area its proper size and shape relative to the whole head.

Curiously enough we already have an acutely sensitive appreciation of the interrelated areas of the head and face, which we use in recognition of individuals, but it is so subliminal that most people find it impossible to extract these stored patterns in order to draw them. To check this, try drawing from memory the complete head of someone that you have never drawn from life, but whose face you know very well. If you produce a good convincing likeness you have a very unusual visual memory.

This problem of familiarity gets in the way of objective vision, and contributes to the difficulty that most people encounter when drawing hands and feet too, but to a lesser extent.

The following projects are designed to help you to see these 'familiar' areas with a more direct and objective eye.

113

Heads, hands and feet

Fig.1

Project 1

Pose your model in any comfortable reclined pose, with head and face resting horizontal to your vision.

Unless you tilt *your* head to get a 'normal' upright view of the model's face, you will now have in view a form in which the two eyes are one *above* the other, the ridge of the nose lies horizontally and all together it is fairly unfamiliar.

Observe and draw it from this angle, resisting the temptation to tilt your head for the normal view. Treat the shapes and volumes as though they were completely new and unfamiliar forms. Look for general linking planes as in the Shape projects.

It may be as well to draw the neck and

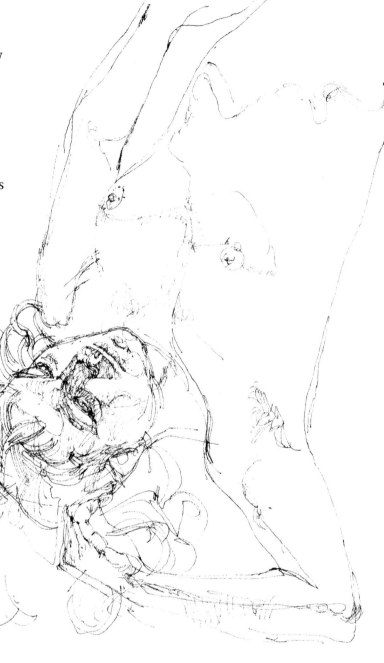

shoulders or even more of the figure as well. The point of this exercise is to view the head and face from an unfamiliar angle, so as long as that is complied with, there is no reason why the figure should not be completed.

Later try drawing a pose where you have a completely upside-down view of the face as in my drawings. The heads of these figures were drawn totally without turning the drawing board round to check that it looked right the

other way up, but after completion a 'normal' upright view of the drawn head revealed that a good likeness had been achieved, which perhaps proves something!

Although my drawings here are in pencil, I suggest that you may find it easier initially to generalize and simplify the forms using charcoal, but it is not important and if you find you need the greater precision of pencil, that's fine.

114

Fig.2

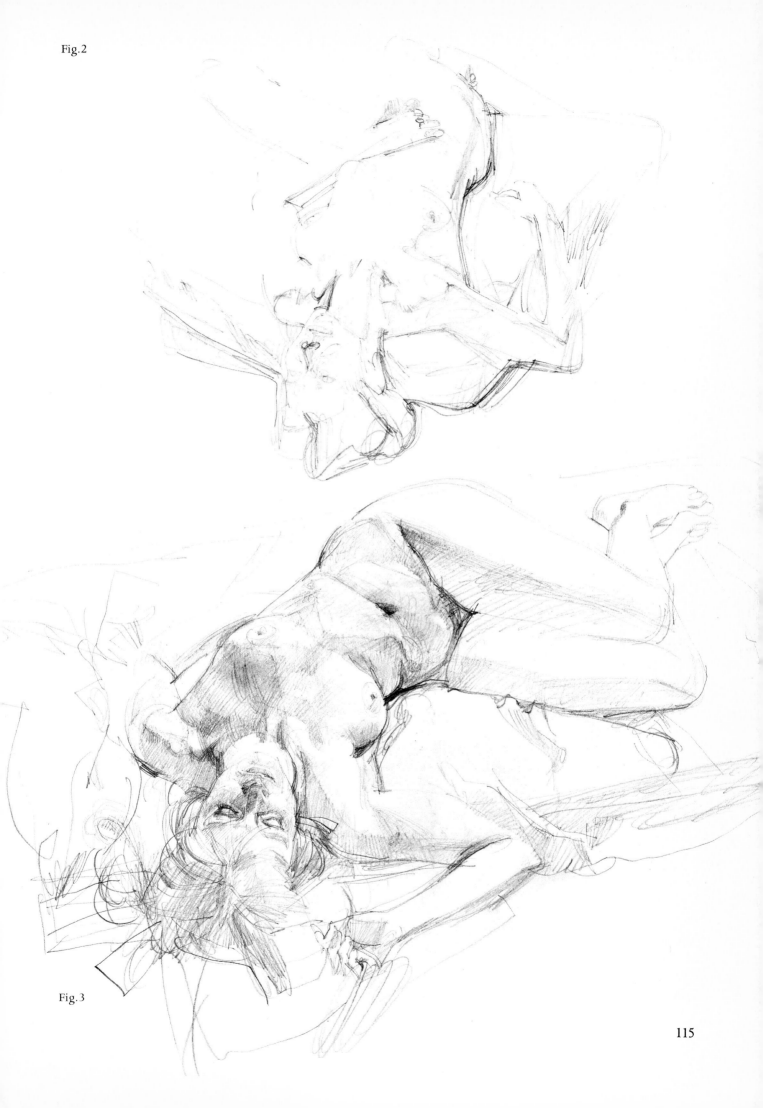

Fig.3

115

Heads, hands and feet

Project 2

For this session a series of poses should be set up involving head, hands and feet in a variety of close associations as suggested by the drawings on this spread.

Hands are capable of many actions but they are especially good at gripping, when they wrap around objects and in a sense take on the shape of the object that they enwrap. If you draw them like this, not only can you use them to help describe the enfolded form, but you can also illuminate their own shape by studying the form that they are holding.

It all helps to keep you looking at composite forms and not getting tied up with surface detail. Fingers can be spread of course and so can toes, but fingers most often combine with the palm to make simple shapes, even a relaxed hand is cupped in shape.

The palm of the hand is often represented as a flat squarish rigid form to which the fingers are attached, but it is not like this at all. It moves *with* the fingers and thumb and should be seen as a form continuous with them, arching when the fingers are stretched and spread, and cupping when they curl.

Feet are much less mobile, but still plagued by preconception-engendered difficulties. They have splendidly strong arched structures which make the under surface concave, so that the middle to inner border of the sole does not touch the ground in the normal standing position. The area that *does* contact the ground however is pressed by the weight of the body to the shape of the ground plane, usually in the studio a flat surface.

You must try to visualize this flattened surface in the supporting foot and make it fit the plane with which you represent the ground.

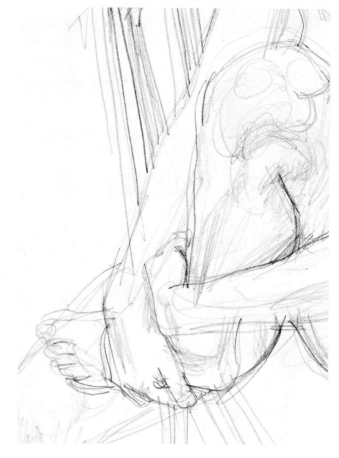

Fig. 1

Fig. 2

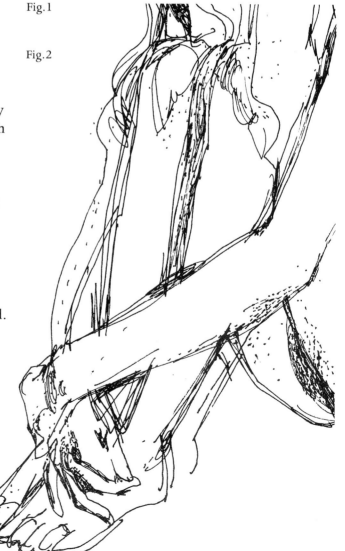

Fig. 3

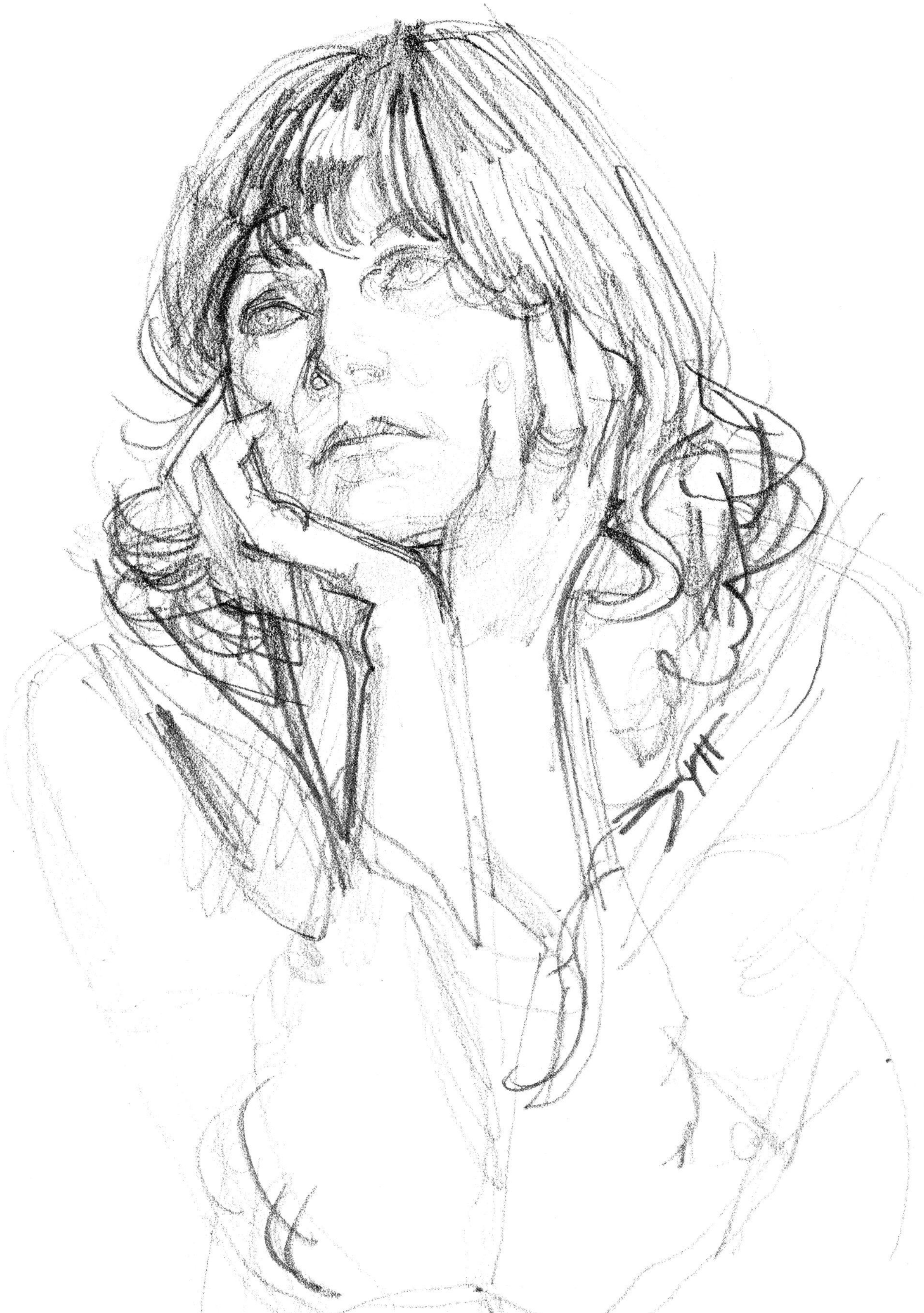

Heads, hands and feet

Project 3

Have the model sit comfortably in good light to give strong modelling to the face and head. A cross light from one side is usually good. If the source is too far behind the head, you will need a light surface to reflect some light back into the shadows of the face.

Having hopefully rid yourself of some of what you think you know about the head and face, this project is to allow you to re-look at the 'normal' view and try to see it anew.

One of the hardest things to get right is the proportion of facial area to the rest of the head. This varies from individual to individual, but it usually comes as rather a surprise, when measured, to see how little of the total head area is taken up by the eyes, nose and mouth features.

The skull gives the shape to the head and face. It is unique in the body in having a complete bony structure near the surface. Most

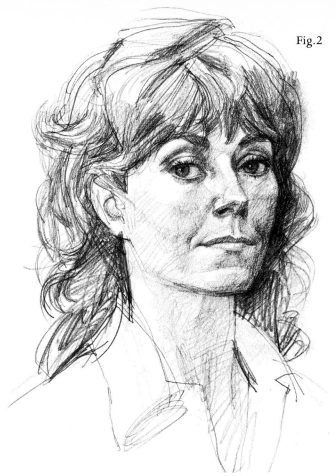

Fig.2

of the cranium is covered by a very thin muscular sheet and the main modification of the facial form of the skull is made by the inclusion of the eyes in their orbits and the extension of the small bony ridge of the nose by cartilage into the familiar nose shape. The only muscles with any bulk are those which activate the jaw bone, the masseters, and even these to a great extent are underlying the angle of the jaw, having no visible effect on the surface form.

It follows that to understand the skull is to understand the basic forms of the head and face, so if it is possible to have access to a good plastic skull, it is worth making some drawings of it from a variety of angles, paying particular attention to the proportions and directions of its main planes.

Failing this, study drawings of skulls and try to recognize the same forms beneath the skin of the live model.

Fig.2 in the introduction to this section shows a skull with the top of the cranium removed. The shape of the section so revealed shows that the side planes are fairly flat and that they are not parallel, but converge a little towards the brow, the widest part of the head being much

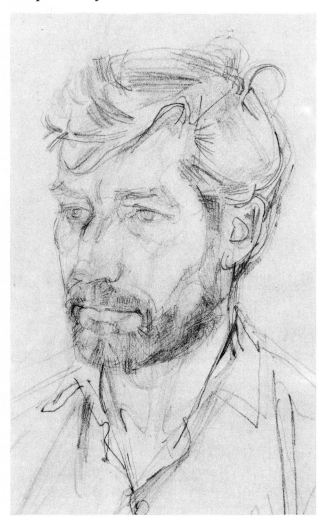

Fig.1

118

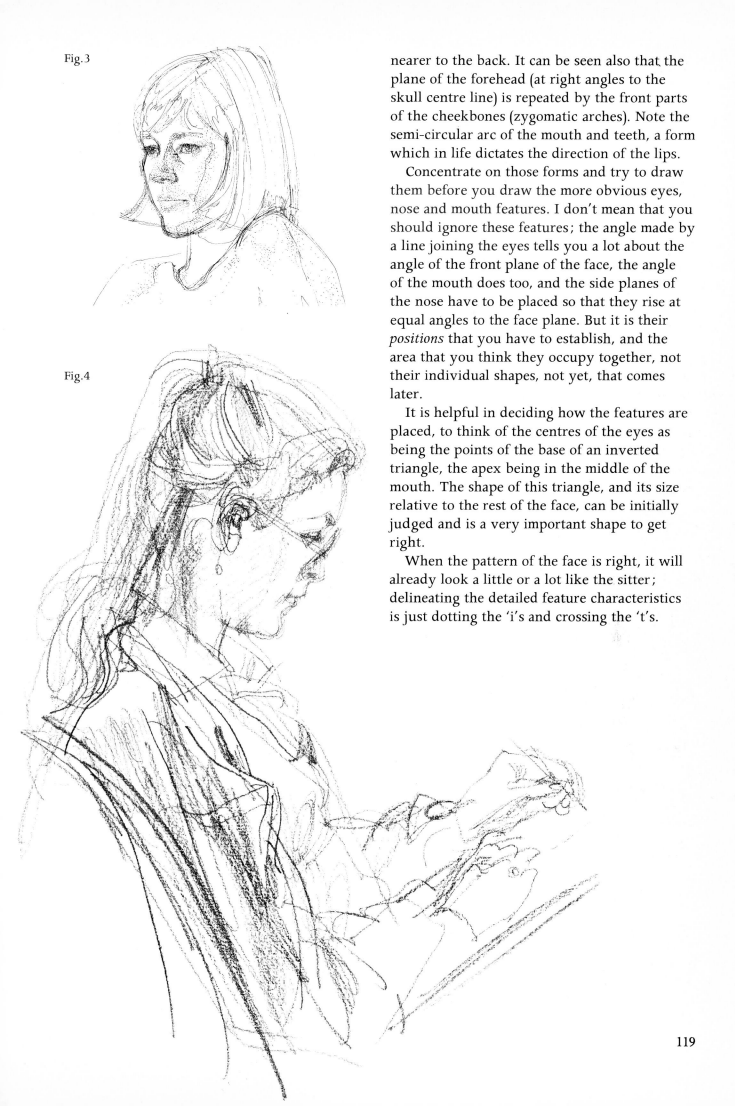

Fig.3

Fig.4

nearer to the back. It can be seen also that the plane of the forehead (at right angles to the skull centre line) is repeated by the front parts of the cheekbones (zygomatic arches). Note the semi-circular arc of the mouth and teeth, a form which in life dictates the direction of the lips.

Concentrate on those forms and try to draw them before you draw the more obvious eyes, nose and mouth features. I don't mean that you should ignore these features; the angle made by a line joining the eyes tells you a lot about the angle of the front plane of the face, the angle of the mouth does too, and the side planes of the nose have to be placed so that they rise at equal angles to the face plane. But it is their *positions* that you have to establish, and the area that you think they occupy together, not their individual shapes, not yet, that comes later.

It is helpful in deciding how the features are placed, to think of the centres of the eyes as being the points of the base of an inverted triangle, the apex being in the middle of the mouth. The shape of this triangle, and its size relative to the rest of the face, can be initially judged and is a very important shape to get right.

When the pattern of the face is right, it will already look a little or a lot like the sitter; delineating the detailed feature characteristics is just dotting the 'i's and crossing the 't's.

119

Weight

In this section we give consideration to the weight of the figure and try to see how its forms react to the constant pull of gravity.

Projects from the first section (Shape) explored forms gradually building from the ground up, so to speak. Now we should look rather at the forces which try to pull them back down again.

Bodies come in all shapes and sizes, but all are composed of comparatively soft tissue, which is prevented from becoming a heap by clinging to a system of hard supports called the skeleton. Some of the soft tissue is purely suspended, the viscera, fat, genitals etc., and some contributes to the stiffness of the skeleton and operates it, muscles, tendons, cartilage etc. More will be said of the bones and muscular systems under the Anatomy heading, but for the moment it is enough to observe which forms seem to resist gravity and those which bend and sag.

Overweight subjects will reveal the omnipresent force more obviously than will very thin models, and the decision to concentrate attention in a drawing on this aspect may well be prompted by the over-powering 'weightiness' of a well-upholstered model, which is a fine and good reason for drawing it so.

But my intention in these next exercises is to draw attention to the way *all* figures are affected by gravity when they are at rest.

The figure in movement, while still being

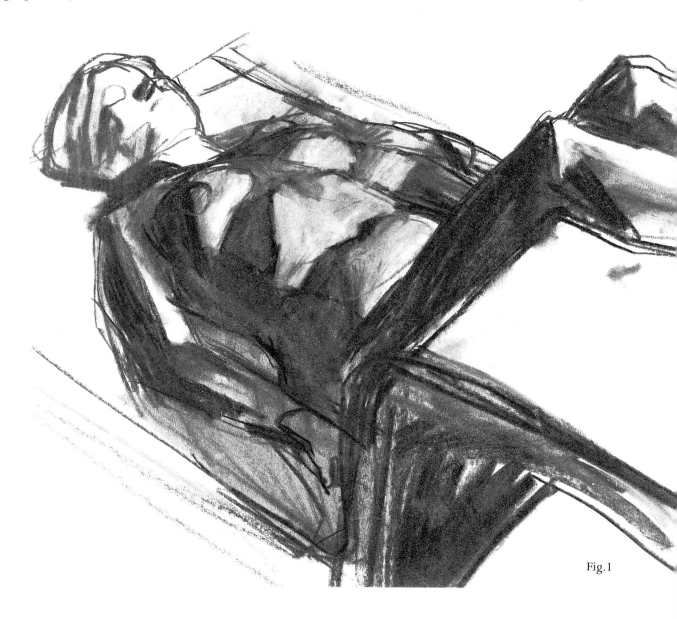

Fig.1

120

subject to the force of gravity, is generating forces and movements of its own, which can be added to the gravitational pull in some places, while subtracting from or multiplying it in others. A leaping figure, for example, immediately before take off from one leg may have transferred all body weight to that leg, which will be tensed and taut under the strain, while the other leg is being thrown upward and outward, its tissues apparently defying gravity.

At rest, on the other hand, the pull on the body is all one way and it is arrested either by contact with the ground or by the limit of its suspension.

It is the way that it adapts itself to the constant pull, the way that, depending on the ground plane, it tells us where that plane is that must be the primary interest. It is this that will enable us to make a drawing that expresses the subjective feeling of mass and weight.

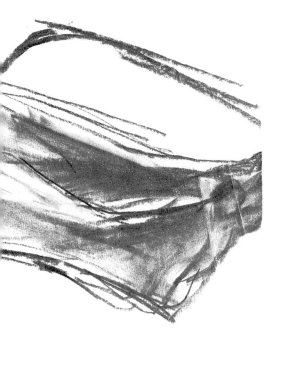

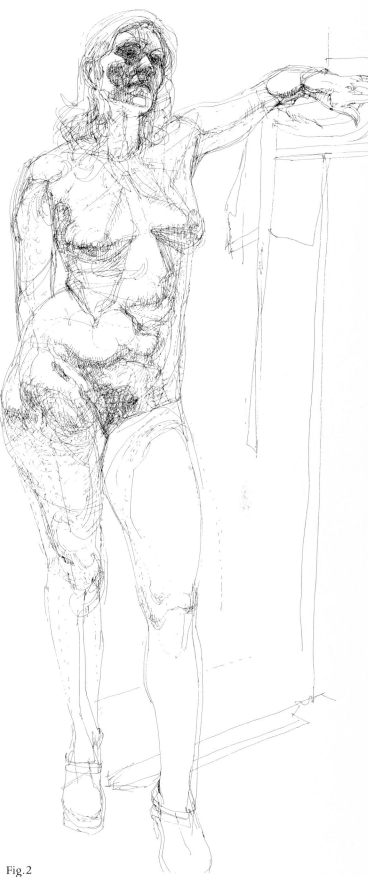

Fig.2

Weight
Project 1

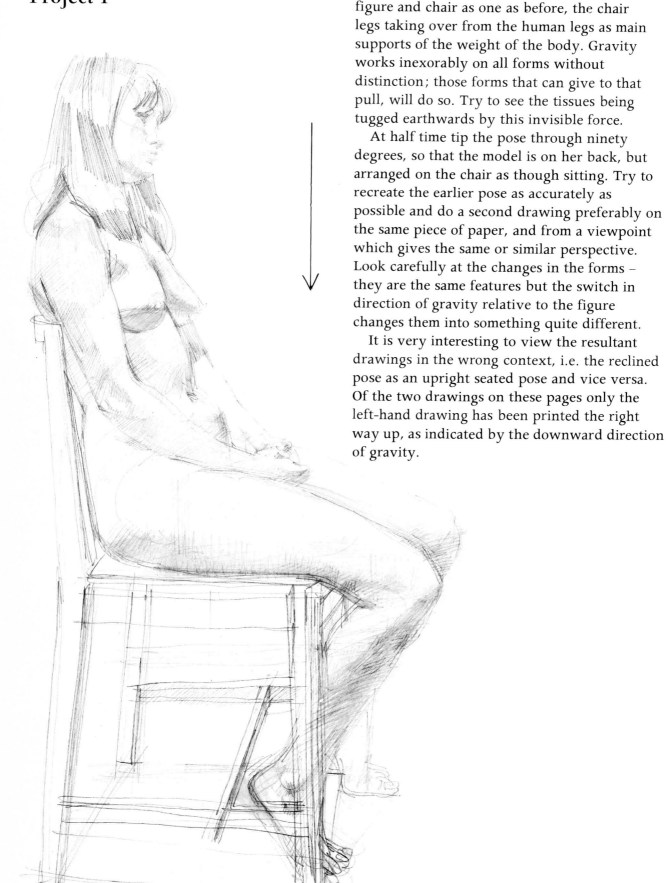

Set the pose with the model seated simply on a chair, legs together, arms by side, feet firmly on the floor, back against the chairback. Draw figure and chair as one as before, the chair legs taking over from the human legs as main supports of the weight of the body. Gravity works inexorably on all forms without distinction; those forms that can give to that pull, will do so. Try to see the tissues being tugged earthwards by this invisible force.

At half time tip the pose through ninety degrees, so that the model is on her back, but arranged on the chair as though sitting. Try to recreate the earlier pose as accurately as possible and do a second drawing preferably on the same piece of paper, and from a viewpoint which gives the same or similar perspective. Look carefully at the changes in the forms – they are the same features but the switch in direction of gravity relative to the figure changes them into something quite different.

It is very interesting to view the resultant drawings in the wrong context, i.e. the reclined pose as an upright seated pose and vice versa. Of the two drawings on these pages only the left-hand drawing has been printed the right way up, as indicated by the downward direction of gravity.

Fig.1

Notice how the soft tissues of the breasts and stomach tend to be pulled downwards along the torso in fig.1 and *across* the torso in the new downward direction in the other drawing. Also, less obviously, in the lying figure the base of the rib cage is left high, the shoulders pulled down and the neck is at a completely different angle in response to the weight of the head.

In short, the main weight of the seated figure is supported on the base of the pelvis, while in the lying figure support is distributed along the length of the back. Gravity acts on facial tissues in the same way, which is one reason why the head should be drawn in the position that you see it, without turning your own head to see the model's face the 'right' way up.

On this page the figure looks wrong, almost like a figure pinned to a wall of death by centrifugal force, but if the book is rotated through 90 degrees so that the gravity arrow points downward, all will be well, and the other drawing will look wrong.

If your drawings *don't* look wrong when viewed the 'wrong' way, you have missed the pull of gravity.

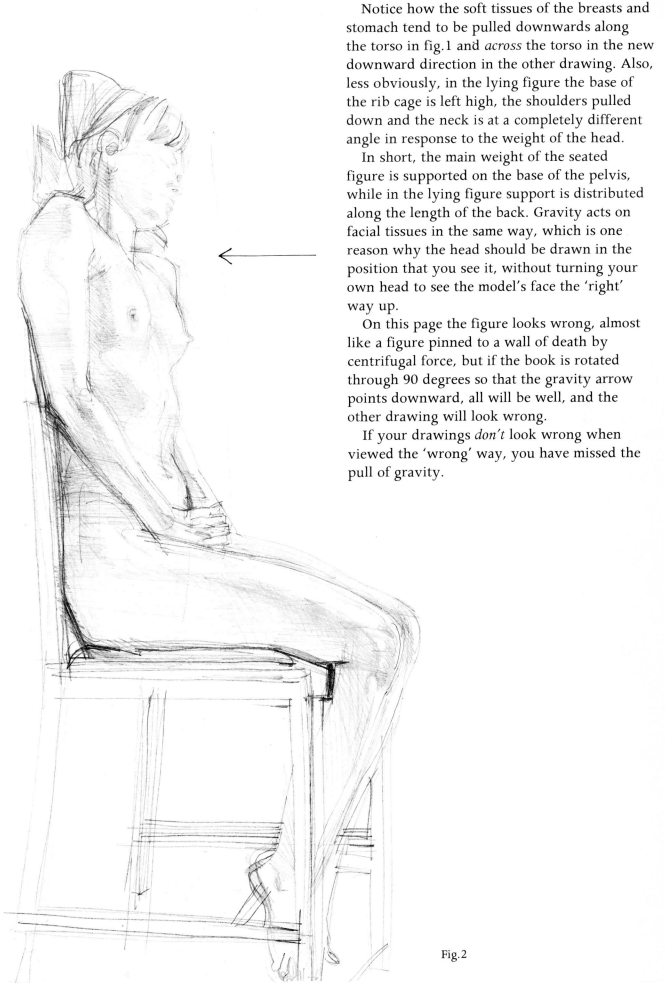

Fig.2

Weight

Project 2

On as hard a surface as your model is prepared to tolerate, set a relaxed reclining pose something like the ones on these pages.

Since the human figure does not have regular side and front planes as a regular geometric architectural block has, it cannot be lain on its side to rest unmodified on a flat plane. In these circumstances it must perforce adapt its shape to the rigid surface as best it can.

As we have seen, gravity tugs continuously at soft and rigid forms alike, but they react rather differently to its influence.

A fully reclined figure initially achieves much more comprehensive contact with the ground plane than does the standing figure, and the action of gravity increases this contact area.

As shoulder and hip are rigidly supported by their bony structures, the major adaptation to the flat surface is made by the sling-like lateral curvature of the back bone, cancelling out the hollow of the waist on the contact side, and greatly exaggerating the curves on the upper side.

Look carefully again for all the outward visible signs of the force of gravity at work. Set yourself the task of expressing just this aspect of the pose above all others.

Try to imagine the shape of the part of the body that has been flattened into contact with the ground. Try placing large sheets of paper or board under the model and drawing a line closely round the contact areas. When the model moves away, the 'imprint' shape is very revealing and interesting. It can be copied while the model is resting and incorporated into your drawing.

In both the very similar poses drawn here, the model has made the hip area more comfortable and balanced by rotating the pelvis a little to distribute weight along the lower thigh. As a result the abdomen (and its quite heavy contents) is tipped forwards to be pulled towards the floor by its own weight. The amoung of sag varies, of course, with the elasticity of the individual model's muscle tone, but some effect is always visible. Breasts too change shape in this position. Note how in fig.1

Fig.1

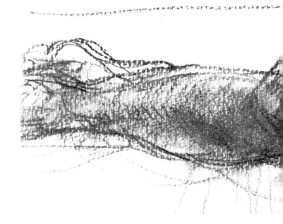

the nearer breast is pulled by gravity away from the chest wall, while her left breast is spread and flattened by its contact with the ground.

Main limbs, with their rigid long bones, cannot bend but must pivot under gravity to achieve a position of rest or else be used as props to support other forms.

Again, in the drawings on this page, see how the legs have adapted their own weight to the ground surface, while one arm is supporting the head, transmitting its weight to the elbow and distributing it along the upper arm.

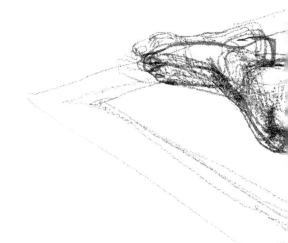

Fig.2

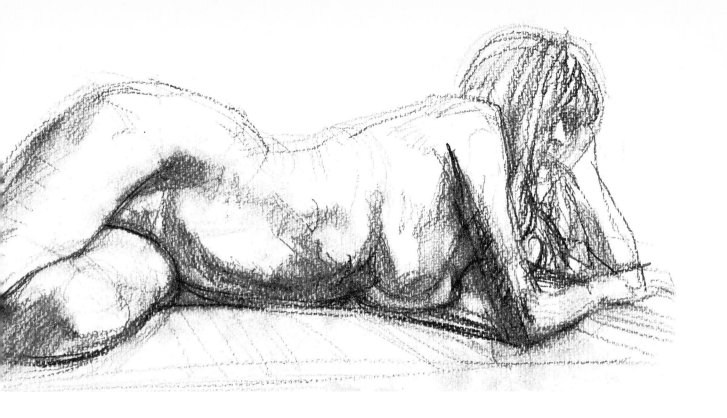

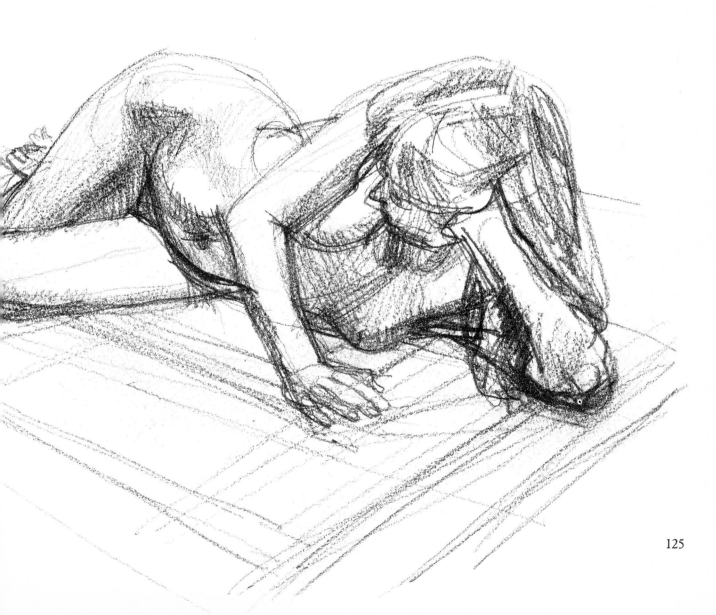

125

Weight

Project 3

This time pose the model on a soft surface that will 'give' to the weight of the reclined or semi-reclined figure. A softly sprung settee or soft mattress is ideal.

Although I have not repeated the poses exactly here, you could do so and then make direct comparisons with the rigid support for the figure in the last project.

On this soft support the hard projections of the figure can make hollows to accommodate themselves and extremes of pelvic swing are not necessary.

Soft tissues are still pulled downwards but where before they made contact with the rigid plane of the floor and were compelled to spread out and flatten, now they bury themselves. Sometimes their line of contact with the soft support is depressed out of sight, so cutting off your view of part of the figure and apparently narrowing it.

It is most important, when this occurs, to understand what is happening and to draw the emergence of the soft support *in front* of the obscured part of the figure so that it is very clear that the rest of the figure *is* there, but sunk out of sight by its own weight.

A combination of soft and hard supports for the figure can be interesting too. In fig.2 all the weight of the model is taken by the settee and transmitted to the floor by its four legs, except for the model's left leg which emerges from the hollow made by the torso, depressing

Fig.1

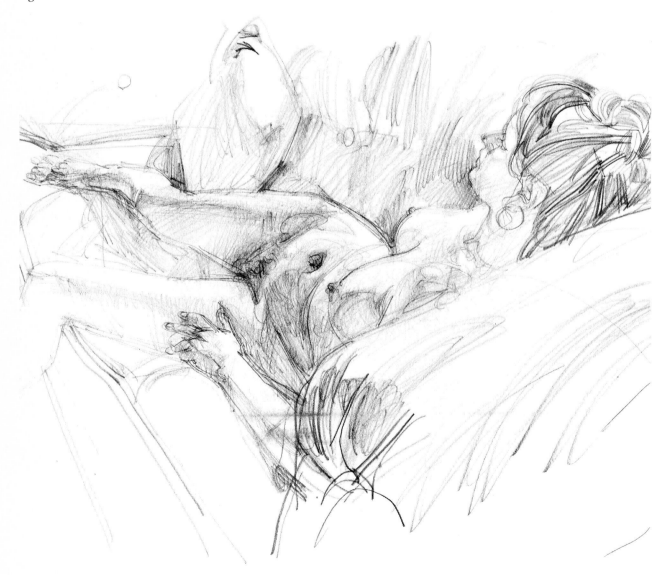

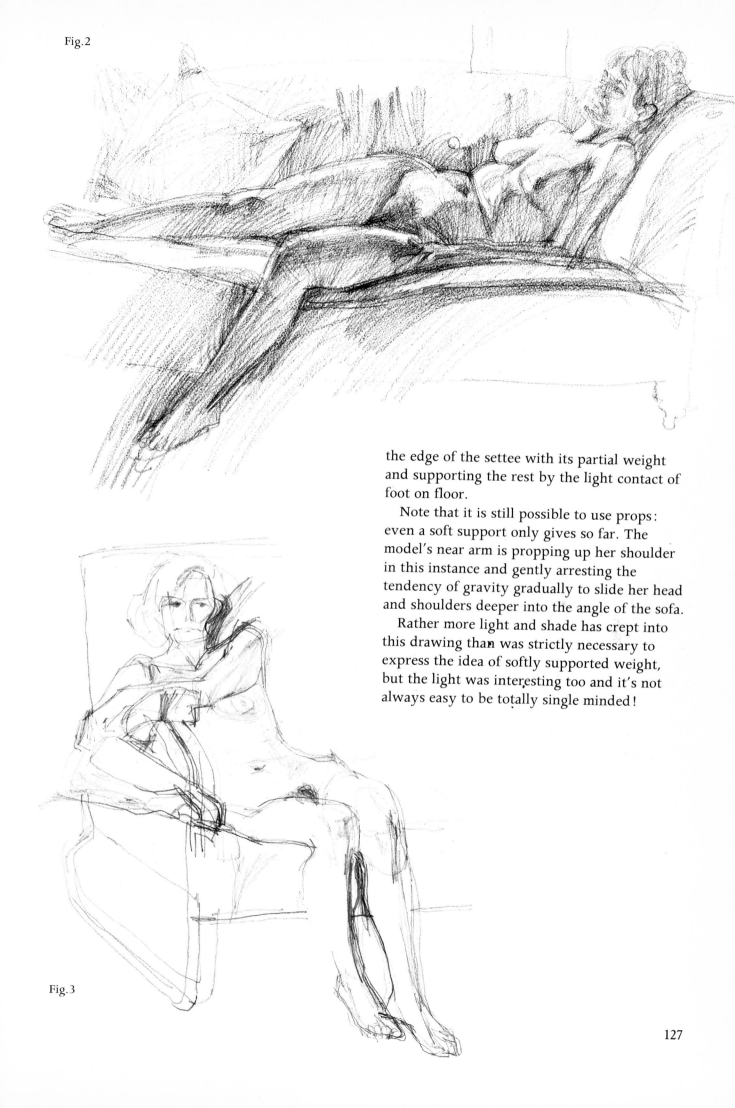

Fig.2

the edge of the settee with its partial weight and supporting the rest by the light contact of foot on floor.

Note that it is still possible to use props: even a soft support only gives so far. The model's near arm is propping up her shoulder in this instance and gently arresting the tendency of gravity gradually to slide her head and shoulders deeper into the angle of the sofa.

Rather more light and shade has crept into this drawing than was strictly necessary to express the idea of softly supported weight, but the light was interesting too and it's not always easy to be totally single minded!

Fig.3

Weight

Project 4

In this project the pose has been set up to involve several supports and props allowing the weight of the body to be widely distributed.

In a semi-reclined position much of the body weight is supported between the pelvis and the shoulder girdle. Hence the model's torso is 'slung' between the support of her firmly lodged right upper arm and her tipped pelvis. The right arm also functions as a prop for the head. Her right leg has been allowed to fall and is in contact with the ground along all its length, in contrast to the other leg in which the weight is balanced and transferred to the firmly planted foot. Neither leg is supporting anything but itself and the far arm is hanging slackly. These are the movements to sort out and express here, and there are many clues.

Note the rounded shape of the model's right breast pulled up by the propped and propping arm contrasting with the slacker form of the breast on the relaxed side. Also the swing of the torso in this position allows the weight of the viscera to round out the lower side while leaving the hard edge of the pelvic girdle visible on the upper side. There is also a flatness to the edge of the weight-taking foot, the whole length of her right lower leg and what can be seen of the model's left buttock – all these forms are flattened by gravity in contrast with a hard base surface.

Incidentally the left hand figure below was drawn *after* the more studied version, in an attempt to express the relaxed weight of the torso more clearly. It often happens that the essential movement becomes clearer as one drawing is completed, either because one's understanding of the pose has become less cluttered or perhaps that the model has relaxed more into the pose. So in either case it is quite reasonable to add a quick statement of the newly seen movement to the original drawing.

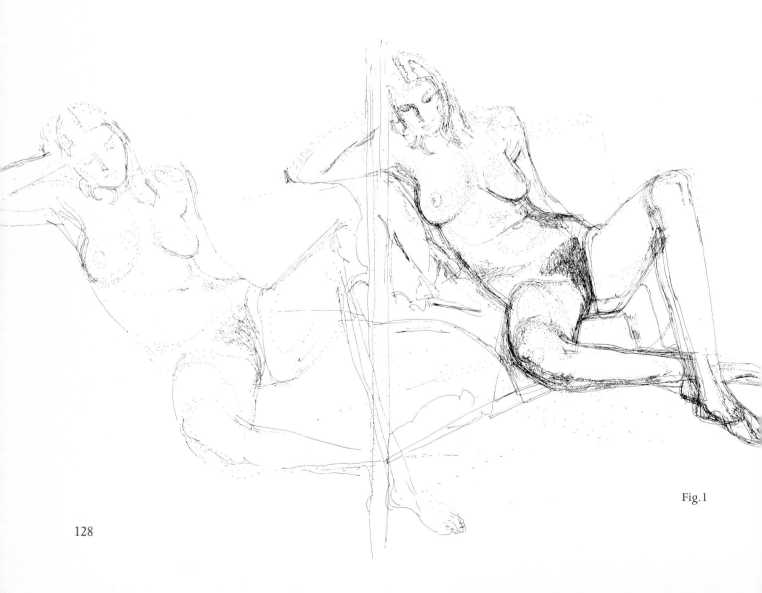

Fig.1

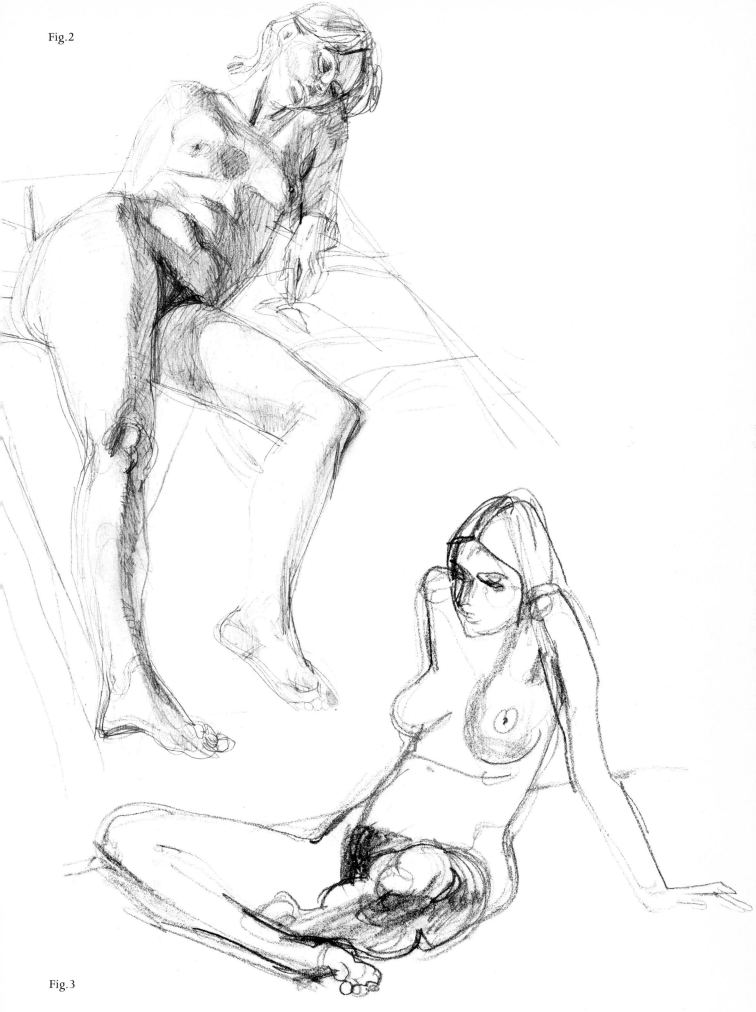

Fig.2

Fig.3

Balance

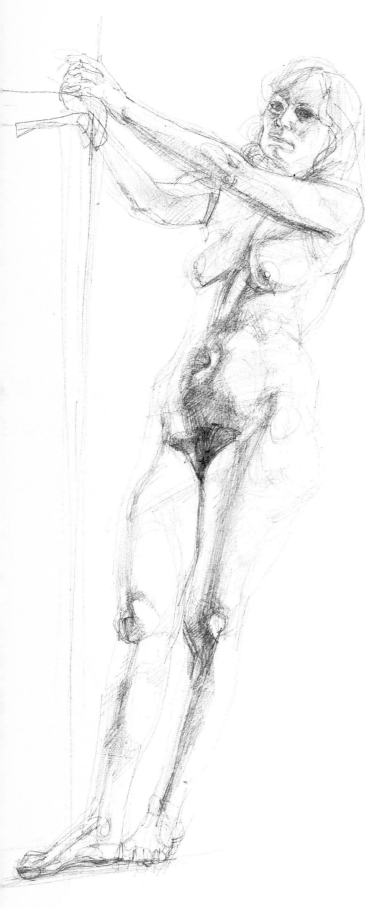

Having learned something about the way that the pull of gravity is made evident in the seated and reclining figure, I now suggest that you pursue the subject of weight distribution by considering the balancing acts performed by human figures when standing upright.

Objects with weight close to the ground and broad bases have no problem maintaining equilibrium.

As objects become taller and relatively smaller based, equilibrium becomes increasingly precarious, until eventually the slightest inequality of the downward pull of gravity, or deviation of the direction of pull from 90 degrees to the base, results in the object falling over.

In this context we have to refer to a vertical line through the centre of a figure about which weight must be distributed equally if the figure is to maintain its balance. We can call this the centre line of gravity.

It is a very useful concept in drawing the figure, as the head of an upright standing pose is nearly always balanced at the top of this imaginary vertical, the centre of weight being directly below it.

Where weight is distributed equally between the feet, as in the soldier's position of attention, the vertical line will descend from the head to a point between the heels, and the same will apply in any position of equal weight between wider spaced feet; the centre of gravity will be directly above a point midway between the weight-taking heels. I say heels, rather than feet, because most of the weight of the body in an erect but relaxed pose is transmitted to the ground via the heels – the rest of the foot is mainly functioning to maintain balance.

If the weight of the figure is mainly supported by one leg, as is the case more often than not, then the weight-taking heel will be seen to be on or near this vertical line from the base of

Fig.1

130

the cranium. Supporting the weight of the body in this way on one leg implies taking the weight *off* the other one, and the relaxed result of this is that the hip on the side unsupported by the non-weight-taking leg, drops to an angle where the base of the spine is supporting itself with the minimum of muscular activity. In this situation the upper part of the body would be thrown to one side of the centre line of gravity and would fall unless some counter balance was made. This is achieved by a counter swing of the upper body so that at the shoulders a

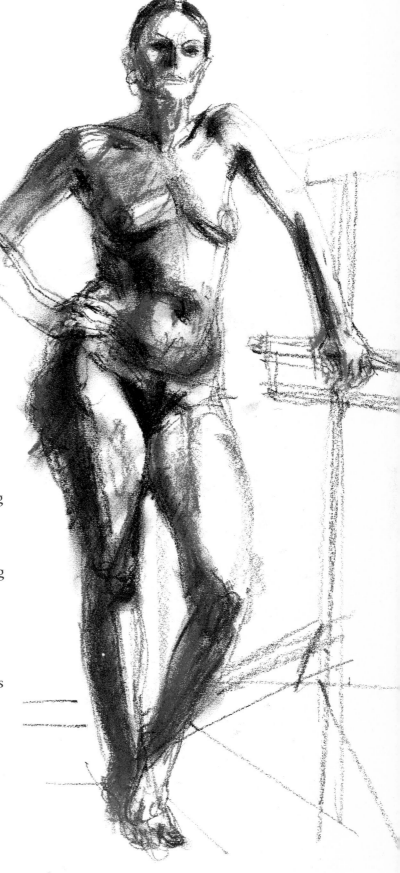

tilt contrary to the hip tilt is maintained at exactly the right angle to bring the head back to its position vertically above the main ground contact.

It should be said that this rule is not absolutely precise or infallible, but drawing a vertical line and observing carefully how the shapes and volumes of your standing figure distribute themselves relative to it is fascinating and informative.

For example, movements of the arms subtly affect the distribution of weight about the centre line. If the arms are actually contributing to the support of the body at all, as in fig.1 where the model's lean is arrested some way from the vertical by the arms, the head is clearly seen to be well to the right of a vertical through the feet i.e. the figure is in a sort of arrested disequilibrium; if the grip of the hands was released, she would immediately fall backwards.

In the figure on this page (fig.2), however, the model's left arm is only really supporting itself on the easel, very little of any body weight being transferred through it, and what little weight is lost there to the equation is balanced by the akimbo right arm.

Balance is fundamental to the understanding of the standing figure and absolutely essential in drawing.

Fig.2

Balance

Project 1

Set a standing pose to throw as much body weight on to one leg as possible, and by separating the feet by at least 8 or 9 inches promote a strong tilt of the pelvis. You should aim for plenty of movement and counter balance in the pose, consistent with the model being as relaxed as possible.

Standing poses, especially if they are free-standing and unsupported, are hard to maintain, and you should mark the feet positions on the floor as soon as the pose is set, and tell your model to shift the bodyweight to the other leg from time to time as it gets painful and to stop posing at the faintest sign of the onset of giddiness. In any case it is probably necessary to rest a standing pose every half hour, although some experienced models maintain hour long poses without difficulty.

When drawing, search diligently for that centre of gravity line, then try to place the centre line of the weight-taking leg at the correct angle to it. If a reasonable degree of pelvic swing has been adopted by the model, the angle of the locked supporting leg will not be vertical and the hip on that side will jut out considerably. Do not *underplay* this move-ment: it is better to overdo it.

Note the positions of the feet, not just relative to each leg, but relative to each other. Try to see the pattern that the contact surfaces of the feet make and what shape on the floor would contain them.

Look for the counterswing of the upper body. Check the centre line of the torso against imaginary verticals if it is a front view, use the line of the spine in a back view.

Look for shoulder-tilt-angle compensating for hip swing; lines linking left and right hip helpful in this respect; see the Skeleton, Muscles and Surface Form sections for more details about these and other useful landmarks.

Above all, question your drawing at all stages.

Put down marks to denote the main movements, add secondary shapes based on them and check the emerging pattern of shape. If it doesn't quite ring true, suspect the first

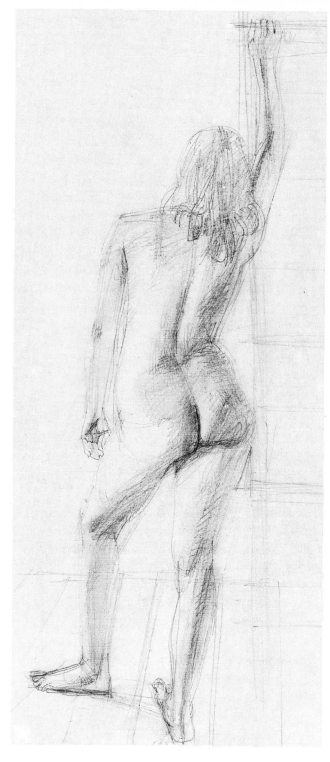

Fig.1

lines; maybe you are building on a false premise – drawing is a process of searching and change. If after two hours' drawing you see something fundamentally wrong, to change which would ruin some beautifully finished bits of drawing on which you have laboured long, don't hesitate, change it.

One statement which says something forceful about the whole pose, is much more worth-while than any number of uncoordinated pieces of descriptive detail, however pretty.

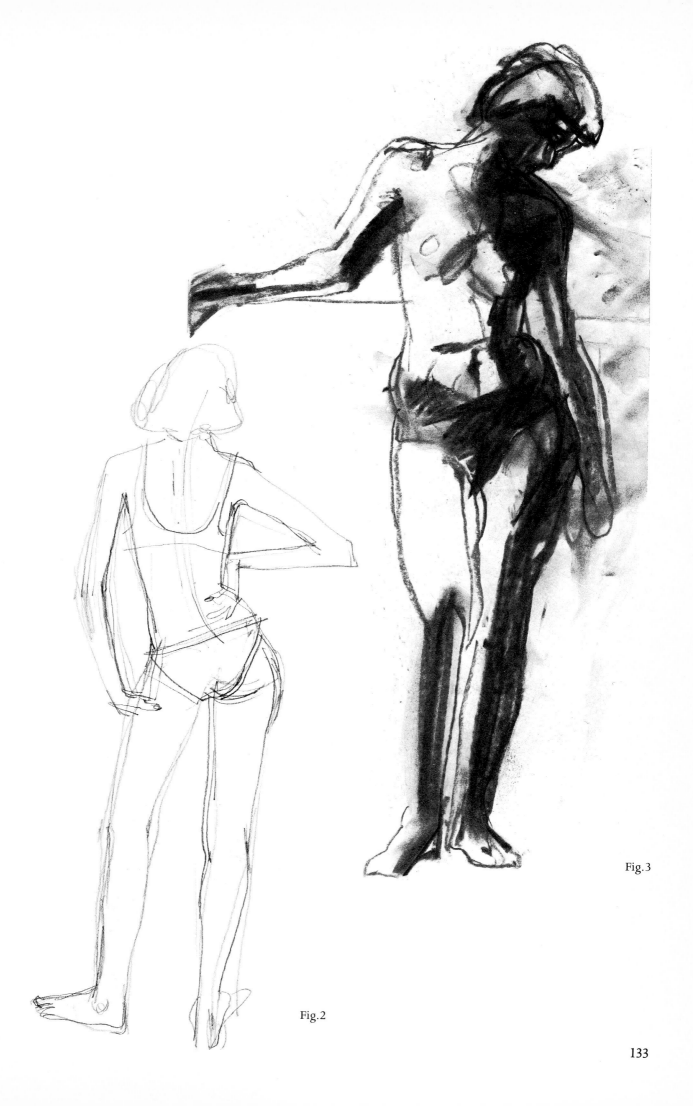

Fig.2

Fig.3

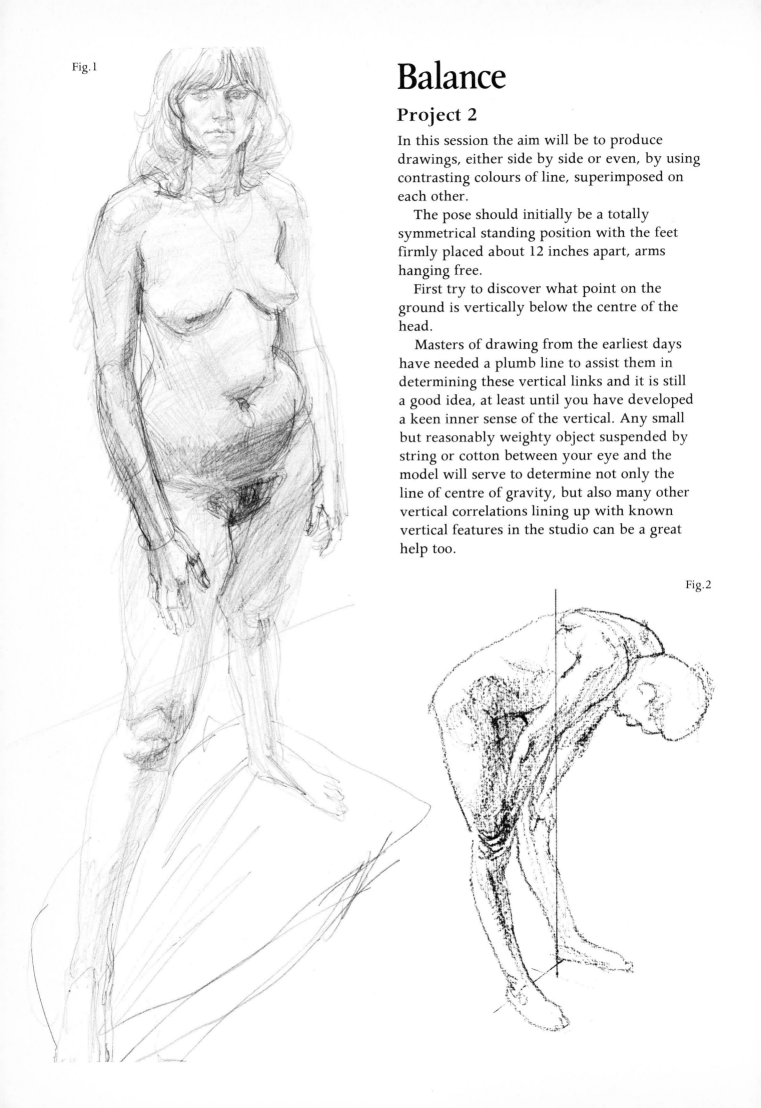

Fig. 1

Balance

Project 2

In this session the aim will be to produce drawings, either side by side or even, by using contrasting colours of line, superimposed on each other.

The pose should initially be a totally symmetrical standing position with the feet firmly placed about 12 inches apart, arms hanging free.

First try to discover what point on the ground is vertically below the centre of the head.

Masters of drawing from the earliest days have needed a plumb line to assist them in determining these vertical links and it is still a good idea, at least until you have developed a keen inner sense of the vertical. Any small but reasonably weighty object suspended by string or cotton between your eye and the model will serve to determine not only the line of centre of gravity, but also many other vertical correlations lining up with known vertical features in the studio can be a great help too.

Fig. 2

As in all the exercises, but in this one especially, move around the pose before you start, and be prepared during the making of your drawing to leave your position and look again from other viewpoints.

Thus while drawing a standing figure from a front view, you may be unsure whether points which lie on the same vertical plumb line from *this* view, are indeed truly above each other in depth. A plumb line check from the side view will tell you the answer immediately, and enable you better to understand and draw the solid geometry from the front.

Having analysed the symmetrically balanced pose, ask your model to move, without significantly changing the feet placement on the floor, so that the body weight is taken up by one leg more than the other. Make sure that this new pose is really relaxed and stable.

Now look and compare what you see with your first drawing. Try to discover the adjustments that the body has made to adapt to the asymmetric support. Look especially for the distribution of body weight each side of a plumb line from the head, and how near to the weight taking foot is the point where this line meets the floor.

Then, try other variations on the theme: twisting, tilting, bending forwards with the arms propping the upper body, or backwards with the arms hanging free (very difficult to hold for more than a few moments).

Analyse and compare each pose, and judge your drawings only by their appearance of stability. If your figures look as though they may fall over, look again at the pose.

Fig. 3

Fig. 4

Fig. 5

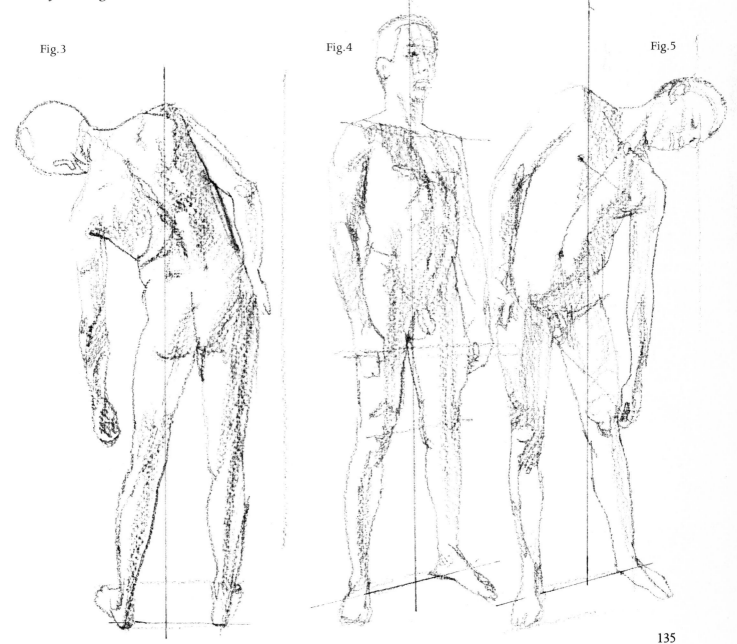

135

Balance

Project 3

In setting up the pose for this exercise, what you should be looking for is a standing position which is receiving some help to maintain balance and so is rather more of a 'lean'.

To have sufficient time for a thorough analysis of the weight distribution the pose should not be too extreme, your model must be reasonably relaxed while supporting some body weight by suspension from, or propping against, a surface or an upright. The secondary support should be just enough for it to be clear that without it, the figure would fall over.

Analyse as before. Try to see the inclined weight being pulled over by gravity and prevented from falling by the prop of arm or shoulder.

The direction of lean need not necessarily be towards a support, but can be the other way as described and illustrated in the introduction to this section, where the model's backward lean is arrested by the extension of her arms from her light grip on the fixed upright. (In this case, the upright was a fixed ladder and was not vertical, hence the opposite lean in this drawing).

In these situations, the greater the degree of inclination of the figure from the vertical, the more tension there must be in the legs to maintain its rigidity, and the more compression or tension there must be in the supporting limbs.

Such considerations, however, are edging in to another area which will be investigated more fully in the Dynamics section. For the moment I suggest that you should concentrate on making sure that the imbalance of the standing figure but for its secondary support is made clear. Later on the pose can be referred to and considered again in the light of later discoveries about dynamics.

This is the whole point. Good poses can be returned to again and again. They are always a little different, very different with different models, and there is always another way to look at them, more to see and discover.

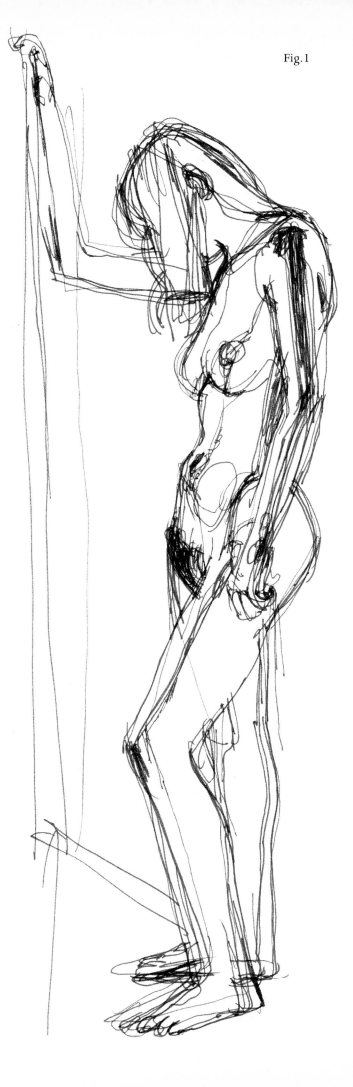

Fig.1

Fig.2

Fig.3

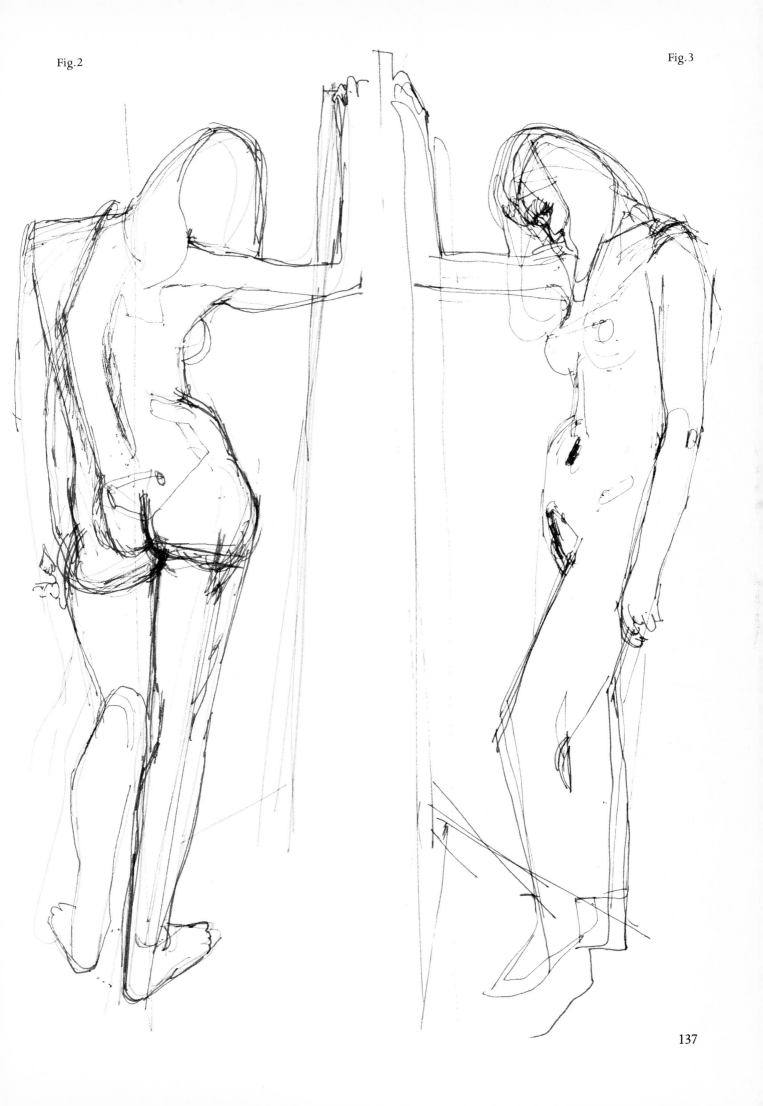

Surface form

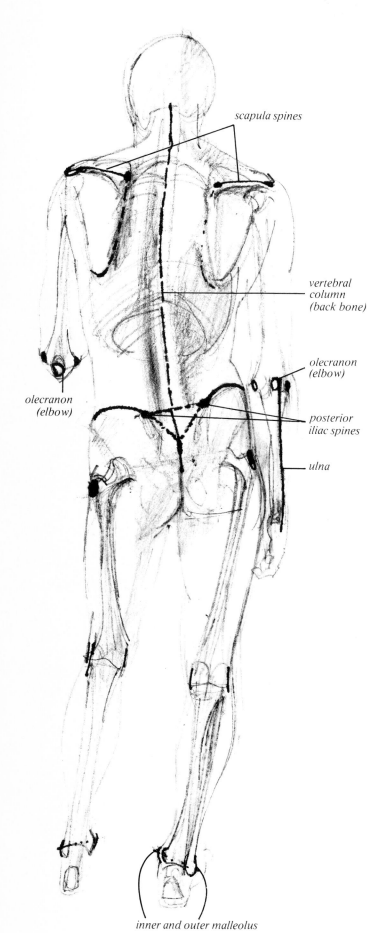

scapula spines

vertebral column (back bone)

olecranon (elbow)

olecranon (elbow)

posterior iliac spines

ulna

inner and outer malleolus

The back 1

In the preceding section mention was made from time to time of certain anatomical features of the body which can be 'read' from the surface form and which help to sort out what is happening in a pose.

This surface form section is intended to help you to link the anatomical features described in the first half of this book with what you see on the surface of a live human body.

The drawing on this page is an analysis of the left hand photograph opposite, in which the basic struts, protective cages and boxes of the skeleton are sketched lightly while the principal recognisable surface evidence of the skeleton is indicated by darker points and lines.

Recognition of these relatively few salient features will enable you to build a clear picture of the structure and dynamics of a pose.

From the back view the obvious primary clue to the posture of the figure is the long central depression which marks the spine, backbone, or vertebral column. It is a depression and not a ridge in most postures because each side of it are the muscular ropes (erector spinae group – see page 57) which underlie the surface muscles.

At the base of the spine the tilt of the hips (pelvis) can be readily judged by reference to the two points rather dauntingly named the posterior superior iliac crests or spines (see page 14). They are often seen as prominent dimples in the female model, but may be slight protuberances in thin models of either sex. Together with the point at the base of the spine, they make a useful inverted triangle reference.

20 Inner edge of scapula
30 Posterior iliac spines

Surface form

The back 2

Muscular structure is usually less easily seen and identified in the female subject than in the male, although by no means always so.

Some figures of either sex may have clearly defined muscle edges unobscured by subcutaneous fat, while in others the fatty layers seem to conceal all clues to the underlying structure.

However, in the roundest individuals the groove marking the backbone is always clearly visible, as are the dimple-like depressions over the iliac spines.

The upper back is probably the most difficult area in which to equate forms seen in the live model to the musculature described in anatomical drawings. Often the observed dimples and grooves seem to bear little relation to the theoretical surface anatomy in this area.

To explain where I think the problem lies I would refer you to the drawing on page 61. Here, as in all anatomy diagrams of the back, the trapezius is a very prominent shape with a clean cut edge at its lower borders. Because it is a very flat muscle, wrapping very closely over the underlying forms, this edge is rarely seen in life.

Instead, it is the spine of the scapula which shows up most, as a groove if the trapezius is active or well developed, and as a ridge or change of plane in a relaxed or lighter muscled subject. (See photos and diagrams on this page and opposite.)

Another often observed feature which can be puzzling is a groove running more or less vertically downwards from the inner edge of each scapula spine, i.e. approximately in the middle of each half of the upper back. Referring again to the anatomy diagram on page 61, this

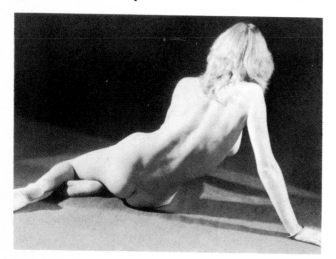

7 *Erector spinae*
24 *Trapezius*
30 *Posterior superior iliac spine*

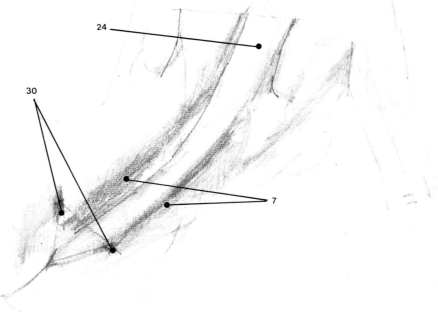

groove is formed initially by the change from flat tendon to fatter body of the trapezius at the inner edge of the scapula spine, and continued by the groove between the underlying infraspinatus and rhomboid muscles. This groove also indicates the medial (inner) edge of the scapula and as such it follows the scapula as it rotates with arm movement.

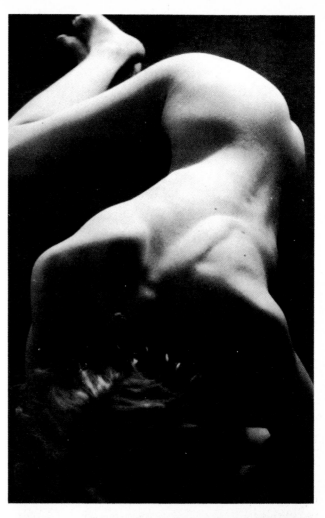

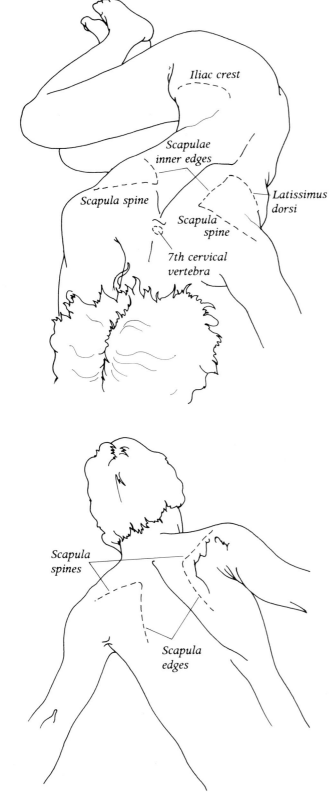

Iliac crest

Scapulae inner edges

Scapula spine

Latissimus dorsi

Scapula spine

7th cervical vertebra

Scapula spines

Scapula edges

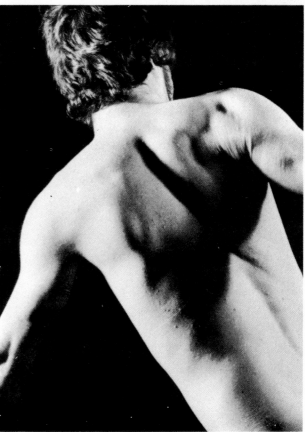

Surface form

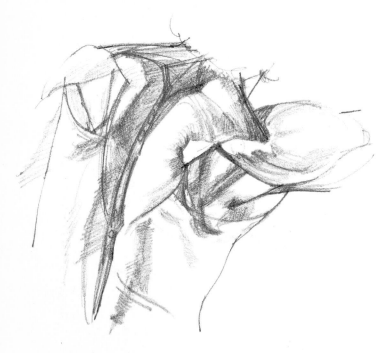

The back 3

It may seem as if the matter of the upper back is being somewhat laboured, but as I have said, it is easily and often misread in anatomical terms.

Shoulder joints are very mobile and as they move the scapulae follow.

On page 68 you can see the groove, which has no name that I know if but which we could call the scapula edge groove, and how it moves as the arm is raised.

A similar situation is illustrated by the photograph and explanatory diagram on this page.

Note how the groove between the infraspinatus and the rhomboideus continues upwards, appearing to cut into the trapezius border. As the diagram shows, this is again the result of the exact coincidence of this groove with the edge between the body of the lower fibres of the trapezius and their angular tendon attachment to the scapula spine.

Raising the arm further rotates the scapula even more and the situation becomes rather like that demonstrated in the anatomy drawing on page 71.

In the photographs and diagram explanation of a similar high extended arm situation it can be seen that the trapezius is strongly active and bunched into a rather knotted form. The scapula edge groove has now swung round to be nearly at 45° and again appears to cut across the lower border of the trapezius.

These rotations of the scapula with all its attendant muscular contractions and extensions can produce a bewildering array of changing forms but with practice and continual observation, combined perhaps with some tactile exploration to distinguish bone from muscle and tendon, visual forms can be recognised that square with the anatomical diagrams.

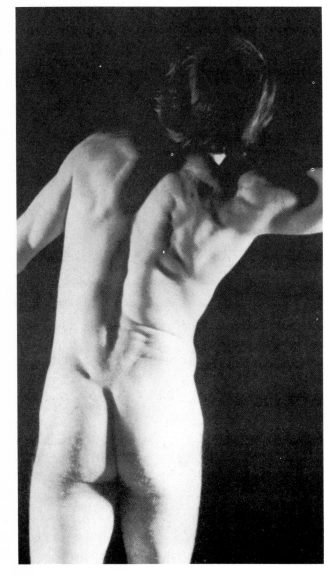

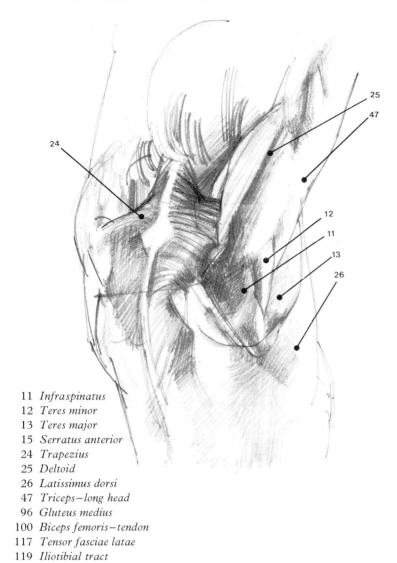

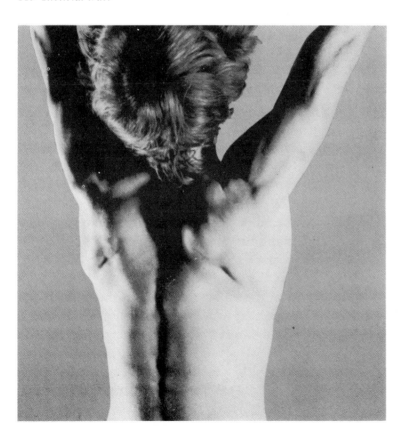

11 *Infraspinatus*
12 *Teres minor*
13 *Teres major*
15 *Serratus anterior*
24 *Trapezius*
25 *Deltoid*
26 *Latissimus dorsi*
47 *Triceps—long head*
96 *Gluteus medius*
100 *Biceps femoris—tendon*
117 *Tensor fasciae latae*
119 *Iliotibial tract*

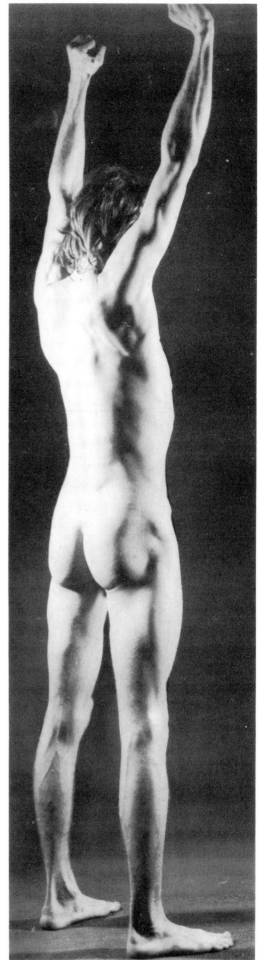

Surface form

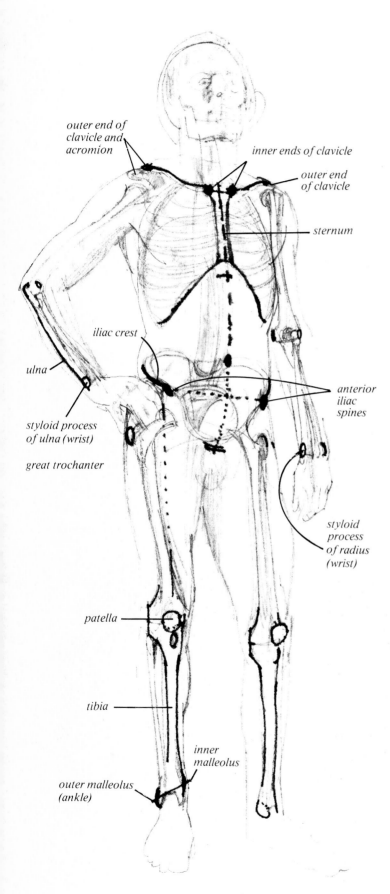

outer end of clavicle and acromion

inner ends of clavicle

outer end of clavicle

sternum

iliac crest

ulna

styloid process of ulna (wrist)

great trochanter

anterior iliac spines

styloid process of radius (wrist)

patella

tibia

inner malleolus

outer malleolus (ankle)

The front 1

From the front view the principal points to look for are as follows:

The collar bones (clavicles), each joined at its outer end to the flat extension of the spine of the shoulder blade (scapula) to form the shoulder girdle.

The breast bone (sternum) is usually clearly visible and the lower opening of the thorax can be partially or wholly traced, depending on the model and the pose.

Similarly the upper edges of the pelvis may or may not be clearly seen, although the iliac crests (anterior superior iliac crests) can almost always be traced.

Although the backbone is well hidden from the front, the centre line of the body can be traced by the line of the sternum continued down between the two vertical bands of stomach muscles (rectus abdominis) to the pubis. The lower centre line is not always evident as the rectus abdominis plunges rather deeper here and fat tends to deposit there too.

Visible from front, back and, with slightly greater difficulty, from the side, are the greater trochanters. In the female they are normally seen at the surface as bumps which mark the widest part of the hips. In males they are often hollows due to the bulk of muscle surrounding them and the different structure of the pelvis. The greater trochanter is actually not a part of the pelvis at all, but a protuberance on the upper angles of the thigh bone or femur.

The remainder of the thigh bones run deep in the leg and only the lower end is seen at the surface where it swells out to meet and articulate with a similar shape at the top of the lower leg bone (tibia), so that, together with the knee cap (patella), they form the rather angular shapes of the knee joint.

At the ankles the salient features are the inner and outer ankle bones (malleoli) which make characteristic downward sloping angles, the inner ankle higher than the outer.

Only at the elbow and wrist is there much evidence of the arm bones, although the major bone of the lower arm (ulna) is very near the surface for its whole length, and the upper rounded end of the upper arm bone (humerus) does round out its muscle covering in a characteristic way.

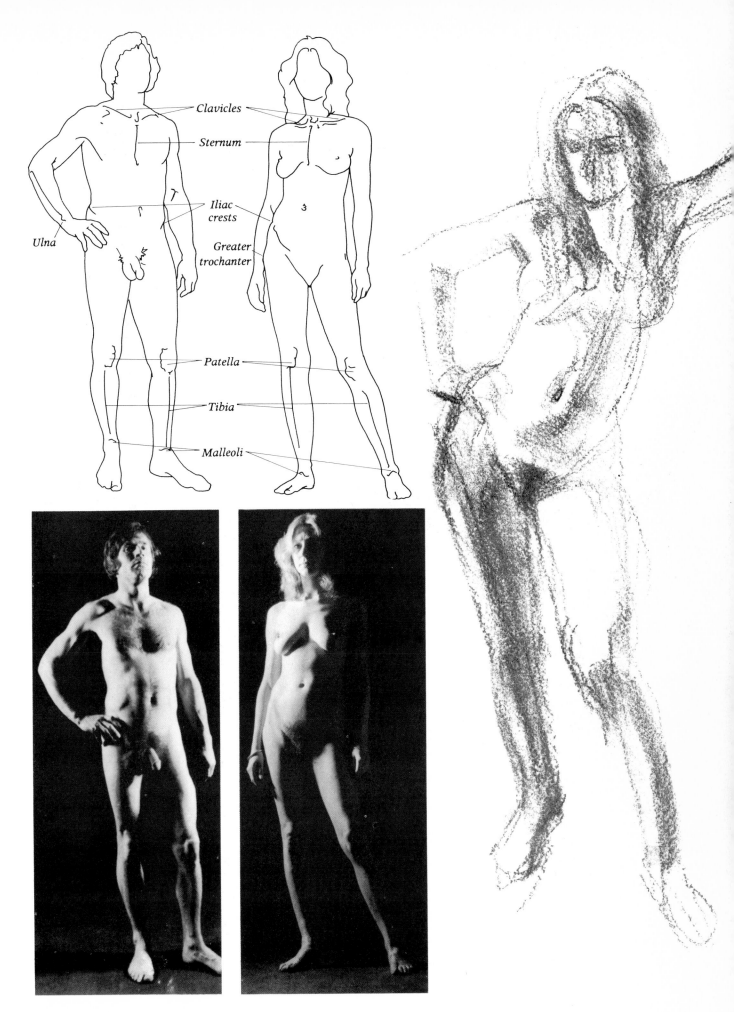

Clavicles

Sternum

Ulna

Iliac crests

Greater trochanter

Patella

Tibia

Malleoli

145

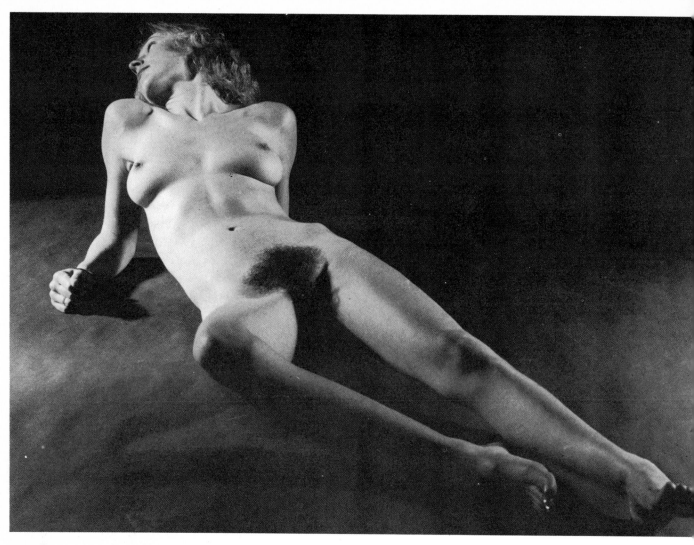

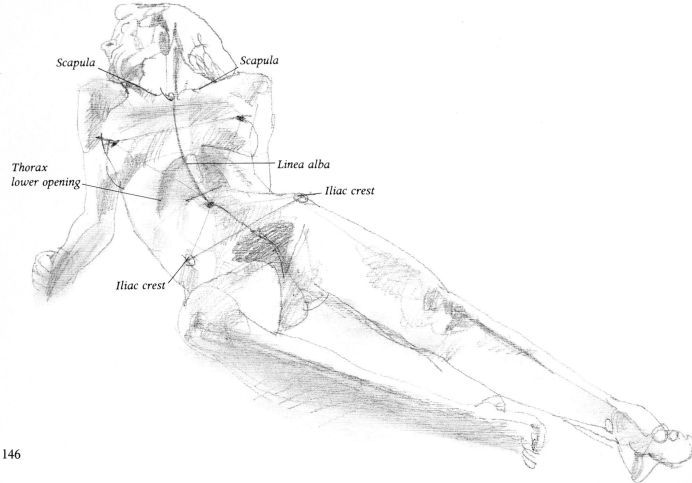

Scapula

Scapula

Thorax
lower opening

Linea alba

Iliac crest

Iliac crest

Surface form

Front view 2

Surface form at the front of the torso differs from the rear view in having somewhat softer shapes with less of the skeleton near the surface.

There are, however, extra marks on the soft tissue which are useful: the nipples and the umbilicus. Because these points have no direct attachment to the skeleton they are not always totally reliable clues to deep structure: it very much depends how soft the flesh is, and how much effect gravity is having. Obviously the nipples on a full-breasted woman move about relative to the rib cage and the pectorals, much more than those of a thin man, and a large and pendulous belly can drag the umbilicus out of the centre line of the body in side-reclined poses. However, taken in conjunction with the evidence, if present, of collar bones, sternum, thorax opening, pelvic crests, pubis and the centre line of the torso, the nipples and umbilicus are useful additional, always visible, points. Lines accurately drawn or visualised joining as many of these points as can be fixed give a specific and characteristic framework of a pose on which the solid forms can be built.

All the observable surface clues to anatomical structure are very clearly seen in the well-defined model on the right.

Note the clear separation of the three surface muscles of the quadriceps and the unusual sharpness of the foot extensors and their retaining fibrous bands (retinacula).

The structures exposed in the front view of the raised arm, especially in the area of the armpit, tend to be rather poorly understood. Reference to the anatomy drawing on page 70 should help to explain the observable forms.

One main thing to remember is that the latissimus dorsi (and the teres major, but this is virtually indistinguishable in the combined form) insert into the upper humerus *between* the triceps and biceps, as can clearly be seen in this photograph.

In this position, the serratus anterior becomes very prominent as it acts to control the rotation of the scapula, and the pectoralis major has been stretched upwards by the raised arm as illustrated and described on page 70.

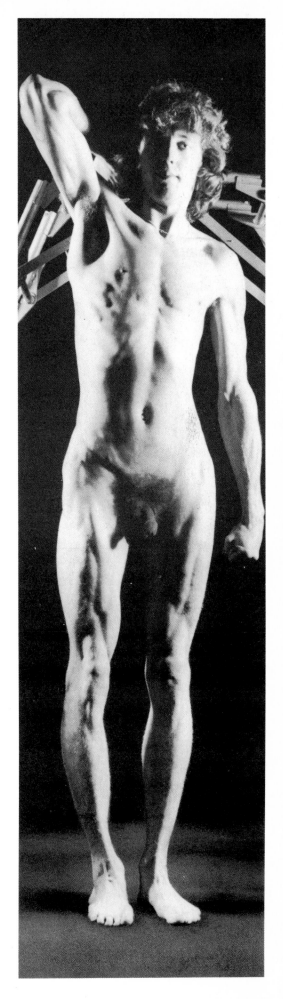

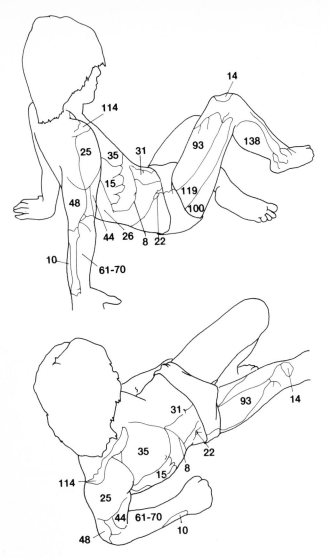

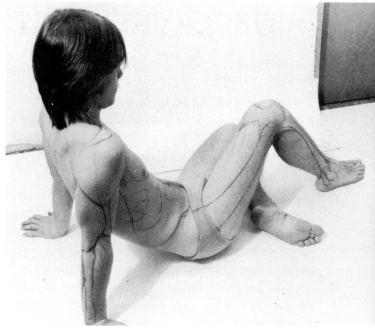

8 Lower opening of thorax	44 Biceps
10 Ulna	48 Triceps
14 Patella	61-70 Lower arm extensors
15 Serratus anterior	93 Quadriceps femoris
22 Iliac crests	90-100 Thigh flexors
25 Deltoid	114 Acromion
26 Latissimus dorsi	119 Iliotibial tract
31 Rectus abdominis	138 Calf flexors
35 Pectoralis major	

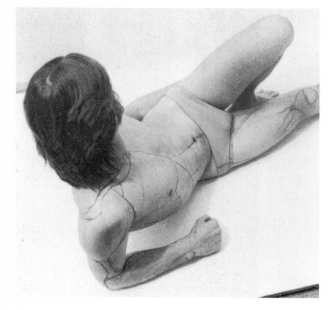

Surface form

Drawing on the live model

In the photographs on these pages I have indicated the main muscles or muscle groups on one side of the body by drawing them on the skin of the models.

If your model is amenable, I suggest you try to do the same, by reference to these photographs and the explanatory diagrams. Make-up pencils are ideal for this. The marks can be left there for a drawing session, which is a very interesting exercise, and they wash off fairly easily. A warning: some of the surface salient features are not as easily seen when you are close to them, so in order to mark them it may be necessary to feel for them, in some cases delving quite hard to make certain of the position of the bone. Make sure your model understands this and does not mind.

A great advantage of drawing and photographing anatomy explanations on the skin of the live model is the infinity of views available of the anatomization. The musculature of the back is well known when viewed 'flat', but it would be very difficult to predict the foreshortened shapes seen from the views in some of the photographs on these pages.

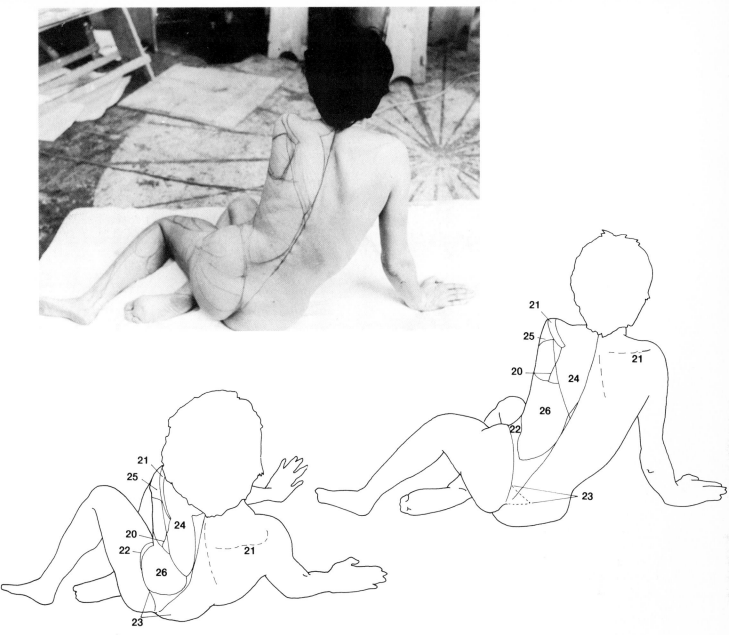

20 Inner edge of scapula
21 Scapula spines
22 Iliac crest
23 Posterior superior iliac crests
24 Trapezius
25 Deltoid
26 Latissimus dorsi
113 Infraspinatus

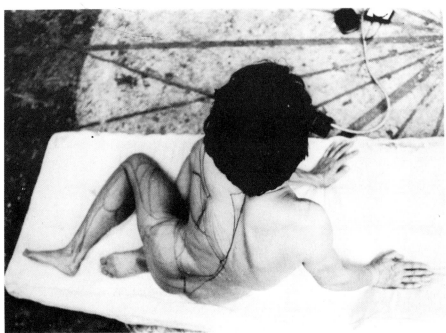

Structure

In this section the emphasis will be on more detailed analysis of the solidity of the human figure and how it holds together. Weight and balance, investigated in previous sections, are part of this, but the logic of structure ties these elements together.

Such a relatively complex form as the human figure with its numerous hollows, mobile limbs, hair appendages, local colour etc., can sometimes be seen more clearly as a wrapped package. It is then rather akin to the first rough stages of a stone carving, where basic directions

Fig.1

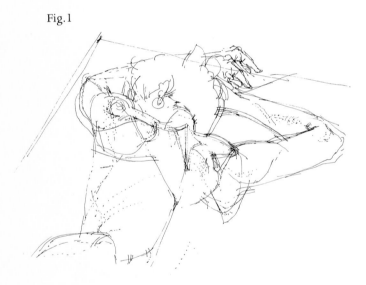

of main planes are established before they are elaborated.

Drawing as a sculptor works, first finding the large forms and progressing in stages towards smaller and smaller detailed forms is a perfectly valid mode of working, but I intend it more as a way of looking and thinking about the structure of the figure.

The two photographs demonstrate this very clearly. Using two models juxtaposed, creates a composite form which is more abstract, less human, and therefore easily seen in terms of inanimate masses, or even of landscape. If it had been possible to coat the models in plaster of paris so as to eliminate details, it would have been ideal; but since this was clearly not practicable or humane we had to try to achieve the same effect by wrapping them in fabric. We tried as far as possible to eliminate folds and revelation of underlying detail by differential tensions in the cloth, trying only to simplify multiple forms into broad, simple ones.

Once one has seen these what I call 'averaged out' planes, it is quite easy to 'see' them still, even when the wrapping is removed.

It is not then necessary to draw these averaged planes explicitly, but just to let their presence in your mind's eye assist you to place the more complex forms accurately.

Remember, when searching for structure, the marks do not need to be pretty – any sort of dot, line, tick or smudge will do if it helps to explain what is going on. Such drawing should be thought of as explanation and analysis, not as description or imitation.

Fig.2

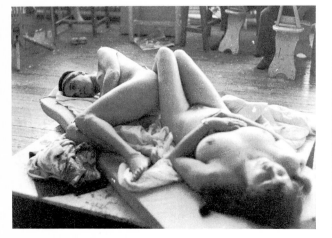

Fig.3

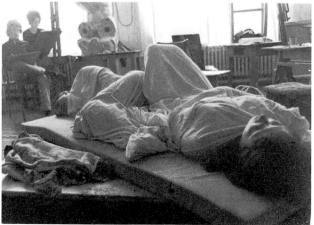

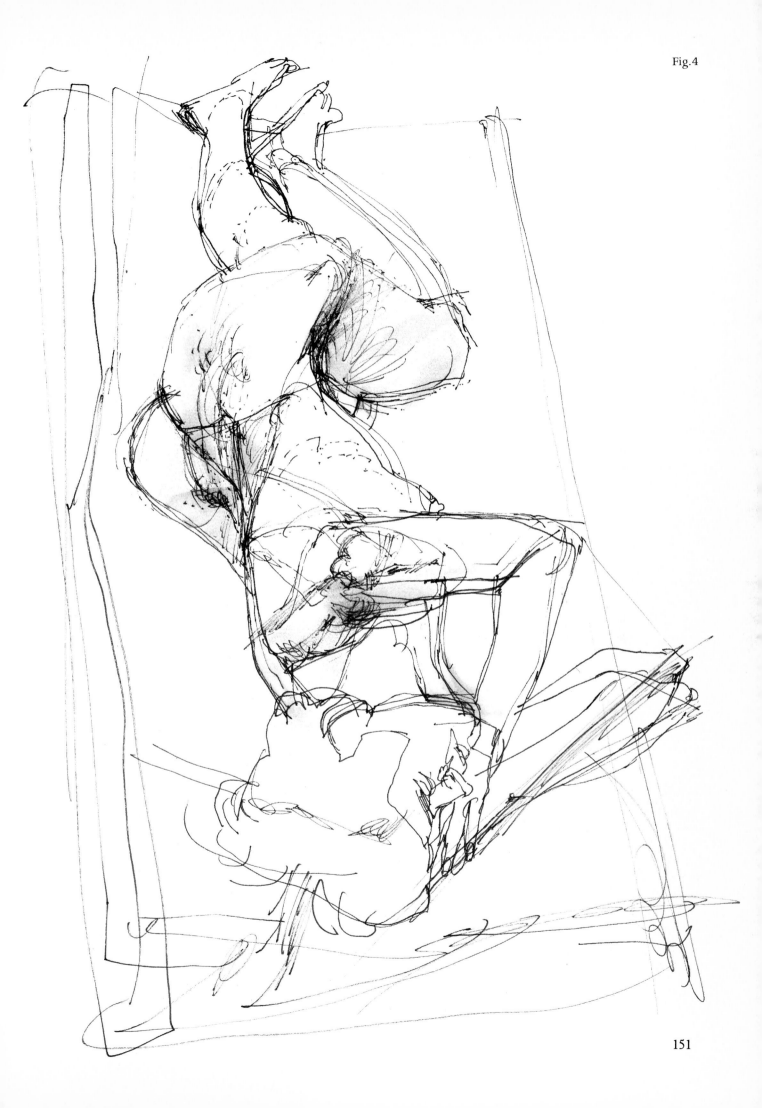

Fig.4

151

Structure

Project 1

Pose the model in a kneeling position, sitting
back on the floor, perhaps splaying the feet, or
with knees apart. This simulates a wide stable
base, in architectural terms, surmounted by a
sort of high-rise block. Such a position is fairly
relaxed, the pelvis firmly seated, the support
pillar of the spinal column held in balanced
upright position by its guy ropes, the spinal
muscles, and surmounted by the head.

Look for the triangular stability of this
structure; think of it in an architectural way
and try to express its internal structure rather
than the external cladding. Charcoal is very
good for this, as structure lines can be

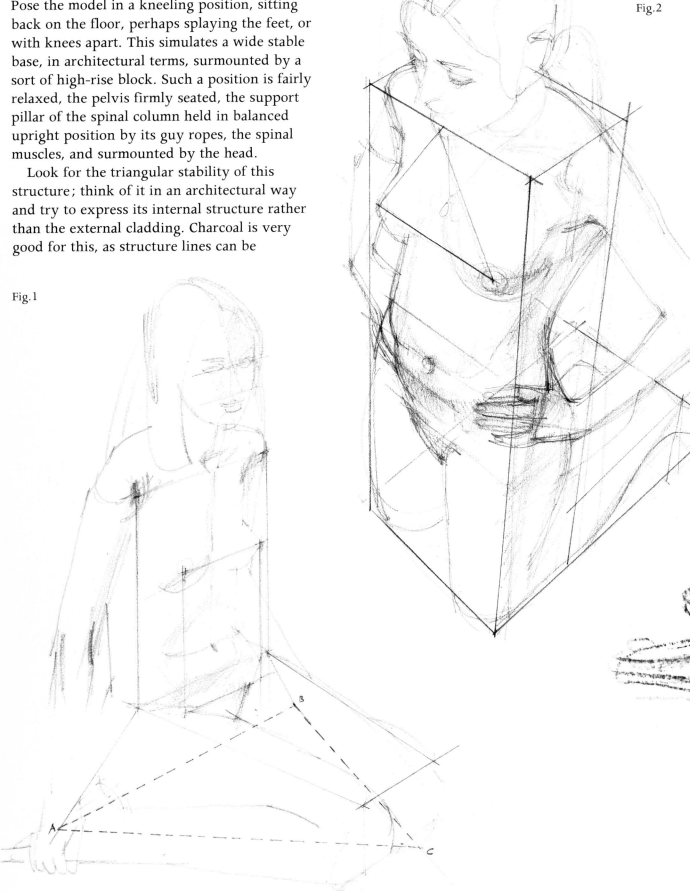

Fig.2

Fig.1

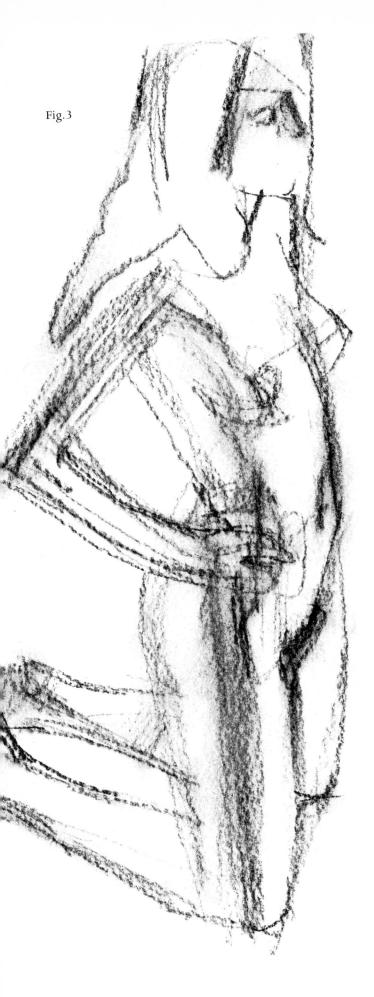

Fig. 3

committed to paper boldly and gradually lost as the cladding is added.

Ask the model to kneel up from the previous position. Now the architecture is less stable, more dependent on adequate bracing. The base is still large, the 'tower block' still upright, but its stability depends on the angle between the upper and lower leg being maintained strongly and correctly.

This angle, as would be expected, is normally a right angle, the lower legs lying on the ground plane, and the thighs vertical. Depending on the stance of the upper body the angle will change to achieve equilibrium, as will be seen by asking the model to raise both arms in front of her when the torso leans back slightly to balance the weight.

Fig. 1 shows a wide triangular base ABC and 'tower block' of torso rising from the stable platform. Note the variations of the torso from the true vertical, and try to place the head in position relative to the vertical structure. Horizontal lines through the shoulders, nipples, pelvic girdle etc. can be seen as storeys in the vertical structure, subject to the same laws of perspective as a building would be.

In fig. 2 I have boxed the vertical block, so as to clarify the way that the human torso swings and counterswings within it, and yet can be closely surrounded by such vertical scaffolding. As can be seen, the front of the thighs and lower stomach are flat against the front of the imaginary box, then the forms swing away until the shoulder blades touch the imaginary plane at the *back* of the box. The neck carries the swing back again, so that her chin is back to the front of the box again, forming the apex of a triangle of which the nipples form the base.

Fig. 3. Rounding the forms to a more human idiom, the architecture can still be the motive for a drawing – even though the scaffolding is not explicit.

Structure

Project 2

Stand the model on a table and move your drawing board up close in order to get a low eye-level view.

If it is not possible to raise the model to table top height, a low eye level can be achieved, albeit less comfortably, by kneeling or lying on the floor close to the model and looking up.

From this view the figure has a monumental appearance. The feet, being on or near eye level, are seen near the same horizontal level but higher up the figure horizontal sections are apparently tipped away from your eye at ever increasing angles. It is essential to get these angles right, to be conscious of the way in which the forms of pelvis and thorax interlock.

This is very much the same as the last exercise but in reverse. The building is taller, with a smaller base and viewed from ground level, but the same rules apply. Wherever storeys can be defined by lines through twin elements like pelvic crests, nipples, shoulders, cheek bones etc. their angles should be determined with care.

Checking points on your by now, I hope, inbuilt mental grid will reveal interesting correlations which differ from more usual eye levels the further up the figure you look.

For example, note on fig.1 that the underside of the model's right breast (left hand in the drawing) is about on the same horizontal grid as the junction of upper and lower near arm, and that, further up, the chin is about on a level with the near shoulder. By contrast the knees are very much on the same level and the pelvis does not seem as tipped as would have been expected from such a low view. The reason for this is that the model is supporting most of her weight on her right leg and relaxing and bending her left leg, so allowing the pelvis to tip *against* and partly cancel out the apparent perspective angle.

You will find it interesting to introduce twists and other movements which you explored in the Weight section, and see how such poses are modified by the extreme eye level. The

drawings 2 and 3 are two views of the same low eye-level pose in which, while the weight is fairly evenly distributed between the two legs, the upper part of the body is rotated relative to the pelvis, thereby introducing more variations of upward perspective.

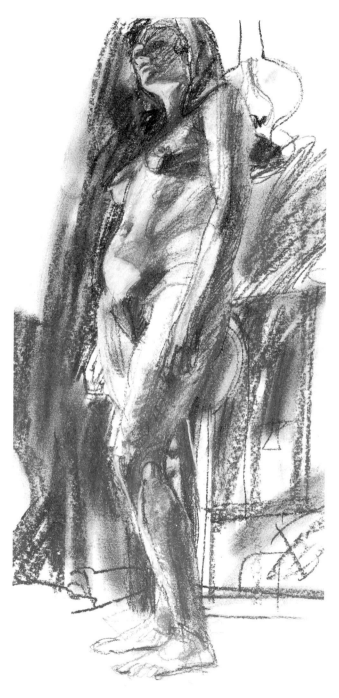

Fig.1

Fig.2

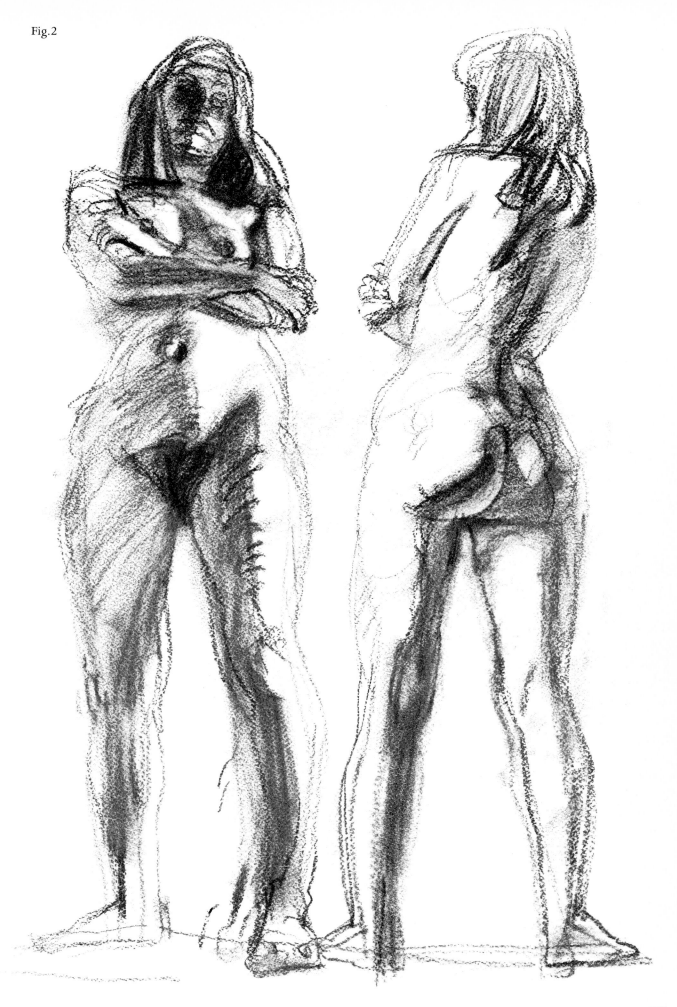

Structure

Project 3

This time the interlocking forms of the figure are to be viewed from a high eye level which is not the easiest thing to arrange in every studio.

To be able to look down on a standing figure your drawing position must be raised by a few feet.

The vantage point for the drawing on this page (fig.3) was a gallery about eight feet above the floor. From this height there is considerable foreshortening of the figure and changes in the section can be easily seen. Such perspective is akin to the view of a skyscraper from a helicopter, while the perspective resulting from standing close to the model and looking down is more like the view of a skyscraper from the top windows of an adjoining block. In the former the floors (or sections) are arranged as fig.1 while in the latter they are more as fig.2.

Clear appreciation of the way that the sections change their angle to your eye and relate to the ground plane, is what you should be after in these exercises.

You should be searching for a strong piece of architecture which stands firmly on a discernable base, and which ascends from that base at right angles to it, so that your viewpoint is consistently verified by your drawing.

Everything must be subordinated to this end, line and tone used only to search for and describe the coherence of the structure, not to copy light and shade or surface texture and detail.

Many students' drawings begin strongly in the search for structure but degenerate into superficial copying in the later stages. It is difficult to maintain your analytical vision,

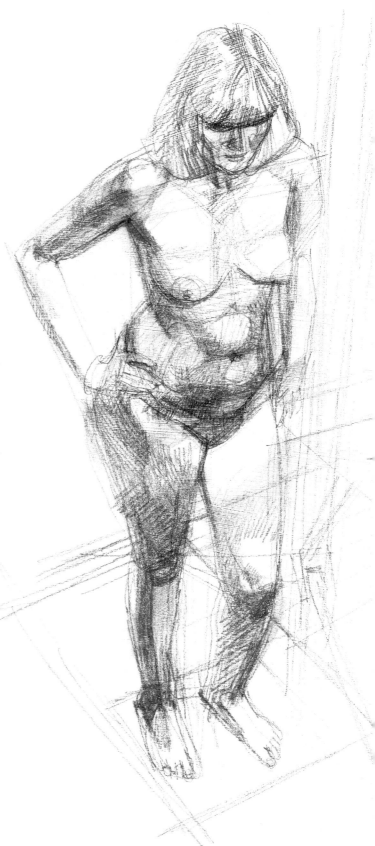

Fig.3

Fig.1

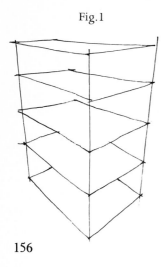

Fig.2

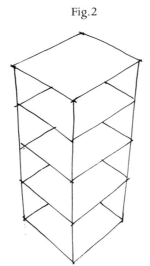

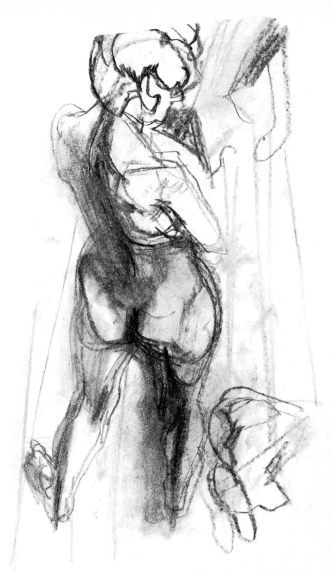

Fig.5

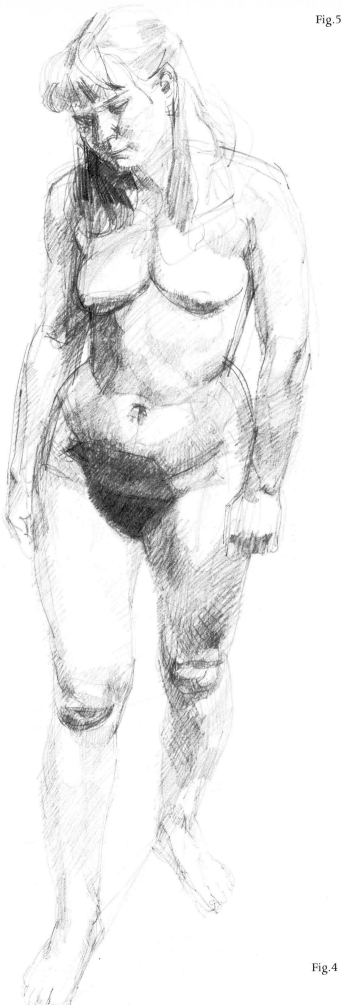

especially as the familiar areas of head, hands and feet are approached. It is relatively easy to see the planes and box structures of the torso, but facial features, fingers and toes tend to deflect attention from the basic planes of which they are only relatively superficial details. You must look past the familiar details and search for the basic form of even these smaller structures.

Breasts on the female model, in this context, need to be seen as they structurally are, as appendages attached to and supported by the thorax or rib cage. It is sometimes easier to link the plane of the front of the thorax above and below the breasts as though the breasts didn't exist, and to suspend them from that plane as you find its structural place. Once this relationship has been clearly seen and understood by drawing in this way, it may only be necessary in future to watch for the continuity of the thorax under the breasts while structuring breast and thorax together.

Fig.4

Fig.1

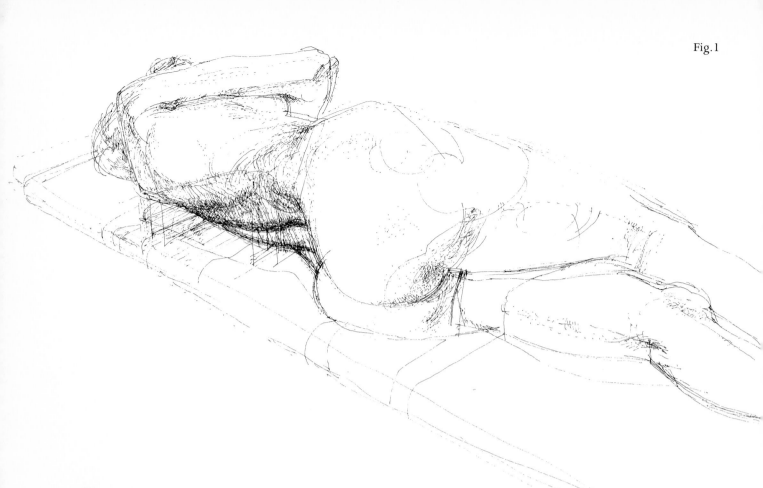

Structure

Project 4

Arrange the model in a simple lying pose. What you should be looking for is a structure reminiscent of a long, low building, or to change the metaphor, a series of slopes, cliffs, overhangs and plateaux. Poses lying on the side as on this page, give good opportunities to explore a variety of low-height structures.

I find it helpful to think oneself into the situation where the foreground ground plane is a beach, the figure representing the cliff.

In fig.1, you would assume that the flat mattress was the beach, then as you approach the small of the back you encounter a sudden vertical cliff face. In fact it is more than vertical, it is tipped back towards you, and this backwards tilt becomes more extreme if you move left. The approach opposite the shoulder blade has a huge overhang, and I have tried to understand and draw attention to these angles by drawing little triangles which would fit under the varying degrees of overhang.

If it had been possible to negotiate these overhanging cliffs at, say, the waist area, the summit attained would be a low ridge leading away, round the higher ridge of the haunch and then presumably to the descent.

Approaching from a point on the beach further to the right presents a completely different aspect. The rounded buttock form is flattened by gravity, and after the initial, mainly vertical face (with a foothold or two in the cleft!), the slope becomes much less steep and culminates in a wide-domed plateau, its high point being the widest part of the model's hip (great trochanter – see Anatomy section).

Other approaches, not necessarily at right angles to the length of the figure, present a different series of planes, all of which can be appreciated the more vividly for the analogy with topography.

As always, viewing the same structure from other directions and heights, deepens your

understanding of the original viewpoint and
presents new problems and possibilities.

The other view of the pose here (fig.2) shows
how narrow is the low ridge at the waist,
giving way quickly to steeply undulating
downslopes. The way that the summit of the
hip gives way to the shallow downslope of the
upper thigh can be more clearly seen, but at the
same time the space under the overhang of the
back is not so obviously appreciated.

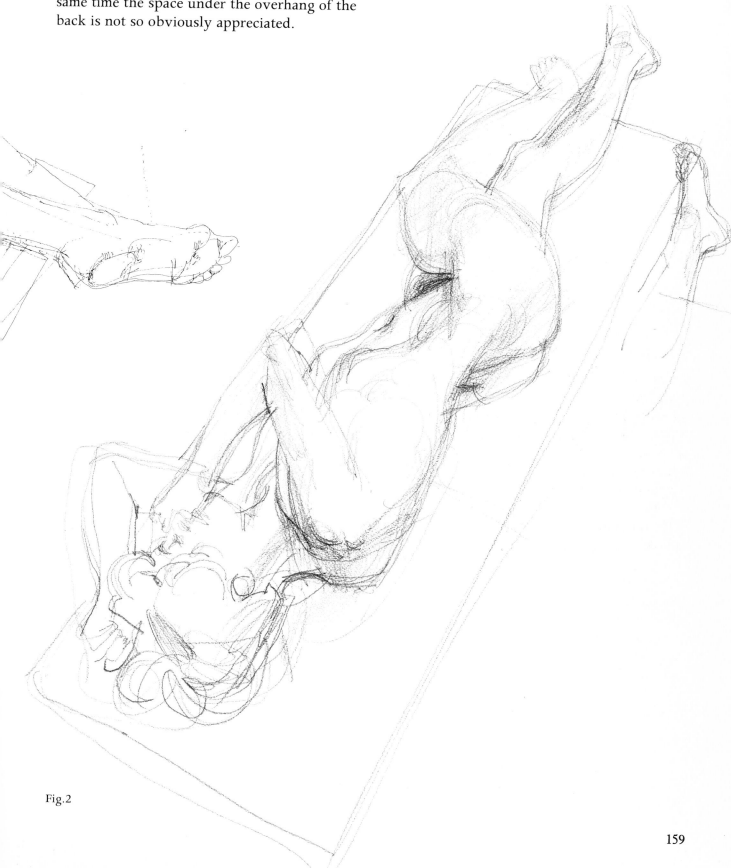

Fig.2

Structure

Project 5

A more complex reclining pose should be tried this time, employing a variety of supports, floor, raised surface and props.

Figure 4 shows what I mean. The support surface in this case was constructed with the use of some boxes and a folded mattress arranged to make varied levels and an inclined plane, all covered by a sheet.

Some, perhaps most of the weight of the torso is being supported by the pelvis, which in turn is supported by a lower part of the raised surface. The torso has relaxed sideways onto the inclined surface, the abdomen falling that way to leave the hip bone (iliac crest, see Anatomy section) prominent, and is also partially propped up by the right arm. Although unseen, it can be deduced that the right arm is propping to some extent by the attitude of the flopped-over head, the weight of which has to be supported.

Also propped is the model's right thigh, held horizontal by the lower leg and foot in contact with the floor. In contrast the other leg falls directly to the floor from the hip, to form what could be thought of as a long sloping ramp, as opposed to the vertical face and plateau of the right leg.

It is probably a good place here to reconsider the problem of foreshortening.

In the introduction to Shape, I cited the example of a wine bottle seen from near to one end and therefore making a shape not far from circular, and yet being recognized as a shape which from a 'normal' viewpoint is long and cylindrical i.e. bottle shaped.

The low and high eye-level views in this section will have forced you to consider the foreshortened shapes of the torso, and in many of the other projects foreshortened views of limbs will have occurred. If you are still experiencing difficulty or are nervous when presented with foreshortened views, consider the diagram fig.2, which demonstrates how the apparent length of the arm diminishes from its actual length to no more than its actual width as it rotates to the most extreme position of pointing directly towards the eye of the observer. In this latter position the hand can be expected to appear bigger than the total space taken up by the complete arm.

Now try looking at your foreshortened arm in the mirror. Prop it so that you can take time to observe it at length and then draw what you see. Forget that it is an arm, which you know

Fig.1

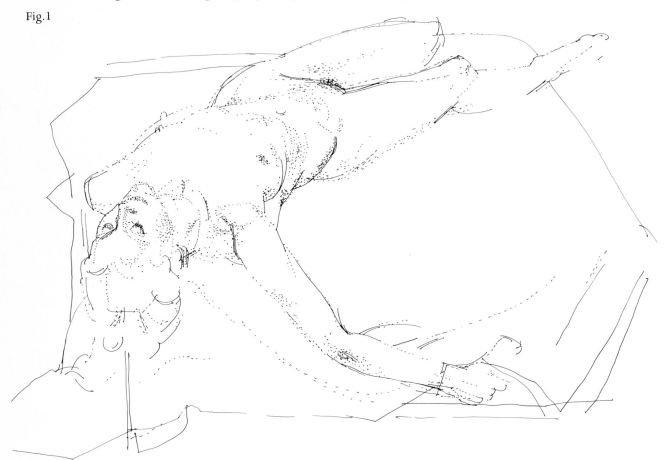

to have greater length than width, and draw
only the two-dimensional area that it covers in
your view, on the picture plane, if you prefer.

You should come up with something rather
like fig.3. More extremely foreshortened views
of the torso than can easily be arranged in a
standing pose, can be arrived at simply by
observing a fully reclining pose from either
end. In fig.1 I have searched for the way that
the cross sections fit together, discovering such
interesting correlations as for example the top
of the model's shoulder being offset to the
right from, or further *down* her body than, her
left hip.

In this drawing, incidentally, the searching
was made initially by the use of dots, lines of
dots eventually being confirmed by a
continuous line. This is a useful way to handle
a completely ineradicable medium which only
makes absolutely black marks.

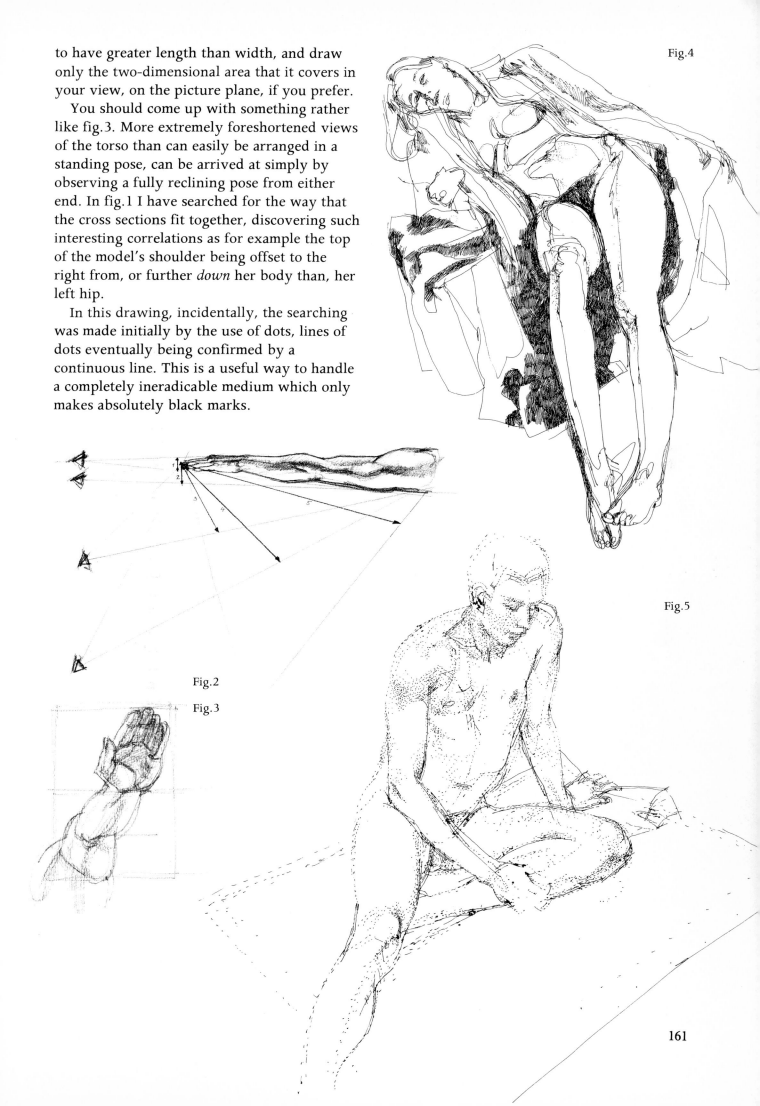

Fig.4

Fig.2

Fig.3

Fig.5

161

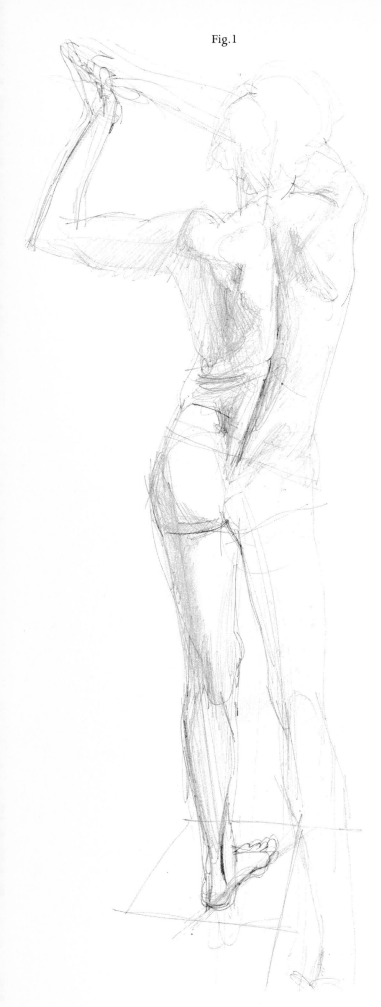

Fig.1

Dynamics

Up to this point we have looked at the figure as a form with structure involving both hard and soft material, acted upon by the force of gravity. We have not yet considered the forces that are contained within the figure, which determine how the body resists or gives way to gravity. It may seem to be a matter of more interest to a physicist than an artist, but I hope to convince you that trying to discover what forms in the figure are doing, will add to your understanding of the way they *look*, and enable you to draw figures which, although not moving, are dynamic.

When I speak of a pose which is balanced but at rest, I mean one in which there is the minimum of muscular activity consistent with maintaining equilibrium, because of course, except in a completely relaxed lying position, some muscular power is always being applied.

In order for the figure to maintain equilibrium at rest, as we have seen, it has to arrange things so that the force of gravity on parts that could be pulled down to the ground, is absolutely equalized and balanced. It does this by delicately sensing a tendancy to be pulled one way, and immediately correcting the position by contracting one set of muscles, extending another set, until the balance is corrected, and then returning to rest.

The forms which are then in a sense stacked one above the other are each taking the weight of the forms above and transmitting the combined weight to those beneath and so on until ground contact is made. They are thus under compression.

A form which is suspended by a part or parts or itself will tend to be stretched, and it is therefore under tension.

It is a slightly misleading term in the context of figure drawing, as in a relaxed figure pose the forms which are subject to tension are being stretched, but only by their own weight, and consequently they appear slack and

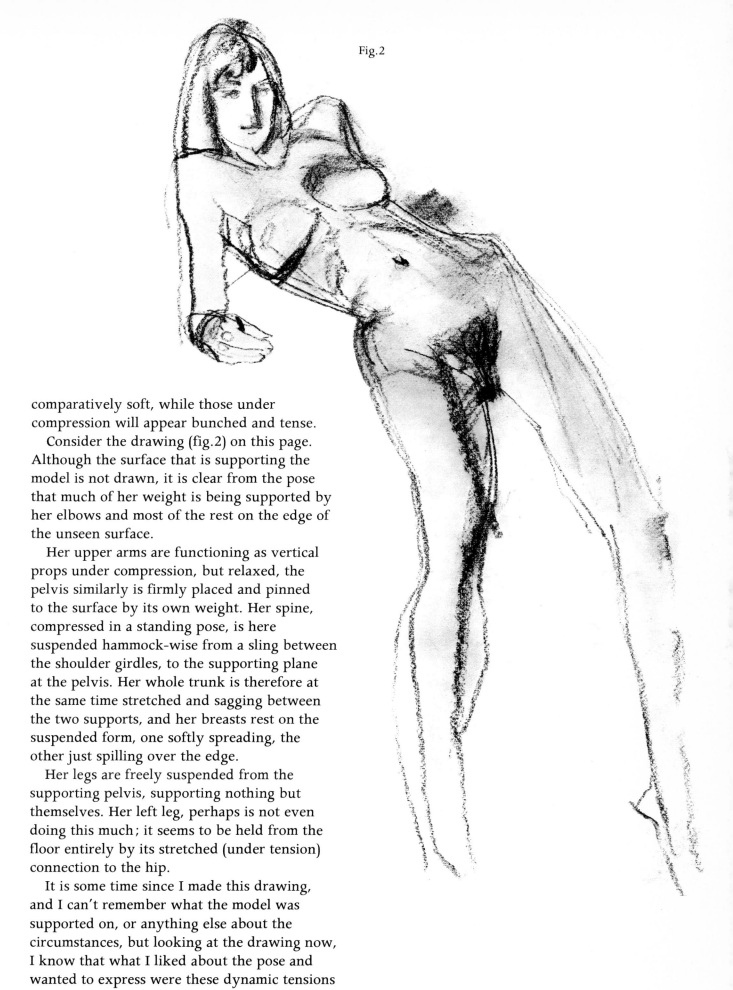

Fig.2

comparatively soft, while those under compression will appear bunched and tense.

Consider the drawing (fig.2) on this page. Although the surface that is supporting the model is not drawn, it is clear from the pose that much of her weight is being supported by her elbows and most of the rest on the edge of the unseen surface.

Her upper arms are functioning as vertical props under compression, but relaxed, the pelvis similarly is firmly placed and pinned to the surface by its own weight. Her spine, compressed in a standing pose, is here suspended hammock-wise from a sling between the shoulder girdles, to the supporting plane at the pelvis. Her whole trunk is therefore at the same time stretched and sagging between the two supports, and her breasts rest on the suspended form, one softly spreading, the other just spilling over the edge.

Her legs are freely suspended from the supporting pelvis, supporting nothing but themselves. Her left leg, perhaps is not even doing this much; it seems to be held from the floor entirely by its stretched (under tension) connection to the hip.

It is some time since I made this drawing, and I can't remember what the model was supported on, or anything else about the circumstances, but looking at the drawing now, I know that what I liked about the pose and wanted to express were these dynamic tensions and compressions.

Dynamics

Project 1

For the first half of this session draw the model in clothes, in a standing pose with as much tilt and swing in it as can be managed. Exactly the same pose will be *unclothed* for the second half of the session.

A pose with the model's weight heavily on one leg with the opposite arm up and taking leaning weight, as here, is ideal for this exercise. Slightly loose garments, in a light-weight cloth in plain colours are best, so that they fall clearly into folds which reveal the directions of the body beneath. When drawing this figure pay particular attention to the pulls in the cloth, analysing where it is stretched i.e. under tension, and where and how it reacts to compression by folding on itself.

Human skin is much more elastic and flexible than clothing, and the pulls of tension and folds of extra material will not be as immediately obvious in the skin of the model when the same pose is adopted without clothes. Nevertheless something of the same thing *is* happening. Skin does fold when an area that it is covering is severely compressed, and it does have a stretched, taut look when the area is under tension.

You should try to find these areas which correspond to the tension and slackness in the clothing. Try to express the differences in tension by the way you draw; if a clue of thrust is sensed, draw it vigorously and assertively. Softer, slacker forms can be drawn more delicately with gently undulating lines or soft tones.

In fig.1 the main movement is shown by the way the cloth is pulled from the model's right elbow across and over the left hip. Note also the angle of the skirt hem line and bunched cloth above the left hand on hip.

Fig.3 clearly shows the straightness and strength of the left leg supporting the transferred weight of the figure via the bunched muscles of buttock and hip, the pelvis tilted leaving the right leg and buttock loose and relaxed (supported only by its own weight), and the resultant curve of the spine. Perhaps now return to the clothed pose and re-look. The line of the spine is no longer visible, the

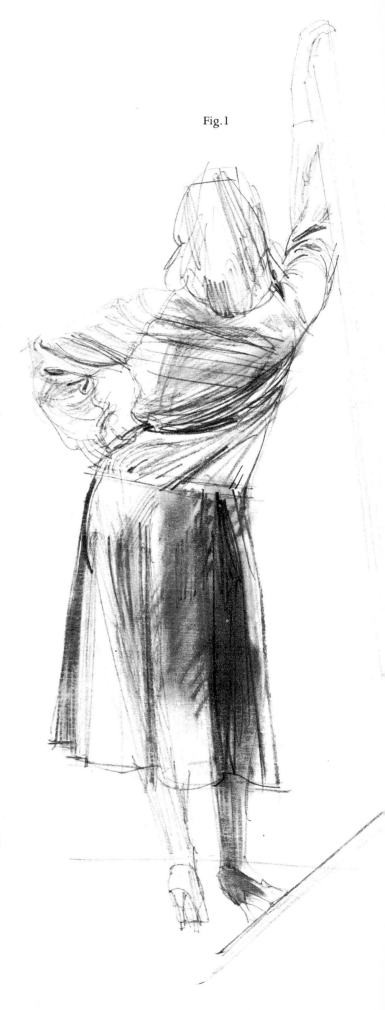

Fig.1

pelvis tilt and the relative bunching and
relaxation of muscle groups cannot be seen
directly. Yet the pose is still immediately
readable because the looser envelope of the
clothing must react to the dynamics beneath.

It is essential to see and describe these
clothing folds in terms of what they are doing
and why, rather than solely copying their
shape. Work out which are the main directions
of stretch and try to figure out what underlying
form is responsible for it. Any linear medium
will do.

Fig.2

Fig.3

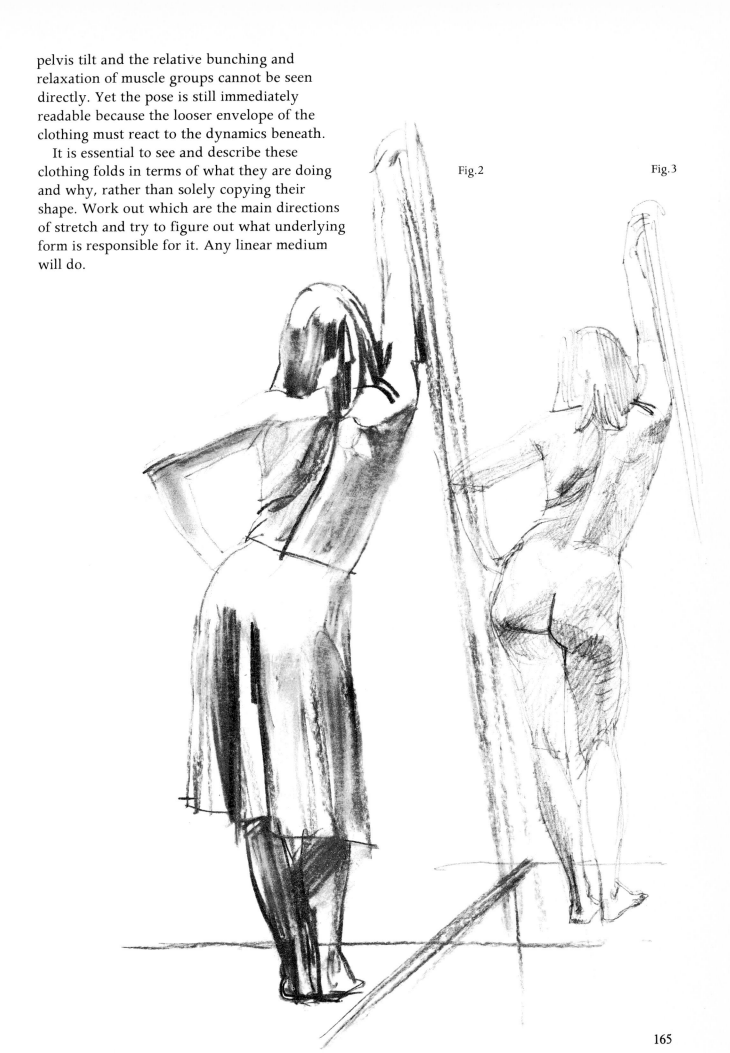

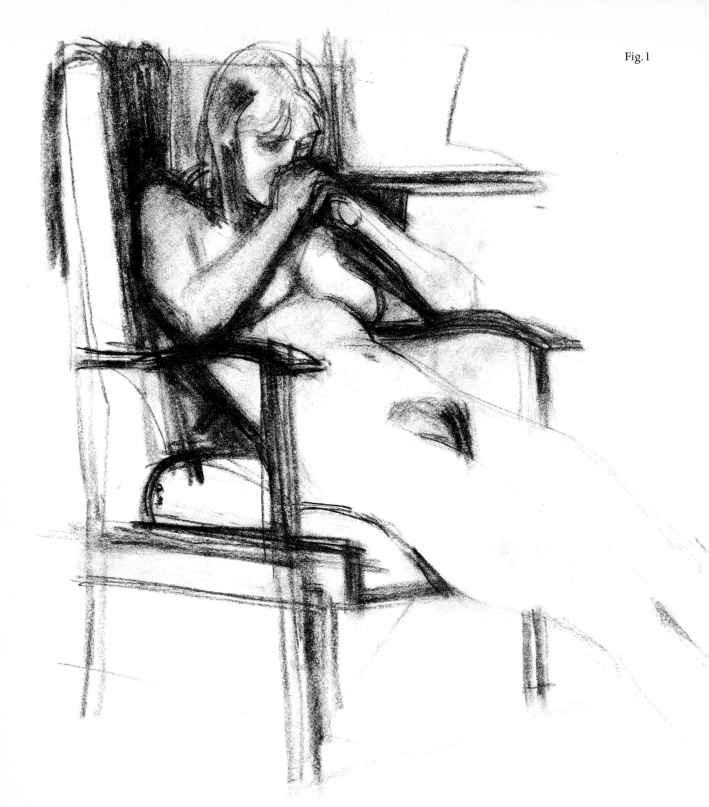

Fig.1

Dynamics

Project 2

For this project a chair with arms will be needed. The aim is to set up a really relaxed, almost reclining sitting pose, the model slumped deep into the chair, pelvis well forward, arms supported by arms of the chair.

In a sense the chair in this situation, takes over some of the function of the skeleton, functioning as a system of rigid supports for the flaccid forms of the figure.

Draw both chair and figure as one object in terms of rigidity and slackness.

This is a position frequently to be seen in gardens or on beaches in the summer, and I have included a drawing (fig.2) of my wife sunbathing in a beach chair in just the pose I have in mind. It was drawn some years ago, when we had time to take holidays!, and while I am not entirely happy with the drawing as a

Fig.2

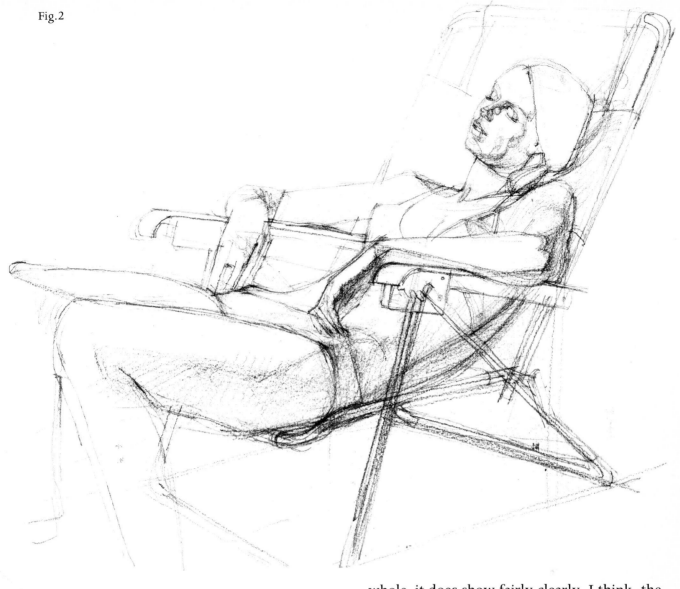

whole, it does show fairly clearly, I think, the contrasting roles of rigid supports and relaxed suspensions. Even the beach chair itself is a model of the pose, being a system of struts and a slung canvas seat and back which falls to its limit under its own weight, and in this case, the weight of the figure too. Note how closely the curve of the spine, suspended between propped shoulder girdles and pelvis, follows the curve of the canvas, suspended between chair front rail and top rail. Of course they are to an extent forming each other, but given the same supports they would fall in a similar curve anyway.

Watch carefully for the way the shoulders are held up by the arm supports while the head and neck sinks with the slump of the body, and notice how the relaxed tissue is pulled downwards where it is unsupported by a surface e.g. the near thigh in fig.1 and the near upper arm.

Dynamics

Project 3

We return now to short poses. Positions which combine stretching, twisting, relaxation and tension are what is needed. Poses like this can only be held for short periods and it is essential to see the dynamics of the pose almost in one look. Try to see the *explanation* of the pose, the forces working within it, and see it *whole*. None of the drawings on this page took more than ten minutes, some only three or even just one minute.

This project and the one preceding, may seem to be repeating former projects. In some respects they are, and I make no apology for this. When drawing the dynamics of a figure, you will inevitably be involved in considering its weight and structure and balance too. It is just the emphasis that, for the purpose of each exercise, is expressly directed towards one aspect in particular.

There is always something new to discover about the human figure, and although there are only so many basic poses, there are infinite subtle variations.

You will find that in practice it is not always absolutely clear from the resulting drawing just what was the original motivation. But I think it is essential to have one, even if, as often happens, discoveries are made during the making of the drawing which lead to a shift

Fig.1

Fig.2

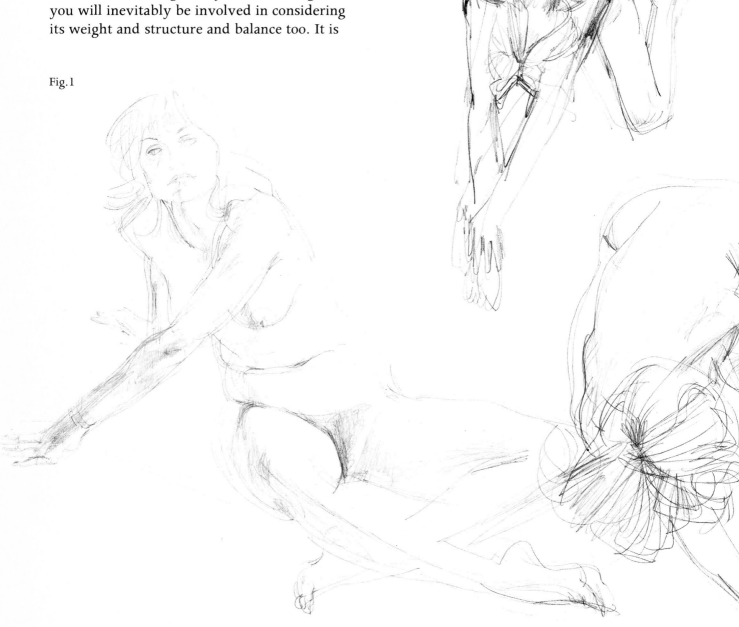

of emphasis. If you try to give too much information about too many aspects of the figure, you will say nothing clearly. This cannot be overstressed (however hard I try!).

By now you may feel confident to try making very quick drawings with pencil and pen as well as charcoal, and as long as you go for the essential action, there should be no need for erasure. Even when you have more time, you should not necessarily rub out construction lines or even gross errors.

You should not even think of errors at all in connection with drawing: every mark made is progress towards the final statement. If you make a mark, say a line denoting what seems to be the main direction of swing in one of those poses for example, and having decided that it is not quite right, rub it out, then you could quite easily put it back in the same place again. Better to leave it, and draw your later estimate alongside it. If that one seems right or nearer right as the drawing progresses, re-enforce it. The earlier lines will diminish by comparison, not affecting the final statement and yet by their presence showing how your thinking progressed.

Fig.3

Fig.5

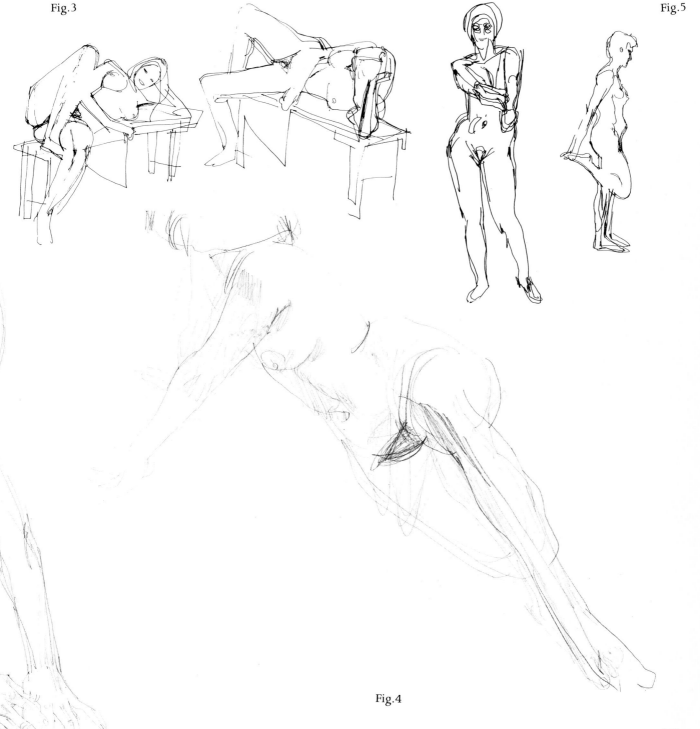

Fig.4

169

Dynamics

Project 4

The most complete situation of tension in which a figure can be arranged, is that where the model is suspended by the hands, or of course the feet. Suspension from the feet has to be ruled out, and total suspension by the hands and arms cannot be maintained for longer than a very few minutes.

However, by providing the model with a secure high support that can be comfortably gripped by reaching up with the feet flat on the ground, a position of partial suspension can be held for periods of time long enough to make reasonable studies. About twenty minutes between rests is probably the most that should be expected.

When as in fig.1, both arms are used to suspend the figure, the whole of the torso is stretched and tensed. The weight of the body falling forward slightly has tensioned the arms so that they are stretched absolutely straight from the supporting bar. At the junction of the arm with the body, the muscles which surround and activate the shoulder joint are all stretched tightly too and this tension has to be expressed forcefully enough to match the strain of the

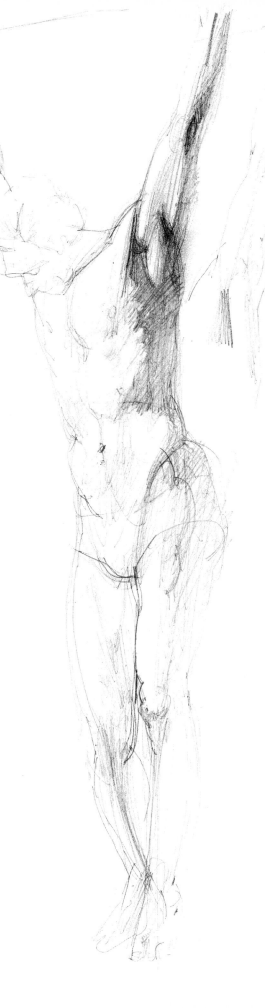

Fig.1

170

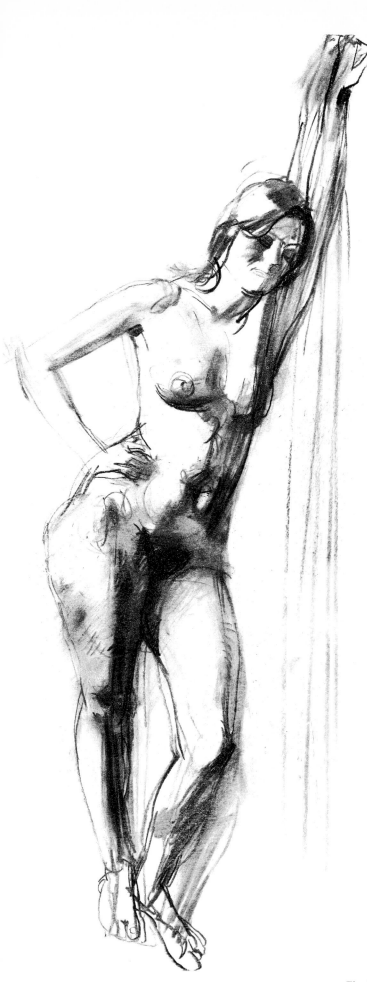

action. In this pose, and in nearly all partially suspended poses that can be held for long enough to draw, much of the body weight is being supported by one leg, only that weight which has been allowed to pivot onto the relaxed other side being in reality held by the arms.

The pelvic tilt will therefore be obvious, as it was in the standing pose showing weight shift, but with the vital difference that equilibrium is not maintained by counterswing, but by suspension. Note how far the head is offset from a position vertically above the weight-taking heel.

Single-handed suspension of course puts the suspended side of the torso into tension, allowing the other side to relax, the main body weight being transferred via the pelvis to the leg away from the suspending arm. The other leg is relaxed to allow the tilted weight to hang from the straight arm.

The top of a door, or a robust easel will do for the one-handed pose. The other one will require a firmly fixed bar or crosspiece, perhaps bridging between two ladders.

Fig.2

Light and shade

There are occasions when the most interesting and visually arresting fact of a figure in situation is not its solidity, its structure, its dynamics, all of which are seen by virtue of the light which falls on it, but the pattern of the light itself.

Up to this point, we have used tone, if at all, as a means of creating the illusion of solidity. Mostly it has corresponded with shadow areas observed on the figure. But not all the shadow areas have necessarily been recorded. Only tone which is necessary to explain form needs to be used, and the depth of that tone need not always match that of the observed shadow area. Moreover, if the areas of shadow or tones of light are judged not sufficient to clarify form or movement, tones can be invented to do the job.

As I have said, linear outlines are inventions; no such line can be seen in reality, it is just a useful and well understood part of the complete visual language.

Now we will look specifically at the figure in terms of light and shade only. Lines

Fig.1

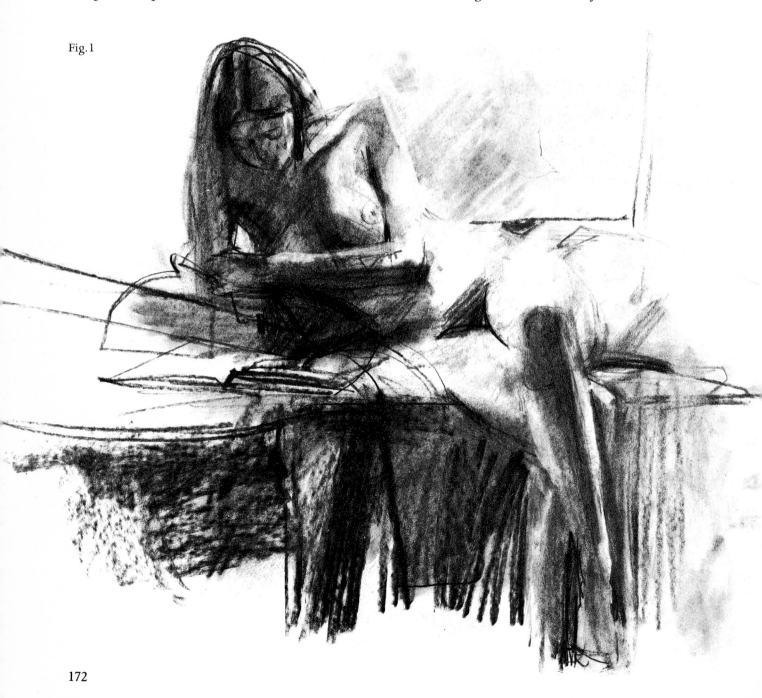

172

representing the edges of objects need not be used. Edges, which after all, only represent the disappearance from view of the outside planes of an object, can just as well be represented by a change of tone as by a line. If there *is* no discernable tonal change, as is sometimes the case, the edge can be *inferred* from adjacent edges that *can* be seen tonally.

In fact one of the excitements of light and shade is ambiguity of outline, now you see it, now you don't, and the artist can use this to advantage. Attention can be directed to selected areas of the drawing by, almost literally, spotlighting it, and whole areas can be lost in shadow to reinforce the emphasis.

So there is still a place for selectivity and exaggeration in drawing light and shade – we are using our eyes to see what the camera records, but we can choose what we use.

Fig.2

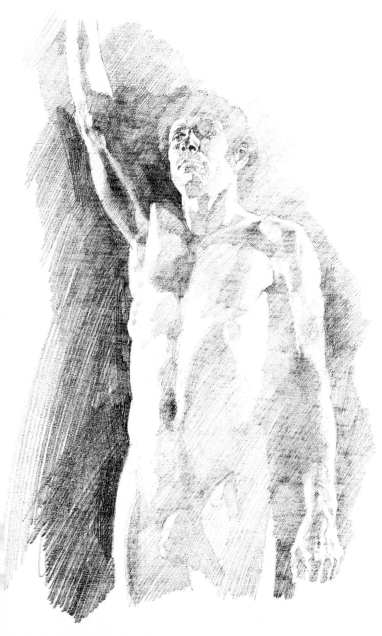

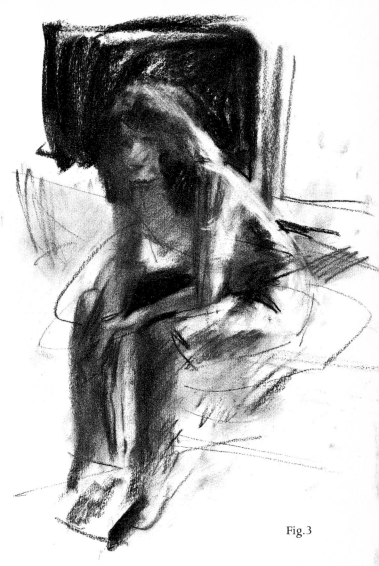

Fig.3

Some line may be used initially to define outer edges, but increasingly you should look instead for the edges of tonal areas, defining these and treating the edges of the figure as of secondary importance unless they are represented by strong contrasts of tone.

It follows of course, that using tonal changes to define outer edges, implies judging and representing the background all round the figure, and this will lead into compositions which place the figure in an environment.

Also completely tonal drawing, where no line is used, only areas of light and shade, comes close to being painting. In fact it is difficult to decide at just what point one becomes the other. Painting has often been described as 'drawing with paint', so perhaps there is no really intrinsic difference.

In the Composition section there will be more on the subject of the figure and background, and 'drawing with paint'.

173

Light and shade

Project 1

Arrange the model in any convenient pose lit by a single light source so as to produce strong definition between light and shade.

It is not the easiest situation to organize, as it is necessary not only to light the model in the right way but also to ensure adequate light to draw by.

If the light in your studio is natural sunlight it is probably best to place the model near to the window so that maximum contrast in lighting can be achieved, and then choose your position rather further from the light source so that plenty of shadow area can be seen in the figure. There will probably be sufficient reflected light from a wall to illuminate your drawing surfaces.

In artificial light, it is a little trickier. A photographic flood lamp or even a spot is ideal, but failing that a reflector lamp in an anglepoise or similar movable light would do. Failing *that*, placing the model near to a low and directional overhead light will have to do.

Depending on how many people are drawing, more directional light will have to be procured to light the drawing surfaces without spilling light onto the model and spoiling the strongly defined light and shade areas.

When all is arranged, look at the model, maybe half close your eyes to merge detail and minor light changes, and try to see, not form, not weight, not dynamics, not structure, but light and shade.

Assess the relative depth of shadow areas one to another, and decide which of the basically light areas is really the very lightest.

For the moment line can be used to help find the outline, but start thinking about a light edge where it gives way to a dark

Fig.1

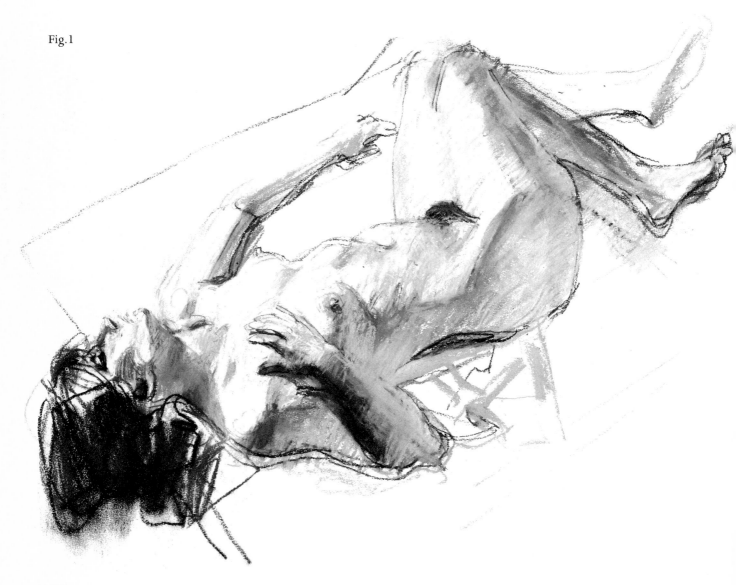

174

background as just that – a change of tone, and draw it so.

Treat this project as an 'easing in' to the idea of light and shade.

It may not be so very different from drawings you have made previously; it depends on how much tone you habitually use.

The vital difference is that, while previously you should have been using tone only where necessary to clarify what you were searching for, now it is the tone itself that should concern you, its area, its depth, the pattern made by it and the light areas.

Fig.3

Fig.2

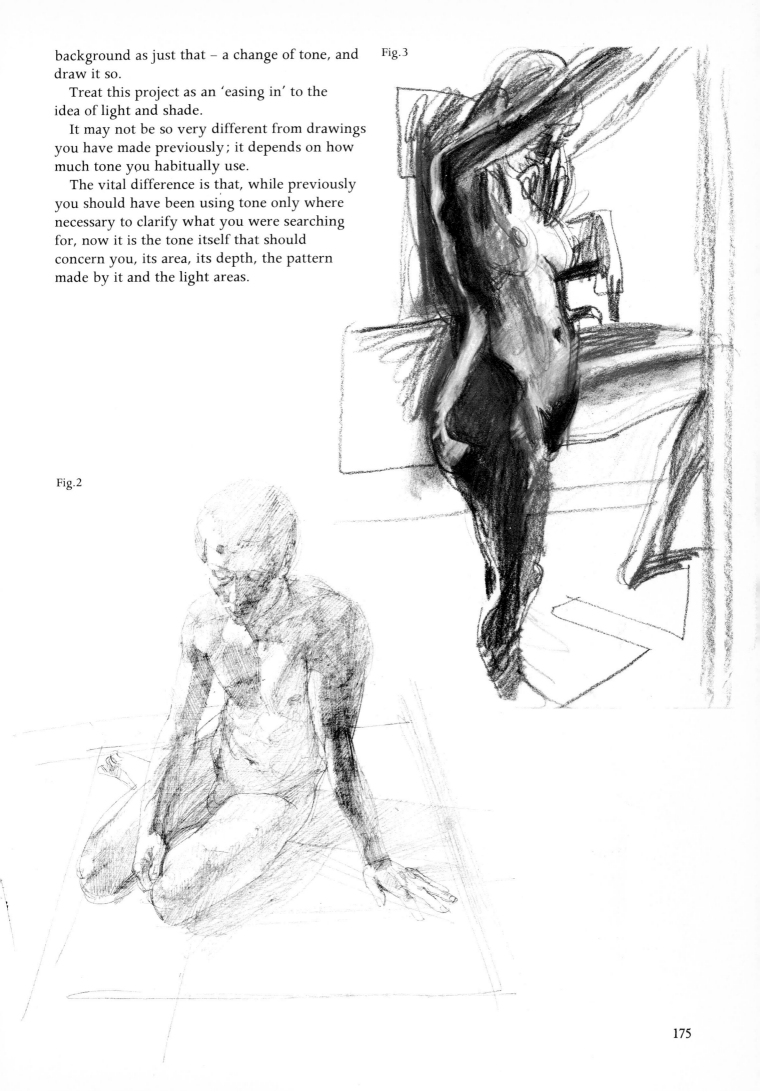

175

Light and shade

Project 2

More dramatic lighting than last time is needed for this project. If the model is posed standing or sitting directly under a bright light source, the tops of forms will be strongly lit and will cast dark shadows on lower forms. Minor adjustments of position under the light will produce big changes in the lighting situation, so a pose should be chosen which can be maintained without swaying or gradual sagging.

Fig.1

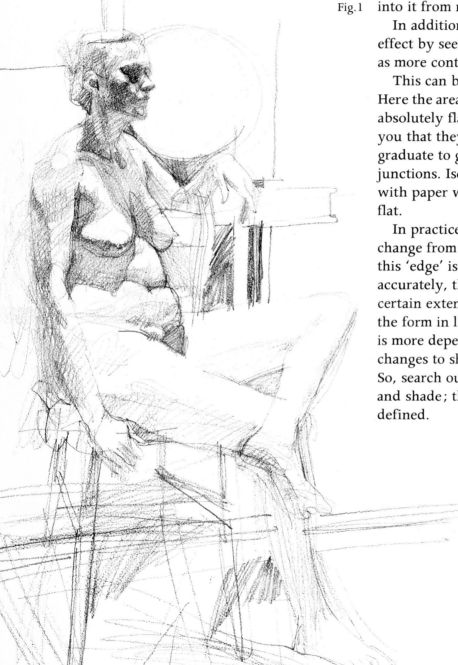

In this lighting situation, every form is thrown into sharp relief, and the head and neck, being closest to the light source tend to be particularly dramatically transformed.

Even in the most dramatic light however, the dark areas of shade receive some degree of reflected light, the darkest parts often being nearest to where the shadow gives way to light.

This apparent darkening of shadow areas where they meet the bright light areas, is an interesting phenomenon and vital to appreciate.

As I have said, it is partly, perhaps mainly, a result of the tone furthest from the light on a rounded form, being in the best position to catch light from the main source reflected back into it from nearby lit forms.

In addition however, the eye adds to the effect by seeing adjacent contrasting tones, as more contrasting than they objectively are.

This can be verified by reference to fig.2. Here the areas of contrasting tone are themselves absolutely flat and even, but your eye will tell you that they are not. Each tone seems to graduate to give maximum contrast at the junctions. Isolation of any one tone by masking with paper will show that the tones really are flat.

In practice this accenting of the line of change from light to dark is very helpful. If this 'edge' is searched out and put down accurately, the rest of the shadow tone can to a certain extent look after itself. The solidity of the form in light and the feeling of strong light is more dependent on the place *where* light changes to shade than by how *much* it changes. So, search out the shapes of the areas of light and shade; they should in the main be sharply defined.

Fig.2

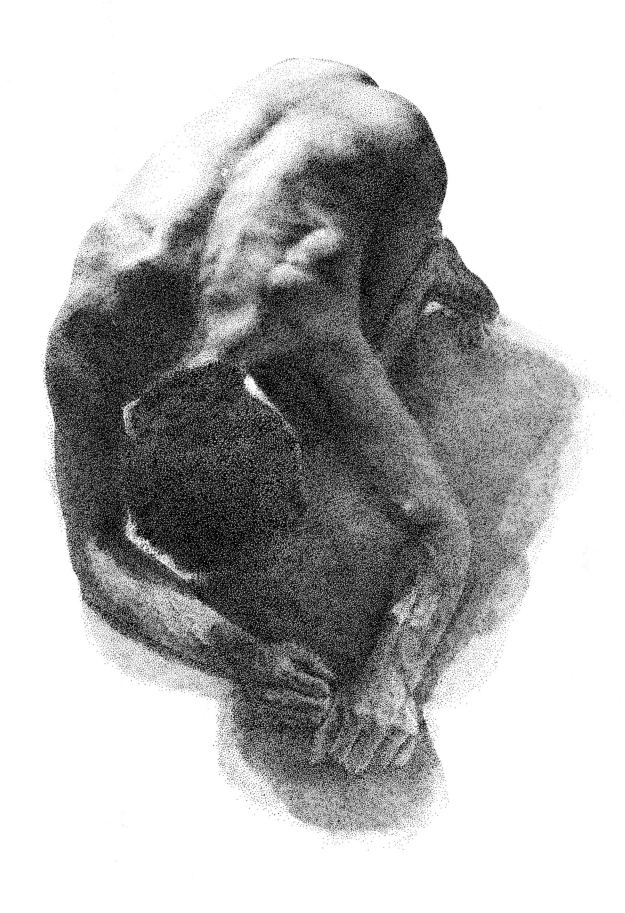

Fig. 3

Light and shade

Project 3

Light illuminating the figure from below always creates an unexpected, unfamiliar appearance.

I am referring of course, to lighting which is from a low level relative to the upright figure; the same effect can be achieved by lighting the prone figure from the feet end. The model's torso in fig.2 is almost upside down so that the same lighting is produced by nearly overhead lighting, the unusual appearance being heightened by the effect of gravity pulling the forms the 'wrong' way.

You should by now, be beginning to make judgements about *all* the tones, not just those on the figure itself. This means much greater areas of paper to be covered and thought should be given to the choice of media.

Given sufficient time, tone can be created with great subtlety by the use of pen line or dot, but in the time normally available with a live model it is not very practical.

Pastel, chalk, crayon and the ubiquitous charcoal are quicker and more malleable.

Ideally you need, not only to work from light to dark, but also to be able to add to and change light areas, even if it is achieved by erasing or moving tonal areas. Charcoal and

Fig.1

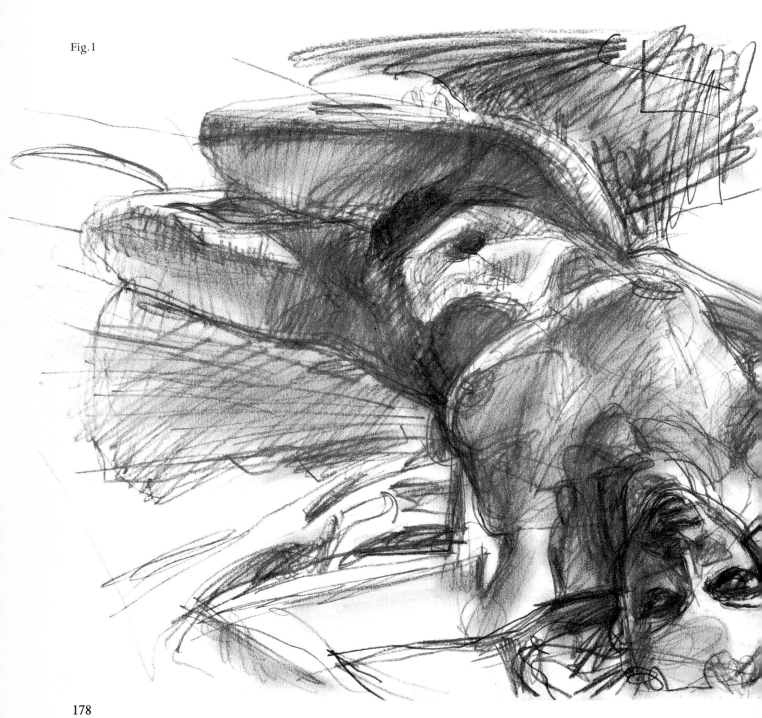

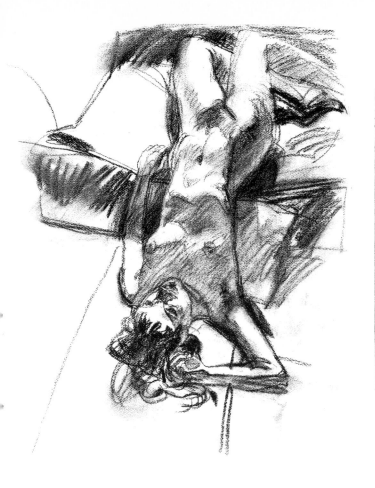

Fig.2

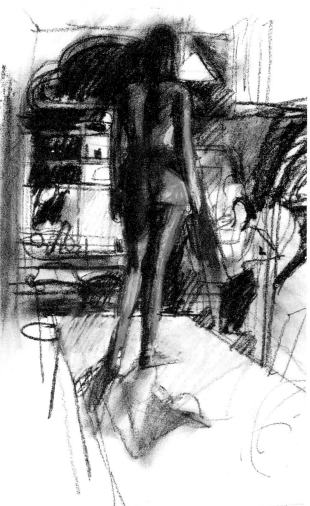

Fig.3

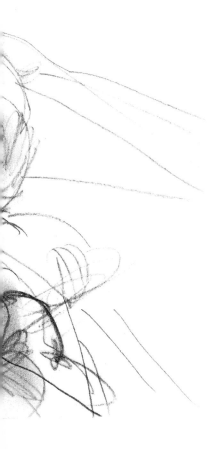

putty rubber (or bread which works well) is ideal for the latter method, but in order actually to apply light areas you will have to use white chalk or coloured pastels.

Elevating the model on a table or similar raised surface as in fig.3, facilitates lighting the standing figure from a low level and allows more background possibilities. In this case the head and parts of the shoulders are virtually the same tone as the background. In such instances, when figure and background merge tonally, let them do so; such uncertainties add to the excitement of tonal studies, as do counterchanges where a tone is at one point a light against dark, and elsewhere, although tonally unchanged becomes suddenly, by virtue of a background variation, a dark against light.

Look for pattern as ever, organize the shapes by reference to your mind's eye vertical/ horizontal grid and try to keep the drawing mobile to the end.

Fig.2

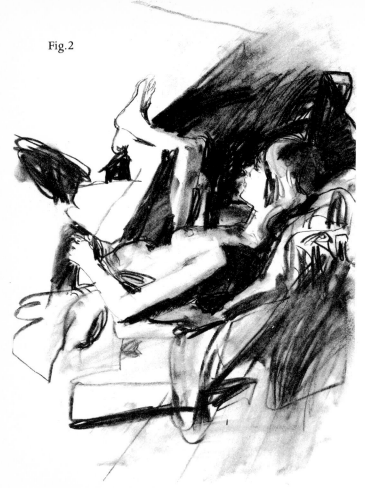

Light and shade

Project 4

In this session I suggest that you take one step further towards a purely tonal representation of the figure in a situation. Pose the model in a shadowy corner, and shed just enough light to catch some of the major forms.

The actual position adopted is not important, but sitting or reclined poses usually give more interesting patterns of light and shade than standing ones.

If the lighting is selective and dim enough, the figure will emerge from the surrounding gloom by virtue of a relatively few well lit forms, much of the edges of the figure being lost or hard to define. If these light areas on the figure and those on surrounding surfaces, are well judged in their positions, shape and relative brightness, a great deal of the rest of the figure which is lost in shadow, will be easily inferred by the viewer.

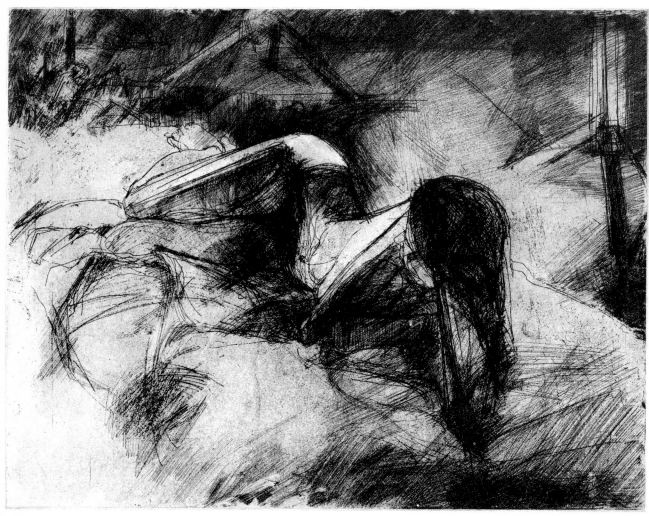

Fig.1

Fig.3

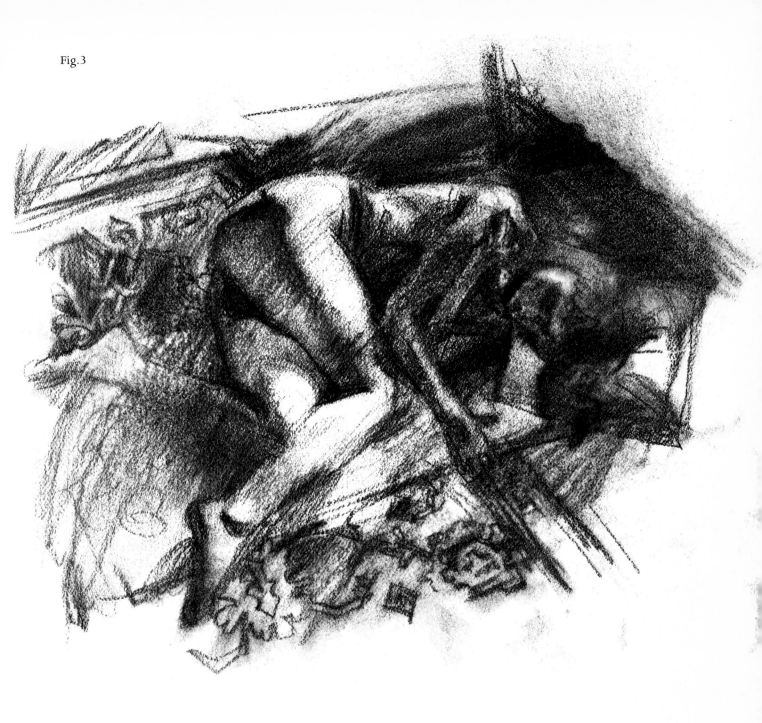

Try to rid yourself therefore of the need to represent outer edges by line at all; let the tones speak for themselves. This applies to edges of limbs within the external outline of the figure. There is an example of what I mean in the drawing fig.3 where the model's right calf rest over her left knee. The adjacent forms are both lit quite well, so they have been allowed to merge with just a small change of tone between them. Their sharing of the sparse amount of available light is more important than the fact that in different circumstances they will become quite separate forms.

Colour too, and pattern need to be considered in tonal drawings. When drawing form and structure, the local colour of tissue, colour of hair and surrounding surfaces and forms, is of no importance and can deflect your attention from the point of the drawing. Drawing light and shade purely means that you have to give a tonal value to *all* the surface, so that colours which although receiving light are themselves tonally dark, must be represented so.

Fully tonal drawings are rather rare in the history of art, perhaps because of the afore-mentioned proximity to painting, but I recommend you to look at the Seurat on page 238, to see how light and shade can be handled completely without line and yet remain unarguably a drawing.

Clothing

It may sometimes be wondered at that so much figure drawing is done from the nude model, when in real life most people are almost always to be seen more or less clothed.

The main reason, I believe, is that the nude human figure is the supreme test of draughts-manship. Not that it is necessarily *the* most difficult subject that exists, but it is the subject that most ruthlessly exposes dishonesty, laziness or plain ineptitude. There are just too many people who will know immediately if a drawing of the nude is basically right or wrong for you to be able to get away with slack drawing.

A tree can be drawn grossly inaccurately and few people will know; only experts know if machines, plants, animals are really well drawn and even they tend to check details rather than subtle proportion and form, but we have a very critical eye for our own kind.

Not many people can use their subliminal sense of the 'rightness' of a figure to draw well themselves; that, as we have seen, needs a new objective vision, and few can always pinpoint exactly what failure of objective vision has made a drawing look wrong. Some flashy

techniques may confuse criticism for a while, but not for long. Honesty shines through good figure drawing for all to see, dishonesty cannot be concealed.

As a result it is generally agreed that drawing the nude figure embodies *all* the disciplines and problems as well as the challenge and excitement of drawing anything.

Having said all this, I feel there is another reason.

Even if all you ever wanted to draw were people in clothes it would still be better to explore and understand the figure *beneath* the clothes first.

Clothes are made to fit the human body; they are not always a close fit, but always they are supported and activated by the structure, form and dynamics of the body they cover. They can be thought of as extra, looser skins, and they have to react and accommodate themselves to the movement of the figure in a similar way. It follows that to understand the stresses involved in the human skin covering will help your understanding of the way clothing behaves.

It is also true that analysis of what would be called the dynamics of clothing, where lack of the elasticity of skin renders the tensions and slackness grosser and easier to read, can help you to sort out the dynamics of the underlying figure.

The following projects in this section therefore, will suggest ways of exploring and clarifying the relationship between the nude figure and clothing, and understanding the dynamics of clothing itself.

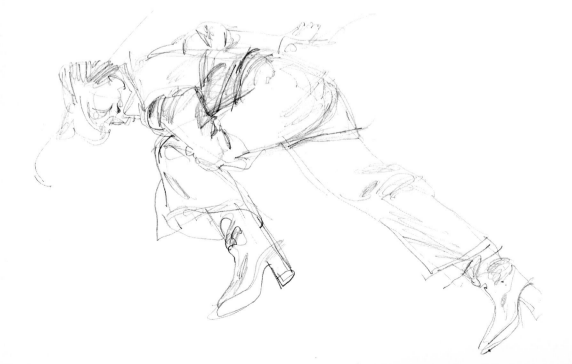

Fig.1

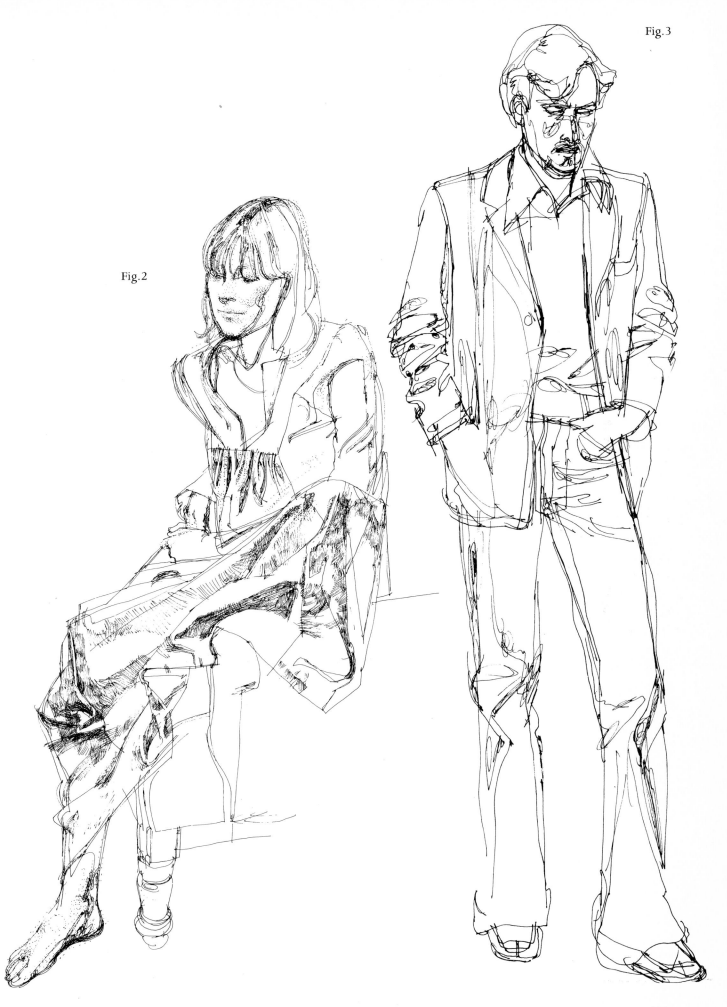

Fig.2

Fig.3

183

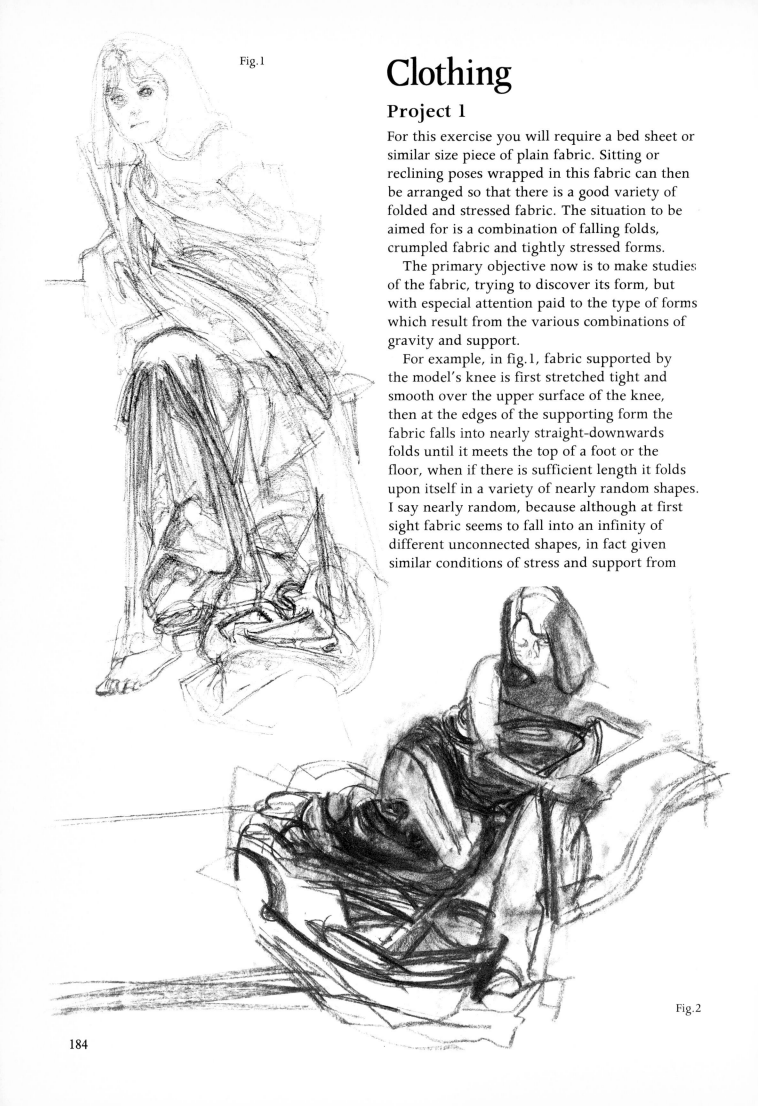

Fig.1

Clothing

Project 1

For this exercise you will require a bed sheet or similar size piece of plain fabric. Sitting or reclining poses wrapped in this fabric can then be arranged so that there is a good variety of folded and stressed fabric. The situation to be aimed for is a combination of falling folds, crumpled fabric and tightly stressed forms.

   The primary objective now is to make studies of the fabric, trying to discover its form, but with especial attention paid to the type of forms which result from the various combinations of gravity and support.

   For example, in fig.1, fabric supported by the model's knee is first stretched tight and smooth over the upper surface of the knee, then at the edges of the supporting form the fabric falls into nearly straight-downwards folds until it meets the top of a foot or the floor, when if there is sufficient length it folds upon itself in a variety of nearly random shapes. I say nearly random, because although at first sight fabric seems to fall into an infinity of different unconnected shapes, in fact given similar conditions of stress and support from

Fig.2

Fig.3

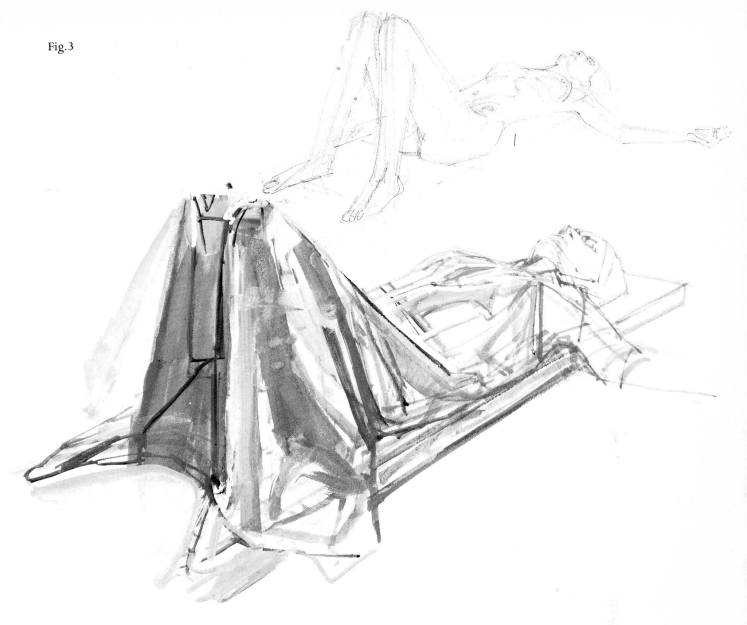

underlying forms, fabrics of similar weight, texture etc., tend to react in a predictable way.

Details of folds may differ each time the cloth in a given situation is picked up and dropped again, but the *type* of folding especially over the stress points will increasingly be recognized as typical.

You may notice in this drawing that the nearest forms are drawn darker and with greater stress than the forms farther back, which achieves a feeling of recession. This is not an entirely conscious device. Indeed, such things never work if they are premeditated. During a drawing all effort is concentrated on discovering the uniqueness of the object, and using whatever marks that may seem necessary at the time.

Once the marks describe your discovery accurately and clearly, no addition or embellishment is necessary. If they do not

describe accurately or are ambiguous they should be changed, and changed until it all works as well as one's capability permits. This is the natural process of drawing. The areas which are giving the most trouble or which seem to be most vital, are changed and returned to again and again, and acquire a more worked on look.

This is how you get the areas of greater stress – they reflect the draughtsman's dwelling of attention; the progress of the search can be traced.

There are occasions in the best-organized life drawing group when for one reason or another you may find yourself without a model for a session. This particular project is a useful one in these circumstances, as a couple of chairs with the fabric draped and wrapped over them will do almost as well as the model as a basis for your studies.

Clothing

Project 2

Have the model wear a loose fitting garment such as a dressing gown. The fabric should be plain, preferably fairly light coloured and of a thin, clinging consistency which makes good folds but hugs forms quite closely too. The objective of this exercise is to discover the figure underneath the cloth through the stresses visible in the garment.

In fig.1 the pose is intentionally simple and undramatic and the garment is fairly loose and shapeless. Because the model's knees and lower legs are uncovered and the contact points of the chair legs and her feet are clearly visible, the basis of the structure can be established without reference to the clothing. Thereafter clues to the underlying form must be sought in the folds and stress lines of the garment.

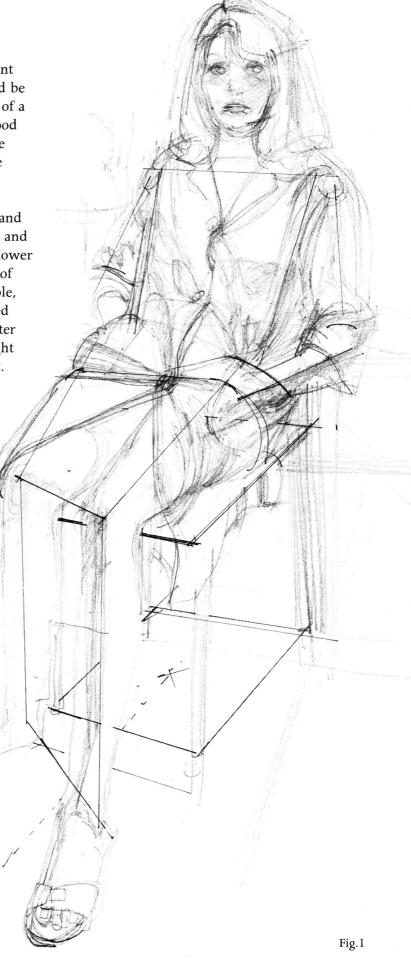

Fig.1

Fig.2

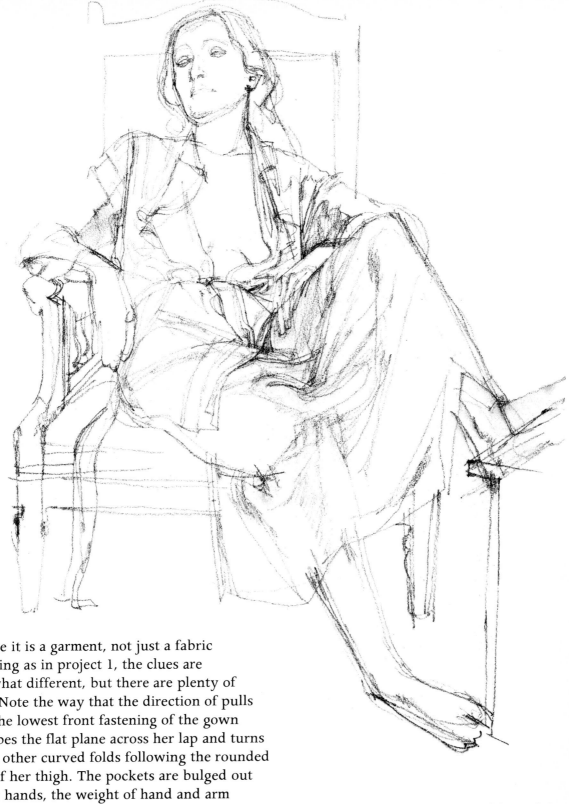

Because it is a garment, not just a fabric wrapping as in project 1, the clues are somewhat different, but there are plenty of them. Note the way that the direction of pulls from the lowest front fastening of the gown describes the flat plane across her lap and turns to join other curved folds following the rounded form of her thigh. The pockets are bulged out by her hands, the weight of hand and arm pulling folds from the shoulders and helping to define the front plane of her chest. Smooth areas above the breast, undulating, slightly crumpled forms beneath tell of the fullness of breasts and slimmer but quite round middle. Sleeves fall from shoulders and are then forced to fold deeply in the bend of the arms – all the main directions of the body can be deduced.

In fig.2 the form of the garment has been searched out with greater concentration on the appearance and quality of the folding of the fabric, but still plenty of information about the pose comes through. The long waist tie, not only defines the waist, but by trailing down the abdomen and then over the near thigh delineates these forms too.

Such garment details as collars, arm seams, back and side seams can often be used to help to define forms in a similar way, as we will see in the next project.

Clothing

Project 3

We come now to garments which are designed to fit the figure more closely, which may be multi-layered but which must allow the figure normal freedom of movement. As you would expect, there are many more seams and much less fabric free-falling into long sweeping folds.

Ask the model to wear normal underclothes, a jacket and skirt or trousers, shoes and socks etc., preferably plain, not too dark coloured materials again, so that the dynamics of folding can be clearly seen. Choose fairly normal sitting poses as here, remembering that if a pose is difficult to hold requiring very frequent rests, the folding of the material will be different after every rest. As I said in the introduction to this section, this does not mean that the *type* of folding will be intrinsically changed each time the pose is resumed, one can learn to draw a sort of stress pattern which represents the function of a set of folds rather than their precise shapes, but it's nice to get a few typical fold forms into your visual memory from explicit observation first.

For the purpose of this exercise, which is to discover more about the stress patterns of clothing that reveal its structure and that of the body beneath, I think that you should not pay too much attention to garment detailing for its own sake.

The number of teeth in a zip fastener for instance is not important, but the direction it takes is. A line of stitching that by its direction defines a form or reveals tension is important, but purely decorative stitching is not. Do not misunderstand me; in another context, decorative stitching, pattern and colour could quite legitimately be your primary interests.

Note that in fig.2 the pocket seams on her jacket have helped to establish the side plane. The seam of the arm hole explains the discontinuity of the jacket fold resulting from the forward thrust of the arms, and those over the upper arm and shoulder. Also the side seam of her jeans tells of how the tube of cloth has had to fold on itself in the inside of the bent knees, while in fig.3, the side seam's discontinuity shows how much the loose cloth of his trouser leg is displaced.

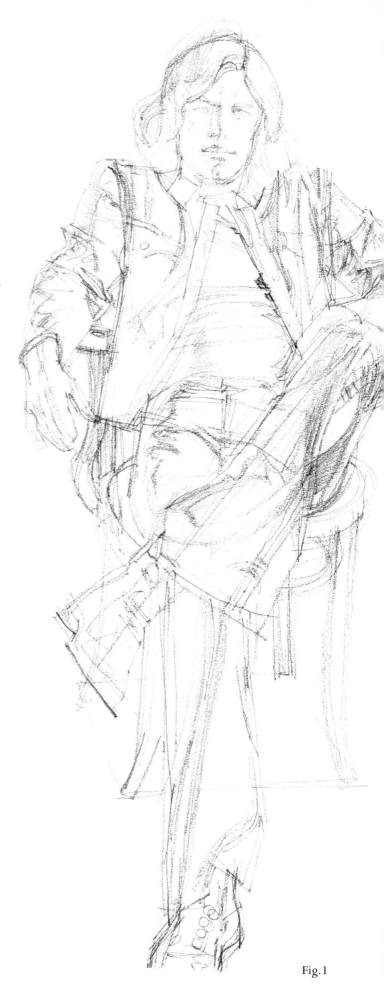

Fig.1

Use tone where necessary to explain form
and function but not to denote colour. That's
a waste of time in this context. Shoes are only
a problem if you let your preconceptions of
what shoes are like, based usually on the
profile view, get in the way of your objective
vision of the often encountered foreshortened
views.

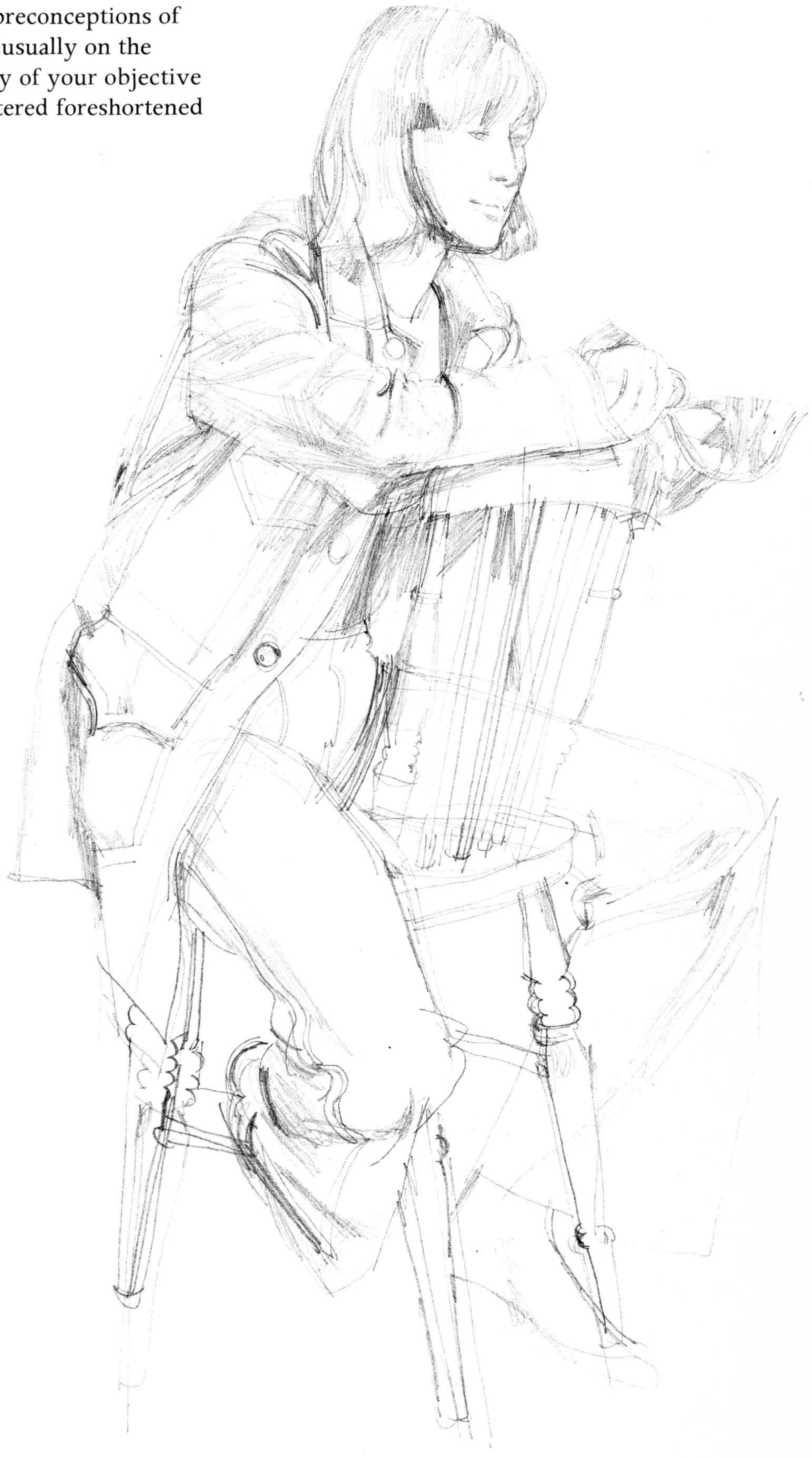

Fig.2

Clothing

Project 4

This project explores further what was begun in Dynamics project 1, that is, the analysis of a standing pose by reference to clothing.

Basically loose clothing which is close fitting at the waist, such as the long skirt in fig.4, most dramatically reveals the nature and degree of weight shift in a standing pose, by so accurately conforming where it can free-fall, to the pull of gravity.

It makes visible the invisible canopy of forces I have asked you to imagine.

I suggest that you extend this exercise over more than one session in order to make a series of drawings of standing poses variously clothed.

Minimal clothing, amounting to little more than a framing shape, as in fig.5, can add interest to a heavily asymmetrically weighted pose by providing a vertical reference to measure the movement against.

The backward swing of the jacket in fig.1 helps to dramatize the balance of the pose.

I have also included two drawings from life of a fashion model (figs.2 and 3). Fashion

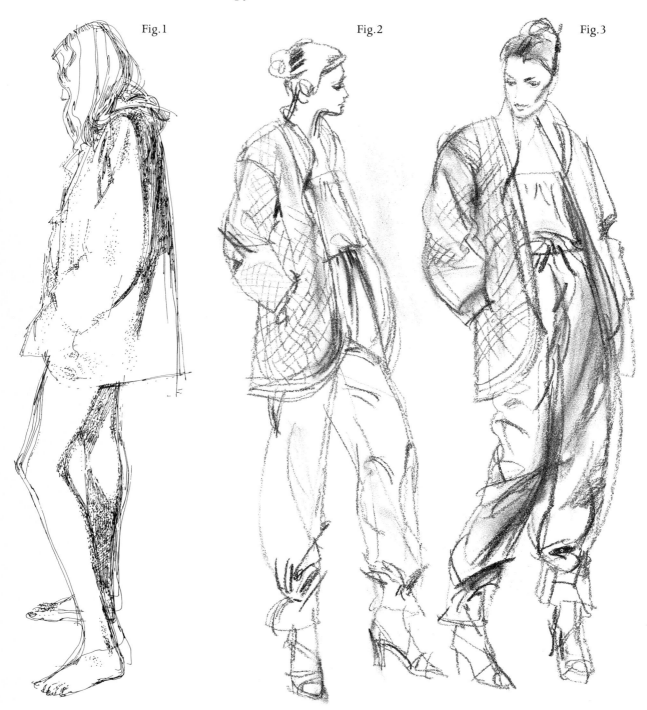

Fig.1   Fig.2   Fig.3

drawings represent a very specialized area of clothed figure drawing, in that it is the garments which are of first importance and the figure is expected to conform to the designer's idea of the shape of his clothes rather than the other way round.

Consequently the distortions of the figure vary in a degree and kind dependent on the currently preferred outline and how far the fashion illustrator is expected to go in fantasising on the theme.

The most constant adjustment generally considered to make clothes look good, is an elongation of the figure so that the head length which is normally about one sixth to one seventh of the total height, goes instead into the body ten, twelve or many more times.

My two drawings, while not being finished fashion illustrations, but just the preliminary drawings from life, have nevertheless been consciously elongated in this way.

There is much more to fashion figure drawing of course than this brief exposition has told, but it *is* very specialized and rather subjective, and therefore strictly outside the declared limits of this book.

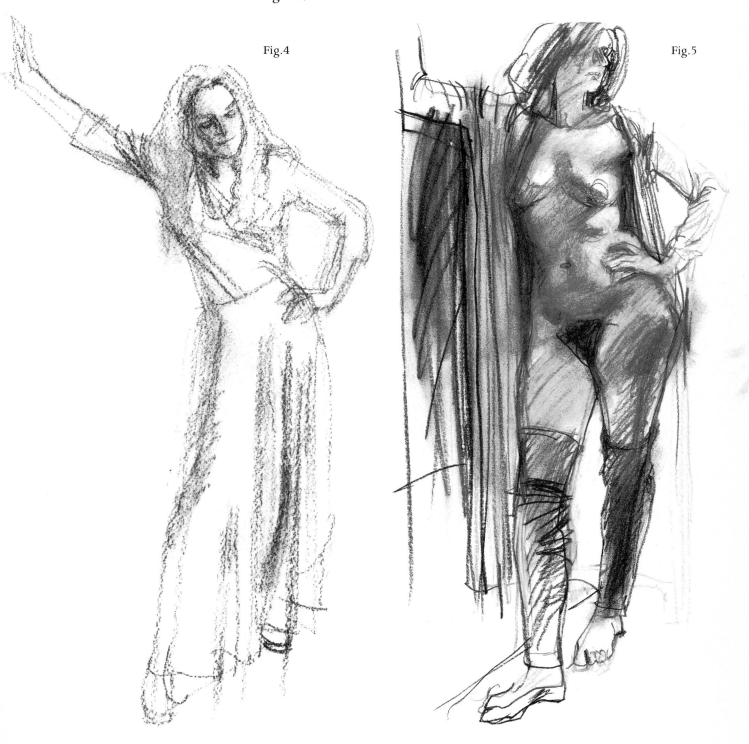

Fig.4

Fig.5

191

Character

In order to define what I mean by character in this context, I think it easiest to recall first what we have been looking for in the previous projects.

I have suggested that you consider shape, weight, balance, structure, anatomy, dynamics, light and shade, clothing – all abstract concepts Even in the section on head, hands and feet I have concentrated on objective, abstract elements. Nowhere have I encouraged you to think of your model as a person. I believe that it has been a necessary constriction. Cezanne's famous advice that a head should be painted as though it was an apple, is an example of the same thinking. To be able to 'see' objectively requires an initial denial of the mass of visual half-truths that we have acquired through social contact and interaction, and its replacement by concentrated objective observation of each form as though it had never been seen before. The point has been made often enough I hope, and I will not labour it further.

A point will eventually be reached however, when the habit of direct analytical observation will have become, if not entirely second nature, at least fairly natural to slip into when settling down to draw. I suggest that now is the time to allow yourself to re-admit some of the originally denied emotional reactions to the model as a person. All the other objective realities have

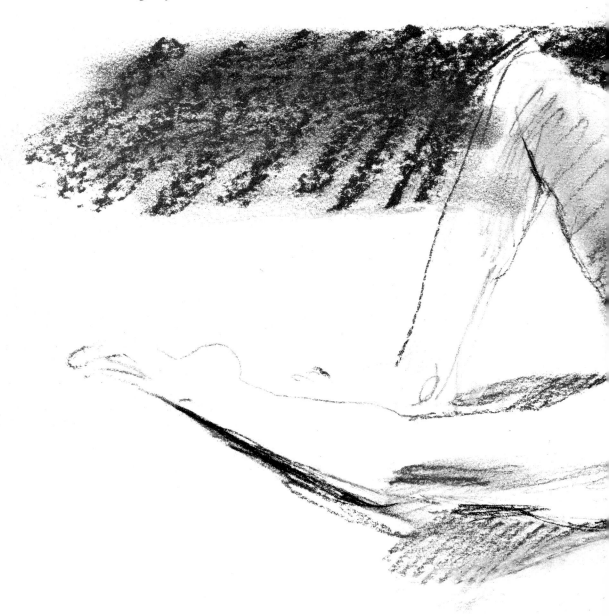

still to be dealt with, but you should in addition, try to discover what makes the human figure that you are drawing specially different from any other.

The face of course is where we normally expect to find the identity of a particular individual, and it is true that we gain a lot of information about current mood and personality traits from looking at the face. But we *recognize* people from distances and angles where the facial expression and details are not discernable. The essential recognizable character of an individual is there in the whole body.

It is this that I suggest you now try to search out. I would not expect the drawings

necessarily to look vastly different – particular 'likeness' still resides in shape and proportion – but the emphasis should be different.

Searching out small asymmetries, where symmetry is to be expected, noting the imperfections or unusual colourations of hair or skin, or any other features which are distinctive and special to the person who is your subject. Be prepared to exaggerate these features a little or a lot, and to subjugate or ignore some of the objective features of form, structure and so on.

It is not easy. It is especially difficult to combine this 'humanity' with still, strong objective drawing, but it is very satisfying when it works.

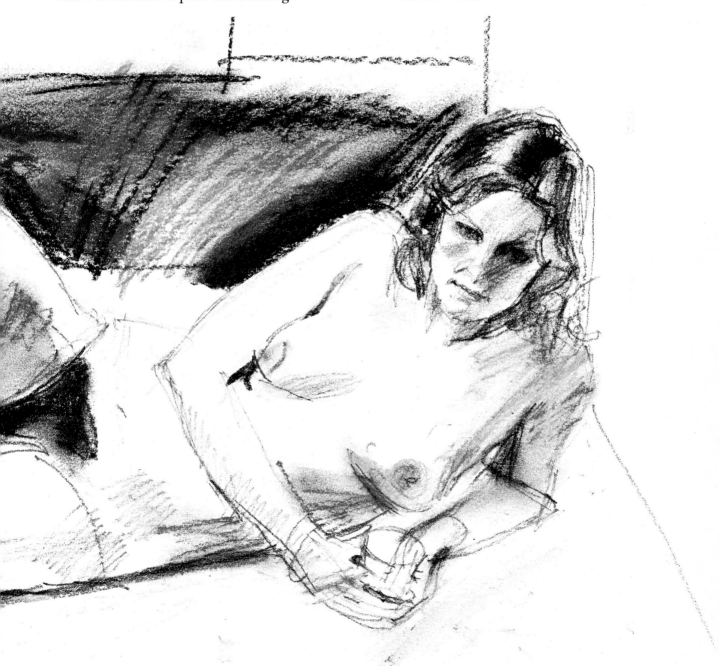

Character

Project 1

Ask your model to adopt a pose which both looks to you and feels to the model, to be natural and comfortable.

It may be that during a rest period in a drawing session, you will catch the model off guard, relaxing unselfconsciously into an attitude which is more natural and typical than the poses which have been formally arranged.

On the other hand, if the model has been a regular sitter for you or your group, there may be poses which you particularly liked in earlier sessions which you feel could be drawn again with a different emphasis.

To catch the essential character it is generally helpful to have a view of the face, the strongest connection being made between viewer and model when there is direct eye to eye contact. This is the situation when the eyes in portraits are said to 'follow you round the room', and you do receive an enhanced sense of there being a real person there, when the eyes are looking straight at you.

However, it is not essential and not possible for everyone if you are drawing in a group. In any case you should not limit your search for character to the face of the sitter alone;

shoulders and upper body or the whole figure should contribute to the complete impression.

Some consideration of the immediate surroundings of the sitter establishes the figure in a real place, rather than the limbo of a figure study on a white page, and helps to create the feeling of there being a real person inside. If the model holds a book or a cup, or is knitting, it can help to reinforce the naturalness of a pose too.

When drawing, look for proportion and form as before but with an especial eye to discovering what makes this particular person different from others.

I repeat that it is only a slight change in emphasis. It means that when you draw, for example, a hand and arm, it is not enough that it should be a well drawn arm, with solidity, weight and good tension or slackness; it should also look like this *particular* hand and arm. If by delving too deeply into its structure, you have destroyed its delicacy, then in this context, you have failed. On the other hand, if the character of the same hand and arm is there but the form or solidity are a little lacking it may be all right. The essential thing is to make sure the whole drawing hangs together – some inaccuracies and exaggerations are permissible as long as the figure is all of a piece and says something about the uniqueness of the person you are drawing.

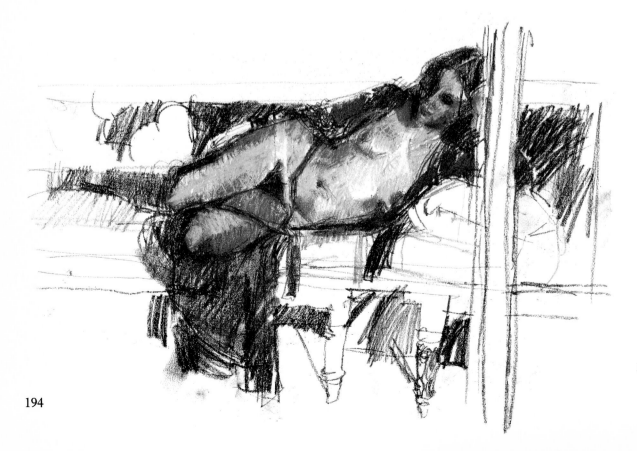

Fig.1

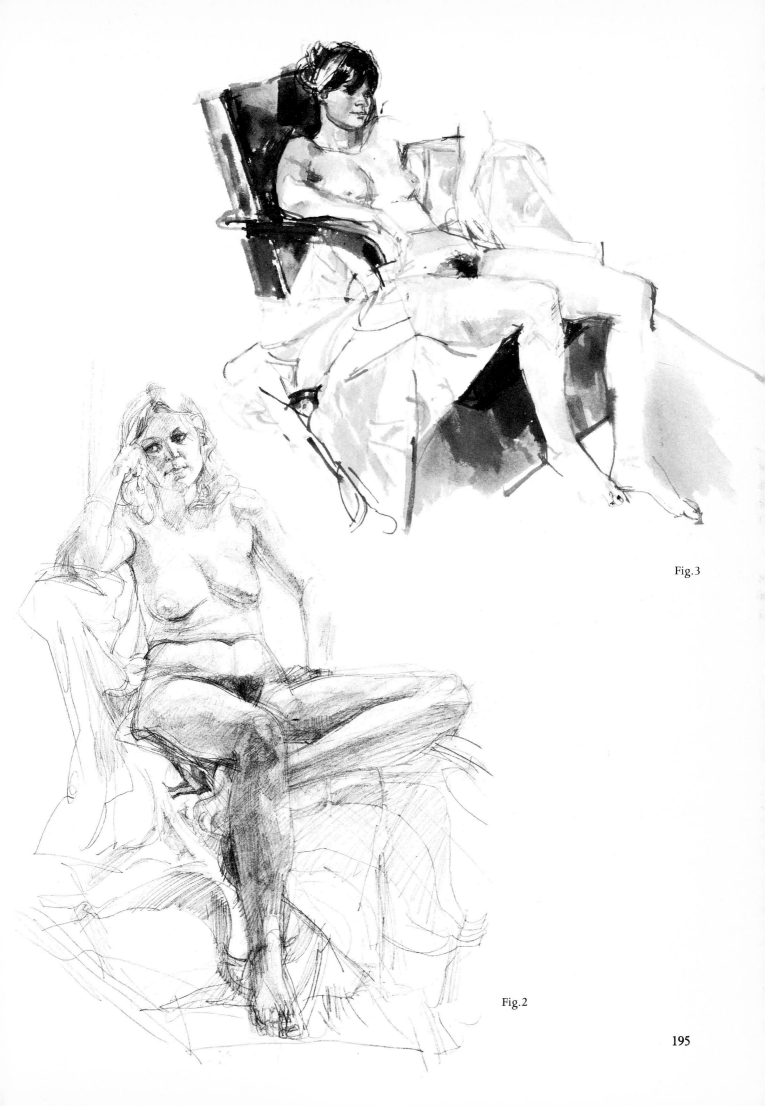

Fig.3

Fig.2

195

Fig.1

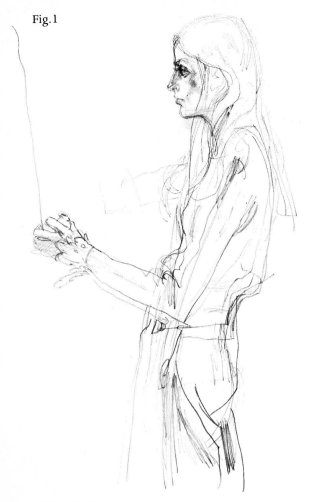

Character

Project 2

This project is another one that can be kept in reserve against the possibility of being without a model for a session. There are three possibilities, assuming that you are drawing as a group.

First each member of the group can take a turn at posing for the others. Each pose should be short enough to allow everyone to do their share of posing within the session. As this means you probably won't have very much time to make each drawing, economy of means is essential. If all your sketches are on one pose, you will be able to see whether you have been able to capture the variety of character and expression rather than drawing a succession of stereotyped heads.

Another way is to all draw each other simultaneously. This is not as complex as it sounds. If you all sit, or stand, in a widely spaced group, each person can choose to draw any other, and may themselves be drawn by the same person or any other. Of course all the drawings will be of people drawing and so there will be a certain amount of movement involved. The shifts in position tend to be minor, however, chiefly confined to looking up at the model and down at drawing alternately, and occasional easing of a position

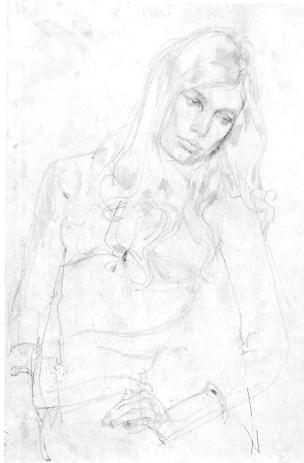

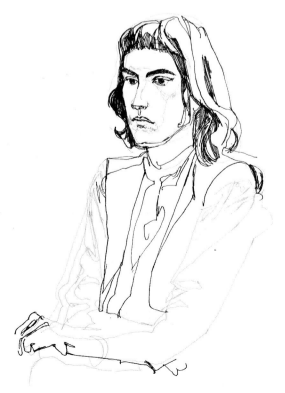

Fig.2

Fig.3

for a slight rest. If you choose to draw the
position which is most frequently adhered to
and ignore the occasional lapses, there should
be no problem. At least your subject will know
that he is being drawn and will try to keep
movement to the minimum. If you draw people
that you see about you in everyday life, as I
think you should, there is no guarantee that
any position will be maintained for more than
a few minutes or even seconds, so it is essential
to develop the ability to see a face or figure in
one look and to put down the essentials in a
very few strokes.

The third alternative for this project is to
draw a self portrait. For this of course you
must have a mirror, large enough if possible
to be able to see the whole of your figure in
one view. Your most available model is after
all yourself and although the necessity to be
in a position to draw and yet be able to see
yourself in a mirror is a trifle limiting, you will
find that with some ingenuity a large number of
poses *are* possible. Two large mirrors can be
placed so that even back views can be seen and
drawn. A great deal can be learned from self-
portraiture; for many artists it has been a
constantly recurring theme, sometimes
combining the self portrait with other figures
seen in the mirror.

You may find it interesting to draw yourself
from the mirror with one or more other figures,
or dressed in a variety of costumes.

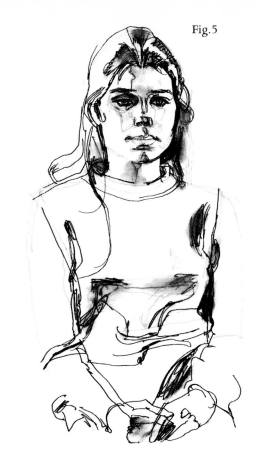

Fig.5

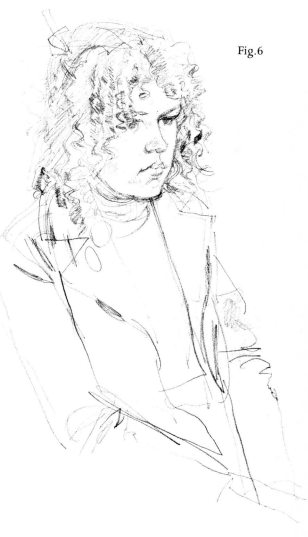

Fig.6

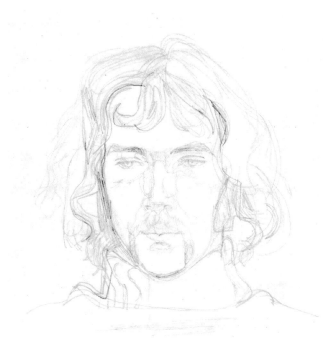

Fig.4

Character

Project 3

I have throughout the preceding sections made no mention of the possibilities of drawing from more than one model at a time.

Perhaps I have been remiss by the omission, but I have been conscious of the difficulty and the cost of arranging sessions with two or more models. If you have pursued the course so far though, you may have acquired a number of model contacts and have enough enthusiastic members of your drawing group to be able to consider hiring or persuading two people to pose together.

The interest and possibilities are heightened enormously, whatever the area of interest, by the juxtaposition of two figures. The composite shapes and volumes which are made by the two figures in contact or even entwined as one, seem almost limitless. There is the added

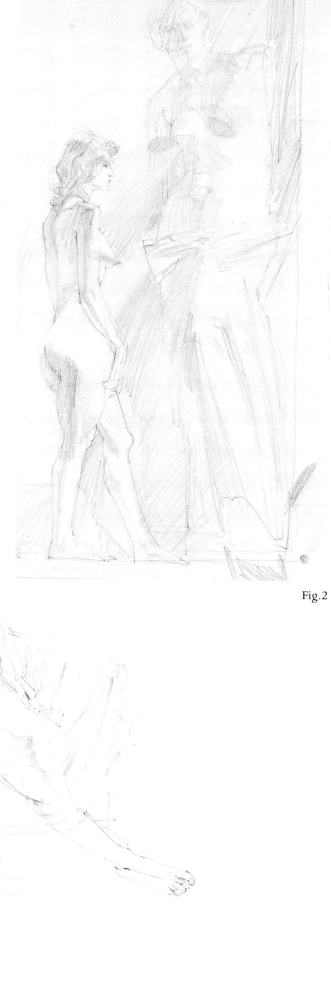

Fig.1

Fig.2

bonus that the 'two headed monster' is an unfamiliar shape and therefore more likely to be drawn without preconception.

Placing the figures physically apart but connected by line of sight, or by compositional tensions (more of this in the section on Composition) opens up further possibilities, and it hardly needs to be said that the introduction of more figures, singly or in groups, expands the permutations to infinity.

For the purposes of this particular exercise you should choose as models, two people of dissimilar type and/or age. The greater the contrast between them the easier will be the task of stressing the differences, but you may enjoy the challenge of discovering the more subtle disparities between similar types.

Fig.3

My two models in the drawings here, while contrasting strongly in terms of bulk and age, seem to be rather similar facially, almost as mother and daughter although they are in fact unrelated.

The drawing of the model with a plaster cast of the Venus de Milo records non-intentional juxtaposition which occurred in the liferoom of an art school, at the time when it was standard practice to surround students with many such greco-roman casts. Most of the great draughtsmen have spent some time drawing from the 'antique'. Unfortunately during the Victorian period in England, the practice of drawing from these plaster casts became so laboriously pursued with such painstaking attention to detailed and highly photographic, rather sterile, rendering that the practice fell into disrepute. As a result very few of these lovely plaster casts are to be found outside the museums nowadays. If there are any accessible to you I suggest that it would be rewarding to go and make some drawings of them, if only to underline the differences between the classical view of the figure and

your own observation of real life. I found the extreme contrast of the sharp forms of the ex-stripper model and the rounded idealism of the Venus, not to mention the enormous size differential, to be rather amusing.

199

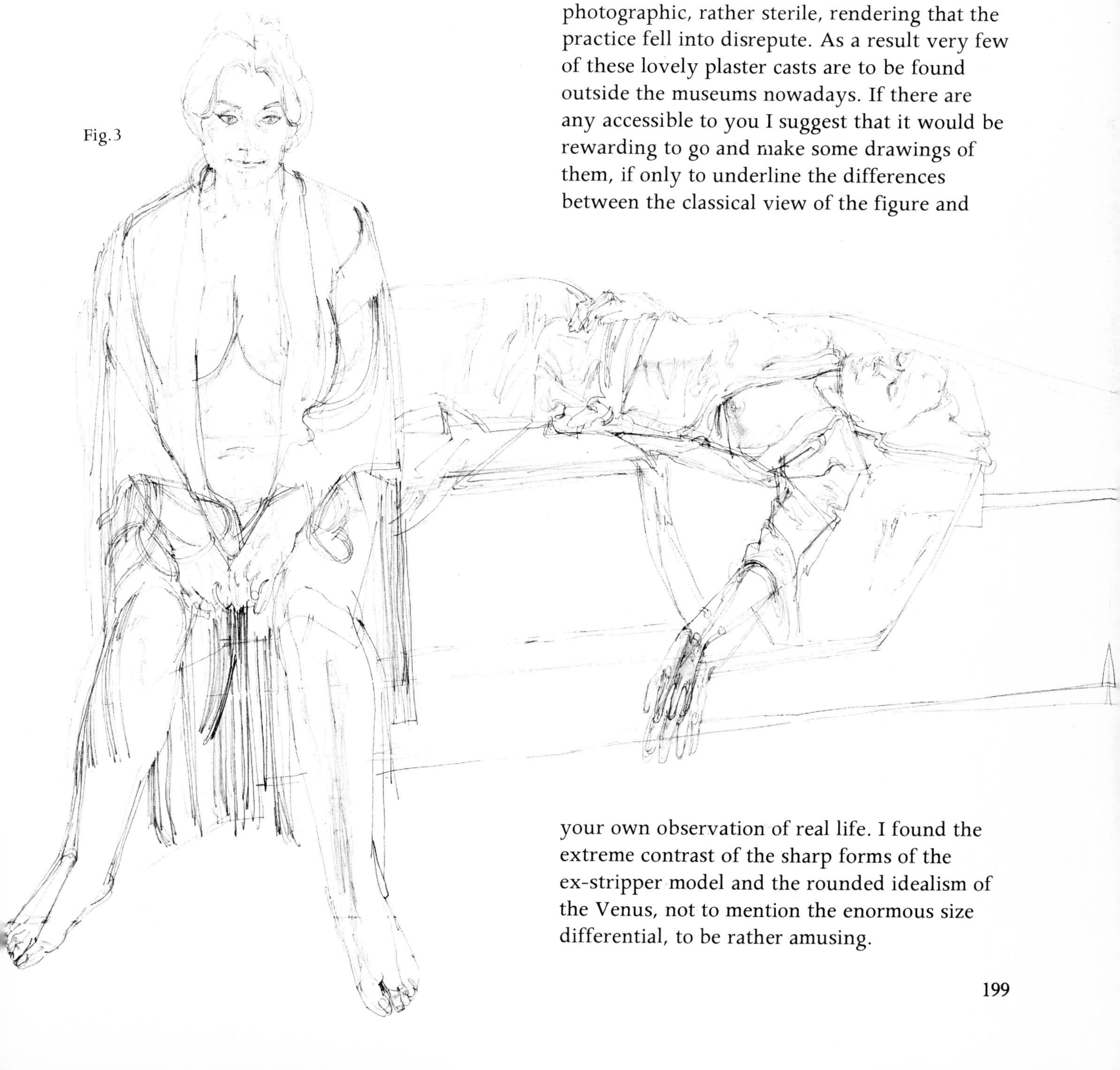

Character

Project 4

Elderly people are always interesting to draw, and are obviously particularly suitable when exploring character.

Habitual expressions gradually become etched on faces as the skin grows less elastic, producing the tracery of lines associated with old age. Revealing though these patterns are of character, if you can persuade an elderly person to pose for you, you will discover that there is more to ageing than superficial creasing.

Allow your elderly model to adopt a pose which is comfortable and natural. Try to establish a relaxed atmosphere, converse with your model, watch carefully and only begin to draw when you are sure that the model is not consciously posing and is truly relaxed.

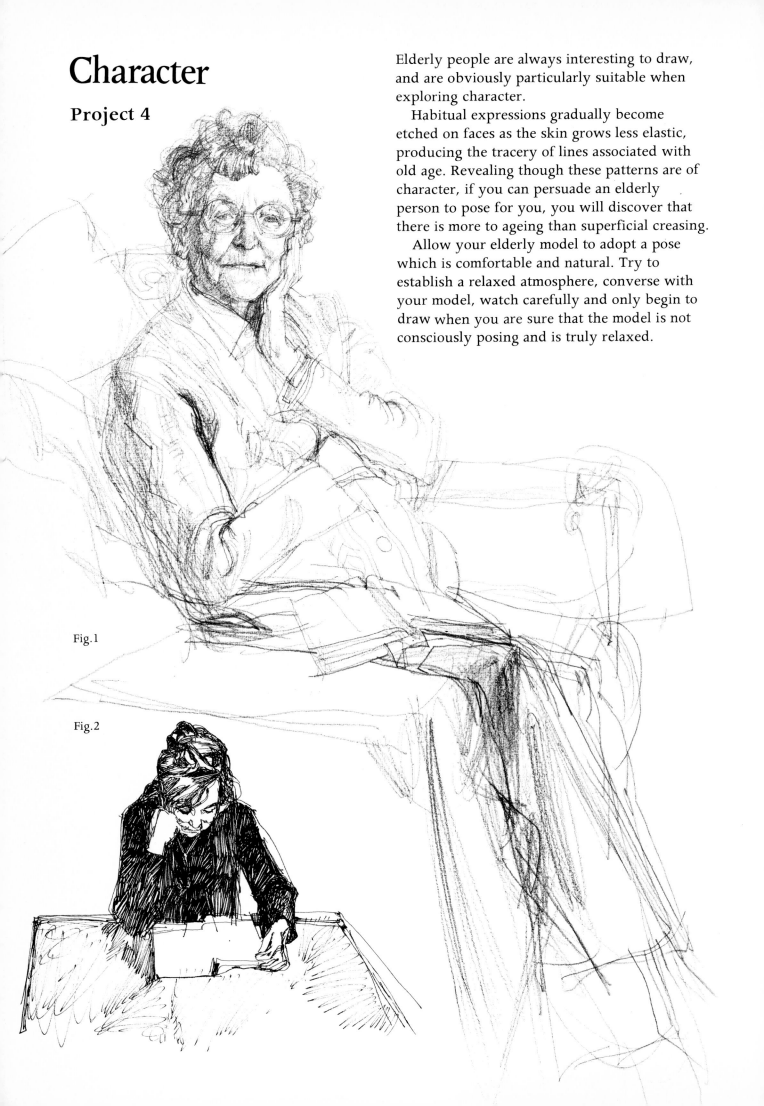

Fig.1

Fig.2

You will find that there will be something about the whole attitude that expresses the age and character of your sitter. Try to analyse this and either establish it first or have it in your mind as you start with the head.

When analysing the face, look for the bony structure of the skull which is often much more prominent in an elderly person, due to slacker tissue and musculature. In many cases atrophy of the lower jaw, especially where most or all of the natural teeth have been lost, contributes to further looseness of tissue around the jaw and neck.

Observe the way the head is held – it may be excessively upright or bowed, but nearly always different from the posture of a young person. Hands and arms too are revealing. Joints in elderly people are often arthritic and enlarged, and seem more so because the musculature has atrophied.

Watch how the clothes hang and what they tell you of the forms beneath. Shoulders, elbows, knees, may be sharper, the chest hollower, abdomen rounder.

On the other hand none of this may apply – I seem to be creating a preconception of total decrepitude – your model may present a picture of blooming health and robustness.

The essential thing is to be looking beyond and beneath the wrinkles to search out more fundamental character features.

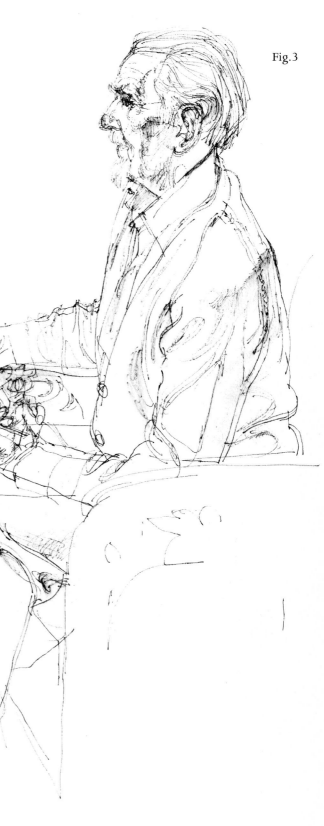

Fig.3

201

Movement

Mobility in the human figure has always posed special problems for the artist.

Before the discovery of photography the only way to draw a figure in the course of violent action was to remember a fleeting momentary glimpse, relate it to the positions at the beginning and the end of the action, and hope that it was somewhere near right. Poses in mid-action could be simulated of course, and held long enough for studies to be made, but such simulations always lack conviction.

The problem is that locomotion on two legs at the most gentle rate is only possible by successively losing balance and regaining it.

This can readily be appreciated by considering what happens when running or walking if the leg which is *not* taking the weight of the body at any given moment, is prevented from moving forward to take *its* turn at supporting – the body crashes to the ground. Running is falling forwards, being caught and pushed forwards onto another potential fall and caught again by the other leg and so on, until the decision is made to stop, when the forward fall is arrested and equilibrium resumed.

It follows that any attempt to hold a pose representing any frozen moment of the action is impossible because it must be a position of total imbalance. Various supports can be devised to enable a basically unbalanced position to be maintained, but this can never be entirely satisfactory, as the dynamics of the body adjust to the newly introduced props, achieving static balance again which is just what running is not.

Slower action *can* be analysed by eye as I will explain in the first project, but really fast ones can only be guessed at or suggested by

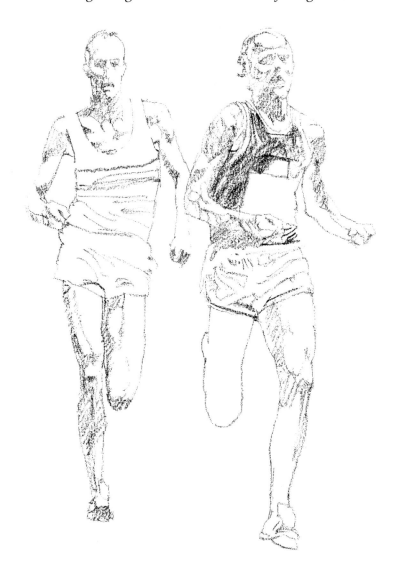

Fig.1

drawing the static beginning or end of the movement.

When the figure leaves the ground altogether, as in jumping, there is just no possibility of making any thorough analysis of the action by eye. Again guesses can be made and universally accepted conventions established for representing certain actions. Horses depicted with the front legs stretched forwards together and the back legs backward, were accepted for centuries as galloping, until high speed photography revealed how the legs really moved in the gallop.

It has to be admitted that artists of the past have made better guesses about the movement of the human figure than they did about the horse, movable models helping in this respect no doubt. Such models range from very simplified to beautifully shaped and articulated versions of the human figure. Usually made of wood and supported somewhere around their centre of gravity, they can be easily manipulated into a great variety of active poses, some possible in reality, some impossible. By experimenting a little it is possible to come up with some convincing looking simulations of actions. However they lack dynamics and I am not sure whether the sense of conviction engendered is not due to the memory of a photographic version of the action – i.e. *before* photography there would have been no correct visual idea to match with the lay figure. The models were probably not developed for the purpose of simulating action anyway. Their primary use was as life size substitutes for the live subjects of portraiture. Clothed in the appropriate garments they would be left in the chosen position indefinitely while the robes and regalia were painted, the important sitter only requiring to be present when the painting of head, hands etc. was undertaken.

So, it seems, if we are to draw movement in these days when the frozen photographic instant is commonplace, we really have no alternative, at least for the speedier actions, but to turn to photographs for information.

The succeeding projects suggest how you can make best use of them.

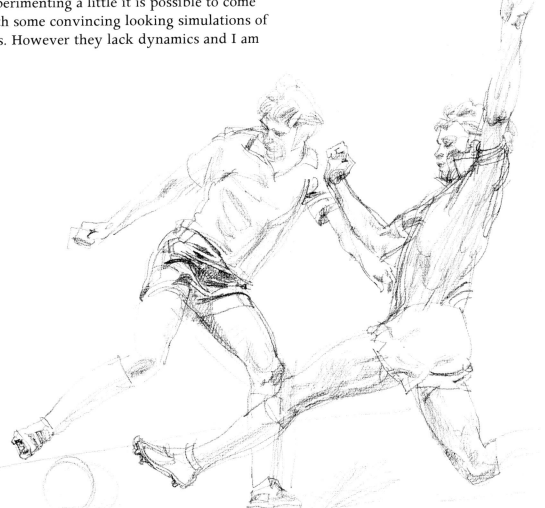

Fig.2

Movement

Project 1

Even an action as seemingly simple as walking was not fully understood until sequence photography made it possible to analyse every stage of the movement. Curiously enough the same kind of analysis *is* possible without the use of the camera.

First ask your model to walk across the studio slowly, turn and walk back again and repeat this sequence continuously. Take any moment in this continuous action and try to freeze some small feature of it in your memory. Draw that feature, wait for the exact moment of the movement to be repeated and note

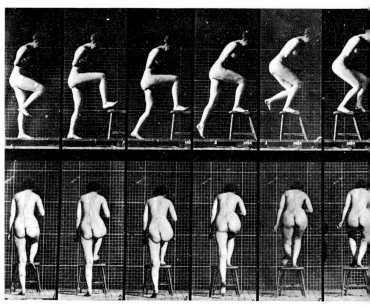

Fig.2

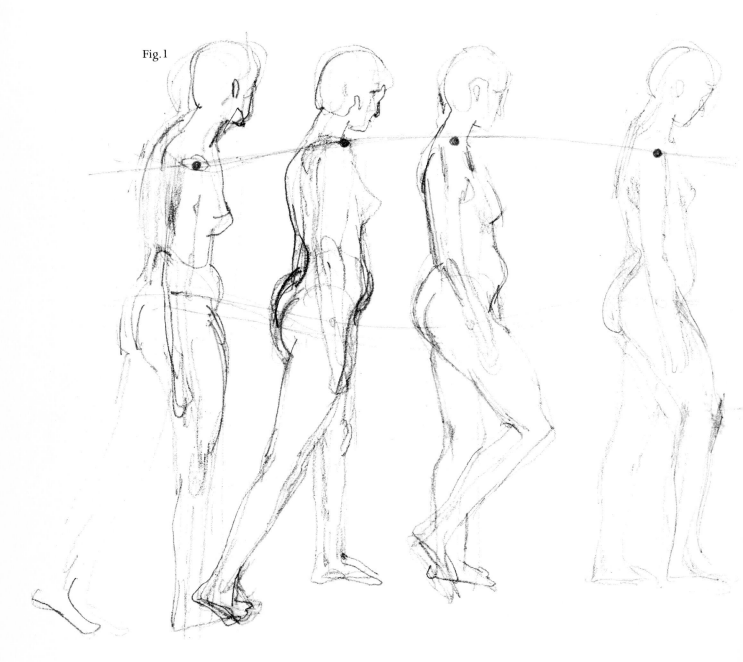

Fig.1

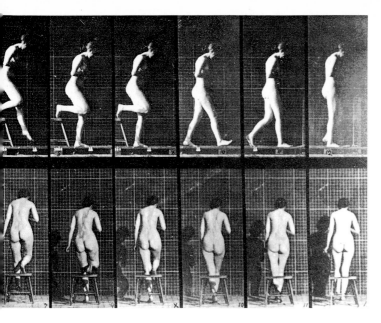

A Muybridge sequence of photographs.

Nude descending a staircase, No. 2. 1912, by Marcel Duchamp. This representation of movement was specifically inspired by Muybridge's photographs. Philadelphia Museum of Art, Pennsylvania. The Louise and Walter Arensberg Collection.

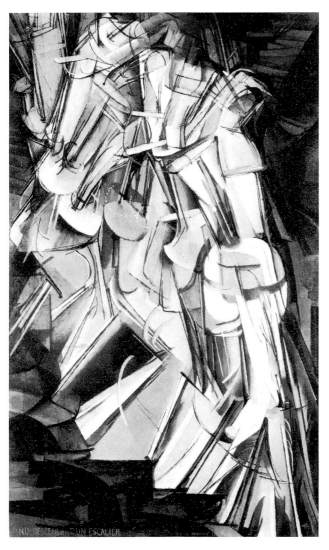

another feature. The sort of things to look for are pelvis swing, head carriage, shoulder tilt, weight distribution and balance shift indicated by position of head over weight-taking foot.

A picture of one instant of the action can be built up in this way.

Next a succeeding moment in the action can be observed and recorded in the same way, and then another, as long as you and your model's stamina lasts.

If you have analysed accurately and in sequence it will be obvious that walking is a succession of changes of balance and imbalance, a sort of falling forward over each succeeding supporting leg. In the first drawing of my sequence (fig.1), the weight is just shifting to the right leg, and at this moment the right shoulder is dropped to achieve balance as the left leg is swung forward. The head is well forward of the weight-taking foot, so we know that the figure is about to fall forward. As it does so the left leg has finished its forward swing and taken up the duty of main support as in stages 2 and 3, the left shoulder dropping to allow the right leg in turn to swing forward. Since it is a slow walk the arms are fairly static, but in faster action they swing forward with alternate legs.

Subsequently two lines have traced the movement of the functionally vital points of shoulder and hip, and show how they rise and fall alternately in a fluid motion.

It won't be possible for you to make very finished or detailed drawings this way; it does require quite intense observation just to produce little sketches like these, but the exercise helps real understanding of the action and speeds up your reactions.

You should find it interesting to compare your results with the Muybridge photographic series. If you didn't manage to make an on-the-move analysis, try analysing the movement by copying the photo sequence. The Marcel Duchamp painting, reproduced on this page, was an attempt to reproduce movement that was specifically inspired by Muybridge photographs.

Fig.3

Movement

Project 2

For this project and the next one a live posed model will not be needed. Instead, collect mid-action photographs of running and jumping athletes from magazines or newspapers or any other available source.

Having found a sharp photograph of an instant of an action, you could of course just look at it and draw from it, tone for tone, until you have produced a facsimile, but this would be a pointless exercise. There must be some selection of the information and some statement made about the action. To do this, you need to be able to understand the complete action of which you are to draw a small part.

In order to understand the action of running, you will need a number of photographs so that all stages of the action, and several views and types of individual, are depicted.

Sort your collection into groups of similar views and try to find examples of every stage of a stride which can then be placed in order. In one photograph of runners together in a race it is sometimes possible to find represented all the main stages of a typical running stride, which is helpful as the view and the lighting are then constant. More probably you will have to look at quite a large number of shots to find complete sets from several views.

To explain what you might be expected to cull from a reasonably full series of related photographs I refer you to the succession of drawings below (fig.1).

Starting from the left, the first two drawings are of stages of the running stride when both feet are off the ground. The body has been propelled forwards by the runner's left leg, the right leg is on the way to the ground for the next stride. In picture 3 contact with the ground has been made by the right leg which is slightly bent to absorb the shock of the body weight.

At the same time the left thigh is being swung

Fig.1

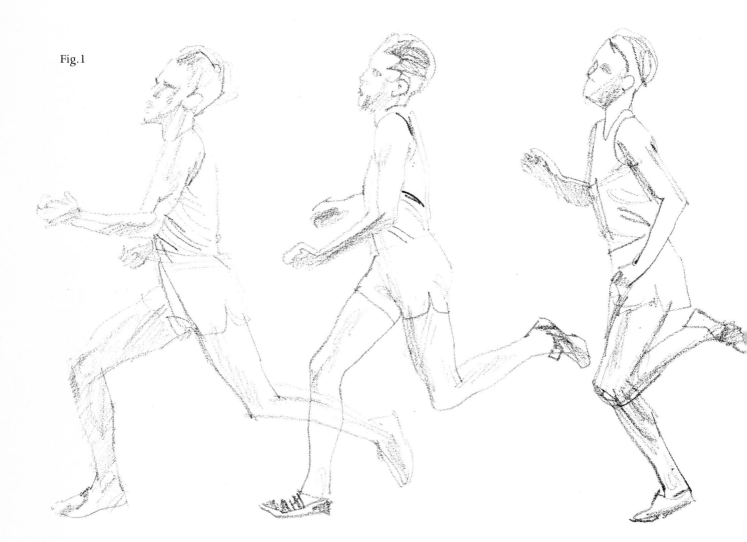

206

forward in preparation for the next stride, the lower leg and foot in typical flexion ready to be kicked downwards and forwards. As take-off from the right leg begins (4th drawing) the swing downwards of the left calf is initiated, until in the last drawing it is ready in its own turn to catch the weight of the body and pivot it forward over the contact point.

Side-to-side balance is beautifully maintained by weight shift from one side of the pelvis to the other, compensated by arm and shoulder movement. Notice how the right arm follows the left leg forward and vice-versa.

So it goes on, until the forward movement is arrested by a backward body lean and check steps. There are small variations dependent on personal style and speed. The smaller stride of jogging does not match the movement of a full sprint, but the basic action is universal.

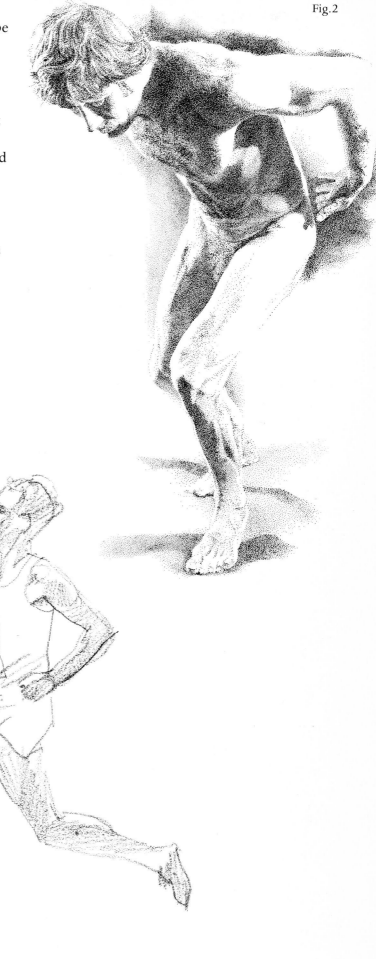

Fig.2

Movement

Project 3

More collections of photographs are now needed, this time of clothed figures in vigorous action, which are rather less easy to come by.

What you should be hoping to find are instances where the violence or speed of the action has thrown or stretched the clothing into interesting or unpredictable shapes.

In the sporting field, there are some activities that are fairly well clothed; golf and cricket are examples in which normal clothing is spasmodically subjected to extreme stresses (figs.2 and 3).

Just copying the photographs without thought or selection will not help you to understand the action, as I have said, and with clothed figures there is the added need to understand the dynamics of the clothing. When drawing from pictures of golfers like these for example, you should look for the tense pulls in the cloth and draw them very firmly, concentrating more on their direction than on their every individual shape. Try to express the comparative slackness of rucked cloth by looser marks, almost letting the pencil feel its way loosely in your grasp in contrast to the firm incisive grip with which you make the stretched folds.

Fig.1 is a drawing resulting from analyses of three stages of a judo throw overlaid one over the other. The resultant pattern of shape has more movement in it than any one of the stages drawn on its own.

Fig.1

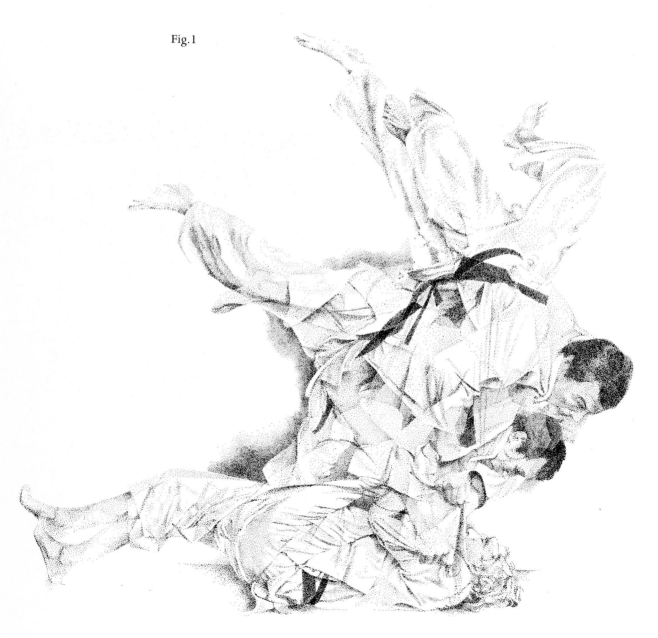

Fig.2

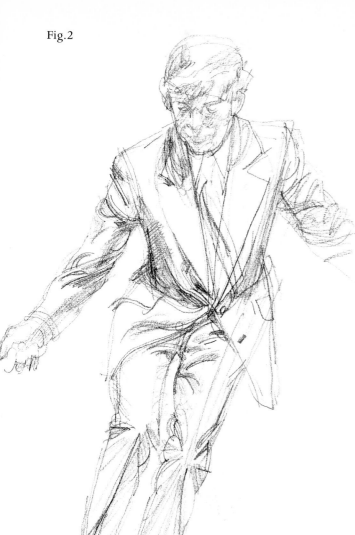

paper and *then* superimpose them. The final
drawing can then be made from the arrangement
that looks best.

How strongly each successive stage is drawn
relatively to the others has to be a matter of
judgement as the drawing progresses, in order
to achieve a pattern of shapes and rhythms
which best express the whole movement.

Lines of tension in clothing, for example,
which are present in all the stages and whose
shapes reinforce the direction of movement can
be treated strongly, while detailed rendering
of one peripheral part of one stage of the
action might tend to arrest it.

Fig.3

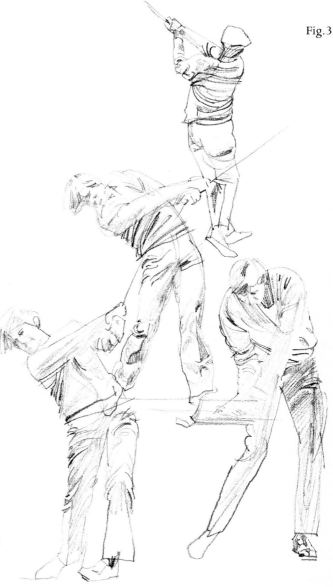

If you are lucky enough to find a series of
photographs like this, usually taken at 4 or 5
frames or more per second with a motor driven
camera, you could try the same. Three
successive actions are usually enough to cope
with, especially if more than one figure is
involved. It helps if there is one part of the
action which remains fairly stable throughout
the stages – a pivot point for example. This will
then be drawn only once while the rest of the
action is repeated one or more times, so
providing the stable point about which the
drawing will appear to rotate.

It is fairly difficult to superimpose stages by
drawing direct, and much easier to make
separate drawings of the stages on tracing

Composition

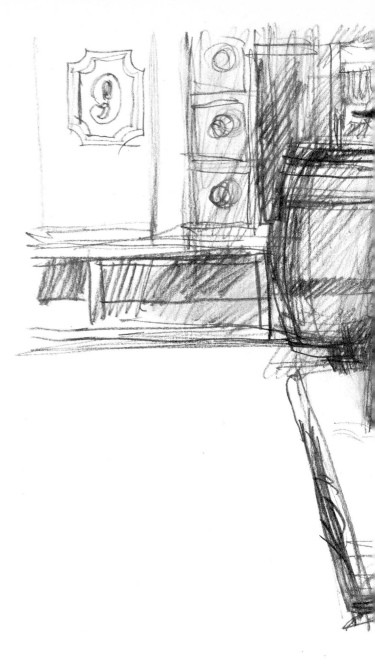

Composition as applied to drawing and painting is nothing more or less than the arrangement of the various elements of a picture on the drawing surface or within the frame.

Drawings, more often than not, do not completely cover the available picture area, but the untouched areas are nonetheless important elements in the composition. Every time you make a mark on an otherwise blank surface you make a start on a composition; the first line, by its placing establishes symmetry or assymmetry to what was immediately before featureless.

When placing a figure drawing on a sheet of paper you should always be conscious of the shapes and areas which are left untouched around it, and how they affect the 'balance' of the page.

Compositional balance is a hard thing to define. Absolute symmetry is clearly balanced and can be very satisfying, but it can also become boring and in any case the human figure is rarely seen symmetrically.

In abstract terms, if a main element, say a sitting figure, is moved away from the centre, it can be thought of as a weight tending to tip the picture about a central fulcrum. Depending on just where and what shape the figure is, the actual area of the larger space may be sufficient on its own to balance the off centre figure.

This concept is more difficult to accept and understand verbally than it is visually. The diagrams here clarify my meaning I hope. Fig.2(a) shows a seated figure placed to the left of the centre of a featureless background. The composition is reasonably satisfying, the shapes of figure and background area seeming to be acceptably balanced. There is however another factor contributing to the success of this arrangement which is underlined in fig.2(b), in which the same position in the composition is occupied by a left-to-right reversed version

of the figure. The reason why this looks unbalanced while the first one does not, is that the figure is facing out of the picture. Whichever way a figure is facing, and in a sense looking, the viewer's eye seems to be directed the same way, so that if it is towards the centre of the picture a larger space is felt to be satisfactory and necessary. When the figure is placed as in fig.2(b), the viewer's eye is led immediately out of the picture.

Fig.2(c), shows diagramatically the way that

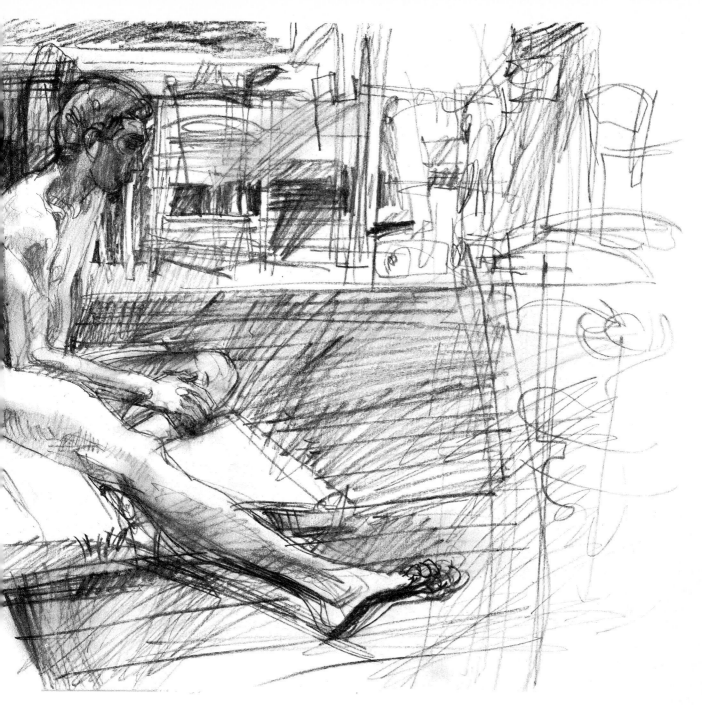

Fig.1

an outward facing figure could be balanced by use of a large area of tone of medium weight. Smaller features of greater contrast can be made to do the same job rather more precariously (fig.2d).

It is almost impossible to be definitive about what is or is not a good composition. I can only introduce some of the elements that have to be considered and urge you to look analytically at the compositions of the past masters.

Fig.2

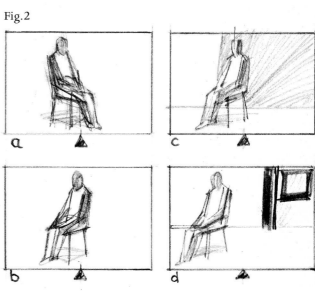

Composition

Project 1

It is always advisable to move around the model viewing the pose from several angles and eye levels before settling on your chosen viewpoint. So often I see a group of students in a life class, having established their places before the model has been posed, placidly accepting their view of the model without question.

While this is no doubt exemplary behaviour I think I would prefer a few minutes of mild chaos as everybody moved about and jockeyed for the best positions. Although it is true that there is something to be said for searching out the interest in a viewpoint that one is stuck with but would not normally have chosen, I think on balance it is better to find a view which strikes an immediate chord.

Hopefully in a fairly small group there will be room for some choice of viewpoint and I suggest that for this project you explore the compositional possibilities of one set-up from several different drawing positions. Don't forget that distance from the model and height of eye level are both variables to be added to the angle changes to produce different compositions.

Figs.1 to 8, give some indication of the variety of compositions available from just one reclining pose on a bedstead, and these are only a few of the almost limitless variations.

If you are sharing the model with other students, they will frequently be in vision as you change your view of the model, in which case I think you should not hesitate to include them in your drawing. This does not mean that everything in your view should necessarily be included – you have the absolute right to reject and select at will to make the most exciting composition.

Aim to make at least two, preferably three or four compositional sketches in a two-hour period, which will require some pretty incisive and economical drawing if they are to be reasonably accurately organised. Obviously too much time must not be spent on the figure alone but it would be pointless to evolve a composition in which the figure lacked conviction.

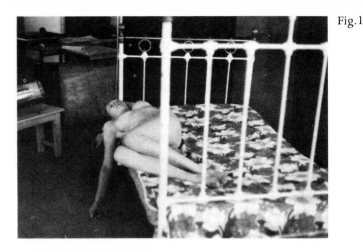
Fig.1

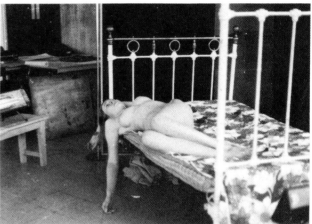
Fig.2

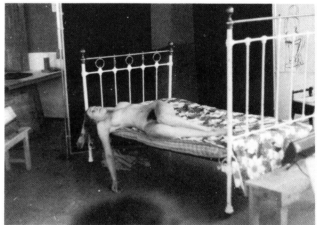
Fig.3

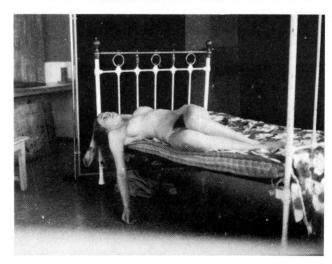
Fig.4

Fig.5

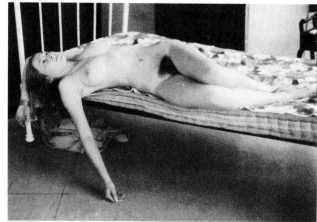

Fig.7

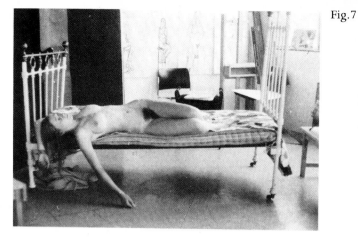

Fig.6

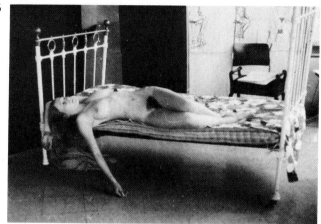

Fig.8

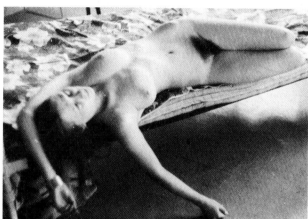

Fig.9

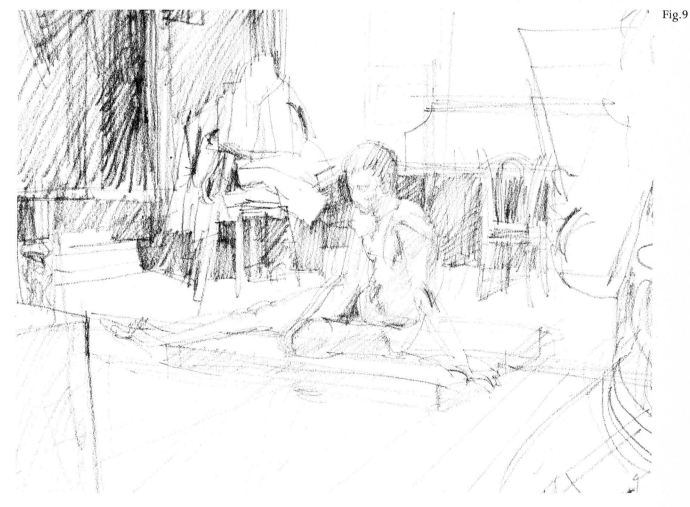

Composition

Project 2

Place the model in a cluttered situation so that the figure is only one of the many objects in view, not necessarily dominant or visible in entirety.

It is to be hoped that you may have acquired a few props in your studio by now, easels, boxes, lengths of material and the like. It is worth taking some time to create an environment for the model which is complex and varied in form and texture. The photographs here show views of the type of arrangement I have in mind, although they can be devised to render the figure even less conspicuous amongst a greater variety of objects. The limits on such compositions are set only by your ingenuity and the time available. One art school that I visited recently had set up an environment of the most incredible complexity and richness of form. Objects as varied as musical instruments, animal skulls, garments, household utensils, were suspended on strings at various levels, and the model was posed in the middle. It took a day or two to devise and it was left up for two weeks or three weeks so that all the possibilities of juxtaposition of objects and figure could be explored.

If a suitable location is accessible to you and climate permits, it is worth doing a composition of this sort outdoors, where natural forms can be used to surround and partly obscure the model. (Fig. 1.)

When drawing your own figure-enclosing environment, look as always, for composite patterns of shape. Parts of the set-up, however recognizable they may be as objects which, when separated, can have an entity of their

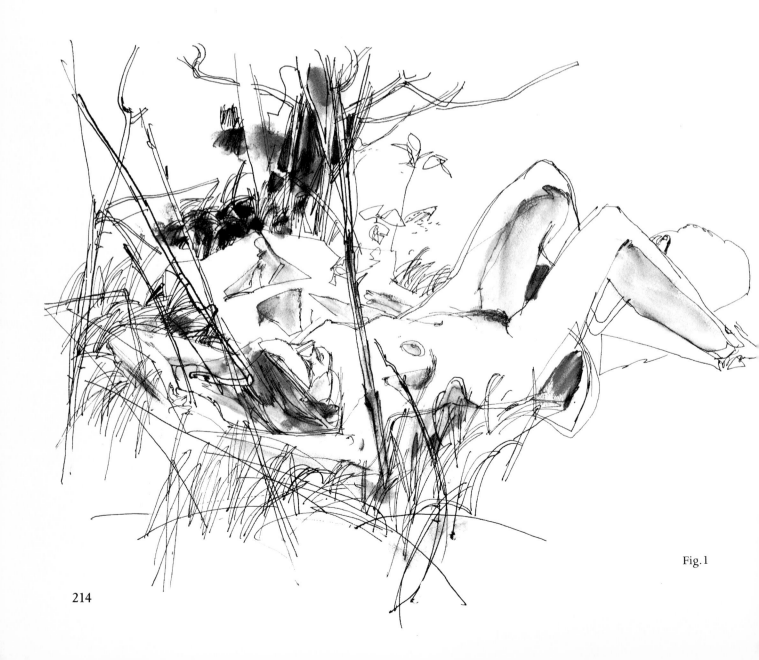

Fig. 1

214

own, should be looked upon only as forms interacting with the whole.

Apertures through or between forms through which the figure can be seen, define the shape of the figure almost as a grid.

In the drawing, fig.3, an aluminium ladder frames the head and shoulders of the model, which makes a mini composition within the main one.

The shapes 'left' around the figure in this frame must be considered as carefully as those of the figure itself. Moreover the amount of her breast that is seen to the left of the ladder upright has to match what is seen and also be in the right position to link with the rest of the figure. For this to work, the *thickness* of the upright must be correct, and so on – every shape is dependent on and helps to define every other one. If one is wrong all are wrong, but there are so many cross-checking points and shapes, that if an honest, diligent search is made the whole thing will hold together and work as a total and satisfying interlocking pattern.

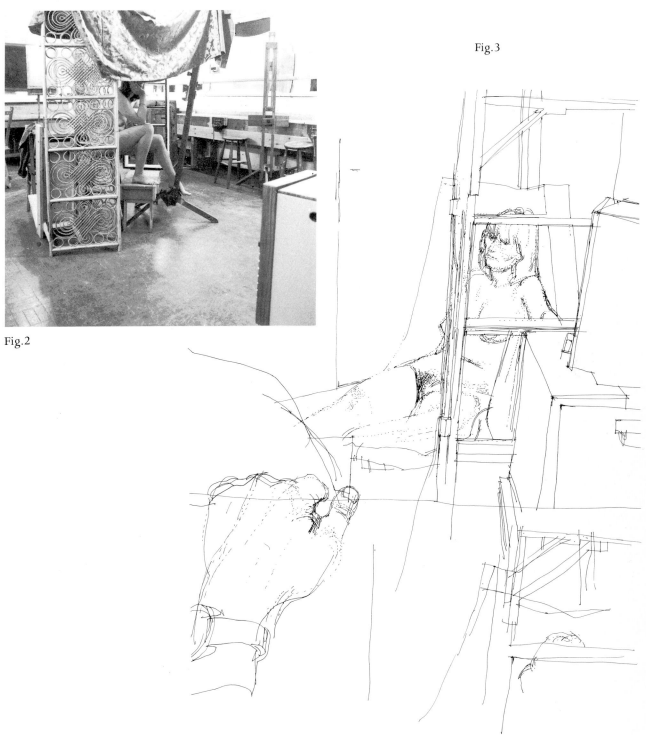

Fig.2

Fig.3

Composition

Project 3

I suggest that you now try some compositions in which space is a major element.

As it is essential to be able to get back some distance from the model, I realize that this could be a problem if only a small drawing studio is available.

If it is impossible to find the sort of space suggested by my composition, you could change venue, either as a group or singly, to a larger room, or even to an outdoor situation, weather permitting. It is not essential that the model should be nude for this exercise which should make it easier to arrange an alternative location.

The object of the exercise is to place the figure in a spacious environment in such a way that although the figure is a small element in the composition, it nevertheless commands attention.

One way to accomplish this is to place the figure absolutely in the centre of the picture with no competing areas of interest.

As I have said earlier, a symmetrical composition is fine if a still, ikon-like image is what you want. Otherwise try for slightly more testing asymmetric compositions.

The compositions shown here were both drawn in the life-drawing rooms of art schools, fig.2 in quite an old one, and the other in a very new college. In the older one, blue and grey painted wooden cupboards, boxes and tables mingled with plaster casts and other paraphernalia in a room dominated by pale grey and white walls.

By seating the model on top of the cupboards, high up in a corner, she was already in a focal point of interest in the composition. The model's throne and a box (or maybe it's a throne on its side) were placed to give more perspective lines leading to the figure, the cloth, feet, supporting table and pieces of plaster cast, adding incident to the corner in

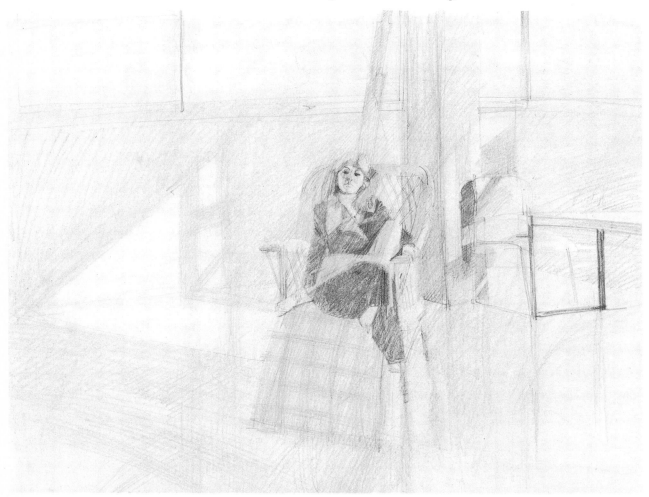

Fig.1

contrast to the large plain shapes elsewhere.

In the other composition (fig.1), the life room is on the top floor of a modern block, surrounded by windows and largely furnished with steel and plastic cupboards, chairs and tables. There are traditional easels, 'donkeys' and a number of the usual props, but the overriding feeling on a bright day is of light and reflection.

I thought that the contrast of the wicker arm chair in which the model is curled, and the thin steel and plastic shapes of modern chair and table, linked by the concrete pillar, was interesting in itself, but the composition is really about light and dark shapes.

What this drawing reminds me that I liked and maybe could develop later in painting, is the interplay of the dart-like shape of light on the floor and wall, the harder shadows of the plastic chair back on the concrete pillar, the reflections in the right hand floor area and the lights and darks of the figure itself.

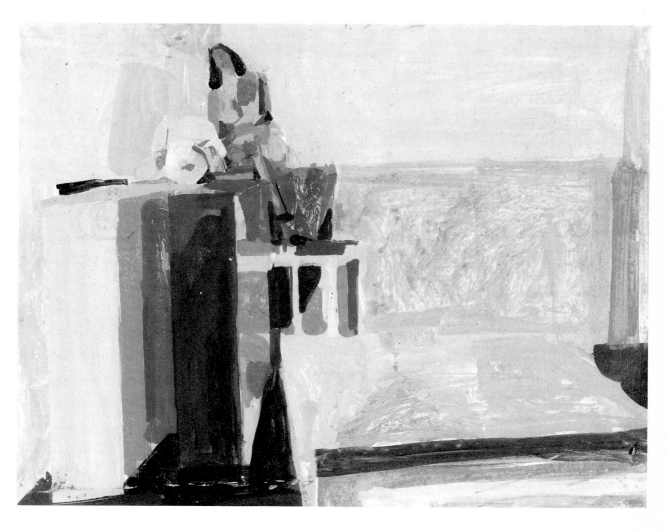

Fig.2

Composition

Project 4

Now move closer to the model to seek out compositions in which the figure is the dominating element.

Although it is possible to be some distance from the model and yet enlarge the figure to fill the picture area, it is generally not advisable, in my opinion.

For the reason why not, we have to consider another visual phenomenon.

When you look at a specific small object, your eye produces a clear sharp picture of that object *plus* a certain area of its surroundings. If your head is kept still, only this central area of vision is absolutely clear although *outside* it there is a much larger area of vision at the outer edges in which you can see movement and light but little else. The outer area of vision is designated peripheral, and the centre area is known as 60° cone of vision.

This cone is visualized in the diagram opposite. As you can see, the further away an object in a situation is, the more surrounding area is included in the cone of vision and the smaller the object becomes proportionately.

Now, there is a tacit assumption when viewing representational drawing or painting, or indeed photography, that the limits of the picture coincide approximately with the limits of the cone of vision. The photographer or the painter, in a sense, puts the viewer into the same position of view so that the complete scene is recreated.

If only part of the cone of vision is represented, or a lot more outside it, the effect is slightly strange and in extreme cases looks grossly distorted. The effect can be more clearly demonstrated by photography. A telephoto lens allows a photograph to be taken of a picture area which is only a small part of the unassisted cone of vision. When this part is enlarged to a normal picture, the perspective looks quite wrong, parallel lines seem not to be converging, and depth looks compressed. It is *not* in fact distorted, the perspective is absolutely correct, *for its original position in the cone of vision.* It looks wrong because the viewer assumes that it represents the complete cone of vision of a normal human eye, when it is in fact only a small, distant piece of it brought nearer by enlargement.

Conversely, a picture continued out of the cone of vision by drawing more and more of

Fig. 1

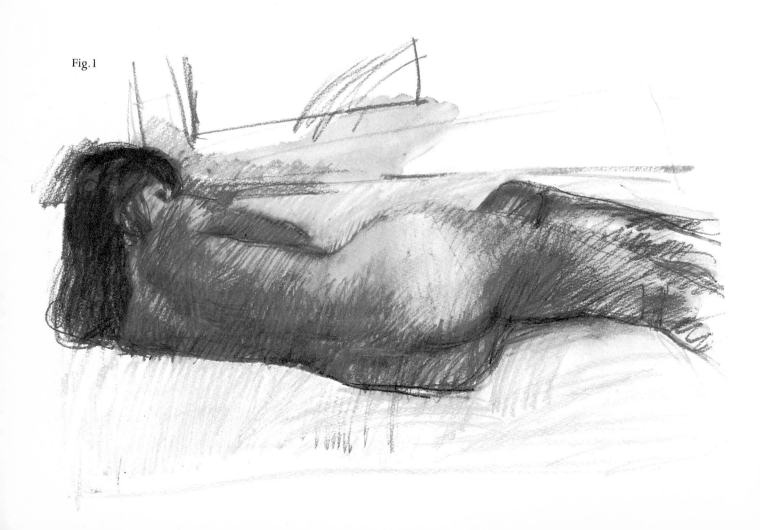

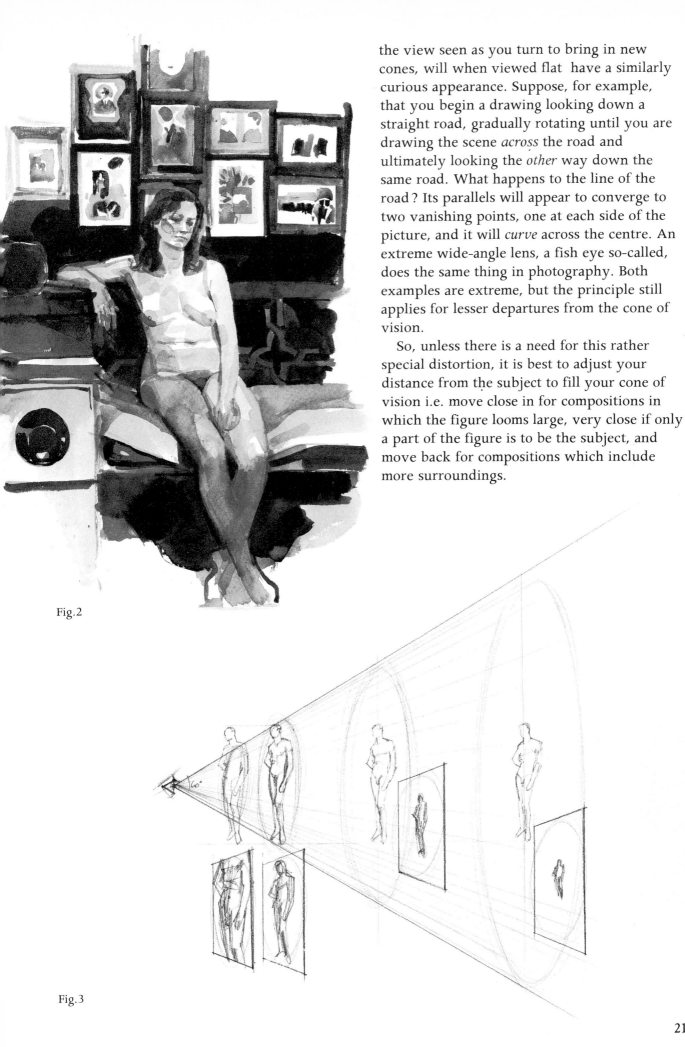

the view seen as you turn to bring in new cones, will when viewed flat have a similarly curious appearance. Suppose, for example, that you begin a drawing looking down a straight road, gradually rotating until you are drawing the scene *across* the road and ultimately looking the *other* way down the same road. What happens to the line of the road? Its parallels will appear to converge to two vanishing points, one at each side of the picture, and it will *curve* across the centre. An extreme wide-angle lens, a fish eye so-called, does the same thing in photography. Both examples are extreme, but the principle still applies for lesser departures from the cone of vision.

So, unless there is a need for this rather special distortion, it is best to adjust your distance from the subject to fill your cone of vision i.e. move close in for compositions in which the figure looms large, very close if only a part of the figure is to be the subject, and move back for compositions which include more surroundings.

Fig.2

Fig.3

Composition

Project 5

In this project the aim is to produce compositions involving several figures, but to do this with the aid of only one model.

In addition to being economical in model fees, it is an interesting and useful exercise in that the composition evolves before your eyes in a way that cannot entirely be foreseen and may produce groupings which you would not have arrived at by any other means.

Preferably there should be sufficient room available for you to be able to position the model at discernibly different distances from your viewpoint – the greater the distances, the more variety of possible scale.

The procedure then is simply to pose the model in your chosen environment, draw this pose with particular care to relate it accurately to the surroundings and then to set up new poses in the same environment, adding them progressively to the same drawing.

The resulting figure composition is never actually seen in totality except in your drawing – the environment only ever actually contains one figure at a time.

It is obvious therefore, that the relationship between the figures cannot be checked as you draw – each figure has to be related carefully to the fixed surroundings, the figure *inter*-relationships only becoming evident as each new figure is added.

It may be necessary to complete parts of the environment covered by the first pose in order to place the second pose accurately, and indeed it may sometimes be considered preferable to draw the environment completely before adding the figures.

For example, in fig. 2, the figures were posed in and on a scaffolding tower which has a dominating coherent structure of its own to which the figures must conform, and which could have been drawn completely and accurately before the figures were added, thereby also performing the function of a grid to help fix the poses. It is not necessary to do it this way though – in such a case each figure can be drawn in its immediate area by observing the interplay between its shape and the framing bars and the spaces, so evolving scaffolding and figures together.

Fig.1

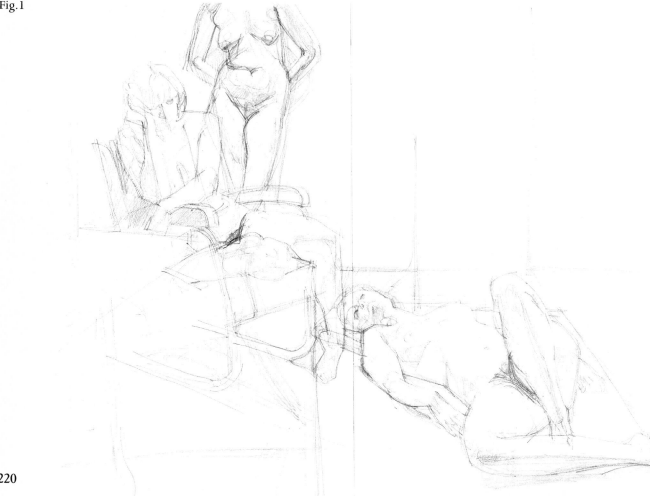

Drawing quickly and simply with charcoal will allow you to explore a number of compositional variations in this way, some of which may suggest groupings which can be contrived and studied rather more penetratingly on later sessions.

There is no reason, for instance, why a composite drawing should not be continued through several sessions, a carefully observed figure being added in each session to a carefully retained identical situation.

Be careful to ensure that succeeding poses do not occupy some of the same spatial volume as a previous pose, which would result in a feeling of unreality without convincing depth.

I feel bound to say that there are many visually fascinating possibilities resulting from multiple figure drawings which are intentionally *not* arranged to occupy space in a 'real' way, but then this is not strictly objective drawing and has moved beyond the declared compass of this particular study.

Fig.2

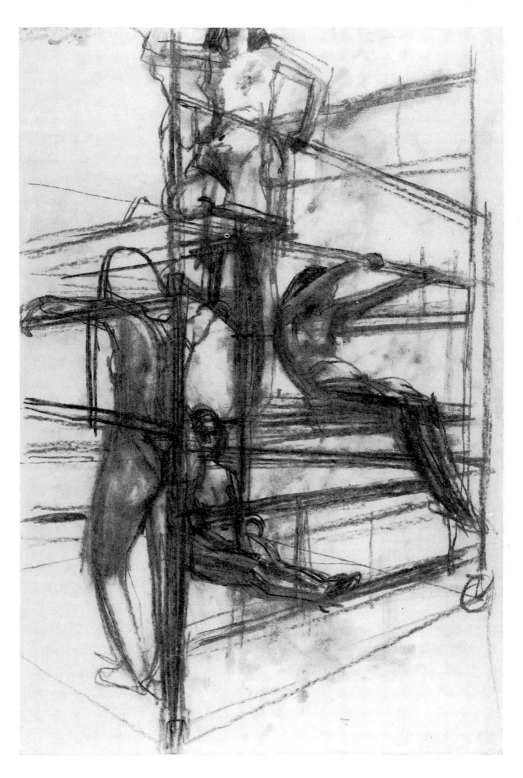

Creativity

We come now to an area that is rather difficult to define.

Until now I have been discussing ways of improving observation in order to make more and more incisive studies of the human form and I have stressed the need to search for information about reality and to record the discoveries in an economical and selective way. I consider this searching out and gathering in of information to be fundamental to objective drawing.

At its most basic level it can be thought of as the energizing and refuelling process for the creativity which is to follow.

Of course it is never quite so clear cut as this; each artist, however like a blank slate he tries to be, brings to observation some emotional response which colours even the most austere information gathering.

It is at the point where the artist turns away from the model, having seen and collated enough from direct observation and wants the emotional response now to be given freedom, that I think the emphasis changes from objective to creative.

Sometimes the transition from one to the other can be almost instantaneous, where information is taken in, emotionally processed and then given out in a variety of forms which may have little obvious objective resemblance to the original.

Letting a method or a medium have its head can sometimes provide the catalyst which pushes an objective study into the area of creativity. Similarly extreme selectivity in use of the discovered shapes can produce near abstractions.

My painting/drawing here is I suppose a bit of both. Certainly I was interested in the interplay of shapes in the figure and those on the floor, tables and walls, but the particular way that the washes took to the rough water colour paper had a lot to do with the decision to leave the shapes and forms so minimal.

Another way to influence the output is consciously to manipulate the input i.e. to change the real object by various devices *before* drawing it objectively. A few ways of doing this are described in the first project of this section.

Perhaps the whole creative idea will come from the imagination or from a desire to give form to a story or myth. The objective drawings may then be made purely to be used as reference material to populate the imaginary composition.

There are so many, many ways to extend drawing into increasingly esoteric areas of creativity that it would be impossible here to do more than suggest a few directions to begin exploring.

The following projects are intended to do just that.

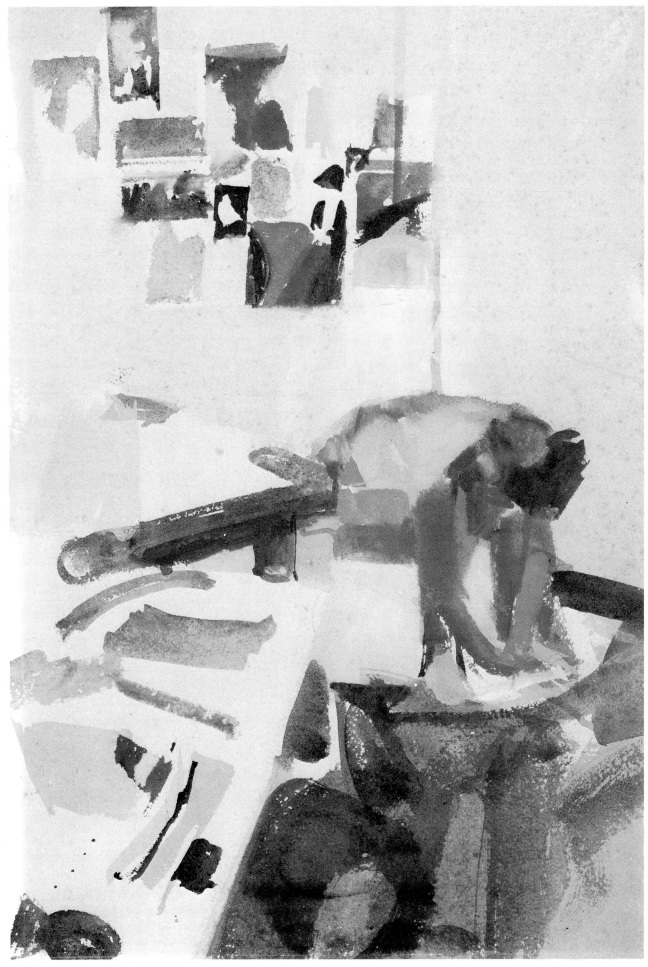

Fig. 1

Creativity

Project 1

Construct a complete situation for the model based on a particular composition or the general style of an established master.

Here are a few suggestions.

Find a reproduction of Manet's *Olympia* (which was itself based on *The Venus of Urbino* by Titian) and base a composition on it. Find fabric and pillows to make up a couch or bed in a similar way, pose your model similarly and draw the whole as a possible variation on the theme. The background figure could either be copied, or posed by the same model later, or even substituted by a vase of flowers or other decoration.

A Francois Boucher type of composition could be simulated if you have a young, reasonably pretty girl as a model. A typical Boucher would be a rather exhuberantly decorative pose with rich surroundings of drapery and bric-a-brac.

In many of his paintings Gustav Klimt nearly submerged the figures in boldly patterned fabrics, flatly represented. A set up of this type was the basis of my water colour drawing here (fig.1), which in black-and-white reproduction may very well conceal the figure even more than it does in the colour original. It is not absolutely necessary to draw these highly patterned compositions in colour, but it does help. The background fabric in this drawing is basically yellow with orange and purple decoration, the fabric wrapped around the figure is green, figured with blue and purple and there are tints and shades of these colours in the figure and around. Many of these colours are tonally undifferentiated and would merge if drawn in black-and-white, where a tonal value of grey must be allocated to represent every colour. It can be done and it can be interesting but it decreases the range of pattern possibilities.

You could try a Matisse *Odalisque* composition, of which he painted several, the name meaning 'female slave in a harem', although they are sometimes entitled *Decorative figure on an ornamental background*.

A 'captured instant' composition of the type inspired by documentary photography and exploited by Degas and Vuillard can be interesting to simulate. A bathed-in-light patterned domestic interior may not be beyond your ingenuity to create, à la Bonnard. There will be many other paintings and artists that will spark off ideas for situations that you can create which are rich and exciting.

Having spent some time making such an arrangement, it will be something of a waste to use it only for a two- or three-hour session. If you or your group can manage to find a few days or a week to extend the drawing into a painting, perhaps on canvas or a primed board, it will be found to be really worthwhile. It is amazing how much progress can be made in the understanding of figure drawing and painting in a concentrated period of a few days, as opposed to two-hourly sessions once a week.

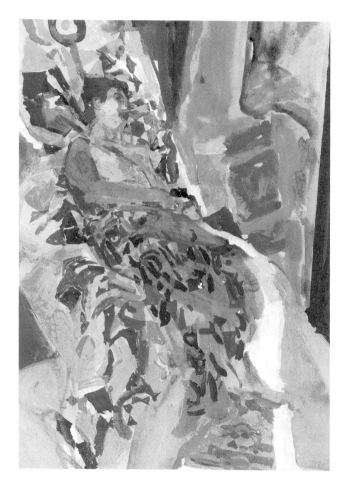

Fig.1

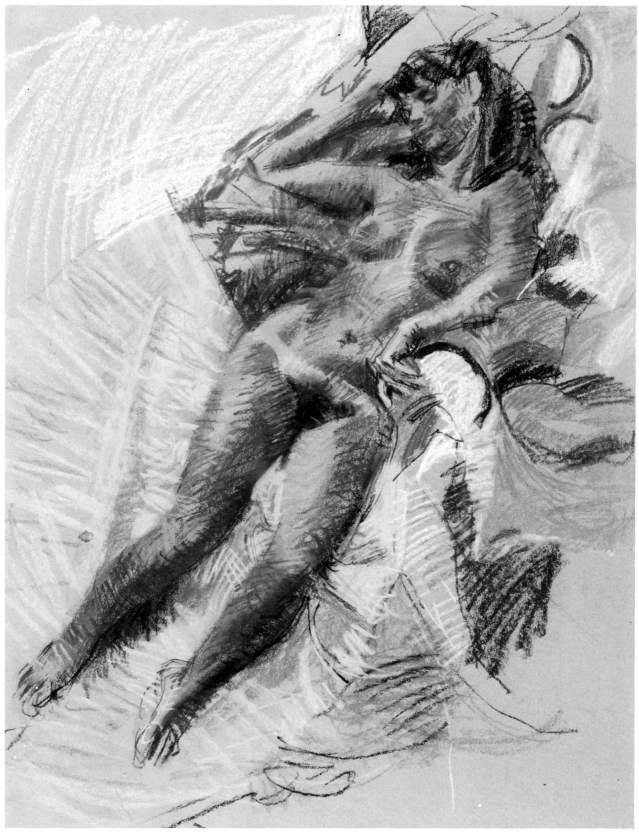

Fig. 2

225

Creativity

Project 2

Another completely different method of modifying reality before drawing involves the use of light, either generated or natural.

It only needs an ordinary 35mm slide projector, some empty slide holders and a few slide-size pieces of clear acetate, to provide almost infinite variations of patterns of light on your model.

Some clear acetates take pen lines or colour better than others – it is usually possible nowadays to obtain pads of clear film specifically designed to take ink and paint without problems. 'Artcel' and 'Drawfilm' are two current product names in this country. The thickness should be about the same as photographic film; very thin kitchen cellophane is no good.

Having found a suitable acetate film, draw a few simple patterns on it in areas equivalent to the picture area of the 35mm slide holder. Very simple regular patterns usually yield the best results, so initially at least, keep to various width and colour parallel lines or square grids. Fix the grids into the slide holders and load them into the projector-carrier.

When these slides are projected onto the

Fig.1

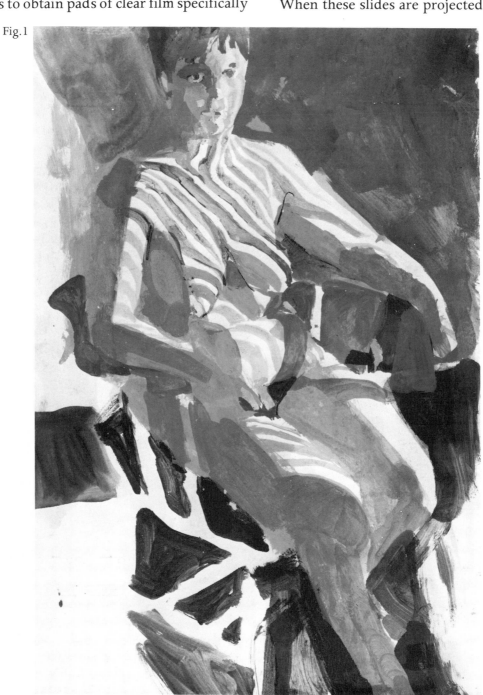

226

Fig.2

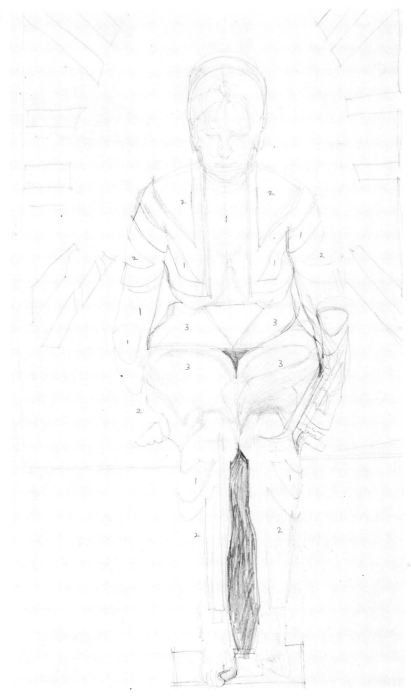

model in a fairly dark room, the most interesting linear patterns result as the projected grids are bent and twisted by the forms of the figure. Every change of position of the projector relative to the model results in a whole new set of patterns and the permutations are fascinating to observe.

Two problems have to be overcome in order to draw these patterns however. Firstly any change in the pose, however small, alters the projected patterns; even the model's breathing is revealed by a close textured regular grid, so it is essential to choose a pose where movement can be kept to the minimum.

Secondly, light for the drawing boards is hard to come by without drowning out the projected patterns. There will be some reflected light from walls, and a few shaded and carefully directed angle-poise lamps should do the trick, and you will probably have to adapt to drawing in more subdued lighting than usual.

The pencil drawing (fig.2) is a record of the result of projecting a slide of the union jack from a low central position in front of the model. Colours and shadow areas are labelled by numerals, No.1 denoting blue areas, No.2 red, and No.3 areas of total shadow.

Creativity

Project 3

As an extension of the last project in which lines were generated on the surfaces *before* drawing, I suggest that, with the patterns that you saw still in your mind, you return to drawing with line but using a line which makes its own patterns.

Choose a black ineradicable medium such as pen and ink, fine felt or fibre-tip pen, rapidograph or similar. Having set any pose which, from the previous projects, has been found to be interesting and worthy of further study, draw with an almost continuous line.

Let the pen wander over the forms, not following exterior outlines only, but wandering almost randomly over the surfaces as though describing the track of a fly as it clambers over the forms.

As you feel your way over the forms, try to sense the planes with the pen tip, almost as though you were running your finger tips over the surfaces with your eyes closed. You may begin to produce lines which surround high forms and proliferate in the hollows, like a computer-generated contour map.

Maybe your line-trailing fly will be attracted to the junctions of light and shade, in which case the wandering line may begin to build up a suggestion of tonality and illuminated form. The aim is to be watching and only loosely in control of a continuous series of random responses to intense observation. It has been called 'taking a line for a walk', and it can produce surprising results. At the very least it may free you from the tyranny, if you are still subject to it, of the linear outline.

The wandering line may actually ignore the outside edge of the figure altogether in places, and later on some tones may be filled in for no other reason than that it seems to make the pattern more interesting.

Another variation of the procedure is to look at the pose and before you start drawing, 'see' it in terms of a linear pattern. Draw that pattern only and then stop. Drawings figs.1 and 4, were of this type and fig.1 was more or less accidently wetted later which blurred the non-waterproof fibre pen line and I thought rather improved the pattern.

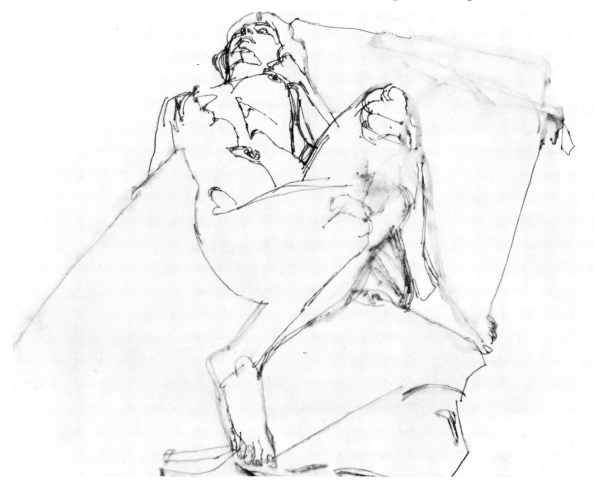

Fig.1

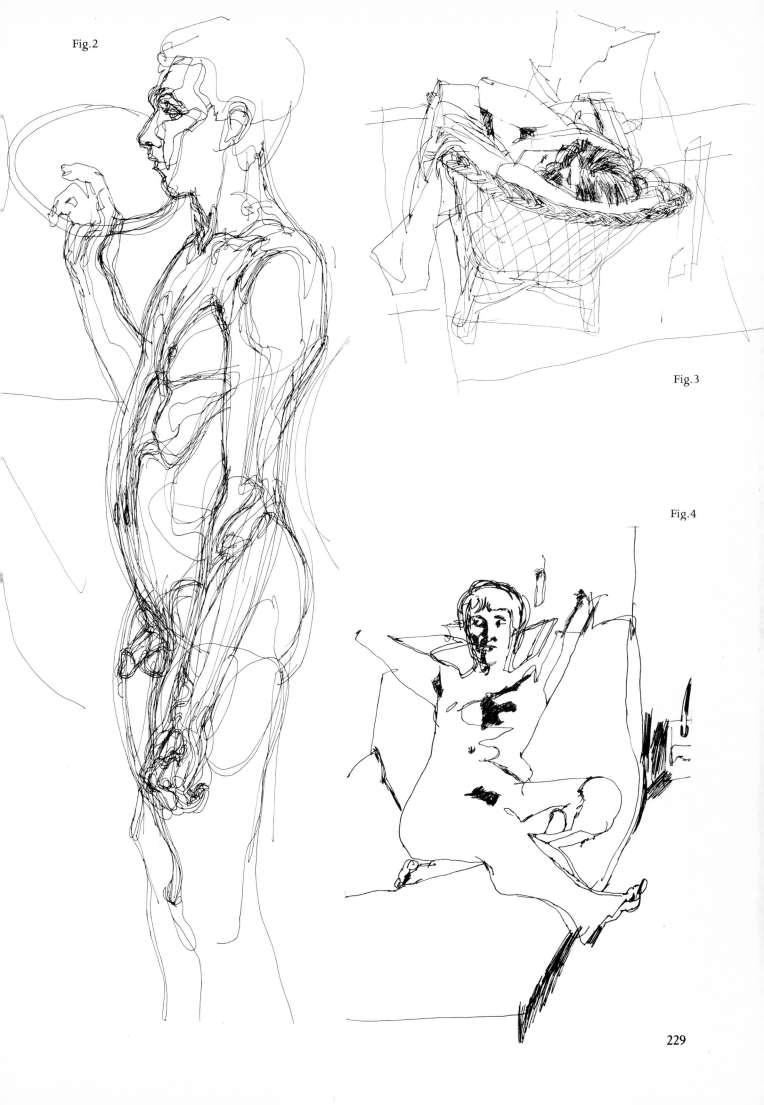

Fig.2

Fig.3

Fig.4

229

Creativity

Project 4

This last project has really just brought us to the beginning of the activity which has been the main motivation of drawing for centuries – that is original composition, for which drawings or studies are made.

Drawings were originally self sufficient perhaps, but since the Italian Renaissance at least, the primary function of figure drawing has been to gather information from life for use in figure compositions.

We now value many of these drawings as works of art in their own right, but they were only intended as working drawings. More recently, especially since the advent of printing, drawings have increasingly been made for their own sake, but the function of drawings as studies still remains relevant.

Moreover the necessity to record information which can be made use of later in a painting, makes sure that the drawing really does say something useful. A superficially pretty drawing which is fundamentally unsound is impossible to work from.

Reproduced here is a compositional scheme for a group portrait. Before this stage is reached a few or perhaps more than a few compositional ideas have been considered on a smaller scale, perhaps as thumbnail sketches, very abstract. One of these ideas is then developed further to determine more precisely the abstract relationship of the figures with all the other elements and areas. Some sketches may be made or polaroid photographs taken at this stage to confirm how much of the imagined grouping is possible. For further development as either a drawing or a painting, studies of the individual figures and other single elements can be made in poses and lighting as required by the overall compositional plan.

As the finished work progresses, figures may not work in the composition as well as you hope, and new studies may be made which in turn suggest new groupings and so on. Some elements of a painting are changed many times and require a large number of studies before final decisions are made.

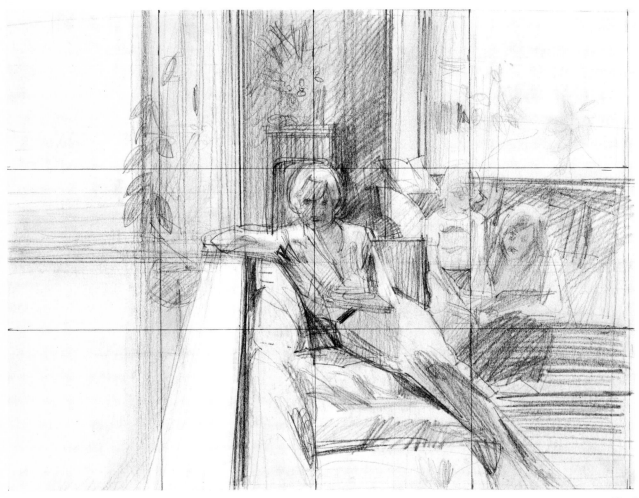

Fig.1

Such drawings may be absolutely straight-forward and ordinary but they should be workmanlike, and they are truly an essential part of a creative process.

Drawings can go much further than this though – as I said at the beginning, this is a book about objective figure drawing. Once you can draw well (and you can always draw better) there is a large range of possible ways of experimenting with figure drawing, to which this section is merely an introduction.

Maybe those possibilities will be explored in my next book!

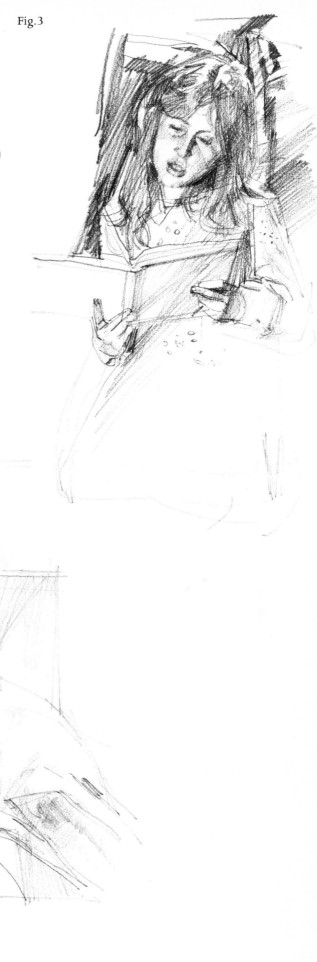

Fig.3

Fig.2

Master drawings

This final section of the book looks at the work of some of the great masters of figure drawing, and attempts to demonstrate some connections between their works and the main themes that I have been discussing in this book. In the limited space available, I am obviously not able to provide anything like a thorough history of figure drawing, and have chosen, fairly arbitrarily, some works that I particularly liked or found interesting. As well as practising your own drawing, you should take every opportunity to look at the works of the masters, and think about what it is that they have achieved in making an especially successful, or especially beautiful, drawing: you may notice things that you would never have seen on your own, or realize how a great artist has found a simple solution to a problem that has been confusing you for a long time. There are many great names in figure drawing; in addition to the ones whose work is illustrated here, I have also to mention Leonardo, Michelangelo, Botticelli, Dürer, El Greco, Raphael, Caravaggio, Rubens, Rembrandt and Velasquez, among the old masters, and Ingres, Degas, Millet, Eakins, Lautrec, Modigliani, Picasso, Pascin and Wyeth as more modern artists. They have all drawn the human figure with sensitivity and understanding.

The drawings in this final section are arranged very roughly in chronological order, but I have also been concerned to put together works that could usefully be compared or contrasted with each other.

The first work shown is a copy by the little-known draughtsman Giorgio Guilio Clovio (1498-1578), of a lost drawing of a Pietà by Michelangelo. It is very subtly drawn, probably in black chalk, and the plasticity of the flesh in the figure of Christ is beautifully expressed; look for instance at the way the flesh of Christ's right arm is squashed as it rests on the knee of Mary. Apart from this figure, there is very little sense of real three-dimensional depth or solidity, as the artist has concentrated rather on the compositional pattern of the work. There is instead a fascinating interplay of the folded patterns of the cloth, the undulating surface of the figure of Christ and the gesturing hands of the other figures. It is clear that, whatever was the emphasis of Michelangelo's lost original, Clovio's work is a study in pattern and composition more than about space and light.

By comparison, the sketch of Sir Thomas More and his family by Hans Holbein (1497-1543) is not so much a compositional scheme as a diagram, a stage on the way to a painting, exploring the proposed figure placings. The sketch gives no indication of light and shade, and, since the finished work was destroyed by fire, we do not know how the tonal balance was organized.

Despite this lack of tonality and weightiness, it is apparent that the figure of More himself dominates the work. He is, in fact, virtually at the centre of the composition. This feeling of dominance is if anything heightened by the comparative simplicity of his figure; the only texture is supplied by the detail of his chain of office, which itself draws attention to his face, with its rapt and concentrated gaze.

Drawing of the Pieta by Giorgio Guilio Clovio after a drawing by Michelangelo, a beautiful composition with a well-observed drawing of the central figure of Christ. Victoria and Albert Museum, London.

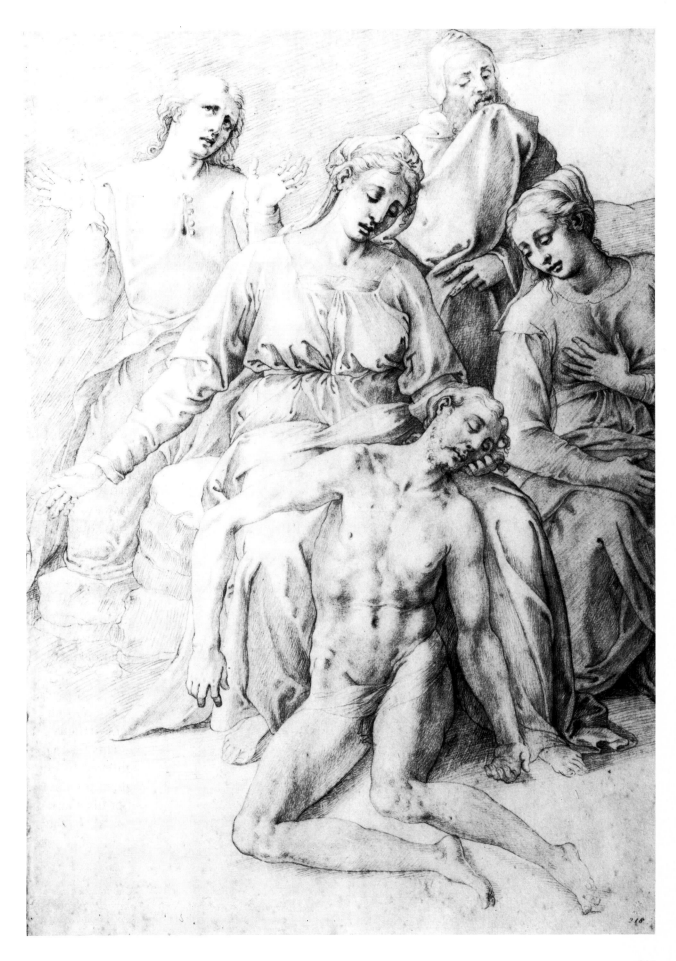

233

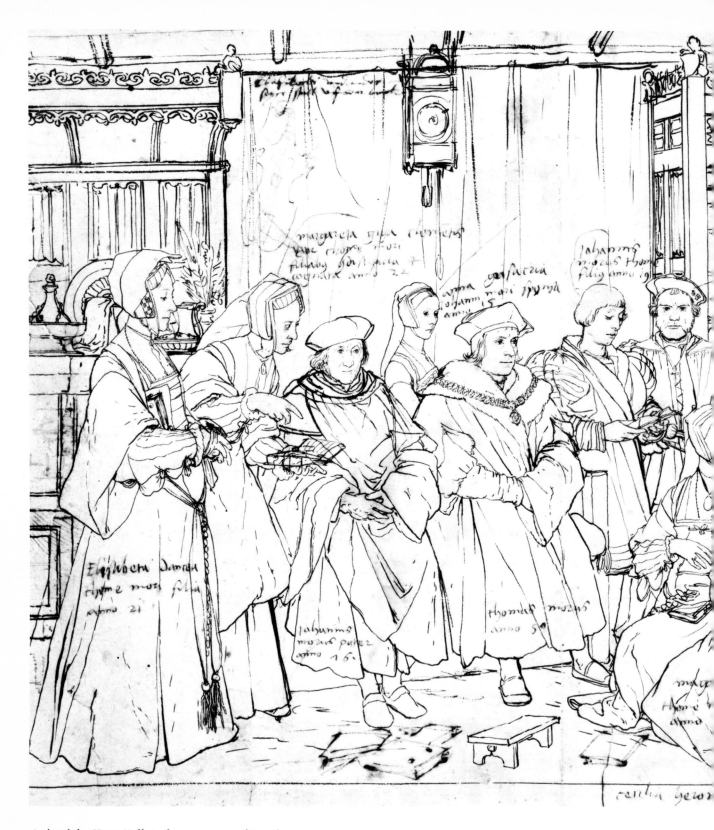

A sketch by Hans Holbein for a painting of Sir Thomas More and his family, drawn in 1526. Though intended as a working drawing, it is an excellent study in the creative use of line. Kunstmuseum, Basel.

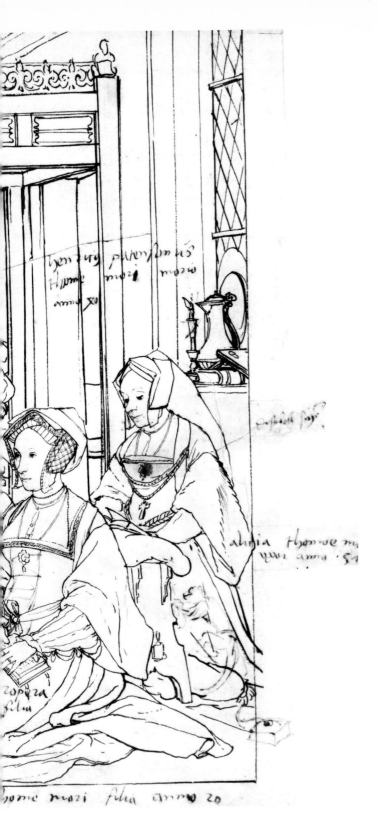

Probably, to judge from other surviving works by Holbein, the shapes of the various garments would have been organized into closely related tones, to draw further attention to the heads of the sitters. Even so, in this drawing the pattern and texture of simple linear outlines creates a decoration which is none the less splendid for being a minor aspect of the final work, or even perhaps being an unintentional achievement.

The back view of a male draped figure on page 236 is a study by the Venetian painter Tintoretto (1518-94) for the figure of the landlord in his painting of the Last Supper which he did in San Paulo, Venice, in the late 1560s. This drawing is appealing in its directness and unity. While it yields some information about the fall of light on the figure, the artist's primary interest seems to lie in the folding and stretching of the simple garment, which manages to evoke the pose of the figure beneath with certainty and conviction.

The nervous, knotted figure is also by Tintoretto, and, like the previous drawing, is drawn on grey paper with black chalk, although this time there are no white high-lights. It is thought to have been a study from a piece of sculpture representing a man bowed down with a heavy burden, possibly the mythological figure of Atlas. It is also an excellent example of the flickering, mannerist style of an artist who tried to emulate and adapt the achievements in draughtsmanship of Michelangelo to his visionary view of the world. The forms are convoluted in a way that they could never be in life, but they are strangely convincing and expressive, and give to the work an extraordinary life and vitality. Most of the bumps and hollows have a soundly observed anatomical explanation, and the way in which the outline has an exaggerated weariness gives a marvellous impression of tottering under a heavy weight. Some of the marks may seem out of place and these are stains that have appeared since the sixteenth century.

It might be interesting to compare these works with the back view of a half-clothed male by Nicholas Lancret in the early eighteenth century. Though drawn 150 years later than the Tintorettos, this displays an equivalent simplicity and conviction; the

235

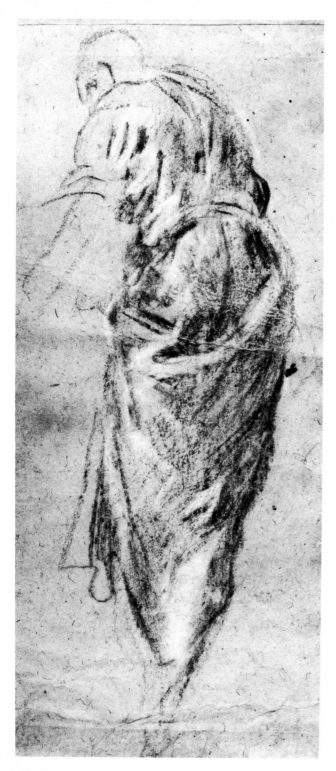

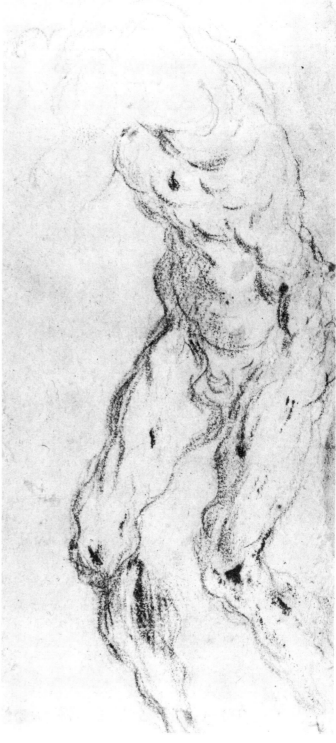

A back view of a draped male figure by Tintoretto, one of the most original figure draughtsmen of the Renaissance. This study explores the definition of the underlying form purely in terms of the folding and stretching of the drapery. Victoria and Albert Museum, London.

Another figure by Tintoretto, combining his heightened, dramatic view of man with his interest in dynamics. Victoria and Albert Museum, London.

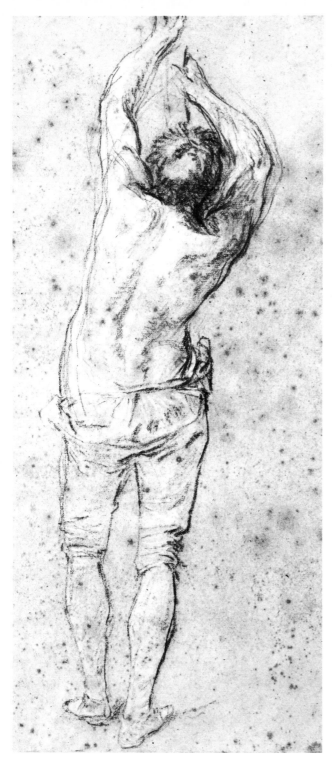

Standing figure of a man by Nicholas Lancret, a pupil of Antoine Watteau, combining robust observation with an elegance typical of the Rococo. Museum Boymano-van Beuningen, Rotterdam.

stylistic differences between the finished works of the two masters are not at all apparent in their working drawings.

The next two drawings are much more modern. First, a typically rich drawing of a standing nude by the post-impressionist painter Georges Seurat (1859-91). It is primarily done in conté crayon, but on close examination it is possible to see a much lighter grey underdrawing, perhaps in pencil. Seurat's work is wonderful for the organization of its tonality; even the brightest of the highlights has a little tone. Although it may not be visible in reproduction, the hip, for instance, carries a delicate, spidery tracery of conté lines, and this becomes stronger and thicker on the lesser lights. As a study in tone it is completely uncompromising – there is no edge line to the figure at all. The hands and feet simply disappear into the background gloom, yet there is overall a splendid feeling of solidity and atmosphere. It may be interesting to compare this drawing with the points I raised in the section on Light and Shade, projects 1 and 4.

The reclining nude by the modern British artist Victor Pasmore (*b.* 1908) is more overtly sexual. It is not, of course, a drawing but one of the two or three paintings I have included for their strict selectivity or for the strong evidence of draughtsmanship. Where the Seuret was a study in direct light, this explores a more complex interplay of direct and reflected light. The structure of the back is simple, and the composition gives depth and atmosphere, but the subtlety of the lighting continually draws your attention back to the delicious fleshy and ovoid shape of the hip and bottom. I suppose it could be called titillating; but it is wonderfully done.

Pages 240 and 241 compares standing clothed female figures by two very different artists, the Viennese *art nouveau* painter Gustav Klimt (1862-1918), and the British portrait painter Augustus John (1879-1961). Klimt was fascinated by flat patterns, which he has explored in the drapery of his figure; yet the evocation of the pose is extremely vivid here. He has managed, with the barest minimum of pencil strokes, to indicate without question that the model's weight is on her left leg, and to show the swing of her torso, the way in which her left shoulder is tilted down and

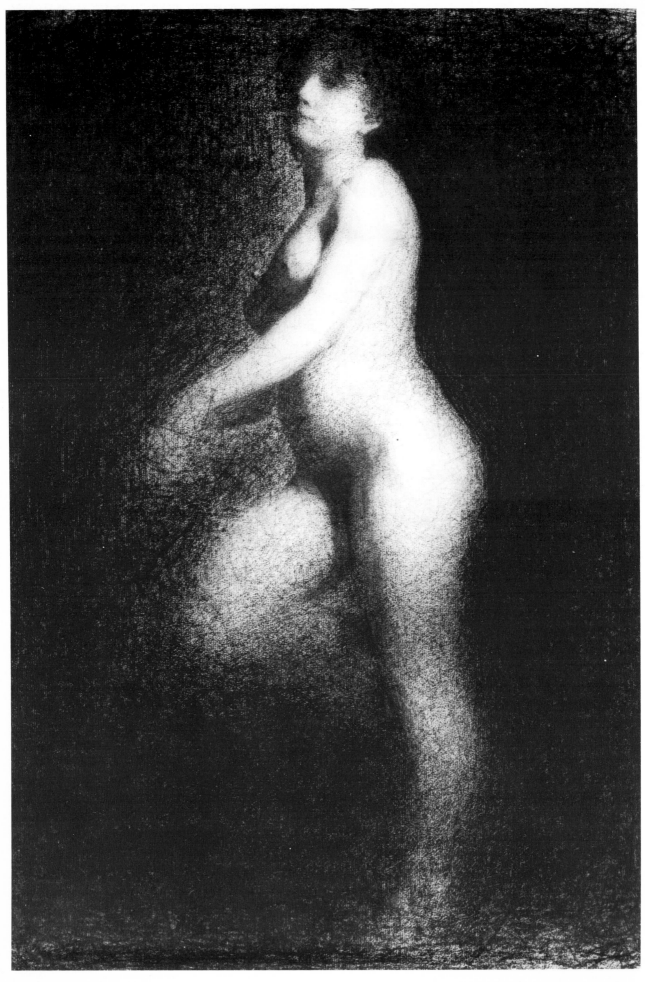

238

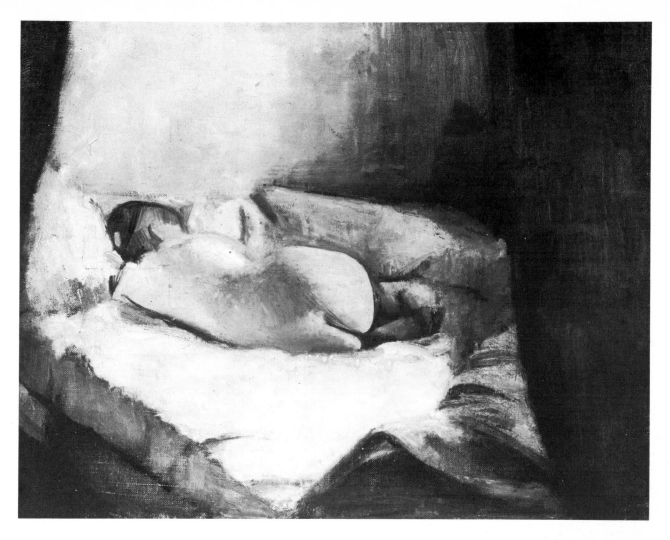

Reclining nude by Victor Pasmore. Another study in light and shade, but one which also frankly delights in the textures of the flesh. Tate Gallery, London.

Opposite: Standing figure by the French Post-Impressionist Georges Seurat. He carried out scientific studies of tonal systems which formed the basis for his pointillist style of painting, and this interest in tone is evident in such careful, entirely non-linear drawings. Courtauld Institute Galleries, London.

her head is counterbalanced. He has also included the hint of exotic mystery in the pose which is characteristic of his art. Equally fine, and also by Klimt, is the study of two reclining nudes; the undulating, flowing line captures the sensuality, and the slackness of the form that were discussed in the section on Dynamics.

The work by Augustus John, of his wife Dorelia John, was done in pencil and watercolour. The pose is strong and balanced, and although the fabric of the dress falls cleanly to the ground, it contrives to suggest the pose underneath. As in the Klimt, the weight is on the left leg. Where the Klimt emphasized flat pattern, this drawing has the form shown with added tone. The tension and weight of the cloth are shown in strong straight lines, while the fold of the cloth at the elbow is freely expressed. The head is nicely inclined to counterbalance the pose, and contrives to suggest a totally different character to the Klimt. Both of these works might usefully be compared with the sections on Balance and Clothing.

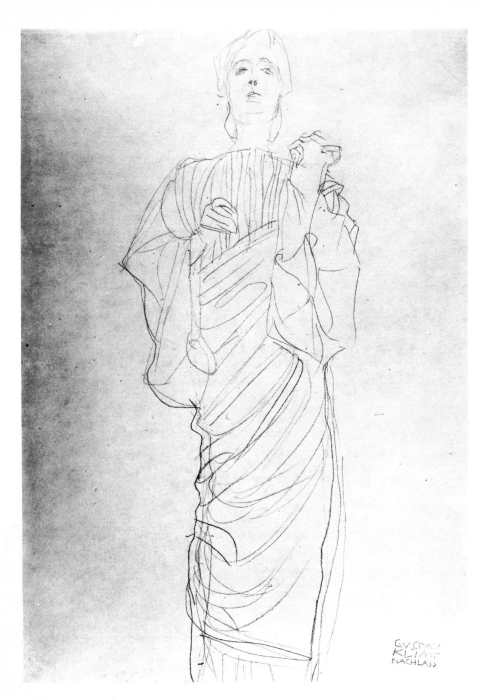

Study for the mythological figure of Hygieia by Gustav Klimt, a study in flat patterns which nevertheless reveals an exactly balanced pose. Victoria and Albert Museum, London.

Opposite: Dorelia standing, by the British artist Augustus John, a study in the tensions and slacknesses of clothing contrasting the tight bodice and full skirting and adding up to a charming pose. City of Manchester Art Galleries.

Study for two reclining female nudes, also by Klimt. The art nouveau lines explore the relaxed flesh and bones of the model. Victoria and Albert Museum, London.

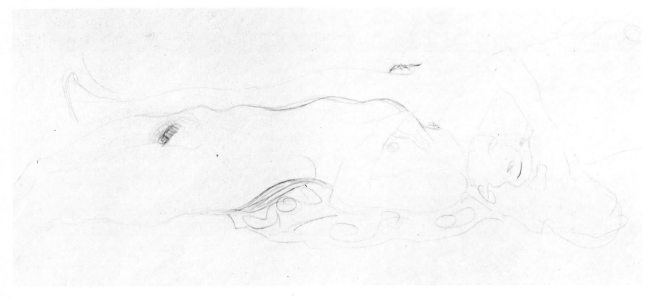

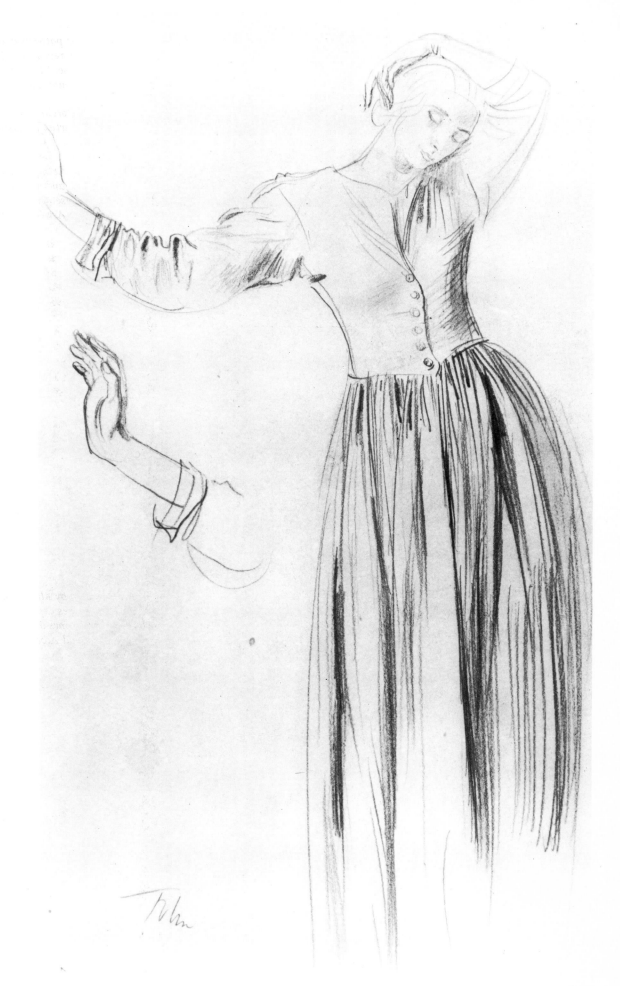

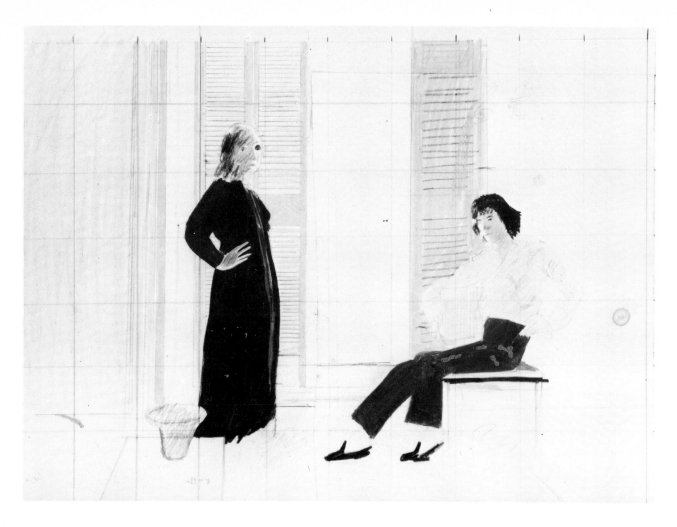

This next spread looks at studies and compositional sketches for paintings by the English Pre-Raphaelite Dante Gabriel Rossetti (1828-82) and the contemporary English artist David Hockney (*b.* 1937). The sketch for Hockney's large painting *Mr & Mrs Clark and Percy* explores the relationships between the characters and the composition of the whole work. Incidentally, as Percy the cat, which features in Ossie Clark's lap in the final work, is here missing, the title to the painting must have been chosen at a later stage. Hockney did a great many studies for this painting, and took many photographs, and he has admitted that he found great difficulty with the portrait of Mr Clark. The pencil sketch here is very similar to the head finally used in the painting, but the body has a completely different pose. Unusually for Hockney, both the figures in this work look straight out and establish eye-to-eye contact with the viewer. Admittedly these two drawings are not masterpieces in their own right, but they are good examples of real working drawings.

The Rossetti drawings show a rather different

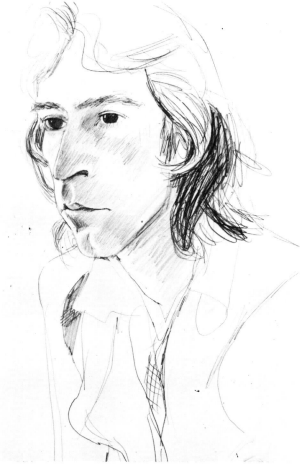

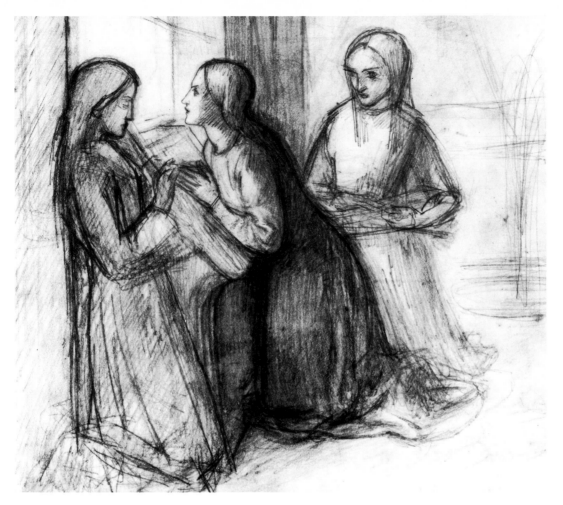

Two studies by Dante Gabriel Rossetti for a never-completed painting, demonstrating a different, more detailed, method of working from Hockney's. Birmingham Museum and Art Gallery.

Opposite top and bottom: Two studies by David Hockney for his painting Mr and Mrs Clark and Percy, *working drawings that demonstrate the importance of composition in Hockney's portraiture. Tate Gallery, London.*

---

emphasis, and different method of working, typical of the Pre-Raphaelites' prediliction for pictures that tell a story, and the requirement of their creed to depict every little detail with 'truth' and 'clarity'. Like the Hockney, the subjects of these studies for an unknown painting are seen against the light source, and where Hockney concentrates on the compositional pattern, Rossetti has paid much more attention to the way the light falls on the figures. It was a common practice of Rossetti and his associates to make nude studies for the clothed figures; the drapery being added so that it clung to the figure, revealed almost as much as it concealed and yet remained superficially pure and chaste. In this case, I

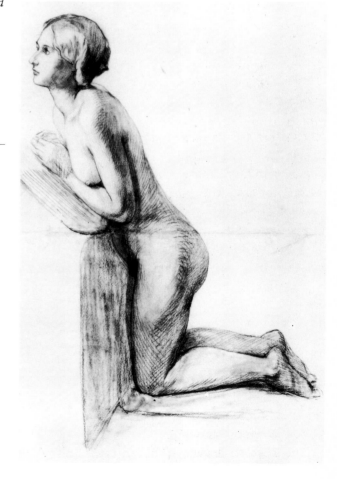

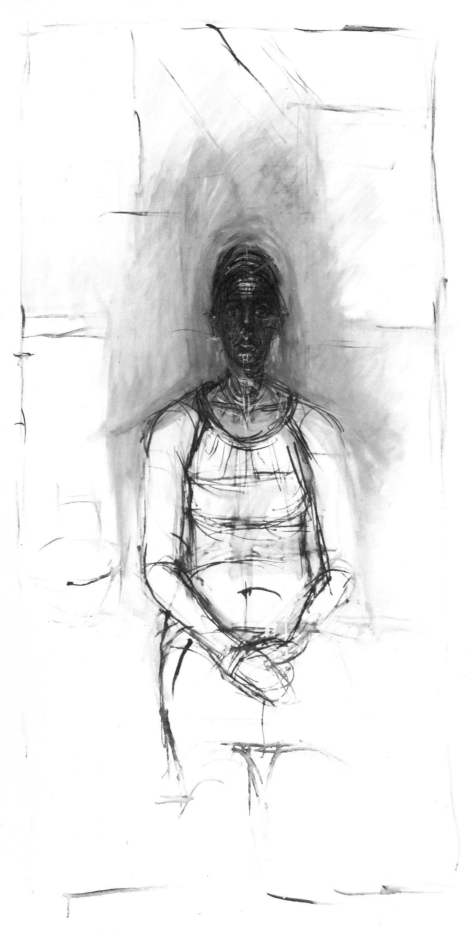

think it unlikely that such a sexually desirable figure was intended and so I think it probable that a draped study of this figure would have been made as well and information from the two combined for the painting.

The painting by the Swiss sculptor Alberto Giacometti (1901-66) seems to have begun as a study of a seated figure and ended up as a strangely concentrated image of a human face. Giacometti primarily produced thin sculpted figures, and here the head has begun to take on the compressed form that is typical of his work; although it will not be apparent in black-and-white reproduction, the painting has even got the colour and sheen of a bronze casting. The artist has obviously made a search for the form of the body, as can be seen in the network of lines, ticks and scrubbed tone, but it is apparent that his attention was drawn again and again to the head. The intensity of his search for form in that region is such that it not only takes on a strong sense of being in the round, but seems almost to be in an atmosphere and space of its own.

Where the Giacometti has sacrificed the individuality of the sitter, the portrait of P J Spencer by the English artist Stanley Spencer (1891-1959) has concentrated on portraying the character of the sitter by seeking out the uniqueness of his face. The portrait is typical of Spencer's work in its interest in the localized asymmetries of the details of the flesh of the face, such as the slightly one-sided nose and eyes which are marginally different in shape. Such asymmetries are to be found in most faces, and Spencer's portrait is notable for its exploration of these without any disturbance of the general symmetry of the whole. This is achieved because he has been able to ensure that the details, such as the folds and undulations of the skin, are not allowed to disturb the strong feeling for the general planes. This drawing is typical of the artist's work also in that the forms are absolutely continuous, and no area of the head is skimped or left unstated.

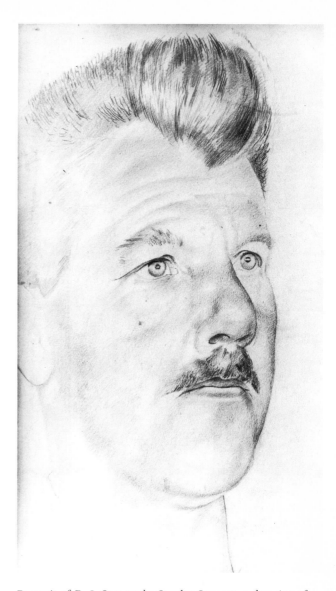

Portrait of P. J. Spencer by Stanley Spencer, a drawing of great subtlety which achieves tonal and structural strength and still manages to pay attention to the idiosyncrasies of the flesh. Tate Gallery, London.

Opposite: Caroline by Giacometti, a painted sketch which has become a portrait; the strong sense of form in the head reflects the artist's sculptural interests. Tate Gallery, London.

The standing figure on page 246 is a study by Pierre-Auguste Renoir (1841-1919) for his painting of *Les Grandes Baigneuses* (1884-87). It is a beautifully strong and simple drawing, bursting with youth and vitality. The figure has great solidity and weight, the tautness of the form around the shoulder-blades seems to me to imbue the whole curve of the spine with a kind of tensed springiness. The angle of the head is just right, and the whole figure is of a piece. In my view this drawing is much more unified, more alive and more successful than the figure in the finished painting, and an excellent illustration of dynamics in drawing.

Like the Renoir, the drawing by Egon Schiele (1890-1918) is a study of a girl's back; but

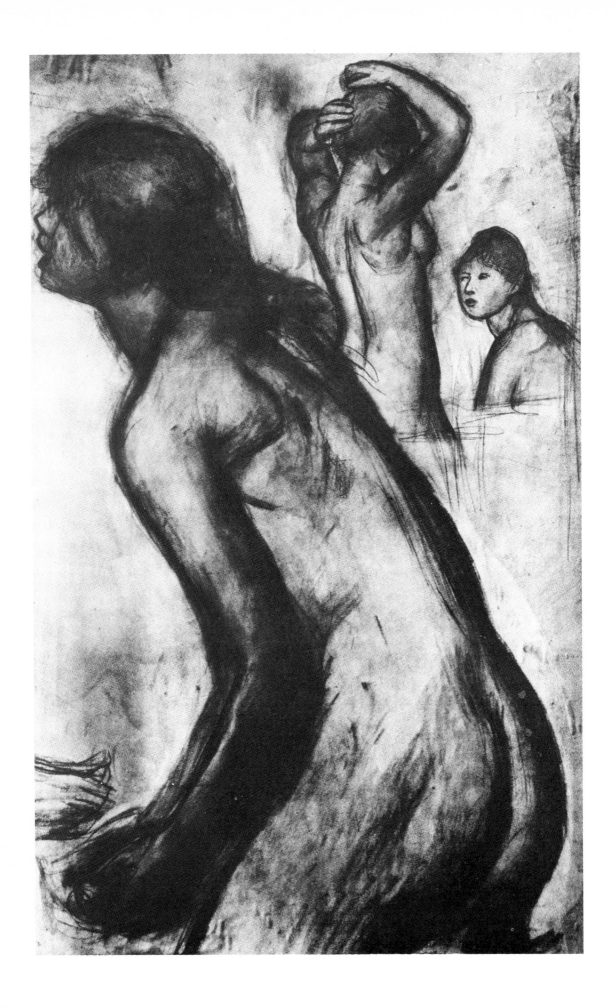

246

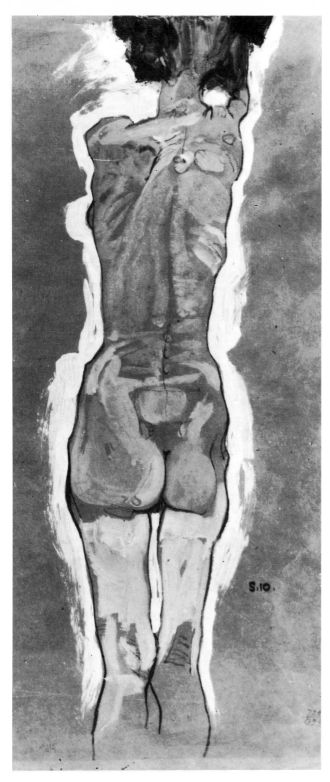

Back view of a female nude by Egon Schiele, a painful but fascinating study of the structure of the body. Graphische Sammlung Albertina, Vienna.

Opposite: Sketch by Pierre Auguste Renoir for his painting Les Grandes Baigneuses, *a vigorous drawing which strongly reveals the artist's control of the dynamics of the figure.*

beyond that, there is no similarity at all between the two works. Schiele's eye is merciless. The almost painful boniness and meanness of the flesh is heightened by the elongation of the torso. The drawing was made on buff-coloured paper, and the artist has used this as the intermediate tone for the figure, heightening the lights with watercolour and gouache. To help clarify the place of the paper's colour in the tonality of the figure, he has isolated it from the background by painting white gouache to delineate the edge of the figure. As well as assisting in using the paper's colour as a ready-made tone, this device also dramatizes the outline shape.

What is not apparent in the black-and-white reproduction here is the way in which smudges of pink and blue are used to accentuate knuckles and joints, and pale acid green and yellow to help round out the fuller forms. Although at first sight these colours usually seem harsh and shocking, I always feel that they contribute perfectly to the overall sense of vitality.

Because I feel that familiarity with Schiele's drawing should be a high priority for anyone interested in figure drawing, I have included two more of his works, *Recumbent nude girl with her legs apart* and the *Man with a red loin cloth* of 1914.

The female figure is typical of his ability to convey a great deal with the minimum of means. The underlying skeleton is always prominent, and line is used to delineate the skeletal structure whenever it comes to the surface. But the linear outline is expressive, and with the linear definition of the edges of the forms, and the small smudges conveying tone, this is a drawing of extraordinary intensity.

The small areas of tone are so few as merely to emphasize the uncompromising directness of the linear treatment, which, though spare, manages to convey sensuously the hardness and softness of the figure. Notice, incidentally, the foreshortening of the model's right thigh has been simply achieved with two loosely ovoid shapes, and the other thigh is made marvellously lucid by similar means.

To add to the eloquence of the line in these drawings, Schiele would blur the line subtly towards the swelling of the form, sometimes by

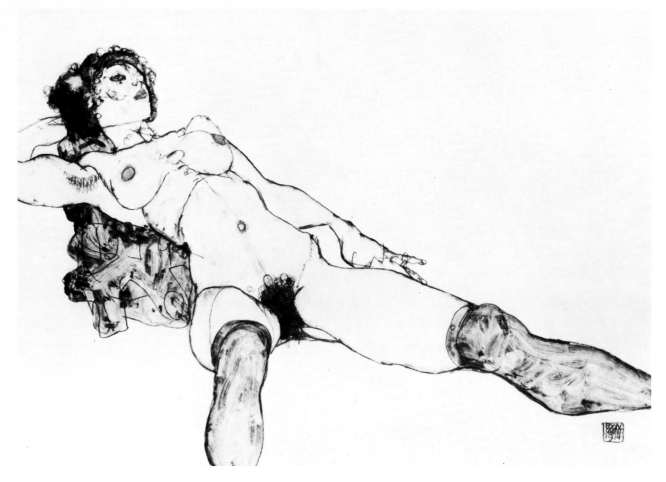

Above and left: Recumbent nude girl with her legs apart, *and* Man with a red loin cloth, *both by Schiele. Both are excellent illustrations of the use of line in the study of the dynamics of the figure, and an original method of portraying character. Graphische Sammlung Albertina, Vienna.*

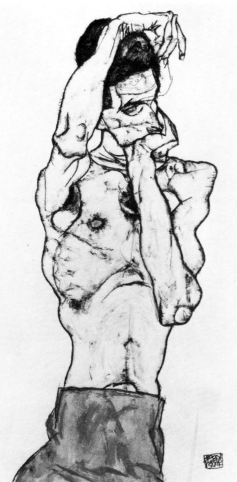

Opposite: Naked portrait by Lucien Freud, an uncompromisingly honest study which maintains a strong sense of structure and composition. Tate Gallery, London.

smudging the chalk, but more often by adding small amounts of water-colour or gouache.

Although it is not apparent from the title, I suspect that the male drawing is one of Schiele's many self-portraits. It is hard to see how he managed to draw it in such a pose, but there is a similar difficulty with many of his acknowledged self-portraits; this pose could have been drawn from the mirror until it was necessary to observe the arm over the head (the artist's right arm). He would have had to hold this arm up to observe it in the mirror, then move it to do the actual drawing.

In this work, the convolutions of the linear

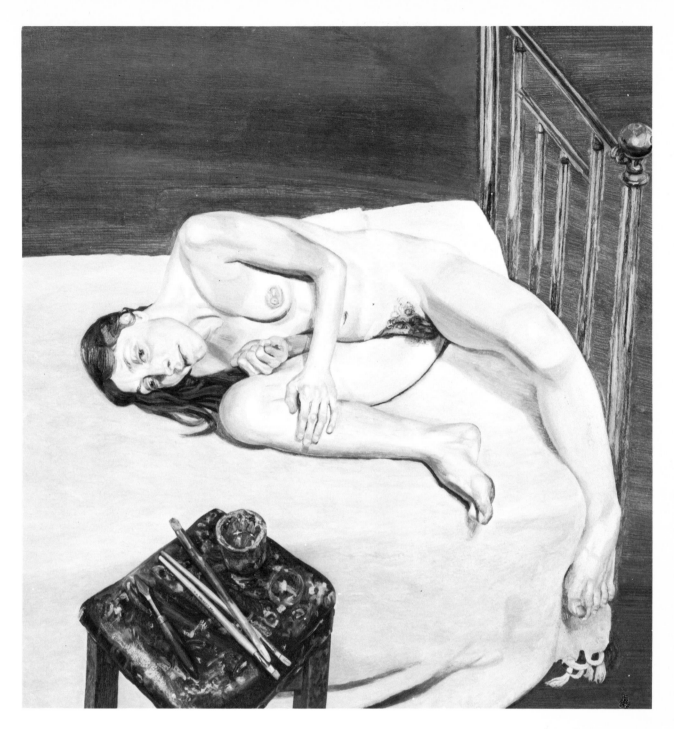

outlines have been pushed beyond any possible objective reality, but all the shapes are based on observation and their exaggeration is just enough to heighten the feeling of tension in bone and muscle which gives the drawing such tortured intensity.

The next two works are by contemporary British painters, Lucien Freud (*b*. 1922) and Euan Uglow (*b*. 1932). Both are, of course, paintings but could be considered as drawings in paint. The Freud includes some extremely subtle colour changes which are lost in reproduction but which modulate between describing the changing colour of the skin's surface and the light and shade to help define form.

But I have included the painting here primarily because it is structurally so strong, not only compositionally but in terms of the figure itself, and the figure's relationship with the flat plane of the bed. And like all of Freud's work, it is uncompromisingly honest and un-idealized, almost cruel in its observation: nothing is sensationalized or hidden.

It is also (although I cannot be sure of how high a priority the artist gave this) a very well organized exercise in light and shade, without any dramatic shadow or highlighting.

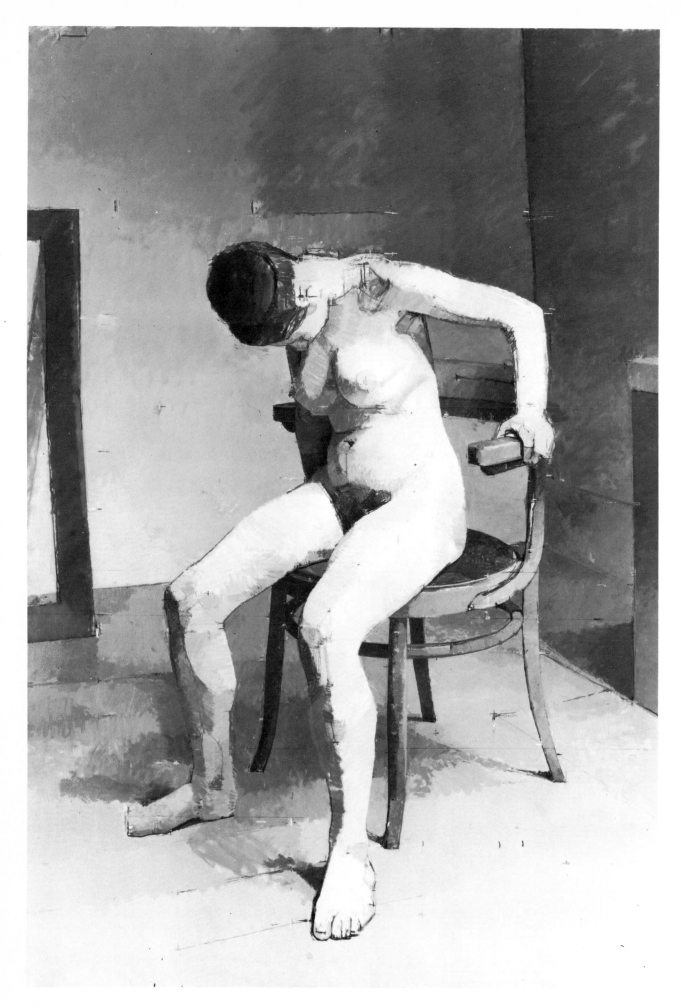

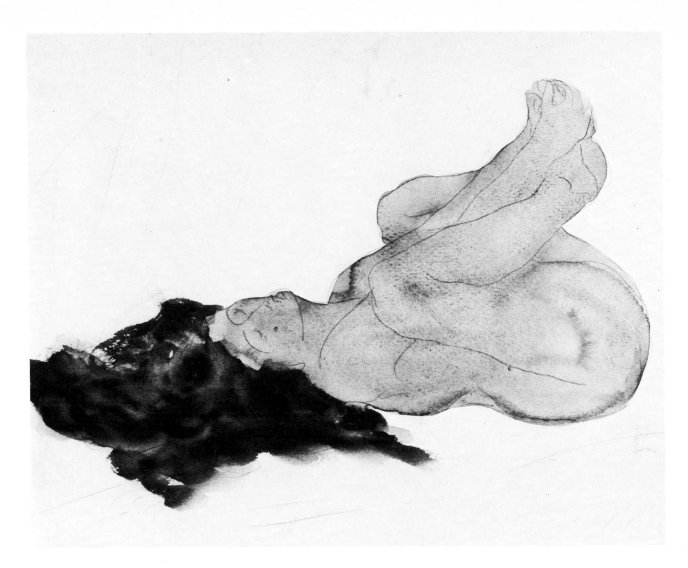

Female nude, by Auguste Rodin, a rapid sketch of a fleeting moment, made in the attempt to capture total movement. Victoria and Albert Museum, London.

Opposite: Seated nude by Euan Uglow, an exercise in structure so complete that the figure and chair almost merge into a single, coherent, form. Tate Gallery, London.

The seated nude by Uglow, done in 1962-63, is equally strong structurally, and indeed much has been sacrificed in the search for the planes. The vertical tip of the head, the parallel planes of the forward-facing shoulders and of the knees are all blocked in with very strong lines (bright red in the original) and there is no attempt to soften these original statements or to make the transitions smoother or more flesh-like. The chair-legs and the model's feet all stand solid on the floor, the plane of which is beyond doubt. Although I am sure that the painting succeeds in capturing the character of the sitter, it is not a genuine portrait with real human presence as is the Freud, and you feel that the light is only there to illuminate the structure.

Pages 251 and 252 compare two very different drawings by the sculptors August Rodin (1840-1917) and Henry Moore (*b.* 1898) Rodin was concerned to explore the human figure in rapid motion, and he used to draw with great speed from models who were encouraged to move freely about his room. He was searching for the 'expressive line', the single bodily gesture that expressed everything about the figure and even about humanity. His drawings are as a result about fluidity of movement and vitality. As in this example, he often used to fill the flowing outlines with freely applied washes of colour. These made no attempt to depict light or form, but somehow they continue to imbue the figures with a degree of fleshy solidity.

The reclining nude by Henry Moore, by contrast, has the effect of an almost rock-like solidity and weight. It, too, was drawn fluidly and rapidly, but it shows the figure as a powerful landscape. This difference between the formal preoccupations of the two great artists can be seen equally clearly in their finished sculptures: Rodin's figures seem to defy gravity while Moore's glory in their weightiness.

Conclusion

Looking at drawings by great artists is, I repeat, very important and necessary to the aspiring figure draughtsman.

Given limitless time and diligence, everything about drawing can be discovered entirely on your own without help, but the whole point is that there is not sufficient time in a life time to discover everything, and without guidance an awful lot of blind alleys will have to be explored, too many trials and too much error.

Climb onto the shoulders of the draughtsmen who have gone before and get a clearer view.

Reclining nude by Henry Moore, in which the artist has concentrated on the weightiness of the figure to such an extent that the result is almost topographical. Victoria and Albert Museum, London.

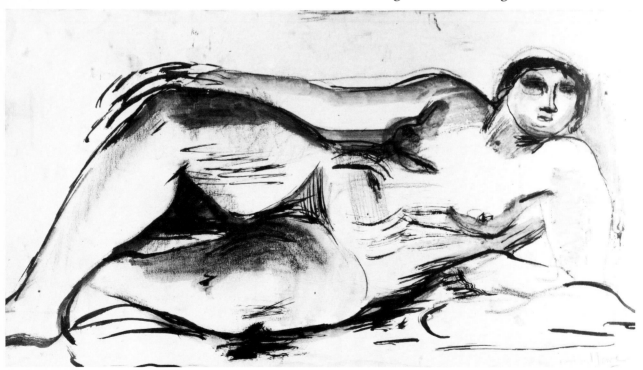

Glossary
of anatomical
terms

Abduction Movement of a limb outwards (laterally).

Adduction Movement of a limb inwards (medially).

Anterior Pertaining to the front side of the body.

Aponeurosis A sheet-like expanse of dense connective tissue, associated with muscle attachments.

Articulation Movement of two bones together at a joint.

Belly The main contractile part of a muscle.

Condyle A smooth knuckle-shaped eminence on a bone, for articulation with another bone.

Costal Pertaining to the ribs.

Crest A marked ridge on a bone.

Digitation A finger-like strap of muscle.

Distal The part of a limb, muscle or bone furthest from the limb root.

Dorsal Pertaining to the back, or to the back of the hand or foot.

Dorsiflexion Flexion or movement of the foot upwards.

Eversion Movement of turning the foot such that the sole faces outwards (laterally).

Extension The movement of straightening a joint or bending the vertebral column backwards.

Facet A small articular surface of a bone.

Fascia A sheet or band of fibrous connective tissue.

Fossa A depression or groove in a bone.

Head (bone) The expanded proximal end of many elongated bones.

Heads (muscle) The origins of a divided muscle.

Insertion Attachment of a muscle to a bone or cartilage, usually at the movable or distal end.

Lateral Pertaining to the side of the body.

Line (linea) A low, narrow ridge on a bone.

Medial Pertaining to the centre of the body.

Origin Attachment of a muscle to a bone or cartilage, usually at the secure or medial end.

Plantarflexion Extension or movement of the foot downwards.

Posterior The rear side of the body, a muscle or a bone.

Process A sizeable projection from a bone.

Pronation Movement of turning the hand downwards such that the bones of the forearm are crossed.

Proximal The part of a limb, muscle or bone nearest to the limb root.

Ramus A branch or arm of a bone.

Retinaculum A fibrous band of strengthened fascia, retaining tendons at a joint.

Septum An extension of the deep fascia, dividing muscles and providing attachments for them.

Slip An attachment for a muscle additional to the main one.

Spine A long sharp projection from a bone.

Supination Movement of turning the palm of the hand upwards such that the bones of the forearm are not crossed.

Synovial A sheath or joint lubricated by the fluid synovia.

Tuber, tubercle, tuberosity A roughly rounded projection on a bone.

Anatomical index